D1739244

BEHAVIOR IN THE
COMPLEX ENVIRONMENT

BEHAVIOR IN THE
COMPLEX ENVIRONMENT

SIEGFRIED STREUFERT

and

SUSAN C. STREUFERT
University of Bielefeld, West Germany

1978

V. H. WINSTON & SONS
Washington, D.C.

A HALSTED PRESS BOOK

JOHN WILEY & SONS

New York   Toronto   London   Sydney

Copyright © 1978, by V. H. Winston & Sons, a Division of
Scripta Technica, Inc.

V. H. Winston & Sons, a Division of Scripta Technica, Inc.,
Publishers
1511 K Street, N.W., Washington, D.C. 20005

Distributed solely by Halsted Press, a Division of John Wiley
& Sons, Inc.

Library of Congress Cataloging in Publication Data

Streufert, Siegfried.
      Behavior in the complex environment.

      1. Social psychology. I. Streufert, Susan C.,
joint author. II. Title.
HM251.S836   301.1   78-2652
ISBN 0-470-26335-0

Composition by **Isabelle Sneeringer**, Scripta Technica, Inc.

CONTENTS

Preface   vii

Chapter 1
An Alternate Focus on Social Psychology   1

Chapter 2
Cognitive Complexity: A Review of Theory, Measurement,
and Research   11

Chapter 3
An Interactive Complexity Theory   87

Chapter 4
Consistency of Motivation   131

Chapter 5
The General Incongruity Adaptation Level (GIAL):
A theory developed in cooperation with Michael J. Driver   163

Chapter 6
Attitudes, Social Influence and Interpersonal Attraction
Written in cooperation with Howard L. Fromkin   207

Chapter 7
Social Perception and Person Perception
Written in cooperation with Glenda Y. Nogami   245

Chapter 8
Concluding Comments
The GIAL and Complexity, A Third Look at Complexity
Theory, Dimensionality and the GIAL in Action,
A Final Comment   273

Author Index   305

Subject Index   311

PREFACE

A preface generally reviews the author's experiences, events, or developments which led him to write the book. He may also present a statement of its purposes and goals and an orientation for the reader's approach to the book. Furthermore, he may utilize the preface to specify the audience to which he addresses the book and for whom it is suited. However, because in this particular case that kind of information would use up more space than befits a preface, we have incorporated it in Chapter 1. Instead, we would like to use these lines for another purpose: to awaken in the reader an awareness of the message and basic motif underlying the ideas presented in the following chapters.

It is, perhaps, unusual for a book that concerns itself with theory, particularly theory in psychology, to attempt as well to convey a "message." This book, as others like it, contains some facts, some findings, some hypotheses and propositions, and some more or less educated guesses. All these revolve around a central theme—dimensionality; or, if we may put it more plainly, "things are not as simple as we may wish." But this theme may also be viewed as our message, one which is directed to two groups of people: researchers and theorists in the field of psychology, and those whose job it is to take the information provided by the first group and make use of it.

For psychologists, the point is relatively clear. So much of the research in psychology is based on theory and methodology that eliminates the possibility of reliably producing results which are relevant to the world outside our laboratories. If it is to be our aim to provide applicable and usable information beyond the scope of psychology for its own sake, it is essential that we study the characteristics of behavior in the world as they really exist. One of the factors which determines these characteristics, and which is too frequently missing in our research, is the very complexity, the multi-dimensionality, of this world. An environment certainly cannot be reproduced in full in the laboratory. But it can be condensed, abstracted, made manipulable, without necessarily destroying its basic features, those characteristics which provide the *essence* of this environment and which contribute to the effects that it has on individuals. If, on the other hand, in order to fit it into the lab, we pare down an environment beyond recognition, we can no longer expect that the effects produced in our subjects are the same effects that are produced in persons interacting with the real-world criterion environment. Further, we should recognize that individuals have different ways of dealing with multidimensional environments and their complexities. We must be aware of the possibility that some of the variance in our data may be created by these "individual" differences. What needs to be measured may, in many cases, be the effects of the interaction between the complexity of the environment and the coping of the subject. The point, then: Let subjects experience at least some of the complexities of the real world in the lab, and take into account their varying abilities and styles in coping with these complexities.

For the applier, the point is somewhat similar. He need not necessarily be concerned with how the theoretical information in this or other books has come to light, but rather with which information to select and how to use it. We would like to urge that in attempting an analysis of, and an application of, psychology to, a specific situation, the environmental *and* the individual factors be taken into account. And beyond that, the complexity, the multidimensionality of this environment in interaction with the individual's capacity or style for dealing with this complexity, should be considered. If, for example, the task is to maximize output efficiency in an industrial decision making setting, it would be necessary to consider not only the decision maker and his various characteristics, but also the characteristics of the setting, of the information on which decisions are to be based, and of the nature of the desired output. If all these factors are viewed in terms of their relevant dimensions, as interactive with each other, as mutually dependent, it is then theoretically possible to put together an optimal combination: Select a decision maker who is best able to deal with the particular dimensional characteristics of a situation and the information, to arrive at the most appropriate results. Only through an interactive view of all these factors can optimalized matching be expected.

The message: The world is complex, and individuals have varying styles and abilities for dealing with this complexity. Both need to be viewed if we intend to apply psychological theory in complex real-world environments. The key is interaction.

We would like to thank the Office of Naval Research (U.S. Department of the Navy) for its generous support for a good part of the research on which these theoretical statements are based; special thanks to Dr. John Nagay and Dr. Bert King for their interest in our projects. Support during the last phase of the relevant research from the State of Nordrhein-Westfalen via the University of Bielefeld is also acknowledged. Many grateful thoughts, as well, for all those persons with whom we have discussed these ideas over the last few years. And finally, a very special thank-you to Elisabeth Wolter for patience, understanding, and a tremendous amount of excellent work.

CHAPTER 1

AN ALTERNATE FOCUS ON SOCIAL PSYCHOLOGY

This book takes a somewhat different look at social psychology and related fields. All of us who have worked in these areas are well aware that data often conflict; that the same theories appear to be sometimes correct, at other times faulty; and that the winning theory is not always the same when experiments are designed for the purpose of pitting one theory against another. Without question, some of the propositions that have been stated by social psychologists are not viable; yet others are often effectively discarded before their final accuracy or inaccuracy—or for that matter their limits of accuracy—are determined. Often it appears that shifts in the interest of social psychologists (for example, from attitudes to consistency to attribution) are due to an inability to provide final clarification of a widely researched theory's status. We can hardly say that letting a theory "get out of fashion" (rather than clearly demonstrating that it needs to be revised or discarded) is done to spare the feelings of the theorist who wrote the theory in the first place. We are not necessarily gentle in our dealings with each other's work. Rather, we seem to

1

be lacking the tools that permit us to reach final conclusions, i.e., we are testing theories in such a way that their final level of usefulness cannot be determined.

To many outsiders, it often appears that we are "playing games." And that impression is not only limited to our theoretical endeavors. For some time now—first through pressure by Congress on the granting agencies, later by public needs as such, and finally through the demands of some of our own colleagues—we have been called upon to aid society; in other words, to demonstrate the applicability of our theoretical concepts or to generate data that would aid in making public policy decisions or solve social problems. Some of us have angrily turned away from these demands, claiming that we believe only in "pure science" and would leave applications to different people, maybe those who would be called "psychological engineers." Others among us have tried to make predictions, to apply theory, to redesign research, and to evaluate programs. We must admit, however, that we have not done as well as we might. In a few cases, we have been able to help, in some, we have clearly failed. In yet others it is not at all certain that the suggestions of experienced practitioners were not (or would not have been) just as good as ours. Here, too, our theories have not served as sufficiently useful tools.

Should we then conclude that social psychology, particularly experimental social psychology, is an endeavor of doubtful value? A number of eminent writers in the field have expressed more or less serious doubts about current social psychology (e.g., Harré & Secord, 1972; Katz, 1967; Moscovici, 1972; Riecken, 1965; Ring, 1967; Scriven, 1964; Shulman & Silverman, 1972). The "critical psychologists" (e.g., Holzkamp, 1970; Sève, 1973) have attacked the field even more harshly. Gergen (1973) has not devalued experimental social psychology as such, but suggested that it has only historical value. Silverman (1975), on the other hand, seems to suggest that we discard current social psychology and replace it with an "exploratory" science. Some of these criticisms seem to us to have more (e.g., Gergen's), others to have less (e.g., Holzkamp's), value. We do not believe that it is necessary to discard current social psychology. Rather, it appears to us that it may be necessary to refocus it without the loss of the previous theoretical gains and without the loss of the data that have been collected in the past. This book is one attempt to point toward the beginning of one potential solution of the problems we have encountered in our field.

ALTERNATE APPROACHES TO THEORY IN SOCIAL PSYCHOLOGY

Without question, the world surrounding us is complex. With "progress" in our civilizations, it has become more so. One does not need "future shock" to view current events as sometimes unexplainable or even chaotic. As scientists, we hope to superimpose a pattern of order over apparent chaos. To do that, we frequently try to find the lowest common denominators of the observed events that might serve to explain them and might predict future events in the same class. However, we often encounter a problem. Typically, if we determine that any small subcomponent of an event which we study can be dissected further, we assume that it is not yet the *lowest* common denominator. The dissecting goes on and on. We have begun the process of infinite regress.

It appears to the authors that *infinite regress often leads us below the level of the lowest common denominator.* How far does it make sense to regress? As psychologists, we would probably accept that all behavioral events of our subjects are the effect of an interaction among atomic or sub-atomic particles. Yet we would not go that far "down" in the level of analysis in an attempt to explain dissonance reduction or success attribution. But how far would we go? If we were to propose any particular point of analysis offhand, there would probably be some who would argue that the reduction already went too far, while others would still find unwanted confounds among the variables. To avoid that argument, let us first take an example from a different science, where we are not as emotionally "involved."

Let us say a biologist wants to study "life." He can find the lowest living (or semi-living) protein molecule and study it. Or he could reduce this molecule to its components, some organic and some inorganic, and study those. If he does the latter, he can tell us much about the *components* necessary for life, but he will not be able to tell us very much about the phenomenon of life itself. Merely reassembling the components into a living organism may prove excessively difficult. In other words, if one wants to study the process of "life," the lowest common denominator is passed when life ceases to be part of the analyzed substance.

In psychology we have a similar problem. Let us again take an example. Early psychologists became fascinated with the views that apparently were underlying people's behaviors in specific situations. Some people seemed to reliably act in ways that were unpleasant to members of certain groups, or were injurious to them. Some kind of psychological mechanism, so it seemed, had to be determining that behavior. The apparent hostility toward outgroups could probably be measured as an "attitude." After some time, the concept of attitude was well defined: unfavorable (or favorable) *evaluation* represented by a mark placed far to the right on, for example, a 7-point scale running from good to bad. Theories were developed, research was designed, confounds were eliminated. And the subjects in the psychological experiment did what they were asked to do. They expressed their evaluative attitudes on the 7-point scales, had their attitudes determined and manipulated. Everything seemed fine.

But then it turned out that these attitudes did not determine very much behavior. They were pure, unadulterated with confounds, but they were (in most cases) sterile. Attitudes seemed to have little predictive value for real-world behavior. To the discomfort of many psychologists, something had to be added (e.g., centrality, intent, etc.) before "attitudes" would predict behavior (other than making a mark on the 7-point scale) to a reasonable degree. Previous divisions of the attitude concept into cognitive, affective, and conative components had to be reconsidered. One might say, it was necessary to "reconfound" the psychologically "pure" concept of attitude.[1] Just as the analysis of "life" is not possible through the study of its components, so the analysis of attitude determined behavior is not possible through the evaluative scale alone, at least not if we maintain the original intent, i.e., studying real-world behavior toward some outgroup (we deal with attitudes in Chapter 6).

Even the evaluative attitude *scale* which we chose as our example is not as pure as one might think. It theoretically should represent only one dimension (cf. McGuire, 1969), i.e., the responses made on it should be valid and reliable. But it takes nothing more than a refocusing of our subject's thoughts to destroy that illusion. Again, an example might help. Let us ask a somewhat puritanical subject to evaluate a prostitute he just (more or less secretly) visited, and let us say the prostitute gave him great pleasure. Is she "good" or is she "bad"? As a puritan, our subject would rate her "bad" if he focused on morality. He would rate her as "good" if he recalled his recent fabulous experience. We do not know which *dimension* of judgment he is using (unless, of course, we tell him what to focus on, taking him even further away from the reality in which he typically behaves). If, on the other hand, he decides to average his two responses and places her in the middle of the scale, we have obtained an entirely inaccurate (supposedly unidimensional, i.e., un-confounded) "attitude."

We do not want to "devalue" social psychological theory and research by these statements (at least not in a unidimensional sense). Theoretical developments have often been excellent. Experimental designs have been useful tests of the theories. Data have added a wealth of knowledge. But we should recognize the limits of these approaches. It appears that rejecting the human psychologies of past decades, as is so easily and often done by Marxist psychologists (e.g., Holzkamp, 1970; Sève, 1973), without proposing a better alternative within the framework of "critical psychology" is of little use. In our opinion, past theory and research probably should merely be viewed from a somewhat different vantage point and should be integrated into a more

---

[1] The many "contingency" theories currently in vogue are, in good part, an expression of the same phenomenon.

general theory that operates at the level of the lowest common denominator of *real-world behavior*, not below it.

Real-world behavior has rarely occurred in the laboratory, unless the lab and the experimental design have specifically allowed for it. In the laboratory, we typically create behavior "of a kind" by focusing the attention of our subject on some single dimension. In the complex world in which people are simultaneously exposed to multiple demands, multiple desires, and multiple stimuli, they are much less likely to focus on a single dimension. This "real behavior" in the "real world," if seen *from the laboratory point of view*, appears hopelessly confounded with variables that most laboratory researchers would not want to admit to their experimental design. Nonetheless, real-world behavior, for example the rejection *behavior* toward an outgroup, just like life in the complex protein molecule, occurs only at this level; i.e., it originates at this level. We might say that it *originates at the level of the confound*.

When we say that the psychological events we need to study originate at the level of a confound, we make this statement from the point of view of the theorist and researcher who prefers "infinite regress." We propose that this regress should not be infinite but finite: that the lowest common denominator of many events in which psychologists are interested is found at levels where *a number of dimensions* can or do simultaneously affect perceptions, information processing, and behavior. From a reductionistic point of view, this complex interaction of several dimensions indeed represents a confound. From our point of view, the minimum number of dimensions that must be present to reliably produce a real-world behavioral event represents the level of optimal analysis. From that point of view, this multidimensional level is *not* confounded. We propose that it is at this level where theory must operate if external validity is of concern and if relatively meaningless conflicts between data are to be avoided.

THE BOOK'S PURPOSE

This book attempts to refocus some parts of psychological theory—and with it research—at a different level of analysis: minimum multidimensionality. Unidimensional behavior, including much behavior in the laboratory, is here seen as a special case of multidimensionality, in contrast to the more usual, although often implicit, view of multidimensionality or curvilinearity as a not yet resolved confound of unidimensional variables. If we choose to view real-world behavior (to the degree to which it is of interest to the psychologist) from the minimum number of dimensions that are necessary to reliably obtain this behavior, then we must permit ourselves to restate theories and to re-think our experimental designs. A number of the chapters deal with theory. Because of lack of space, less is said about designs and data. To quickly state one means of research at this more complex level, we may suggest that for every behavioral area we wish to analyze, we should first ask—and determine—the number and kind of the dimensions underlying the relevant behavior. Only then can theory be applied and specific research designs (see, for example, those suggested in the handbook article by Fromkin & Streufert, 1976) be developed. This point of view does not at all argue against experiments, not even against laboratory research. Rather, it proposes that lab research should not be reduced in dimensionality of design below the "lowest common denominator" of the real-world situation which it represents.

We also are not arguing for "ideographic" rather than "nomothetic" research. Indeed, some researchers have given up on multidimensionality or "complexity" when they found that their research produced primarily noise. If we take a number of dimensions as given—say those of Osgood, Suci, and Tannenbaum's (1957) semantic differential—measure many subjects' responses, and factor the data *across* people, we will obtain the most common factor (evaluation) as the largest, and all other factors to some degree oblique to it, or loading to some degree on evaluation. If every subject's dimensionality is different, but evaluation is more or less common to all, that would be the expected result. If we intend to work with multidimensionality, we have to (1) permit our subjects to determine their individual dimensionality and let them work with that, rather than let other or average subjects' responses determine the dimensions (or worse, have the experimenter determine them in advance); (2) develop research designs that are ingenious enough to measure across subjects, i.e., nomothetically, what our subjects do with these (their own) dimensions[2] (see, for example, the decision matrix in the analysis of decision making responses by subjects of Streufert and associates).

Plan of the Book

As already stated, this book is concerned with theory; the related methodological approaches or relevant research are not covered due to space limitations. We review theoretical approaches in the two central areas in which we intend to propose theories ourselves and, in subsequent chapters, give

---

[2] We do not agree with Silverman (1976) that complex social phenomena *cannot* be studied fruitfully by the experimental laboratory methods. Rather, we propose that it is the sterility of the laboratory and the sterility of experimental designs and measurement that eliminate any possibility of external validity. Indeed, research should be carried out in more naturalistic fashion. Unfortunately, we often lose experimental control in the field settings that provide us easily with a natural environment. In many cases, however, natural environments can be created in the experimentally controlled laboratory, e.g., in the simulations of Drabeck, Streufert, and Zimbardo. (We do not mean those studies—for instance in legal research—where the term simulation has often been applied erroneously to paper and pencil tasks.)

(merely) *examples* of some other theoretical approaches (e.g., in areas like attitudes, social influence, social perception, person perception, and attribution) that may be interpreted or re-interpreted in terms of the two theories which we are proposing in this book. No attempt is made to exhaustively review and/or interpret theory in *all* those areas that might be viewed as relevant to or related to our multidimensional views. Theories and research that appear unrelated to multidimensionality will not be considered at all. Omissions are due to lack of space. They do not imply value judgments. We have selected a few theoretical areas for discussion that appear to us to be particularly in need of multidimensionality.

We are also not suggesting that we believe to have the answer to the "final" level of dimensionality in the various theoretical areas, i.e., the precise level of the lowest common denominator at which the events with which a theory is concerned do occur in the real world. But we hope to get closer to that level in our discussions, and in the process we hope to integrate some well-known theoretical propositions and to point out that apparent contradictions between them (often supported by research) may not, in fact, be contradictions at all.

The first concern of this book is a set of theories that have for some time argued for multidimensionality *within* the subjects: complexity theory. Complexity theories have not been extensively reviewed in the past (with the exception of a technical report by S. C. Streufert, 1972). Consequently, Chapter 2 reviews these theories and related research, and shows where commonalities do or do not exist among them. The review also deals with some newer forms of complexity theory, which view behavior as an interaction between the dimensionality of the person(s), the dimensionality of environmental information, and the dimensionality of the resultant behavior.

In Chapter 3 we describe the current state of our own complexity theory, which hopefully will serve to integrate some of the previously disparate propositions of complexity theorists, and will aid in developing tools for the construction of multidimensional theories in a number of areas of social psychology and related fields.

Chapters 4 and 5 are concerned with a set of well-established—and now nearly passé—theories of social psychology that have been in conflict with each other. The conflict has not been resolved so far. Consistency theory in its many forms has typically proposed that people seek reliability, constancy, i.e., want to make their world highly consistent and highly predictable. In contrast, a different group of theories have proposed that people seek novelty, variety, i.e., would like to increase the complexity of their world. Chapter 4 reviews the apparent contradiction with emphasis on the affective components of these two sets of theories. In Chapter 5, we (laboriously) develop a new multidimensional theory that attempts to integrate the two points of view. We attempt to show that both views represent components of an overall behavior.

Chapter 6 is concerned with attitudes and social influence. It attempts to show that many of the theoretical predictions in this area (which sometimes are and sometimes are not supported by research) can be best made for certain specific conditions of dimensionality. Alternate and more general theoretical propositions are provided.

Chapter 7 deals with social perception and person perception, including attribution. It tries to show how multidimensional approaches can aid us in understanding these phenomena, and points out that current attribution theories have already allowed multidimensionality of a kind to enter into explanations and experimental designs. As an example for the value of the multidimensional approach, the chapter concludes with a focus on one particular area of attribution research, where an apparent contradiction between data from different researchers can be resolved through multi-dimensionality.

Chapter 8 attempts to demonstrate the interactive relationship between the complexity theory proposed in Chapter 3 and the General Incongruity Adaptation Level (GIAL) theory proposed in Chapter 5. It also considers some possible further developments of complexity theory. Finally, Chapter 8 cites some examples of expected person–situation interactions on the basis of the person's perceptual or behavioral multidimensionality and his GIAL.

The theories presented in this book are, in part, new developments; in part, they have been discussed in previous technical reports. Segments of the theories have, in some cases, been considered in chapters of other volumes. All the information is brought together here under a common theme. Those theories which have been discussed elsewhere are extended and updated. Each overall theory is written so that specific testable propositions can be derived. A number of propositions are stated in each case. The propositions are numbered by the chapter in which they occur (identifiable to the theory discussed in that chapter) and in numerical order within the chapter. In other words, since complexity theory is discussed in Chapter 3, proposition 3.1 would be the first proposition of our complexity theory. All in all, more than a hundred hypotheses are stated, many of which are immediately testable without further work on development.

Merely one thing still needs to be said. As social psychologists, we typically approach our own subject matter with the same kind of biases that we tend to investigate in others. We would like to ask the reader—as much as possible—to put those biases aside. It appears more than ever necessary to explore alternate points of focus on social psychology. We can, of course, throw out all or most of the previous work and follow those who propose a "critical psychology" of Marxist learnings (Holzkamp, 1970; Sève, 1973) or we might attempt to find salvation in redefining social psychology as an exploratory rather than an experimental science (Silverman, 1976). Neither of those approaches, however, appears to help us answer the questions the public is asking of us today. Neither of those approaches is likely to help us regain the research funds which we might already have lost. And neither approach values or makes use of the research data that have been collected. On the other hand, a return to the blissful purity of restricted laboratory research will hardly gain us public support. And—admittedly—we can hardly expect such support for an esoteric science that has little external validity at a time when social problems require solution.

We need new tools and new views of our field, without being forced to discard all the valuable knowledge that we have already obtained. The present authors believe that the multidimensional approach is one such tool (among others) that can provide—after considerable further work—a more unified and a more externally valid approach to social psychology. We hope the reader will agree to examine our proposals without either a bias in favor of or a bias against the theoretical and methodological approaches of previous social psychology that we are in part using as a basis for our own theory. And we would like to ask the reader to add to the thoughts we are suggesting. The multidimensional approach might well serve as an integrative force in social psychology, and it might make our science more externally valid, i.e., more applicable to behavior in our complex environment. But before that goal has been achieved, the work of many excellent theoreticians, methodologists, and researchers is needed.

REFERENCES

Fromkin, H. L., & Streufert, S. Laboratory experimentation. In M. D. Dunette (Ed.), *Handbook of industrial and organizational psychology.* Chicago: Rand McNally, 1976.

Harré, R., & Secord, P. F. *The explanation of social behavior.* Totowa, N.J.: Rowman & Littlefield, 1972.

Gergen, K. J. Social psychology as history. *Journal of Personality and Social Psychology,* 1973, **26**, 309-320.

Holzkamp, K. Zum Problem der Relevanz psychologischer Forschung für die Praxis. *Psychologische Rundschau,* 1970, **21**, 1-22.

Holzkamp, K. Wissenschaftstheoretische Voraussetzungen kritisch-emanzipatorischer Psychologie. *Zeitschrift für Sozialpsychologie,* 1970, **12**, 5-21, 109-142.

Katz, D. Editorial. *Journal of Personality and Social Psychology,* 1967, **7**, 341-344.

McGuire, W. J. The nature of attitudes and attitude change. In G. Lindzey &

E. Aronson (Eds.), *The handbook of social psychology* (Vol. 3). Reading, Mass.: Addison Wesley, 1969.

Moscovici, S. Society and theory in social psychology. In J. Israel & H. Tajfel (Eds.), *The context of social psychology: A critical assessment.* New York: Academic Press, 1972.

Osgood, C. E., Suci, G. J., & Tannenbaum, P. H. *The measurement of meaning.* Urbana, Ill.: University of Illinois Press, 1957.

Riecken, H. W. Research developments in the social sciences. In O. Klineberg & R. Christie (Eds.), *Perspectives in social psychology.* New York: Holt, Rinehart & Winston, 1965.

Ring, K. Experimental social psychology: Some sober questions about some frivolous values. *Journal of Experimental Social Psychology,* 1967, **3**, 113–123.

Scriven, M. Comments of Professor Scriven. In T. W. Wann (Ed.), *Behaviorism and phenomenology.* Chicago: University of Chicago Press, 1964.

Sève, L. *Marxismus und Theorie der Persönlichkeit.* Frankfurt: Verlag Marxistische Blätter, 1973.

Shulman, A. D., & Silverman, I. Profile of social psychology: A preliminary application of reference analysis. *Journal of the History of Behavioral Sciences,* 1972, **8**, 232–236.

Silverman, I. *Why social psychology fails.* Paper presented at the convention of the American Psychological Association, Washington, D. C., 1976.

Streufert, S. C. *Cognitive complexity: A review* (Tech. Rep. No. 2). Lafayette, Ind.: Purdue University, 1972.

CHAPTER 2

COGNITIVE COMPLEXITY: A REVIEW OF THEORY, MEASUREMENT, AND RESEARCH

INTRODUCTION

Through the ages, man has displayed an overwhelming concern about himself. He has attempted, through philosophy, religion, science, and even mathematics, to determine his own nature and to understand his interaction with his physical and social environment. That this search for understanding continues is a tribute either to man's stoic perseverance or to his stubborn refusal to admit defeat: The ultimate answer may be that man is unable to ever know himself *in toto*.

As we move from the world of philosophers and theologians into the realm of scientific thought, a note of enlightenment may be detected. For in science we find not the all-encompassing, indisputable proclamations regarding the nature of man, favored by the humanists, but, instead, the more tentative and cautious proposals called theories. And, although every theorist holds somewhere in his heart the vague dream of "Eureka," he allows for and admits the possibility of error by speaking in terms of the hypothesis.

The present chapter shall review one set of these theories, those of cognitive complexity. This, too, is an attempt to understand the nature of man, or at least a portion of that nature: the structure and functioning of his cognitive domain. And it also is filled with the possibility of error and the certain need for unification and clarification. This review will not attempt to be exhaustive. It will focus rather on the major assumptions, points of agreement and contradiction in the several theories, and on the body of research data which has emerged from them.

Cognitive Complexity

The term cognitive complexity has appeared with increasing frequency and increasing confusion in the psychological literature of the last two decades. In reviewing the literature, both theory and research, the reason for the confusion becomes apparent. There exists no unitary *theoretical* phenomenon called cognitive complexity, although some researchers may treat it as such, adding to the confusion. In addition, the opinion is held by many that there is no unitary *psychological* phenomenon that can be called cognitive complexity (e.g., Gardner & Schoen, 1962; Scott, 1963b, 1974; Streufert & Driver, 1967; Vannoy, 1965). Doubt about the generality of the complexity phenomenon is justified and, in part, created by the fact that this is an "area" comprised of a number of theories which purport to address the same concept, yet do so in ways which produce noncomplementary, incompatible, and sometimes outright contradictory conclusions.

The ways in which the theories differ are many, including the underlying assumptions upon which they are based and the definitions of terms. As a result, the methods and measurement techniques utilized in the research stemming from these theories differ as well. Further, the results of this research are not always consistent from theory to theory, leading at times to varying interpretations and conclusions upon which further theoretical development may then be based.

Perhaps a unitary "complexity" phenomenon with high generality does not exist. But the evidence may be viewed in such a way that it may have a higher probability of emerging if it is actually there.

Complexity is typically viewed as one aspect of personality structure. The concept of personality structure was formally introduced into the field of psychology fairly early, as one attempt to understand the O in the S-O-R chain. Freud, in his postulation of the Id, Ego, and Superego (Freud, 1949), was presenting a structural theory. Lewin (1936) and Piaget (1952) also dealt with the concept of personality structure. With increasingly greater insights into the organization of cognitive space, an ever-growing number of structural relationships have been identified. As the feasibility of studying these relationships between internal states and behavior increases (Pribram, 1966), psychology may move further into the direction of increasing the study of structure (Foa & Turner, 1970).

Inclusions and Exclusions

It is always necessary, when writing a chapter of this type, to make certain decisions about the relevance of materials to the scope of the chapter. The present discussion is limited in three ways:

(1) The period of time covered is somewhat limited. Very early antecedents of the current theories of cognitive complexity [e.g., the developmental "states" views of Freud (1938), Lewin (1936, 1951), Mead (1934), Schachtel (1959), Werner (1957), and others] are omitted.

(2) Developmental or applied points of view are excluded. Much of the literature dealing with cognitive complexity is related to theory or research on human development, child development, socialization, etc. (e.g., Emmerich, Goldman, & Shore, 1971; Signell, 1966; Wolfe, 1963). In addition, many attempts have been made to apply complexity theory and research to clinical psychology (e.g., Bieri, Atkins, Briar, Leaman, Miller, & Tripodi, 1966; Harvey, Hunt, & Schroder, 1961, ch. 9); to education and training (e.g., Cross, 1966; Felknor & Harvey, 1968; Gardiner, 1972; Harvey, 1970a, 1970b; Harvey et al., 1961, ch. 10; Harvey, Prather, White, & Hoffmeister, 1968; Harvey, White, Prather, Alter, & Hoffmeister, 1966; Hunt, 1966a, 1966b, 1970a, 1970b, 1971, 1975; Hunt & Hardt, 1965; Hunt & Joyce, 1967; Hunt & Sullivan, 1974; McLachlan & Hunt, 1973; Moerdyk, 1973; Osofsky & Hunt, 1969; Posthuma & Carr, 1974; Reynolds, 1970; Schroder, Karlins, & Phares, in press; Tomlinson & Hunt, 1971; Townes & Carr, 1973); to training of underpriviledged children (e.g., Hunt & Dopyera, 1966; Hunt & Hardt, 1967); to management (e.g., Driver & Streufert, 1969; Schroder, 1971b); to political processes (Streufert & Streufert, 1978; Suedfeld & Rank, 1976); and to vocational choice (Lawlis & Crawford, 1975). None of these application areas—no matter how interesting—is considered in this chapter.

(3) Theoretical and research areas of tangential relevance are not discussed in detail. There are many such areas which can be interpreted in the light of complexity—for example, many of the cognitive styles and controls. These include such styles as field dependence—field independence and global vs. articulated functioning (Witkin, 1965), focussing-scanning (Holzman, 1966), cognitive interference (Jensen & Rohwer, 1966), flexible-constrictive style (Klein, 1954), and category width (Bruner, Goodnow, & Austin, 1956; Pettigrew, 1958).

Among the cognitive styles and cognitive controls, only some might potentially relate to complexity as conceived in this chapter. Some work on differentiation (a complexity-relevant process, to be described below) has employed measurement techniques which were originally designed to tap other perceptual phenomena. For example, Uhlman and Saltz (1965) believed that they could establish individual differences in differentiation by measuring flexible-constrictive cognitive style (Klein, 1954) via the Stroop Color Word Test and by measuring field independence on the Concealed Figures Test. Those who scored high on both tests were viewed as differentiators. Witkin and associates (1962) have also used a number of primarily perceptual indices as measures of differentiation.[1] For most researchers who have worked with differentiation as a predictor, however, Kelly's (1955) Role Construct Repertory Test (in various forms) has been used.

The cognitive style that is potentially the most closely related to components of structural complexity is category width, or the characteristic of individuals to be consistently broad, medium, or narrow categorizers (Bruner et al., 1956). For example, "categorizing" may be similar to the processes of differentiation and integration. Several researchers have been concerned with establishing potential relationships between the two sets of variables (cf., Bieri, 1969; Bruner & Tajfel, 1961, 1965a, 1965b; Gardner & Schoen, 1962, 1965). It appears that the two concepts are not related in any meaningful way. Even when differentiation is viewed as the number of different meaningful categories in which stimuli are sorted (as by Gardner and associates), only low correlations with category width are obtained, typically accounting for less than 7% common variance.

Since category width tends to be concerned with categorizing on a *single* dimension (Bruner & Tajfel, 1965a; Gardner & Schoen, 1965), one might argue that it should be more closely related to discrimination than to

---

[1] The meaning of the term "differentiation" here is quite different than the use of it by many of the researchers concerned with forms of cognitive complexity (to be defined below). Witkin, Goodenough, and Karp (1967) stated that with the accumulated evidence now available psychological differentiation has come to serve, for them, as a construct to conceptualize the particular communality they have observed in a person's functioning in different psychological areas, and they conceive of the individual differences they have found in clusters of interrelated characteristics as differences in extent of psychological differentiation.

"Extent of differentiation is reflected in the area of perception in the degree of field dependence or independence." This definition of differentiation is specifically relevant to visual-motor tasks based on perceptual theory. In contrast, differentiation for research in complexity theory is based on cognitions involving verbal "concepts," "dimensions," etc. In other words, the work of Witkin and associates (Oltman, Goodenough, Witkin, Freedman, & Friedman, 1975; Witkin, 1950, 1964, 1965, 1973; Witkin & Asch, 1948; Witkin & Berry, 1975; Witkin, Dyk, Faterson, Goodenough, & Karp, 1962; Witkin, Goodenough, & Karp, 1967; Witkin, Lewis, Hertzman, Machover, Meissner, & Wapner, 1954) is not relevant to this review and will not be covered.

differentiation (see Definitions, below). Bieri (1969), however, has found that this relationship (at least for physical stimuli) does not hold, either. It had been assumed that tendency to narrow categorization reflects a greater ability to discriminate. This assumption was not supported by Bieri's results. Rather, he found the reverse: Subjects with low category width could not discriminate as well as subjects with high width.

Because of these indications that other structural cognitive styles, even the one most likely to be related, have little in common with cognitive complexity, these areas are not covered in the present review. What is included is a discussion of theory and theory-relevant research and measurement pertaining to cognitive complexity which has appeared since approximately 1955. A description of what is defined here as cognitive complexity is presented in the following section.

Definitions

Due to the disparity among the terminologies used in the various complexity theories, it becomes necessary to state a set of working definitions of certain key terms to create a common language. As the theories are discussed, the specific terms used by their authors will be restated or reinterpreted into this common language, whenever applicable. This process in itself may serve to point out some of the bases for the differing conclusions of the various theorists and researchers. That is, in many cases it may be that two theorists utilize an identical term but define or conceptualize it in very different ways. Similarly, completely different terms may be used, when in fact the identical process is discussed.

Dimension: A bipolar semantic scale in a person's cognitive semantic space. The scale may have as few as two points of discrimination among stimuli (i.e., the poles), or it may have many more. The scale represents an individual's grouping or ordering of those stimuli which have meaning in the semantic space defined by the endpoints of the scale. This last point may be elucidated by an example, similar to one used by Kelly (1955). If an individual has in his cognitive space a dimension (scale) of short–tall, the endpoints of that dimension have meaning to the stimuli *man* or *building*, but do not have meaning in relation to the stimulus *weather.*

Discrimination: The process of dividing (or the degree to which division has been accomplished) a cognitive bipolar semantic dimension into parts (subsections) for the placement of stimuli which have semantic relevance to the endpoints (poles) of that dimension. Discrimination is meaningful only to the degree that sharp distinctions can be made, i.e., to the degree that the distinctions can either be labeled or to the degree that they can evoke differential outcomes in behavior. The minimum number of discriminations on any dimension is two (pole A vs. not-pole A; or, pole A vs. pole B). The maximum number of discriminations on any dimension is limited only by the capacity of the organism to meaningfully divide the semantic space of any dimension.

The process of discrimination, although unidimensional, is related to the processes of differentiation and integration (see below). As in differentiation, it involves the dividing of a segment of semantic space (here, of one dimension only); and as in integration, it involves the assembling of various semantic points (meaning) into a (here, unidimensional) subsegment of semantic space.

Differentiation: The process of dividing cognitive semantic space (or the degree to which this division has been achieved relevant to specific stimulus configurations) into two or more orthogonal or oblique (but near-orthogonal) bipolar semantic dimensions—i.e., the ordering of stimuli in intransitive fashion on two or more scales in semantic space.

Integration: The process of relating a stimulus configuration to two or more orthogonal or oblique dimensions of semantic space (or the degree to which this relating has been achieved) to produce a perceptual or behavioral outcome which is determined by the *joint* (weighted or unweighted) demands of each dimension involved.

Hierarchical integration: The fixed, unchanging relationship among dimensions with regard to a number of stimulus configurations, producing a joint weighted or unweighted, but stable, response to stimuli. Specific stimuli would always affect the same dimensions in the same way.

Flexible integration: The varied, changing relationship among dimensions with regard to stimulus configurations, producing various diverse (over stimulus type, presence/absence, or frequency) weighted or unweighted, more or less unstable, responses to stimuli.

Content: Represents the location of any specific stimulus object or configuration on any specific discriminated point on a cognitive dimension to which it is assigned by the individual (e.g., an attitude). In other words, cognitive content is concerned with the relationship of various stimulus *objects* to each other on that dimension (as contrasted to the structural relationship among dimensions). Content represents *what* a person thinks about a stimulus, not *how* he thinks about it.

Structure: Represents the differentiative or integrative use of *dimensions* of semantic space with regard to a specific stimulus object or configuration. Structure is concerned with the number of dimensions and the number and pattern of relationships among them (i.e., the *organization* of cognitive semantic space), rather than the meaning of the specific dimensions involved. In other words, while content is concerned with what an individual thinks about a stimulus and what response he makes to it, structure is concerned with the cognitive processes underlying a response, i.e., how he thinks about the stimulus.

Cognitive complexity-simplicity: Represents the degree to which the entire and/or a subsegment of a cognitive semantic space is differentiated and integrated.

THEORY

It should be noted that the treatment of each theory in this chapter does not follow a uniform outline or structure. The structure of each of the following sections is determined by the nature of the discussed material, rather than by an attempt to fit each theory into a fixed pattern.

The Psychology of Personal Constructs

The theoretical propositions of G. A. Kelly (described in detail in his 1955 volumes) were originally set forth as a guide to psychotherapy and client-therapist interaction. They are included here because his theory of personal constructs and his Role Construct Repertory (Rep) Test measurement technique have served as the basis and inspiration for many subsequent theoretical developments which deal more directly with cognitive complexity. Use of the Rep Test has been widespread, and it seems important to understand Kelly's notion of personal constructs which became the theoretical basis for the test.

Kelly presented his basic theory in the form of one "fundamental postulate" and 11 corollaries. It may be helpful to list these and then discuss them together with their implications as a unit.

Fundamental postulate: A person's processes are psychologically channelized by the ways in which he anticipates events.

Construction corollary: A person anticipates events by construing their replications.

Individuality corollary: Persons differ from each other in their construction of events.

Organization corollary: Each person characteristically evolves, for his convenience in anticipating events, a construction system embracing ordinal relationships between constructs.

Dichotomy corollary: A person's construction system is composed of a finite number of dichotomous constructs.

Choice corollary: A person chooses for himself that alternative in a dichotomized construct through which he anticipates the greater possibility for extension and definition of his system.

Range corollary: A construct is convenient for the anticipation of a finite range of events only.

Experience corollary: A person's construction system varies as he successively construes the replications of events.

Modulation corollary: The variation in a person's construction system is limited by the permeability of the constructs within whose range of convenience the variants lie.

Fragmentation corollary: A person may successively employ a variety of construction subsystems which are inferentially incompatible with each other.

Commonality corollary: To the extent that one person employs a construction of experience which is similar to that employed by another, his psychological processes are similar to those of the other person.

Sociality corollary: To the extent that one person construes the construction processes of another, he may play a role in a social process involving the other person.

The basic unit upon which Kelly's theoretical formulations are built is the "construct." The construct is viewed as a bipolar dimension which results from the individual's process of construing, or interpreting, events. In the process of construing, the individual observes a series of events and takes note of the similarities and differences among them. Therefore, the constructs which the person creates are cognitive dimensions of similarity and contrast. In its most basic sense, a construct is a way of organizing or interpreting the relationship among three elements (events, objects) of which two are similar and the third is in contrast. An individual creates for himself a construction system, which involves the ordinal, hierarchical relationship among constructs. Both individual constructs and the construction system are continuously changing to adapt to the development of events. Constructs are relevant only to a limited range of elements; that is, not all dimensions can be used to interpret all events. An individual places relative values on the endpoints of his constructs, and chooses that endpoint, in any particular case, in interpreting (placing) an element or stimulus event, which is most likely to assist him in predicting the ensuing events. Some of these values are relatively stable, serving as "guiding principles," while others are changeable, serving only for the convenience of the moment. There are individual differences in specific constructs as well as construction systems, although individuals may be similar in these factors to a certain extent. Finally, Kelly proposed that in order to most effectively interact with another person, an individual should understand that person's way of looking at the world (i.e., his construction system), even though he does not necessarily have the same way of construing the world.

It may be useful at this point to attempt, wherever applicable, to fit Kelly's theoretical concepts in the present set of working definitions:

Dimension: The "construct" is, in effect, a dimension. Its fit into this definition is furthered by the assertion by Kelly that a construct, like a dimension, has meaning only when applied to elements which are relevant to the meaning of the poles of the construct.

Discrimination: For Kelly, discrimination appears to be on the most minimal level, i.e., pole A vs. pole B. An individual chooses that end of a construct which best fits his needs, a process of bifurcation. However, Kelly does allow for the possibility of utilizing "shades of gray," for using a construct in a relativistic manner. For this, however, he proposes the introduction of another, subordinal, construct (in the hierarchical system) called "less gray vs. more gray."

Differentiation: The process most closely related to differentiation postulated by Kelly is that of building hierarchical "scales" or a hierarchy of constructs. This process refers to an individual's ability to utilize a *number* of bipolar constructs in a binary fashion (i.e., pole A, not-pole A, on any specific construct) to interpret a given stimulus. The "scale" is the number of possible binary combinations of the constructs, dependent, of course, on the number of constructs involved. In this way, a person may place stimuli on a number of different dimensions in a "simple" manner (if placement is either pole A or pole B on all constructs, indicating a cognitive collapsing of the constructs into one real dimension) or in a more "complex" differentiated manner by placing the stimulus on pole A on some of the constructs and pole B on others.

Integration: Kelly discussed the hierarchical organization of constructs, and the fact that this organization is changeable. He may, in effect, be referring to something called integration by the present authors. However, it is impossible to make a definite statement regarding integration. If anything, it appears that in referring to the ordinal relationships among constructs, Kelly assumes, at most, some kind of differentiation. What could be viewed as integration appears, in fact, to be the mere collapsing of constructs onto one dimension, i.e., simplicity.

Content and structure: These two concepts appear not to be distinguished in Kelly's conceptualizations. A construct has both content and structural characteristics. An example may be the fact that in many cases a construct is referred to as a dimension of attributes (black-white), while in some cases such things as table vs. not-table are referred to as constructs.

Cognitive complexity-simplicity: There is some evidence, in Kelly's circumspection-preemption-control (C-P-C) cycle of the judgmental process, that although perception may be multidimensional, and the cognitive structure is multidimensional, the final output (judgment) is conceived of as totally unidimensional. Output (decision, judgment) is determined by the choice of a single dimension on which a stimulus object is to be placed.

It must be noted here that any reinterpretation of theoretical concepts into the current set of definitions should be viewed as tentative. In addition, it is not possible to determine, with complete certainty, what the conceptualizations of one theorist mean in terms of the conceptualizations of another. One must rely here on verbalizations, and, in Kelly's terms, may not be able to "construe" the underlying cognitive processes accurately. Further enlightenment should be possible when the research evidence (i.e., "behavioral outcomes") is analyzed.

Cognitive Complexity-Simplicity (Bieri)

The theoretical propositions of James Bieri are viewed as a development based on the work of Kelly (Bieri et al., 1966). Similar to Kelly, Bieri is concerned with the effects of an individual's cognitive dimensional structure on the judgments he makes about input from the environment. Specifically, Bieri focuses on the individual's social or interpersonal judgments. In fact, he explicitly states (Bieri, 1968) that cognitive complexity is concerned *only* with social stimuli and with an individual's "dimensional versatility" in his social judgments.

Cognitive complexity is a measure of the degree of differentiation in the cognitive system for perceiving others (Bieri, 1961). As such, it is considered to be a structural characteristic which serves as an information processing variable affecting the way in which specific (social) stimuli are transformed into judgments (Bieri, 1966). The degree of cognitive complexity is related to the number of dimensions of judgment a person has available to him. The more available dimensions, the higher the degree of complexity.

Bieri refers to two important aspects of psychological dimensions. The first is differentiation (Bieri, 1966; Bieri et al., 1966). Differentiation can refer to either cognitive or stimulus structure. With regard to cognitive structure, differentiation refers to the relative number of dimensions used by the judge in construing others (Bieri, 1966). So, for Bieri, complexity of cognitive structure equals degree of differentiation of cognitive structure. This is true, however, only if it is remembered that the degree of differentiation refers to differentiation of independent *dimensions,* not of categories, concepts, or regions (Bieri et al., 1966). On the other hand, differentiation of the stimulus refers to the number of dimensions possessed by that stimulus. Bieri stresses the importance of the interaction (in terms of output) between stimulus and cognitive complexity. A number of studies relating to this problem have been reported and will be discussed in the section concerned with research results.

The second aspect of dimensions is termed "articulation" (Bieri, 1966; Bieri et al., 1966). Articulation refers to the process of making discriminations *within* a dimension rather than *between* dimensions, as in differentiation. The degree of articulation is reflected in the number of categories or intervals which can be discriminated on any dimension. This process is obviously closely related to the process of discrimination as it has been defined in this chapter.

Finally, Bieri refers to a process which he calls "discrimination." Discrimination in this sense (Bieri et al., 1966) refers to the judgmental process of making unique distinctions among stimuli. It is not necessarily related to dimensionality (stimuli which are unidimensional or multidimensional may be discriminated) and is very different from the definition of discrimination used here, which (as stated above), is akin to Bieri's process of articulation.

There is a long list of variables which, in Bieri's view, can be related to complexity, including concept attainment, information transmission, judgment of inconsistent information, etc. Research by Bieri and others on the various effects of complexity upon these types of variables are reported in a later section.

Categorizing (Zajonc)

Robert Zajonc (1960) presented a set of theoretical formulations based upon an earlier unpublished study of cognitive characteristics. Its main importance in relation to complexity theories is its influence on later theorists and researchers, particularly with regard to methodological considerations. Zajonc first presents a description of the cognitive processes that take place within an organism; these processes mediate between the stimulus and the response. He then describes the nature of cognitive structure.

The first assumption is that stimuli (objects and events) are perceived and discriminated on the basis of psychological dimensions, thereby providing for the O in S-O-R. A *psychological dimension* is defined as the organism's capacity to respond to stimuli in such a way that, given a set of stimuli and a set of responses made to them, the stimuli and responses form two ordered sets with a determinate correspondence between the elements of each set. It may be noted that a "dimension" as described here is not necessarily the bipolar scale which has been previously defined. Instead, it appears to be viewed as a set of points in semantic space.

Dimensions (in the terminology of Zajonc) consist of values which can be inferred from responses. In perception or discrimination, a stimulus is placed on certain of these dimensions and the values of these dimensions are then attributed to the stimulus. *"Attributes,"* then, are the elements of cognitive structures. They are those values which are assigned to a stimulus. An attribute is conceived as a category, which usually characterizes a whole class of objects, rather than merely a single stimulus.

The *"cognitive universe"* is the set of all such attributes or categories which a person possesses for the identification and discrimination of environmental stimuli. The cognitive universe can be divided into cognitive structures. A *"cognitive structure"* is an organized subset of the cognitive universe which pertains to a specific object or event.

There can be various relationships among the attributes or categories in a cognitive structure, including differentiation, complexity, unity, and organization. (It may be important to remember that these may refer to relationships among points or categories, not necessarily among dimensions. This fact may have implications for interpretation of research stemming from the Zajonc theory, particularly when it is related to other conceptualizations of complexity dealing with dimensionality.)

Differentiation: The degree of differentiation is equal to the number of attributes constituting a given cognitive structure.

Complexity: Attributes in a cognitive structure may come from only one or from many classes of "discriminanda." These classes may be subdivided into smaller classes. The definition of complexity is based on the extent to which classes of attributes in a given cognitive structure are thus subdivided.

The degree of complexity is obtained by weighting each attribute by the level of inclusion of its class in the structure and then summing the weighted scores:

$$\text{Complexity} = \sum_{r=1}^{n} rn_r$$

where r is the level of inclusion of a given class, such that if class K_i does not include another subclass, $r = 1$; when K_i includes some subclasses, which in turn do not include other subdivisions, $r = 2$; when K_i includes subclasses which themselves contain other indivisible subclasses, $r = 3$, etc.; n_r is the number of attributes in the rth level of inclusion.

Unity: Unity refers to the degree to which the attributes of a cognitive structure depend on each other. The more interdependency among attributes, the higher is the unity of the structure. The dependency relationship is defined in terms of mutual change. That is, if a change in attribute A_i produces a change in attribute A_j, then the dependency of A_j on A_i equals 1. If a change in A_i produces no change in A_j, then the dependency of A_j on A_i equals 0:

$$\text{Unity} = \frac{\sum_{i=1}^{n} \text{dep}(A_i)}{n(n-1)}$$

where n is the degree of differentiation, or the number of attributes in the structure. (For comparing structures relative to their unity, the measure must be normalized if those structures possess different degrees of differentiation.) $n-1$ is the maximum dependency of a given attribute; $n(n-1)$ is the maximum sum of dependencies in the cognitive structure; and dep (A_i) is the total dependency of the ith attribute. This can be obtained by constructing a dependency matrix for all attributes of a given structure and then summing in the appropriate row.

Organization: The degree of organization is conceived in Lewinian (1951) terms as the extent that one part or a cluster of parts dominates the whole. To obtain a measure of the degree to which the interdependence among attributes of a given structure is "concentrated around a single core," one calculates:

$$\text{Organization} = \frac{\det (A_i)^{\max}}{\text{Unity}}$$

where $\det (A_i)^{\max}$ is the determinance of the strongest attribute (obtained from the appropriate column in the dependence matrix).

Cognitive Structure (Scott)

The theoretical propositions of William A. Scott are based on the early work of Lewin (1936), Heider (1946), and the methodological formulations of Zajonc (1960). Earlier distinctions between personality content and structure are clarified and elaborated by Scott into an encompassing theory of structural characteristics which has considerable implications for social, personality, and clinical psychology (Scott, 1969). Scott (following Lewin and Heider) distinguishes between two forms of cognitive characteristics: content and structure. Content refers to objects in perceptual space and to their attributes (how they are viewed). In other words, cognitive content refers to such psychological characteristics as attitudes, beliefs, and values, and is thus similar to the definition of content presented earlier. Structure, on the other hand, describes relationships among cognitions, that is, characteristics such as differentiation, integration, rigidity, flexibility, etc. (Scott, 1962a). Again, this definition is similar to the present working definition of structure.

Scott's major interest is focused on structure, and he proposes and defines a number of structural characteristics. Among these are balance (separated into evaluative and affective) and consistency (Scott, 1963a, 1969, 1974), unity and hierarchic integration (Scott, 1959, 1962b), centrality, articulation, and ambivalence (Scott, 1969). Since the use of these terms by Scott differs from the definitions presented here, it might be useful to review the definition used by Scott. Such definitions not only refer to structure itself, but also to other cognitive characteristics that help to define structure (cf. Scott, 1969):

Cognitive domain: Consists of those phenomenal objects, or images, which are treated by the individual as functionally equivalent plus the attributes with which he interprets those objects.

Attribute: A line in multidimensional space which is divided into segments representing characteristics recognized by the individual. Attributes are distinguishable to the extent that they order phenomenal objects in different ways. In terms of the present definitions, an attribute is a dimension which has been discriminated.

Images (or concepts of objects): Points in multidimensional space, understood as combinations of characteristics. Represented graphically, an image is the intersection of normal projections from the segments of several attributes corresponding to characteristics assigned to an object. Images are distinguishable to the extent that they include different combinations of characteristics.

Dimensionality: The number of "dimensions-worth" of space taken by the attributes of a cognitive domain.

Articulation: The number of reliable distinctions made by an individual on an attribute. Articulation is equivalent to the previously defined process of discrimination and to Bieri's concept of articulation.

Differentiation (among images): Depends on the number of attributes (dimensionality) in the cognitive domain and the degree of articulation (discrimination) on these attributes.

Integration: The way in which images are related within a cognitive domain. There are various kinds of integration:

  Centralization: A "primitive variety" which treats a number of attributes as central. The limiting case would have all images in the cognitive domain defined only by their positions on a single common attribute.

  Image comparability: Judging all phenomenal objects on the same set of attributes.

  Affective balance : (cf. Heider, 1946) A form of integration in which objects are cognitively grouped according to their affective meaning for the individual. Liked objects are seen as belonging together and disliked objects are seen as belonging with each other.

  Affective-evaluative consistency : A form of integration in which objects are liked to the extent that they are seen as possessing desirable characteristics; alternatively, objects are evaluated according to one's affective reaction to them. This process and the affective balance process would lead to low dimensionality of the cognitive domain, since attributes which correlate highly with liking would also be correlated with each other.

Ambivalent image: An image which includes both desirable and undesirable characteristics. The occurrence of ambivalent images would be reduced if the processes of affective balance or affective-evaluative consistency were operating.

To summarize: Any perception by a person based on the phenomenological world results in an image which represents a point on one or more dimensions (attributes) of cognitive space. Where, on any dimension, the image falls depends on the number of segments of the dimension (degree of articulation of the attribute). The number of independent dimensions (attributes) into which a person sorts information reflects the degree to which he differentiates the specific cognitive domain into which he has placed the perceived stimuli.

It should be noted that Scott views both dimensionality and discrimination (in his terms, attributes and articulation) as parts of the differentiation concept. In this way he differs from other theorists (e.g., Driver & Streufert, 1966; Schroder, Driver, & Streufert, 1967; Streufert, 1970) who view discrimination as a separate process.

Scott's view of "integration" also differs from that of other theorists who have have been primarily concerned with that concept (e.g., Driver & Streufert, 1966; Harvey et al., 1961; Schroder et al., 1967; Streufert, 1970). While all writers would agree that integration refers to the manner in which images are related, Scott includes a much greater number of cognitive operations in his "integration" concept. For example, if (to use one of his integrative processes) various attributes (dimensions) are highly correlated with "affective-evaluative consistency," then this form of association would be viewed by other theorists as the absence of complexity. Integration theorists would argue that integration must follow differentiation. The use of divergent verbal labels for what is otherwise known as the good-bad (evaluative) dimension would suggest to them that identity (unity) of these attributes has been learned, and that a differentiation process did not take place before the association was made. Alternatively, the structure which once was differentiated may have become resimplified through a process that may be called hierarchical integration (Streufert, 1970), as distinguished from what Schroder et al. (1967) called integration proper, and what Driver and Streufert (1966) and Streufert (1970) have discussed as flexible integration.

A final distinguishing characteristic of Scott's theory is his repeated emphasis (e.g., Peterson & Scott, 1974; Scott, 1963b) on the limitations of complexity across cognitive domains (cf. also Cohen & Feldman, 1975). He questions the assumption of the existence of structural *types*, i.e., the description of a person as "simple," "complex," etc. He considers it to be probable that the number of persons who have consistent structural characteristics among many areas of their experience is quite small, and further suggests that such individuals may well be pathological. Scott states, however (personal communication, 1975), that the attempt to describe such types is of value if developed empirically, rather than on an *a priori* basis. Recent evidence (Peterson & Scott, 1974; Scott, 1974) suggests the existence of at least a limited typography: Some degree of generality of cognitive style across domains was obtained. Which style is utilized in a particular situation appears to be dependent upon an interaction between the structural characteristics of the person and the characteristics of the situation.

Most of Scott's theoretical work is concerned with the description and definition (in order to aid measurement) of structural characteristics. Predictions are primarily made for interrelationships among characteristics of structure. Note that such concepts as consistency, centrality, and the like are considered to be structural characteristics. Scott predicts, then, that: (1) Differentiation is inversely related to balance; (2) differentiation is positively correlated with flexibility (willingness of subjects to redifferentiate); and (3) cognitive structure is similar to social structure.

Impression Formation Theory (Crockett)

Impression formation and its consequences are of interest to those who wish to study attitudes under conditions where subjects are provided with inconsistent information. Asch (1946) was concerned with the primacy and recency effects of such information and, depending on the manipulation, both effects have been obtained. Anderson and Barrios (1961), Asch (1946), and Luchins (1957a, 1957b) have all obtained primacy effects. Luchins (1958), on the other hand, obtained recency effects. Whether primacy or recency occurs depends, for instance, on whether or not the subject is required to write a response to univalent (one-sided) information before a block of discrepant information is presented.

It has become apparent to several researchers, however, that some subjects produce neither primacy nor recency effects. Rather, they tend to present integrated information. If the description of the stimulus object is negative in one set and positive in the other, their total response (after hearing both kinds of information) tends to be mixed or ambivalent, rather than either positive or negative. Further, such subjects present a "whole," i.e., meaningful and complete, description of the stimulus person, when asked to do so.

Bieri (1955) suggested that complex persons should produce more veridical perceptions of others. Miller and Bieri (1965) advanced the "vigilance" hypothesis, which assumes that persons will differentiate (discriminate) more finely among negative, potentially threatening people.

A "tight" methodological paradigm in this area which is subject to sequential investigation was developed by Walter Crockett (1965) and associates. He and his students carried out an extensive research program which focused specifically on the "impression formation" process in lieu of the more vague and more varied area of "interpersonal perception."

Crockett's work is based primarily on Werner's (1957) developmental psychology. His theory and the measurement based on it appear to be an integration of the Wernerian emphasis on the development of cognition via increased "differentiation and articulation" of cognitive elements and a simultaneous "increased interdependence of elements" by virtue of their integration into a hierarchically organized system. Combining this view with the work of Kelly (1955) and Lewin (1951), Crockett (1965) makes specific predictions for the complexity of the structure of a cognitive system. Such a system can be considered relatively complex when (a) it contains a larger number of elements, and (b) the elements (constructs) are integrated hierarchically by relatively extensive bonds of relationship. The relative number of constructs in a cognitive system is then referred to as its *degree of cognitive differentiation.*

It should be noted that Crockett uses the term "relative," that is, relative to others, in the same group, working on the same task, etc. This view permits him to do median splits for dividing subject populations into simple and complex individuals.

Beyond these statements, Crockett's theory appears to be relatively pragmatic. His 1965 paper bases theoretical statements on a series of interpretations of research by himself and his associates, and on some research by others where it relates to impression formation. Crockett concludes by listing a number of components which would be important parts of a theory of complexity. These components are based, to a great extent, on his assertion that complexity increases with exposure: the *frequency of interaction hypothesis* which holds that one is most complex in that interpersonal realm where the most experiences with others have been had. He states:

(a) The degree of differentiation of a subject's cognitive system with respect to some domain of events will vary as a function of his experiences with objects in that domain.

(b) Subjects who develop an extensive set of interpersonal constructs, compared with those with a sparse set of constructs, make more inferences from a standard set of information, are more likely to view others in ambivalent terms, and are better able to assimilate potentially contradictory information about another person into a unified impression.

(c) Such differences in the effects of cognitive complexity may be limited by differential experience with particular categories of people, or by differences in the values or motivational states of the perceiver.

(d) The empirical test of one large body of hypotheses depends upon the development of more elaborate methods for observing the structural aspects of cognitions.

Crockett (1965) is concerned, as are several others, with the question of generality. Based on the results of data collected by a number of his associates, he concludes that we have already rejected the assumption of generality of cognitive complexity in the broad sense, i.e., to mean generality across different domains of content. After referring to research by Nidorf (1961), he further concludes that it appears that some degree of generality of complexity held in these data, despite the fact that such factors as frequency of contact with particular categories of individuals were operating to produce systematic differences in the number of constructs used to describe others from these different categories.

In other words, Crockett believes that predictions from a measure of complexity to interpersonal judgments (as required in impression formation tasks) can be made. Much of the data he presents (to be discussed in a later section) does indeed support such a generality, and he carefully explains why research which did not obtain parallel data cannot be expected to produce such data because of differences in manipulations, populations, etc.

Systems Theory (Harvey, Hunt, and Schroder)

Systems theory is a mixture of a structural[2] theory and a system-specific content theory. The theory is, in part, developmental, and, in part (the primary interest here), predictive of current behavior. It assumes that individuals develop concepts about sets of stimuli which reach their sense organs. Concepts define the relationship a person has with differentiated aspects of his environment. A variety of functions of the conceptual matrix can be postulated: For example, shared concepts become group norms. As schemata for evaluating impinging stimulus objects along some specifiable dimension, they serve as a kind of psychological yardstick to which the impinging world is compared and is differentiated and integrated; they operate as kinds of programs or cognitive metering systems through which reality is defined and read (Harvey & Schroder, 1963) (cf. also, Harvey et al., 1961; Schroder & Harvey, 1963.)

Applying concepts to environmental input at times produces mismatches, problems in the conceptualization of new stimuli. As a result, saccadic processes of differentiation and integration (structural reorganization) occur.

---

[2] Abstractness–concreteness is the structural dimension underlying the systems. Structure is defined as the relationship among various parts of the system (Harvey, 1966).

Out of the saccadic process of differentiation and integration, of breaking down and interrelating, variations occur on the important dimensions of consequent systemic organization. One of the most important of these is referred to as concreteness–abstractness (Harvey et al., 1961). "Concrete" is defined as being equal to minimal differentiation; "abstract" is defined as equal to maximal differentiation *and* integration. Greater concreteness (as opposed to abstractness) implies (Harvey & Schroder, 1963): (a) fewer differentiations, incomplete integration; (b) a tendency toward bifurcated evaluation; (c) dependence on external criteria of validity, e.g., authority, precedent; (d) greater intolerance for ambiguity, e.g., quick judgments in novel situations, susceptibility to salient (and potentially false) cues; (e) inability to change set, stereotyping in attempted solutions of complex problems; (f) greater resistance to change when stress is low, greater likelihood of collapse when stress is high; (g) poor delineation between means and ends, hence a paucity of different routes toward the same goal; (h) poorer capacity to act "as if," empathize, simulate a hypothetical situation; (1) less well-defined self, consequently, less perception of self as a causal agent (external vs. internal control).

Progressive development from more concrete to more abstract passes through certain plateaus or stages for periods of time. Dependent on training, development may be arrested at any one stage, or at a point where a transition between stages occurs. The stages (or "systems") are:

Stage 1: Related to authoritarianism, resulting from fate control in childhood training by the parents. Greater dependence on external authority and causality. Positive self-worth is defined by conformity. Violation of rules is seen as sin, and guilt is experienced.

Stage 2: Similar to Stage 1, but the self is better differentiated since the individual must rely on himself for rewards. Developmental arrest at Stage 2 results from an unpredictable environment, where reward and punishment for specific acts cannot be predicted; the training agent is unpredictable. The result is rebellion, negativism, avoidance of dependency and of external control. While representatives of Stages 1 and 2 are content-wise very dissimilar (approach vs. avoidance of same referents), structurally they are quite similar, both possessed of a poorly differentiated conceptual system, strong avidities, high stereotypy, and inability to delineate and try alternate approaches to complex problems (Harvey & Schroder, 1963).

Stage 3: Rules and other extrapersonal forces have not been as influential in the person's upbringing. The training agent was not seen as omniscient or omnipotent. There is greater perception of self as a causal agent and greater fate control. The self is further articulated. Extreme System 3 functioning comes from overindulgence and overprotection by the training agent. In contrast to the preceding systems, one finds here an interactive influence of training agent and trainee. Often there is a symbiotic dependence between the training agent and the trainee. The trainee gets minimal experience with the "outside world." Consequently, a System 3 person is fearful of coping alone with external situations. He becomes dependent, displays greater conformity, wants to be liked. Dependency is upon a finite number of persons, not upon rules (as in Systems 1 and 2).

Stage 4: Characterized by information or task orientation to situations. Training conditions rewarded the trainee for exploration and independence. His demands and his reasons for them were considered, but he was not overindulged. The training agent neither dominated nor was dominated by the trainee. The trainee develops the ability to try alternate approaches to the environment. He engages in self-correction through a process of environmental feedback. Highly integrated, he can cope with a variety of conditions. He places a high value on information. He is an independent individual, without negative or positive dependency on external criteria or negative or positive control, of or by others.

Selection of persons from these "systems" permits a variety of predictions based on the characteristics of O in the S–O–R chain. Harvey, Reich, and Wyer (1968) view Systems 1 and 2 as similar, and Systems 3 and 4 as similar, so that for purposes of structural analysis, these systems are combined (1 with 2; 3 with 4) to obtain a "concrete" and an "abstract" category.

Underlying the more generic characteristics of abstractness–concreteness are such intrasystem properties as clarity–ambiguity, compartmentalization–interrelatedness, centrality–peripherality (Harvey, 1966) and openness–closedness (Harvey & Schroder, 1963).

Harvey (1966) pointed out some of the problems with systems theory: The one source of inconsistency has been the responses of System 3 representatives, who on such things as evaluativeness and categoricalness of the TIB (This I Believe system measure) completion fall next to System 4 (where they should be according to their assumed position on the concreteness–abstractness dimension), but who on such things as authoritarianism and ability to change set fall next to System 1. This inconsistency is, no doubt, due partially to lack of clarity in theoretical formulation of System 3 functioning, which in turn results in somewhat ambiguous criteria for scoring this system.

Systems theory does, admittedly, place values on the various types of structure described. The theorists' stance on the desired state is rather clear. They believe that abstract conceptual structure and its associated characteristics of creativity, flexibility, stress tolerance and broad spectrum coping power, is a desirable adaptive stage. In short, it is a good thing (Hunt, 1961, 1966b).

Hunt (1966a) and others have demonstrated the applicability of conceptual systems to education, with the aim of increasing individuals' level of abstraction. Hunt (e.g., 1966a) also adds a "sub 1" stage to the stages and transitions proposed by Harvey et al. (1961). "Sub 1" stage persons have not developed a single dimension of judgment with regard to a specific stimulus. They operate instead in terms of inclusion (good) vs. exclusion (the bad and the unfamiliar, alike).

Interactive Complexity Theory 1
(Driver, Schroder, and Streufert)

Driver and Streufert (1966), Schroder, Driver, and Streufert (1967), Streufert and Driver (1967), and Schroder (1971a) have presented an interactive theory of cognitive and environmental complexity. The basic components of the theory are the processes of discrimination (division of a unidimensional scale, i.e., a dimension defined by bipolar endpoints, into articulated parts), differentiation (orthogonal dimensionality in the cognitive semantic space), and integration (the flexible relationships among various dimensions with regard to specific stimulation). Simple persons are those who operate primarily unidimensionally, while complex persons operate primarily multidimensionally, integrating and/or differentiating.

These authors suggest that differences between complex and simple persons can be obtained only when (a) the task to which subjects are exposed permits a multidimensional (differentiated or integrated) approach, and (b) when environmental conditions are favorable. Complex information processing (i.e., integration and/or differentiation) should occur, all other things being equal, when an optimal (intermediate) level of environmental complexity is achieved (i.e., when the environment is neither depriving nor overloading). Under conditions of too low environmental complexity (e.g., sensory deprivation), no differentiation or integration should occur and, consequently, no differences between simple and complex persons should be expected. Similar findings are predicted for overloading environmental situations. Both overload and deprivation are described as "stressful."

Intermediate, optimal environments should permit more complex information processing.[3] At that point, discrepancies between simple subjects and complex subjects should emerge. Simple subjects should obtain a lower peak point on the inverted U-shaped curve relating environmental complexity to differentiation and integration, and should reach this peak point at a lower level of environmental complexity than is expected for complex subjects. Since differentiation is viewed as a necessary precondition for integration, the

---

[3] Suedfeld (1978) has recently warned that optima may be too general in theoretical formulations to have extensive meaning.

effects of changes in environmental complexity should be similar or identical for the two processes.

These authors view environmental complexity as a composite of at least three components: information load (the quantity of information impinging on the processing organism per unit time), eucity (success), and noxity (failure). These three components are expected to sum to produce a joint effect on information processing. The possibility that other variables might be added to these three is left open.

The authors suggest that the theory should have considerable implications for decision making, performance, aggression, relationships between individual and group structures, and attitudes. Specific predictions from the theory are limited to research areas where some data have been obtained, e.g., the work of Driver (1962) with Guetzkow's (1959) INS simulation including noxity and eucity components, and the work of Streufert (1966) with attitudes and information search. Based on these studies, attitudes are viewed as being affected by salience for simple subjects more than for complex subjects, and information search is seen as more likely to occur in complex than in simple persons. Schroder (1971a) extends the attitude predictions somewhat. He states that if we view the attitude in this way (structurally), we can expect to find the same U curve relationship for problem solving. Differences in the organizational properties of attitudes may be expressed as a family of U curves mediating between situational factors and levels of information processing.

Interactive Complexity Theory II (Streufert)

Based on a program of research designed to test the previous hypotheses, Streufert and associates have modified interactive complexity theory toward greater parsimony and toward more precise predictions (Driver & Streufert, 1969; Streufert, 1969, 1970, 1972; Streufert & Castore, 1971; Streufert & Fromkin, 1972). Streufert and associates maintain the inverted U-shaped curve hypothesis, but discard (a) the prediction that the optimal point on the environmental complexity dimension is different for complex and simple subjects, and (b) the prediction that environmental complexity consists of a number of components. Rather, the effects of success, failure, etc., are viewed in terms of the inherent information load in these constructs (success results in decreased, failure results in increased information load).[4] Predictions for

---

[4] This view does not mean that the affective components of failure and success information are ignored. Rather, they are viewed as primarily content variables, probably responding to (learned) individual difference in tolerance for success and/or failure, something that cannot be obtained on a measure of complexity.

greater information search by complex persons are limited to tasks or situations which contain inherently novel components. A number of specific predictions are made:

In the realm of attitudes and social influence, Streufert and Fromkin (1972) have suggested that optimal communication is achieved if source complexity matches target complexity. A mismatch is produced if source complexity (as evident in message complexity) exceeds target complexity. The opposite combination is inefficient, but not a mismatch. These authors further hypothesize that simple persons, as opposed to complex persons, will respond to either the message or the source, whichever is more salient, but not to both. Predicitons for delayed retest of attitude change are based on this hypothesis. In addition, Streufert and Fromkin predict that messages with implicit cues (unless they are made salient) would have little effect on simple persons. Effects of such cues on complex persons should be greater.

For primacy–recency effects, again the most salient grouping of information should affect simple subjects, while the complex subjects are expected to integrate the information and, in the case of evaluative messages, resolve the conflict by becoming "ambivalent." Streufert and Fromkin also hypothesize that dissonance predictions (e.g., for persons in selective exposure experiments) should fit simple subjects, but not complex subjects.

Streufert (1970) has suggested that the often proposed 1:1 relationship between differentiation and integration is probably erroneous. Rather, integration should be based on a moderate amount of differentiation. Excessively high levels of differentiation in a cognitive domain would likely contain too much information to permit integration at high levels. Similarly, superoptimally increasing information input produces a decrement of integrative information processing. Streufert points out that there is no reason why differentiation should be affected, at least until environmental complexity becomes extremely superroptimal. Additional changes in interactive complexity theory are more relevant to the "environmental complexity" component and are not discussed in this chapter.

MEASUREMENT

Role Construct Repertory Test (Bieri)

The Role Construct Repertory Test (Rep) as originally conceived by Kelly (1955) has been utilized by many researchers in many different modifications. An example of one of these modifications, which may serve as fairly descriptive of the others, is Bieri's (Bieri et al., 1966). The Rep Test is designed to assess complexity as Bieri conceives the concept, i.e., degree of differentiation.

In general, the Rep Test is administered as follows: The subject is provided with a grid which contains a number of spaces (e.g., 10) for the person to be judged (columns), each labeled with a role title considered to be personally relevant to the individual (e.g., yourself, father, boss, friend) and including both liked and disliked persons. A corresponding number of rows is provided for constructs. In some research using the Rep Test, these constructs are generated by the subject (as in Kelly's original test) while in other studies the constructs (bipolar dimensions of similarity–contrast) are provided by the experimenter. It has been demonstrated by some researchers (Jaspars, 1964; Tripodi & Bieri, 1963) that the indices of complexity derived from own and provided constructs are comparable. However, others (e.g., Kuusinen & Nystedt, 1972) have reported results indicating that considerable differences between the effects of the two kinds of constructs may be obtained. Results appear to depend upon such factors as the type of provided constructs which are compared with individual constructs. Metcalfe (1974), on the other hand, found no differences between own and provided constructs for complexity (i.e., hierarchical structure) and for differentiation, but concluded that the use of own constructs is preferable, because his obtained correlations between results based on own and provided constructs were statistically significant, but not high. It appears, then, it may safely be assumed, in most cases, that the results obtained with the use of own vs. provided constructs are fairly comparable, although not necessarily identical.

In the subject-generated construct procedure, the subject identifies each of the roles in the columns with a real person. Then he is asked by the experimenter to consider three of these persons (which three are specifically designated) at a time. The subject generates the constructs by indicating, for each triad he considers, a way in which two of the persons are similar and the third is different. Different triads are considered in this fashion until all construct rows are filled. Each time the subject produces a construct, he places a check in the cells of the matrix under the two similar persons and leaves blank the cell of the differing person. After all rows have been labeled with constructs, the subject reconsiders all dimensions and places additional check marks in the cells of those persons (in addition to the two original ones) who are also similar on that construct. This procedure yields a matrix of check patterns which represents how S perceives and differentiates a group of persons relative to his personal constructs (Bieri, 1955).

Scoring is accomplished by comparing each construct row with each other construct row, for a particular person. All possible comparisons for all rows and all persons (e.g., 450 in a 10 × 10 matrix) are made, with a score of one (for example) given for every exact agreement of ratings on any one person (Bieri et al., 1966). The scores for all comparisons are then summed, yielding a total score. (In a 10 × 10 matrix, the highest possible score would be 450, indicating that the subject rated all persons the same way on all constructs.) The higher the total score for a subject, the lower his level of complexity, since the high score is indicative of the fact that he uses all his constructs in the same way, that they all have the same meaning to him. In other words, he is more unidimensional. A low-scoring subject is considered higher in complexity, using dimensions differently. Scoring procedures on the Rep Test differ among experimenters, but the interpretation of complexity as inversely related to total score is consistent.

Smith and Leach (1972) developed a "hierarchic measure" of complexity, based on the Rep, which taps structure (a form of interrelatedness of dimensions, or hierarchical integration) as well as differentiation. This measure was found to correlate positively with Harvey's This I Believe test (see below), and to produce scores unrelated to standard Rep differentiation scores (cf. Metcalfe, 1974). And, in an analysis of the discriminant validity of the Rep for various indices, Adams-Webber (1970) determined that the operational definition of constellatoriness (Flynn, 1959) cannot be distinguished from a measure of cognitive complexity (differentiation).

Bieri has also discussed and utilized other "potential" measures of complexity. He expressed concern about the generality of complexity across domains, but decided that complexity was strictly an interpersonal judgment phenomenon. For example, Bieri and Blacker (1956) addressed a methodological problem and a theoretical problem: Can different measures be used to assess complexity and are conceptual styles such as complexity consistent across stimulus domains? These authors utilized the Rep Test and the Rorschach ink blot test (the latter as a measure pertaining to noninterpersonal stimuli). Only one Rorschach determinant was significantly correlated with complexity, the human movement response M. The authors conclude that "some" degree of generality of complexity can be demonstrated. Similarly, Bieri and Messerley (1957) and Bieri, Bradburn, and Galinsky (1958) investigated the relationship between the Rorschach test and cognitive complexity. The findings of these studies indicated that some relationship does exist. Finally, Epting (1972) constructed a Rep measure in the domain of social issues, rather than interpersonal judgment. He obtained results for complexity and for stability of complexity (over time and across issues) which are comparable to those obtained using interpersonal judgment procedures.

Categorizing (Zajonc)

Zajonc (1960) describes a method for obtaining his measures of the four properties of cognitive structures: differentiation, complexity, unity, and organization. This method has been utilized in various forms by several subsequent researchers.

Subjects are first asked to read a letter written, supposedly, by an applicant for a job to a potential employer. Subjects are told to try to get a general idea about what kind of person the writer is. They are then given a set of 52 blank cards, each marked with a letter from A to ZZ. Subjects are asked to write one characteristic which they feel describes the applicant on each of the cards, using as many cards as necessary (they are only required to use as many cards as attributes they can think of). *Differentiation* then is merely the number of attributes (via number of cards used) which are ascribed to the person. Subjects are asked to consider the cards on which they had written characteristics and to arrange them into any "broad natural groupings" they feel are appropriate. After this task, they are then asked to look at each group separately and decide if it could be further broken down into subgroups. They are to continue this process until they have broken down the groups into as many subgroups as seem appropriate. These groupings and subgroupings then are used to determine the level of inclusion of attributes, the basis for the computation of the Complexity score.

Subjects are then asked to list all the characteristics which would change if Characteristic A were changed, absent, or untrue of the applicant, etc., for all the characteristics. Dependency matrices are then constructed on the basis of these responses, from which the measures of Unity and Organization are derived.

The object person used here was fairly specific (job applicant). Of course, any kind of description could be used.

Cognitive Structure (Scott)

Although Scott has derived a number of measures of structural characteristics, we will review here only those that are concerned with complexity *per se*. This discussion will focus only on measures of differentiation (dimensionality), discrimination (in Scott's terminology, articulation), and overall complexity.

Scott bases his measures on information theory (Attneave, 1959). His formula for differentiation is a measure of the quantity of information obtained from a modified sorting task (Scott, 1959, 1962a, 1962b, 1962c, 1963b, 1966, 1969). Scott asks subjects to generate a list of "important" nations, or provides subjects with such a list. Subjects are then asked to sort the nations into (potentially overlapping) groups on the basis of some attribute they possess in the mind of the subject. Absence or presence of the attribute is determined via inclusion of the nation in a specific group. If subjects obtain only one grouping, then two distinctions are made. Nations are viewed as possessing or not possessing a particular characteristic, i.e., they are placed on a single dichotomous dimension (in Scott's terminology, attribute).

If the subject sorts nations into two groups (with overlapping membership), then four distinctions may be made. For k independent groups, the maximum number of distinctions would be 2^k, permitting description of the information contained in the sorting outcomes via logarithms to the base of 2 (Scott, 1962a). Scott makes a number of additional assumptions. He suggests that two groupings (even if named differently) which have identical members (and nonmembers) are empirically seen as representing the same attribute (dimension). He further proposes that groups with no overlapping members are likely to represent antithetical attributes (dimensions) or form different categories on the same dimension.[5] In either case, no differentiation is implied.

The experimenter would be most certain that differentiation did actually occur when a subject orders groups in different ways along different dimensions (intransitivity). This would occur most clearly where there is 50% overlap among dichotomous attributes (dimensions) into which the stimuli (nations) are sorted. The measure of absolute complexity can be expressed by the formula (Scott, 1962a):

$$H = \Sigma p_i \log_2 \frac{1}{p_i} = \log_2 n - \frac{1}{n} \Sigma n_i \log_2 n_i$$

where n is the number of objects (nations) obtained from the subject; n_i is the number of objects that appear in a particular combination of groups; and $p_i = n_i/n$ the proportion of objects falling in the ith group combination.

Further, Scott obtains a measure for the relative complexity of a subject's sort by correcting for the number of nations generated (Scott, 1962a):

$$R = \frac{H}{\log_2 n}$$

In addition to the problem discussed in footnote 5 (see also, below), Scott (1962a) points out some potential problems with the use of the H statistic as a measure of differentiation or complexity. Subjects are asked to make dichotomous judgments, which may not be the kinds of judgments people make in any specific cognitive domain that happens to be tested. Subjects'

[5] Non-overlapping groups may indeed merely form different points on the same dimension. However, particularly for Ss who make very limited inclusions along various (orthogonal) dimensions, there may occur assignments to several separate categories. Such assignments would represent limited discrimination (articulation) but high differentiation. The frequency with which this form of differentiation does occur remains to be examined.

category systems are not tested exhaustively, so that H may describe the lower boundary of their complexity, and any randomness in assignment of objects (nations) to groups would inflate the measure. In any case, high complexity scores would be obtained only when groups are dichotomized at 50%, producing (if groups are indeed orthogonal) a probability of 50% overlap in membership among groups.

Scott has also proposed a number of measures of discrimination (in his terms, articulation). Since they tend to be positively correlated (Scott, 1966), only his "preferred" measure is listed here. Subjects are given the task of rating k objects on n attributes (dimensions) twice (to control for randomness). The number of distinctions made by the subjects are obtained in the measure C (Scott, 1966):

$$C = \sum_{i=1}^{k} \frac{2}{\displaystyle\sum_{x=x_1}^{x_2} f(x)}$$

In this formula, x_1 is the pretest rating which the subject assigns to an object i, and x_2 is the posttest rating for the same object. The total number of ratings made by subjects (pre- and posttests combined) which fall between and include x_1 and x_2 becomes the denominator of the fraction for each object. C is the sum of these fractions over k objects.

Perhaps influenced by Scott's interest in measurement techniques for cognitive structures, several of his associates have also published measures which are of some interest. Wyer (1964) developed a measure of differentiation based on a person's attributed rating matrix (not unlike the Rep Test). Differentiation is defined as the number of distinct concepts in the cognitive domain, i.e., the number of distinctively rated stimuli. For example, if on a number of attributes (dimensions) persons are always rated in the same order, then only one dimension is present. To the degree to which any point on the dimensions is used more than once to place a person, and to the degree to which that placement is unique, a score for differentiation is given. If, on the other hand, two persons are placed together at that point who are also placed together on other points of other attributes, then differentiation is scored only once.

Wyer finds that his differentiation score correlates with that of Scott (1962a)—+.05 (NS). He states that the number of categories which could be formed from a respective portion of the cognitive domain (his measure) varied independently of the distinctiveness of the dimensions from which the domain was structured (Scott measure H). This suggests to him that the original conception of differentiation, which originally included characteristics of both frequency and distinctiveness, should be modified to include one or the other, but not both.

Wyer also presents two measures of integration. Integration is defined as the degree to which concepts and attributes contained in the cognitive domain are interrelated. Measure 1 calculates the number of subject responses which would infer other responses; e.g., if placing a person on Scale-point 3 on Scale A implies that he will then also place him at point 1 on B, 6 on C, etc., then the placement on Scale A can be inferred from two other placements: Score = 2. The effort necessary for calculating all these values would be enormous, so Wyer limits himself to calculating only inferences for placement of persons on the three dimensions which the subject claimed were *most important.*

Wyer's second measure of integration again uses the three most important scales. Subjects are asked to indicate the probability (0–1.0) that a person scoring high or low on each of these three dimensions would also score high or low on the other dimensions which the subject had generated (total of 10 dimensions, so there are 7 left for this purpose). For each pairing of one of the three "most important" with one of the seven other dimensions, the differences in the probabilities for the statements of high or low similarity were calculated. For example, if the probability that a person scoring high on dimension 1 (most important) is also high on dimension 7 is .9, and the probability that he is low is .1, then the difference is $.9 - .1 = .8$. If they are equally probable, then the probability is $.5 - .5 = 0$. The number of pairs which showed differences of greater then .5 was taken as a measure of interrelatedness of the structure (integration).

Wyer's two measures of integration correlated .66 ($p < .005$). Neither of Wyer's integration measures correlated significantly with his differentiation measures (correlations vary from $-.10$ to $+.10$). He states that neither a large number of concepts in the domain nor a high degree of distinctiveness among dimensions from which they are formed are by themselves sufficient conditions for producing a high degree of interrelatedness among the concepts obtained in this domain.

Wyer used the Impression Formation Test adapted from Asch (exactly in the form discussed by Streufert & Driver, 1967) as an additional measure of *integrative ability.* With verbal ability partialed out, IF complexity did not correlate significantly with either of Wyer's integration measures ($+.16$ and .00). He states that this finding is in direct contradiction to the conceptual definition of the structural characteristic itself. Integration, as assessed in this study, while it may reflect the tendency of individuals to interpret aspects of experience in a manner which is conducive to being interrelated, may not necessarily reflect the ability of these individuals to form these inter-relationships. If this is true, the integration measures under consideration may not relate to measures in which ability is assessed. The above findings may also indicate that structural characteristics reflecting the present state of the cognitive domain being assessed do not necessarily reflect the ability of the individual to utilize the processes required to attain this state. This distinction between structure and process is also reflected in Signell's (1966) distinction between experiential and didactic learning. However, Wyer is comparing a measure of flexible integration (IFT) with, at most, a measure of hierarchical integration (or identity), and should therefore not expect a correlation.

The work of Signell, another of Scott's associates, is primarily concerned with development and, as such, is not of relevance to this chapter. Signell has, however, produced a set of complexity measures as well, which may be useful in this context. Her measures are:

(1) Number of intervals of a concept as a scale: An attribute is represented by a 7-point scale, and subjects are required to rate stimuli on that scale. If all checks are at one point, then the score is one. If all seven points are used, then the score is seven (24 objects were used).

(2) Distribution of objects over intervals, a refinement of the previous scale: The highest score would be obtained if, for example, 28 stimulus objects would be distributed on a 7-point scale by placing 4 of the stimuli at each scale point.

(3) Number of labels: The score for each subject is the number of concepts on the List of Concepts yielded by the Rep Test Sorting Task.

(4) Number of dimensions: The concepts' degree of linear covariation is measured via Key Cluster Analysis (yielding individual multidimensional space). This provides an approximate measure of the number of ways in which concepts can differ from each other. The number of dimensions yielded by a subject's cluster analysis (after eliminating those dimensions where the mean square decreased) constitutes the Number of Dimensions score.

(5) Number of substantial dimensions: This is the previous measure, corrected for substantiality of the dimensions (how much communality is accounted for by each dimension). Proportions in communality are transformed to probabilities and assigned an H value. A second measure, the variance of the proportion of communality, is also calculated.

(6) Stereotypy: Based on the unifactor structure cluster analysis (above). The number of clusters obtained is counted. A tendency toward few clusters is seen as stereotyping; multiple clusters are seen as differentiation among stimuli.

Signell does not provide the intercorrelations of her measures. However, in her analysis of the effect of age, discrimination measures (1) and (2) correlate with age when the stimulus objects are persons but not when they are nations.

Measures of differentiation correlate with age when the stimulus objects are nations, but not when they are persons. There is an implication of difference between the two sets of measures. She interprets the data as indicating that there are clear-cut and important differences in the development of cognition in the two domains—based on time of learning in two domains or kind of learning (didactic vs. experiential).

Role Category Questionnaire (Crockett)

While many researchers have used the Rep Test, Crockett and associates have developed a measure of their own, which derives from the conceptualization that complexity represents the quantity and integration of "constructs" in the cognitive structure. Crockett (1965) states that differentiation of a cognitive system will refer to the number of constructs that it contains. The degree of hierarchical integration of the system will refer to the complexity of the relationships among the constructs, and to the degree to which clusters of constructs are related by superordinate, integrating constructs. This point of view results in a measure which primarily "counts" the constructs which subjects generate.

Crockett's measure of complexity (differentiation), the Role Category Questionnaire, is a count of the number of concepts that are used to describe different persons. The subject is asked to identify eight persons he knows. Half of them must be older than he, half peers; half must be liked, half disliked; half must be male and half female. The subject spends a few minutes comparing his persons mentally, and then describes each of the eight persons (with a 3 minute time limit per person). The measure of complexity is represented by the number of different interpersonal constructs which the subject uses in the description. High complex subjects are above the median split of the distribution obtained from all subjects; those below the median, are low in complexity. For example, Rosenkrantz and Crockett (1965) obtained low complexity subjects who generate 18-42 (males) and 19-45 (females) constructs, while their complex subjects generated 46-87 (males) and 49-77 (females) constructs. On the other hand, Meltzer, Crockett, and Rosenkrantz (1966) obtained subjects scoring between 40-188, with a median split at 73.5. This measure is used throughout the research by Crockett and associates. It does not correlate meaningfully with the Rep Test (personal communication).

Crockett apparently prefers the Zajonc procedure as a measure of integration. However, in his 1965 paper he writes in some detail about statistical measures which might be useful. He considers factor analysis and multidimensional unfolding. Referring to research by Todd and Rappoport (1964), who used data based on Rep Test and other scales which failed to produce similarity in the dimensions generated by the methods, Crockett criticizes the measures because they use different analytic techniques, based on divergent assumptions of multidimensional space to obtain dimensions. The only assumption they have in common is that of Euclidian space, and that may not even be justified (e.g., a word, person, etc., may have different meaning in different contexts). Such a problem, he feels, can be handled with Zajonc's phenomenological method by permitting subjects to sort the constructs repeatedly, e.g., into more than just one group.

Systems Theory

Harvey, Hunt, and Schroder (1961) discuss measurement only in general. They do not present any particular test with stated reliability, validity, etc., but rather rely on a general statement about what measures and what kinds of measures are likely to be useful. Further, they strongly suggest, based on propositions of Oppenheimer (1956) and Campbell and Fiske (1959), that measurement should be multiple. Such multiple measurement seems worthwhile in this context, since their "systems" do not represent a unitary dimension.

Harvey et al. state that measures for the systems may be obtained by measuring subjects' responses based on system functioning and system organization. (The first appears to be a content characteristic, the second a structural one.) They suggest that several functioning characteristics may be used: sensitization, interpretation, behavior and affective arousal (Harvey et al., 1961). The operation for such assessment of "dispositional tendencies" (systems) may be summarized as follows: (1) The presentation of controlled system-specific stimuli; the nature of the responses indicate individual differences in *sensitization* to the system represented by the stimuli. (2) The presentation of relatively ambiguous stimuli; differences in *interpretation* should reflect the subjects' systemic position. (3) The presentation of stimuli, some of which are specifically relevant to one system, some to another, noting which leads to *affective arousal*. (4) The presentation of stimuli on a given dimension; the number or range of concepts generated indicates the degree of abstractness.

Harvey et al. (1961) provide some examples for measurement of system membership. They refer to the work of: (1) Schroder and Hunt (1958), who asked subjects to account for criticisms from sources that varied in attractiveness (with sensitivity to attractiveness as a mediator). (2) Hunt and Schroder (reported in Harvey et al., 1961) who measured the relationship between Ss' perceived self-confidence and self-evaluation following criticism. (3) Hunt and Schroder (reported in Harvey et al., 1961) who used a variation of Rep Test to tap differential system specific sensitizations. (4) Schroder and

Hunt (1957) who utilized subjects' interpretation of relatively ambiguous interpersonal stimuli to infer personality disposition.

These examples are designed to provide discontinuous data, relevant to specific systems. In contrast, measures of "abstractness" should provide information in continuous terms which, however, is less precise for purposes of dispositional (system) classification. Examples of such measures are: (1) Goldstein and Scheerer's (1941) object sorting test; (2) Bieri and Blacker's (1956) measure of cognitive complexity; and (3) Witkin's (Witkin et al., 1954) field independence.

Research by systems theorists which have used measures to determine the system characteristic of their subjects usually have been based on "interpretation of ambiguous stimuli which may or may not be refuting to the subject." The kinds of measures utilized will be covered here in sequence: Schroder and associates have used the Situational Interpretation Test (SIT), a forced choice measure. Subjects are asked to think of attitude areas where they hold strong pro and con views toward statements someone might make. They are then to imagine that someone criticizes their view and are asked to make forced choices between hypothetical responses to such a criticism, as well as indicate their agreement with each statement on a 6-point scale. The responses are taken from systemic "typical" responses, and are matched so that an equal number of System 1 responses is paired with System 2 responses, System 3 responses, etc. The score is determined by counting the number of preferred responses representing each system, and by the extremity of agreement for each of the ratings for each of the statements. As a rule, the researchers have quartiled the distribution of response choices, obtaining supposedly 1/4 System 1 subjects, 1/4 System 2, etc.

An extension of this test is Tuckman's (1966a) Interpersonal Topical Inventory (ITI). It was designed to tap complexity differences among subjects generally lower in intelligence and complexity. This test derives some of its construction from the Sentence Completion Test (Schroder & Streufert, 1962; Schroder et al., 1967) and the SIT. The test again uses a forced choice design. Subjects are asked to choose one of a pair of items that best represents their feelings about interpersonal topics. These topics are "when criticized," "when in doubt," "when a friend acts differently toward you," "beliefs about people in general," "feelings about leaders," "feelings about rules." For each topic there are six pairs of alternatives, and subjects must pick one from each pair. The six pairs are obtained for system-specific responses for all systems paired with each other system. Although Tuckman has found that his ITI has satisfactory levels of relationships with other measures of complexity and has been useful for predicting certain behaviors (MacNeil & Rule, 1970; Sawatzky & Zingle, 1971; Tuckman, 1966a, 1966b, 1967), other researchers have not been able to obtain satisfactory correlations between the ITI and other measures of complexity (see, e.g., Suedfeld, Tomkins, & Tucker, 1969). Part of the reason for this lack of correspondence may be an emphasis on "content" in Tuckman's test, i.e., authoritarian orientation, antiauthoritarian, interpersonal orientation and information orientation for Systems 1, 2, 3, and 4, respectively. Results obtained by Tuckman (1966b), indicating that his System 3 subjects revealed more about themselves in interpersonal contacts, and that System 3 persons probed friends more, but System 4 persons probed strangers more, would support a strong association of the ITI with the content portion of systems theory. In other words, Tuckman's test may not be a test of structural (complexity) characteristics.

Harvey's This I Believe (TIB) test is a subjective measure consisting of 12 sentence stems, beginning with the words "This I believe about . . . ," where the concept that follows is successively replaced with one of the 12 stems. For example, one item reads, "This I believe about the American way of life . . . ." Subjects respond in two to three sentences. The responses are scored by three or four judges in line with the descriptions given by Harvey et al. (1961) as typical of the specific systems. Interrater reliabilities tend to be above +.90. Subjects on whom raters cannot agree are discarded. The test has been used and discussed in a number of publications (e.g., Harvey, 1964, 1965, 1966; Harvey, Reich, & Wyer, 1968; Harvey & Ware, 1967; Ware & Harvey, 1967; White & Harvey, 1965). An extensive discussion of the test is provided in Harvey (1966).

Schroder and Streufert (1962) used a similar instrument to determine systemic functioning in response to interpersonal stimuli. Their Sentence Completion Test was later adapted to measure differentiative and integrative complexity (cf. Gardiner & Schroder, 1972). It consists of stems such as "When I am criticized," "When others criticize me it usually means," "When I am in doubt," "When someone disagrees with me it usually means." Scoring of the test again is performed by a number of judges who match the several sentence length responses to the system descriptions provided by Harvey et al. (1961). Interrater reliability is typically above +.93; however, some judges could not be trained to such a high criterion. Subjects' complexity scores are averaged across all responses to obtain a single score. Suedfeld (1968) has demonstrated that subjects' scores on this test and the Impression Formation Test could be significantly modified by "instructing" them to be more or less complex in their responses. Suedfeld concluded that this finding has implications for researchers and emphasized the importance of standardized test instructions. Other researchers (e.g., Baldwin, 1972) have also demonstrated that training can have various effects on complexity scores.

In his research on child development and the relationship of "conceptual level" (i.e., systems) to education, Hunt employs the same Sentence (and later, Paragraph) Completion Test initially proposed by Schroder and Streufert

(1962). While he initially utilized the manual for scoring included in that publication, the proposed "sub-1" stage required additional scoring instructions. Consequently, Hunt developed his own manual, which apparently was revised again later. Unfortunately, neither of the manuals have been published (Hunt & Halverson, 1964; Hunt, Kingsley, Massari, Shore, & Sweet, 1967).

Carr (1965b) has developed the Interpersonal Discrimination Test (IDT). Subjects are instructed to list six persons fitting a given role title (e.g., good friends of your own age whom you like, an older man whom you admire, a young man whom you do not particularly like, etc.). For each person, the subject must list a "quality" and its opposite. Further, the subject is asked to list three favorable characteristics about himself and their opposites, and three unfavorable characteristics about himself and their opposites. The net yield is 24 conceptual dimensions, on which the subject orders all 6 persons, and indicates differences among the persons by drawing dividing lines between persons or groups of persons who differ from the next person or group of persons. Discrimination is assessed via the number of dividing lines per dimension. Differentiation is assessed as the number of nonidentical (verbally or in terms of ordering) dimensions. Test–retest reliability for the IDT (with an intervening task interpolated) was between .82 and .84. After two months, reliabilities were .58 and .65. However, the persons listed may change over time, altering the stimulus array.

Claunch (1964) devised a set of categories for the scoring of unstructured essay materials. His Polar Contrast Index (PCI) is obtained through the formula:

$$PCI = \frac{PC}{PC + QC + IC}$$

where PC = Polarized Contrast, when two points of view are treated as polar opposites; QC = Qualified Contrast, when two points of view are compared or contrasted with the implication that differences are not simple and absolute opposites; and IC = Integrative Comparison, when a commonality between two differing points of view is stated or implied.
A high PCI is indicative of a relatively low level of complexity.

Finally, Harvey (1967) reports the development of an objective measure of conceptual systems, the Conceptual Systems Test (CST). Items on the CST are derived from responses of subjects on the TIB and certain tests purporting to measure personality aspects relating to dimensions of conceptual systems. Using a method of cluster analysis, Harvey has arrived at seven theoretically meaningful factors in five independent samples. These factors are: (a) Divine

Fate Control (DFC); (b) Need for Simplicity-Consistency (NS-C); (c) Need for Structure-Order (NS-O); (d) Distrust of Social Authority (DSA); (e) Friendship Absolutism (FA); (f) Moral Absolutism (MA); (g) General Pessimism (GP). By measuring systems on the TIB and then comparing the ways the various systems scored on the seven factors of the CST, Harvey demonstrates a close relationship between the theoretical attributes of the systems and their profile on the CST factors.

Interactive Complexity

The most frequently used test for complexity developed by researchers in this group is the Sentence Completion Test (Schroder & Streufert, 1962), sometimes (and probably more correctly) called the Paragraph Completion Test. The test is subjective. Subjects write paragraph length (3 to 4 sentences in a 2½-4-minute period, depending on the population) responses to each of a number of incomplete sentences, such as "When I am criticized . . . ." The sentence stems are selected to provide conflict settings to which subjects can respond unidimensionally or multidimensionally. Scoring of the tests is relatively easy, and one-day training will typically result in interrater reliabilities of above +.85. More extensively trained personnel tend to obtain reliabilities in the low 90s. Test–retest reliability of the measure (if the tests are administered properly) is near .85. The scores obtained on the two highest responses are usually taken as an index of the subject's complexity.

In an attempt to gain responses which are more relevant to the domain differences discussed by Driver and Streufert (1969) and Streufert and Driver (1967), Streufert and associates have modified the stems so that responses can be obtained for the following domains: (a) social complexity, (b) nonsocial complexity, (c) perceptual complexity, (d) executive complexity. Intercorrelations among these domains are typically .4 to .6. It should be noted that the test is scorable for both differentiation and integration *separately.* Scoring for differentiation alone produces low scores for integrators.

A second test that is used with some frequency is the Impression Formation Test (Streufert & Driver, 1967; Streufert & Schroder, 1963). As Crockett and associates have established, complex persons tend to integrate conflicting blocks of univalent information. Simple subjects, however, tend to respond with either primacy or recency, depending on the manipulation. This finding has been useful in establishing criteria for estimating interpersonal perceptual complexity on the basis of subjects' responses (cf. Streufert & Driver, 1967).

The Integration Style Test (Driver & Mock, 1974) measures an additional component, thought by the authors to be related to complexity. This component involves a subject's ability to reorganize perceived information around different foci, and leads to four potential different decision styles: refocusing complexity and nonrefocusing complexity, refocusing simplicity, and nonrefocusing simplicity. This is probably similar to what has previously been termed flexibility. Subjects are presented with the description of a complex, ambiguous social situation and with six items of relevant information. They are required to then interpret this situation (make decisions) and receive a score on each of four decision styles based on the amount of information integrated in any decision and the number of foci around which information can be reordered. The four styles are: hierarchic complexity (high use of information, a single focus), integrative complexity (high use of information, several possible foci), decisive simplicity (low use of information, a single focus), and flexible simplicity (low use of information, several possible foci). A score of over 30 on any one of these styles indicates that it is a dominant one. An individual may have more than one style which is dominant or strong.

Attempts at development of objective tests which would have to measure integrative complexity by inference (a complexity self-description—CxSD test) have been made by Driver and Streufert, but so far have not produced the desired results.

Some Additional Comments on Measurement and the Nature of Complexity

The problem of measurement in the area of cognitive complexity has been raised many times in the literature. A striking phenomenon, which has created much of the concern, is the fact that the various measures of complexity seem to be more or less unrelated to each other, either conceptually or statistically, while at the same time a surprisingly large degree of similarity exists in the behavior predicted by these apparently "unrelated" measures. (This will become evident in the following section reporting data.) These factors have led to much speculation as to the nature of the complexity concept *per se*; specifically, the question of whether or not there exists such a thing as a *unitary* phenomenon that may be called cognitive complexity. Several examples of arguments pertaining to this question, as well as data reflecting the relationships among measures, will be presented.

Gardner and Schoen (1962), based on previous work of Gardner and associates (Gardner, 1953; Gardner, Holzman, Klein, Linton, & Spence, 1959; Gardner, Jackson, & Messick, 1960), argue that "abstractness," as proposed by Harvey, Hunt, and Schroder (1961), should be a unitary phenomenon, and consequently cannot exist. Similarly, these authors reject the work of Bieri and others who utilize the Rep Test, since such tests (a) measure complexity indirectly, as compared to a free sorting test in which S is required to group all items simultaneously, and (b) may actually measure some form of ideational fluency rather than the assumed inherent complexity in cognition. A person with higher differentiated conceptions of similarities and differences could therefore select a few key attributes as the most essential ones and use these repeatedly, thereby limiting the number of distinct constructs and revealing nothing of his true conceptual complexity. In addition, Gardner et al. believe that the term cognitive complexity seems grossly overgeneral. They suggest that there is ample evidence that most persons are relatively complex in some areas of cognition, relatively simple in others.

Although not specifically directed toward a refutation of the attack by Gardner and Schoen on complexity theorists, Bruner and Tajfel (1965b) point out that Gardner and Schoen's views are produced by their specific way of defining "differentiation" via the measurement task employing sorting. For this particular measure (Gardner, 1953), the subject sorts 50 stimuli into groups which are then labeled. A score is given for each separate (non-identical) group. In cases of dual naming of a group, the experimenter determines whether the subject actually views the labels as independent and scores accordingly. The score obtained consists of the number of "abstract" (in the linguistic sense) groups divided by the number of abstract groups *plus* other groups (e.g., "waste basket" or "concrete") (cf. Gardner & Schoen, 1962). Gardner and Schoen have determined that this measure does not correlate very highly with other measures of "abstractness" and differentiation.

Vannoy (1965) compared a number of different measures of cognitive complexity (e.g., Rep, SCT, Scott's measure) and a number of measures which could be construed as measures of such a variable (e.g., F Scale, Category Width, test of verbal ability) in a factor analytic study. His analysis produced eight factors, none of which included all measures or even a large proportion of them. The SCT, for example, loaded on a factor of its own. Vannoy concludes from these results that complexity is not as general a trait as has sometimes been implied in the literature. However, it is not surprising that he obtained the results he did. There is no reason to expect these measures to load highly on a single factor, since the measures are based on very different conceptualizations of what cognitive complexity is. The three broad classes of behavioral tendencies, which Vannoy proposes based on his factors (sensitivity to one or many judgmental variables, making few or many distinctions on judgmental variables, maintenance of narrow perspective and ordered view of the world), may very well reflect these differing conceptualizations of complexity. It is possible, however, that these three kinds of behavioral tendencies (perhaps restated as openness–closedness to new information, discrimination, and cognitively simple vs. hierarchically integrated) are all parts of an overall complexity phenomenon, which has yet to be tapped in an overall measure.

In another factor analytic study with 23 variables, Bottenberg (1970) obtained five factors. The first, accounting for 27.6% of the variance, contained tests for category width and field dependence. The Rep test loaded on the second factor (17.1% variance) along with a marking test and arithmetic examples. The SCT again loaded on its own factor, accounting for 14.9% of the variance. The object-sorting test was positively correlated (0.45) with this factor, as was the Rep test (0.37).

In other studies comparing various measures, similar kinds of results were obtained. For example, Leventhal and Singer (1964) found only a weak relationship between the Rep Test and Zajonc's measures. This finding may have been due to measuring differentiation in one test and integration in the other test. Shrauger (1967), employing two Rep-type measures, one with familiar and the other with unfamiliar persons, obtained no correlation between the two. He concludes that differences between people which are thought to be due to cognitive structural characteristics may be more parsimoniously explained via affective orientation. Little (1969) found sex differences between two forms of the Rep test, with males scoring higher with provided constructs and females higher with nonoverlapping sorting. Reed (1966), in a factor analytical study of a large number of ability measures and the Sentence Completion Test, found that the SCT did not relate to any of the other measures. In fact, it appeared on a factor of its own. In a comparison of the measures of Harvey and Schroder, Cox (1971) found that the correlation between them was nonsignificant, that both correlated with such things as vocabulary, and SAT verbal and math scores, and that reliability for Schroder's measure is poor. Bailey (1970), in a study of the underlying factor structure of Super's self-concept dimensions, also obtained a factor for complexity (Rep).

In a multitrait–multimethod study, Richardson and Soucar (1971) found no convergence for two tests of complexity (SCT and the Omnibus Personality Inventory). Carr (1965a, 1965b) compared subjects selected on the Sentence Completion Test for Systems 1, 2, and 3 with performance on his Interpersonal Discrimination Test. He found only a partial relationship between the measures with respect to his hypotheses for System-specific performance on the IDT. In a factor analytic study, Suedfeld, Tomkins, and Tucker (1969) found no evident relationship between measures of cognitive (e.g., SCT, ITI) and perceptual (preference, estimation) information processing. Epting and Wilkins (1974) obtained no evidence that measures of differentiation (Rep and Crockett's RCQ) correlate more with each other than they do with measures of integration (Harvey's CST and Schroder and Streufert's SCT).

Miller (1969) found no significant correlation between Bieri's Rep Test and Crockett's measure. He point to the problems in comparing measures based on different theoretical assumptions. Miller suggests that complexity may be multidimensional, and different researchers make different assumptions about what complexity is. He states that cognitive complexity is probably a more general trait than has been thought. Other authors (e.g., MacNeil, 1974; Zimring, 1971) have pointed to the problem of the *components* of complexity, with the implication that complexity may very well be a multidimensional phenomenon.

There seems to be some confusion in the various discussions of complexity with regard to the terms "unitary" and "general." The first term refers to the "structural" characteristic of complexity; the second refers to its applicability. Two arguments have been presented on the problem of "unity": (1) If complexity is indeed a unitary (i.e., unidimensional) characteristic, then it has not been measured properly. The various measures might merely obtain correlates of complexity, and consequently could not be expected to predict the same behavior. (2) Complexity may not be a unitary concept at all. Rather it may itself be a multidimensional or at least a multicomponent phenomenon. If that were the case, the various measures would be tapping part of the whole phenomenon of complexity (e.g., only one dimension of toal complexity might be assessed by any particular measure). In this case, the measures would be expected to predict similar behavior (just as subtests of the IQ scale tend to predict segments of an overall ability to cope with the environment).

The next section will demonstrate that persons selected on the various complexity measures (which often appear uncorrelated) tend to behave strikingly similar to others of the same complexity level across a number of tasks. Common behavior for more complex subjects and common behavior for more simple subjects tend to be the rule; diverse behavior is the exception. One might then propose that the *different tests of complexity, even though appearing on different factors in a number of factor analyses, may in effect measure subcomponents of a common multidimensional or multicomponent phenomenon.* Of course, one cannot expect any one person to be equally complex in all areas, or show the same level of complexity in all his cognitive domains. This phenomenon would add further to obtained low correlations among measures. These issues will be discussed again later on.

The problem of generality relates to the question of how (if at all) domain-specific complexity is. Shrauger and Altrocchi (1964) emphasize the importance of viewing personality-situation interaction. Other theorists and researchers (e.g., Bieri et al., 1966; Schroder et al., 1967) have stressed the importance of dealing with environmental or situational (stimulus) factors as well as cognitive factors. The impingement of situational, motivational, or affective influences is likely to have effects on cognitive performance in a given situation and makes the determination of the generality of operation for complexity more difficult. However, this question goes beyond concerns with cognitive complexity and is important for all personality traits [cf. the comments of Alker (1972) and the response of Bem (1972)].

RESEARCH

Research which uses measures of cognitive complexity as an independent variable or as predictors of complex behavior has been quite varied. Nonetheless, most of the data reported in the literature can be classified under certain topics and, unfortunately, at times under two or three topics. For example, impression formation techniques may produce attitudinal data, person perception may operate via a consistency principle, etc. In other words, it is, in some cases, difficult to make decisions about where to place reported data: Should they be grouped under the heading "impression formation" or "attitudes" in the first example; should they be listed under "social perception" or "consistency," in the second.

One solution to the problem would be to categorize results under any and all topics to which they may be applicable. At times this is done here, particularly if the respective articles report results from areas which are normally considered closely related. However, in most cases, the data are presented only once to save the reader from repeated exposure to the same information.

Since there are a number of measures of cognitive complexity which tend to be (at least at the statistical level) uncorrelated, or show only moderate common variance, every report of data is accompanied by the respective complexity measure on which the results are based (assuming information about the test used is available). Some simplifications are made. For example, there are several versions of the Rep Test. This chapter refers to all modifications of that test without "discriminating" among them. Abbreviations are used to designate each of the measures. They are:

Rep—Modifications by Bieri and others, based on Kelly's Role Construct Repertory Test.

IFT—Impression Formation Test of perceptual social complexity (Streufert).

SCT—Schroder and Streufert's Sentence Completion Test (also called Paragraph Completion Test) and its modifications.

TIB—This I Believe measure developed by Harvey.

ITI—Interpersonal Topical Inventory developed by Tuckman.

RCQ—Crockett's Role Category Questionnaire.

SIT—Situational Interpretation Test and the earlier version, Situational Interpretation experiment, developed by Hunt and Schroder.

H-Sc(N)—Scott's measure of cognitive structure based on the H statistic (uncertainty). The designation in parentheses indicates the domain on which sorting of objects is based. Since nations are most often used, they will be designated as (N). If the objects of sorting are different, they will be so designated in the parentheses.

Relationship between Complexity and Consistency

Several complexity theories state, either explicitly or implicitly, that cognitive consistency should be more closely associated with simple functioning than with complex functioning. Consistency theory assumes that an imbalance produced must be resolved, implying a unidimensional discrepancy between two associated stimuli. For a person who perceives and acts on the basis of a single dimension (typically an evaluative dimension), some resolution of the conflict seems to be imperative. On the other hand, complex persons who hold several dimensions (either generally or within the domain of the stimulus, depending on the theoretical definition) could either decrease the weight of a dimension on which conflict occurs, or might even resolve the disagreement via an integrative process without changing perceived stimulus values. Data tend to bear out this prediction.

Press, Crockett, and Rosenkrantz (1969) used the RCQ to select simple and complex persons. Subjects were asked to learn the like–dislike relationships existing in 4-man groups. One of the groups contained balanced relationships; two contained different degrees of imbalanced relationships among the members. Simple subjects learned the balanced structure most rapidly, while they learned the unbalanced structure without a simple rule least rapidly. Complex subjects produced no consistent differences in the speed with which the balanced and unbalanced relationships were learned.

Scott (1963a), based on the prediction of Scott (1959), obtained responses from students and adults on his nation sorting task [H–Sc(N)]. In addition, subjects rated the nations on evaluative scales. Comparisons of the H value obtained in the sorting task with imbalance in nation groupings yielded correlations from −.24 to −.46. Greater uncertainty (complexity) was associated with lesser cognitive balance.

Ware and Harvey (1967) selected simple and complex subjects via the TIB measure. Subjects viewed a number of slides showing desirable or undesirable acts by a stimulus person. After viewing 12 acts by the stimulus persons, they indicated the likelihood that the depicted behaviors (prerated as desirable or undesirable) would be plausible for the stimulus person. In addition, subjects were asked to indicate how certain they were about their responses. When inputs and depicted behaviors were consistent, simple subjects generalized the induced impressions further than complex subjects. When the two were inconsistent, complex subjects generalized them further. Simple subjects were more certain of their impressions and made up their minds more rapidly (cf. also Sieber & Lanzetta, 1966; Tripodi & Bieri, 1966).[6]

In a similar experiment, Harvey and Ware (1967), using the same measure (TIB), described the past behavior of a stimulus person in either favorable or unfavorable fashion. Subjects were then presented with that person's present behavior, which ran counter to the previous behavior. Subjects wrote two-paragraph explanations of the perceived consistency-inconsistency. As compared to complex subjects, simple subjects perceived greater inconsistencies, were negatively aroused by those inconsistencies, attributed the inconsistencies to temporary changes in the person, provided few explanations for the inconsistencies, provided poorly integrated accounts, and used stereotypic labels. Further, simple subjects were less tentative about their statements (again, cf. Sieber & Lanzetta, 1966).

Crano and Schroder (1967) asked simple and complex subjects (selected on SCT) to rank 10 professions on intelligence, and to rate 3 colleges (one of them fictitious) on semantic differential scales. Subjects then received information on how "461 students" from the fictitious college supposedly had rated the same professions. The feedback rankings were individually prepared to that some of the rankings differed from Ss' own. Subjects then rated the colleges and the professions again and recalled their own previous rankings. Crano and Schroder found that simple persons used a single resolution process or a group of internally consistent processes. Complex subjects utilized more, though not necessarily consistent, processes.

Janicki (1964) used the SIT to select subjects on four conceptual systems (Systems 1 and 4 may be seen as partially selected due to differences in structure. Other differences among the systems are probably due to content.) Janicki found, on the basis of a praise or criticism manipulation, that the use of predictions from the system's descriptions aided in making better predictions using Osgood and Tannenbaum's (1955) model of congruity. Lower systems yielded better congruity predictions.

Certainly, the number of consistent results about the relationship between complexity and consistency, based on various measures of complexity, appears impressive. The proposition that complexity is inversely related to consistency seeking appears to be supported.

Impression Formation (Interpersonal Perception)

The work of Harvey and Ware (1967) and Ware and Harvey (1967) has been discussed in the section above. Both sets of data are related to

[6] While Sieber and Lanzetta (SCT) obtained parallel results in a decision making task involving uncertainty, the results of Tripodi and Bieri (Rep) suggest that certainty among complex subjects is higher when conflicting stimuli are presented than when stimulus information does not conflict. The discrepancy may be due to task differences.

impression formation as well. Similar results are reported by Miller (1969). Using the RCQ as a selection instrument and predicting responses on a Rep Test-type sorting task, Miller found that complex subjects who responded to a (confederate) partner generated more descriptive traits and constructs describing him. Leventhal and Singer (1964), using a Rep Test and predicting behavior on a Zajonc-type sorting task, found that the relationship between these measures is positive but relatively weak. They did demonstrate, however, that simple judges obtained "clearer impressions" of the stimulus objects. Crockett (1965) has suggested that the lack of results is likely due to a manipulation where the stimulus person presented information about himself (rather than in the third-person format). Any positive statement about self may then be seen as boasting, decreasing its positive value.

Bieri (1955) proposed that a complex (Rep) person should be able to predict the behavior of known others more veridically. In an experimental test of this hypothesis, he obtained a low but significant relationship between complexity and accuracy of prediction. On further analysis, Bieri concluded that the result was produced by complex subjects who were more able than simple subjects to recognize when others' responses would be different from their own. Similar results were obtained by Campbell (1960) and Leventhal (1957). However, Sechrest and Jackson (1961), who used the Rorschach measure previously discussed by Bieri and Blacker (1956) and a measure of the "complexity" of subjects' "family backgrounds," were unable to obtain the same results. Campbell (1960) found that subjects low in complexity (compared with highs) were more likely to separate people into two groups on the basis of a good–bad dichotomy. Also, lows were more likely to view relationships among their associates as balanced [cf. the above reported data by Scott (1963a) and Press, Crockett, & Rosenkrantz (1969)]. Supnick (reported in Crockett, 1965) found that high complexity subjects (on the RCQ) produced fewer univalent (one-sided) descriptions than low complexity subjects. These results can be viewed as related to consistency predictions as well.

In a somewhat different design, varying the complexity (Rep) of the target person, Adams-Webber (1973) found that subjects' judgments of complex persons were significantly less accurate than their judgments of targets of moderate or low complexity.

A number of researchers have used the standard Asch-type format for measuring the effects of differences in complexity on impression formation. Nidorf (1961; see also Nidorf & Crockett, 1965) found that complex subjects (RCQ) are better able to reconcile the presence of potentially contradictory adjectives than simple subjects. Mayo and Crockett (1964) found that simple and complex subjects (Rep) were equally affected by the first block of univalent (all similar) adjectives (cf. also Mayo, 1959). However, complex subjects gave multivalent final impressions after being exposed to the second set of (potentially) contradictory adjectives, while subjects low in complexity demonstrated the standard recency effects which are typical in that situation. Rosenkrantz and Crockett (1965) obtained similar results for males, but failed to obtain them for females. Crockett (1965) suggests that this failure is likely due to the peculiarities of the test population.

Meltzer, Crockett, and Rosenkrantz (1966) measured subjects' complexity (RCQ) and their religious values, and then exposed them to a taped description of a stimulus person ("Joe"). The tape contained three positive and three negative descriptions, and, in a departure from the standard format, a seventh description of Joe as either religious or nonreligious. It was found that subjects who had high religious values used more constructs to describe him. When Joe was similar to the subjects in religious values, complex subjects produced more constructs than simple subjects. When Joe was different, complexity had no effect. Subjects who scored high in complexity and low in religious values formed favorable impressions of Joe. All other subjects formed unfavorable impressions.

The finding that simple subjects are greatly affected by the last block of information they received (recency effect) has been challenged by Petronko and Perin (1970). They point out that this result is likely due to the experimental procedure that has been employed. Rather, they suggest that simple subjects should form impressions on the basis of the information that has been procedurally maximized (cf. Hovland, 1957). For this purpose, the authors exposed complex and simple subjects (Rep) to one of four conditions: (a) block 1, block 2, interspersed task, measurement of impression; (b) block 1, interspersed task, block 2, measurements; (c) block 1, block 2, measurement; (d) block 1, interspersed task, block 2, interspersed task, measurement. They found, for (a), greater primacy for simple Ss compared to complex Ss; for (b), greater recency for simple Ss compared to complex Ss; for (c), no difference; and for (d), no difference. They interpreted the data to indicate that simple subjects are indeed affected by the characteristic of greatest salience, not by position in the information sequence.

Research on the effects of complexity on impression formation has partially supported two divergent theories which are concerned with this process. Crockett (1965) viewed a number of studies as proof for his "frequency of interaction hypothesis," suggesting that greater complexity (here differentiation) is obtained for persons with whom the subject interacts for a considerable amount of time. He discussed research by Mayo (personal communication to Crockett) indicating that among male students, fraternity members show more complexity than nonmembers. Crockett also considered the work by Bieri and Messerley (1957), reporting a significant relationship between extraversion and (Rep) complexity as providing supporting evidence. In addition, he called upon an unpublished study by Supnick (reported in

Crockett, 1965) in detail. The research showed that subjects used more constructs (RCQ) to describe individuals they like than to describe those in similar role categories whom they dislike. Further, she found that subjects used more constructs to describe peers than older persons (this discrepancy was greatest when the person described was female), and female subjects used more constructs than males. Crockett suggests that this result may be due to the greater interpersonal orientation–differentiation of females. Subjects used more constructs to describe others of their own sex than of the opposite sex (greater familiarity is viewed as leading to greater differentiation). Finally, Crockett reported that Nidorf conducted interviews with subjects to determine how they arrived at their impressions of others. Nidorf structured the interview so that subjects were asked to question the experimenter about a stimulus person. When the stimulus person was from the same social stratum as the subject, more questions were asked, questions covered more content areas, and impressions given by the subjects were less stereotyped than when the stimulus person was from a diverse social stratum. Again, familiarity is seen as leading to greater differentiation.

A hypothesis opposing that of Crockett has been suggested by Bieri (Miller & Bieri, 1965). These authors found that socially distant persons are better differentiated (Rep) than socially close persons. Vigilance (leading to complex differentiation) serves, in their opinion, an adaptive function in order to anticipate the behavior of potentially threatening persons. In two studies, Irwin, Tripodi, and Bieri (1967), using the Rep Test, found support for the hypothesis: The results of both studies supported the proposition that individuals differentiate more among persons who evoke more negative affect than among persons with whom strong positive-regard tendencies are associated. Soucar and DuCette (1971) obtained similar data. They asked subjects to rate a set of political figures and found that disliked figures were more highly differentiated than liked ones. Irwin et al. (1967) suggested that the divergent results obtained by Crockett and associates (Crockett, 1965) are likely due to the measure used by Crockett to assess complexity. Irwin et al. present the criticism that the responses on the RCQ are not checked for functional independence.

In an attempt to resolve the disagreement, Carr (1969) measured the degrees of differentiation of the perceptions of others by using (a) a Rep test-like measure and (b) the SCT. In general, his data supported the Bieri position. Subjects differentiated more clearly among disliked persons than among liked persons when the Rep test was employed. Persons scoring high on the SCT (integrators rather than differentiators) differentiated well for liked as well as disliked persons. While the data indicated that subjects did differentiate better among negative than positive persons when the entire sample selected on the SCT was considered, these results were produced specifically by subjects scoring low on the test.

Soucar and DuCette (1971) studied differentiation among political leaders using the Rep test as a measure of differentiation. Since no subject selection was included, the results (based on the previously reported data by Bieri and associates and Carr) should produce the vigilance effect. Greater differentiation among disliked political figures was obtained. Soucar (1970) also found that high school students' perceptions of disliked teachers were more differentiated than their perceptions of liked teachers.

Using the TIB test, Harvey, Reich, and Wyer (1968) tested for differentiation among social beliefs under different levels of attitude intensity. They found that neither the vigilance nor the frequency of interaction hypothesis was supported. Subjects differentiated best among neutral stimuli; no differences among positive or negative stimuli were obtained. Harvey et al. suggested that attitudinal intensity,[7] not direction, accounts for variation in differentiation. Optimal differentiation for simple subjects occurs at a lower level of intensity than for complex subjects.

It should be noted that the data of Harvey et al. are probably not directly comparable to those of Bieri and Crockett. As in Carr's SCT study, the data for complex subjects are here obtained from *integrators,* not differentiators. Further, the stimulus objects were social beliefs, not persons.

Other target characteristics which have been varied include trait consistency (Fertig & Mayo, 1970) and abstract qualities vs. concrete examples of these qualities (Crockett, Gonyea, & Delia, 1970). Fertig and Mayo found that moderate levels of trait consistency produced more highly organized impressions than either low or high levels of consistency, and that complex subjects' impressions were more organized than those of simple subjects. Crockett et al. (1970) obtained results indicating that the impressions written on the basis of abstract qualities were more differentiated and integrated. These results were interpreted in terms of the inconsistency levels probably produced by abstract qualities, which are less easily reinterpreted than concrete examples.

In studies which varied both the complexity of the perceiver and the set or orientation he was provided with, Crockett, Mahood, and Press (1975) and Press, Crockett, and Delia (1975) found that a "set to understand" produced more highly differentiated and organized impressions among complex subjects. A "set to evaluate," on the other hand, produced no differences between complex and simple subjects. Simple subjects' performance did not seem to be affected by set differences.

Finally, Gourd (1973) obtained significant differences in subjects' responses to two dramatic productions as a function of an interaction between the

---

[7] Intensity of attitudes implies associated affect, possibly even anxiety. That anxiety and defensiveness are related to lowered complexity has been demonstrated by Krohne (1971, 1973).

complexity of the perceiver and the complexity of the play.

A number of investigators have measured the effect of stress conditions on impression formation. Supnick (reported in Crockett, 1965) told some subjects that they were doing poorly, and urged them to hurry. Impressions formed under these conditions were more univalent than multivalent, and differences between complex and simple individuals were not obtained (RCQ). Similarly, Krohne and Schroder (1972) found that telling subjects they were specially selected and indicating that subjects were carefully watched depressed their ability to interrelate informational units in impression formation. Using the SCT (Streufert & Schroder, 1965) and the IFT (Streufert & Driver, 1967), and varying the amount of information with which subjects had to deal in a complex (multidimensional stimulus configuration) decision-making task, Streufert found considerable differences between complex and simple subjects in their perception of an opponent's strategies. However, these differences were obtained only under moderate amounts of information. Stressful information deprivation (low information loads) and information overload decreased the quality of impressions formed by subjects and diminished or eliminated any differences among complex and simple subjects (here, groups). It appears, then, that impressions which are differentiated and/or integrated are best formed under optimal (intermediate) stimulus conditions.

Information Orientation

To some degree, the concepts of vigilance and effects of frequency of interaction are dependent on the information with which the subject has to deal and how he deals with it. A number of theories have made the information orientation central to their predictions. In addition to the above concern with differentiation among liked, disliked, or neutral stimulus objects, the interactive theories deal directly with information, and Systems theory (although probably as a content component of the various system orientations) has described openness and search for specific forms of information as one of its basic premises.

Research on information transmission, information search, information utilization, etc., is available from a number of researchers with different points of view. Tripodi and Bieri (1964), in a study concerned with clinical judgments, found that three negatively correlated dimensions are most difficult to transmit (in an information theory sense) when compared with two negatively correlated dimensions, three positively correlated dimensions, etc. Complex subjects (Rep) transmitted more information for negatively correlated dimensions than simple subjects. In another study of clinical judgment, Watson (1976) found that complex judges (PCT) used and sought more different kinds of information and considered the client over more time frames. Results were also presented for length of clinical experience, indicating similar results for most experienced and most complex judges.

Suedfeld and Hagen (1966) selected subjects on the SCT and asked them to identify Kent-Rosanoff stimulus words from response words (clues) which differed in probability of occurrence. Complex subjects solved problems of higher informational complexity (where no single word was highly informative) better than simple subjects. In a complex decision-making task, Streufert, Suedfeld, and Driver (1965) and Suedfeld and Streufert (1966) measured the information search behavior of complex and simple subjects (SCT). Streufert et al (1965) demonstrated that groups of complex subjects did not generally exceed groups of simple subjects in amount of information search. However, complex groups were less affected by changes in information load in their environments, and utilized information gained through search better than their simple counterparts. Simple subjects exceeded complex subjects in searching for information when very little information was provided externally. The inverse held when large quantities of information were provided. Suedfeld and Streufert (1966) focused on individuals and demonstrated—although differences in the quality of information search by simple and complex subjects do not exist—that simple subjects want information about ongoing events while complex subjects search for information containing greater novelty.

Similar findings were obtained by Karlins and Lamm (1967) and Karlins, Coffman, Lamm, and Schroder (1967). These authors developed a different complex task where all information search would have to be search for novel information. It was found that complex subjects (SCT) were more active in information search in such a setting. Tuckman (1964), using a stock market game, also found that complex subjects (SCT and SIT) were more active in information search. Schneider and Giambra (1971) employed a concept identification task and found that complex subjects exposed to insufficient information were more efficient in obtaining additional information than simple subjects.

Streufert and Castore (1971) investigated the effects of failure on information search, utilizing the same complex decision-making task employed in previous research of Streufert and associates. They found that groups of simple subjects exceeded groups of complex subjects on *delegated* information search but did not engage in more active search moves than groups of complex subjects. Groups of complex subjects again exceeded their simple counterparts in two measures of information utilization. Highest levels of self-initiated information search and of information utilization were obtained under intermediate failure levels.

The results of the various studies seem to suggest that complex persons exceed simple persons in information transmission or utilization when the information requirements are complex (e.g., stimulus arrays are multi-dimensional and nonredundant), that complex persons search for more *novel* information, but not for more information in general, that simple subjects search for more factual information or call on standardly available channels for their information needs, and that the search of complex persons is less affected by information levels already present in their environment.

The divergent information orientation of simple vs. complex persons is also evident in their orientations toward "stimulus complexity." While earlier research on stimulus complexity is not relevant here since it tended to be confounded with symmetry, two more recent studies should be mentioned. Bryson and Driver (1972; cf. also 1969) demonstrated that complex subjects manifest higher GSRs in attending to random polygons. Preference for polygon complexity interacted with the subjects' introversion–extraversion score. Complex introverts preferred the simplest, while simple introverts preferred the most complex stimuli. Lilli (1973), using the Rep measure, established that complex subjects generated more complex figures than simple subjects, but when presented with experimenter provided figures preferred the less complex ones. Similar results were obtained by Hill and Kuiken (1975) indicating that simple subjects (ITI) responded more sensitively to abstract art then complex subjects.

Sensory Deprivation

The lowest possible level of information input under experimental conditions tends to be reached under various conditions of sensory deprivation. If the data obtained by Streufert, Suedfeld, and Driver (1965) hold, both complex and simple persons should be highly information oriented under such conditions, with a potentially greater information need present in simple subjects (who are supposedly more dependent on external as opposed to internal stimulation). Suedfeld and associates have carried out a number of studies relating sensory deprivation experience to complexity (as measured by the SCT).

Suedfeld (1964a) exposed structurally complex or simple subjects to 24 hours of deprivation. At the end of the deprivation period, they were exposed to a two-sided propaganda message. As expected, attitude change was obtained for simple but not for complex subjects, and for the deprived but not for the control group. This finding is particularly interesting if one considers that complex subjects rated sensory deprivation as more pleasant than simple subjects did (Suedfeld, 1964b). In an extension of the previous work, Suedfeld and Vernon (1966) rewarded subjects for responding in the direction of the intended attitude change while *S*s were still in deprivation. Complex deprived subjects complied more than simple subjects or complex controls. However, complex subjects showed less (internalization) attitude change than simple subjects.

Attitudes and Social Influence

The suggestion of the sensory deprivation data is that simple subjects are likely to change their attitudes if salient cues necessitating an attitude modification are provided. Less important cues (e.g., on other dimensions) may not have this effect, however. A number of researchers have demonstrated either one or the other of these propositions. Harvey (1965) had his subjects present a message counter to their own attitude in public or in private. Simple subjects (TIB) changed their attitudes more as a result of this experience than complex subjects did. Simple subjects were more influenced by a public statement, while complex subjects were more influenced by a private statement.

Heslin and Streufert (1968) placed groups of complex and simple subjects (SCT) in Streufert's complex decision-making task. Although complex and simple subjects did not differ from each other in the initial periods (about 2 hours) in the task, complex subjects began to rely less and less on environmental cues with increasing familiarity, while the environmental information remained a greater cue for simple subjects (both in terms of actual and ideal ratings provided by the subjects). Such a lack of external influence is also demonstrated by Streufert (1965). His subjects were exposed to differing proportions of supporting and refuting attitudinal messages from tape recorded others of the same status. Similar others were evaluated highly, and dissimilar others were given a poor evaluation. However, when subjects were requested to rate the others under the additional influence of a second variable (amount of predicted interaction with the other), simple subjects (SCT) did not modify their ratings, while complex subjects rated the similar other as positive and the dissimilar other as negative only under conditions of minimal interaction distance (when projected interaction in the future was very close).

The invariant attitude of simple subjects (SCT) toward others was also obtained by Streufert and Streufert (1969) in a complex decision-making task where groups of subjects experienced experimentally induced increasing failure. Simple subjects viewed their own dyad group as consistently moderately responsible for the failure conditions and did not change their attitudes toward their decision-making partner. The complex subjects varied their perceptions and attitudes with the degree of failure they were experiencing. Under success inductions (again increasing over time), simple subjects took increasing credit for the events, and increased their valuation for their partner.

Attitudes obtained from complex subjects were not influenced by the induced failure or success levels alone.

Two studies have reported research on the relationship of attitudes to Systems theory. Greaves (1972), using Harvey's TIB test, exposed subjects to attitudes toward the U.S. and Sweden from a high status source. For one half of the subjects, the attitude statements were biased toward either country. System 1 subjects recalled information for the country toward which the statement was biased. System 3 subjects recalled pro-U.S. information only, no matter what the condition.

Corfield (1969) selected subjects on Tuckman's ITI. Subjects performed a task and were then evaluated by a high status source. Self-evaluations were obtained before and after the source evaluations. System 3 subjects changed their evaluations in the direction of the external evaluation more than subjects in any other system.

In a field study of attitudes related to violence, war crimes, and especially, the Calley case, Suedfeld and Epstein (1973) obtained significant differences among a group of peace demonstrators, army reserve officers, and controls (persons in airport waiting rooms). The data indicated that peace demonstrators scored highest on measures of general "value of life" (a scale developed by Streufert & Nogami, 1970), on the approval of violence as a means to affect social change, and on complexity, while army officers scored lowest on these measures. Feldman and Hilterman (1975) presented subjects with a set of information about manipulated stimulus persons who varied in race, occupation, and social background. Subjects were required to attribute to these stimuli various traits, including conservatism, upward mobility, successfulness, and racial and occupational stereotypes. It was found that the differentiation level (Scott's R) of subjects, their racial attitudes, sex, and the awareness of the study's purpose, interacted with characteristics of the stimulus person. High differentiators used more information in their judgments, including their affect toward the stimulus, and such characteristics as stimulus occupation and background. Low differentiators did not make discriminations among stimuli on the basis of race, regardless of their racial attitudes. In a study of national attitudes in children, Jaspars, Van de Geer, and Tajfel (1972) found that attitudes of children toward other countries decrease with increasing differentiation.

Interpersonal Attraction

According to Byrne's (1971) paradigm, similarity of attitudes leads to attraction. Some other researchers have suggested that the same holds for certain personality characteristics. To determine whether similarities in complexity have an effect on attraction, Streufert, Castore, Kliger, and Driver

(1967) factored the social choice raw data matrix of students who had been familiar with each other for a considerable period of time. Factor structures were obtained for choices in four social conditions: (1) at a party, (2) working under the leadership of, (3) leading, and (4) working together on an academic task. Groups of subjects choosing each other tended to be similar in complexity scores (SCT). Some modifications, depending on the social conditions, were obtained, but complexity accounted for nearly 50% of the choice variance throughout.

In a replication of that research, Streufert, Bushinsky, and Castore (1967) obtained social choices from students living on the same dormitory floor. Complexity and openness again accounted for a large proportion of the variance in the choice matrix. Scores obtained from complex subjects were particularly closely clustered.

Crouse, Karlins, and Schroder (1968) obtained ratings of marital happiness and complexity scores (SCT) for married couples. Couples were most happy when both partners scored high on complexity.

Although replicating results which show that strangers with similar attitudes are more liked and more attractive than those with differing attitudes on Byrne's Interpersonal Judgment Scale, Black (1971) failed to support the prediction that cognitive complexity would affect judgments of liking or attraction. However, in a manipulation of the complexity (Rep) of both subjects and fictitious strangers, Johnston and Centers (1973) found that attraction was highest between persons of similar complexity level. That is, complex subjects were more attracted, on the IJS, to strangers of high complexity; simple subjects, to strangers of low manipulated complexity.

Creativity and Flexibility

Whether the interest in novel information (see above) that has been obtained for complex subjects will also make them more creative has been the subject of considerable speculation. A number of researchers have attempted to address that problem. Karlins (1967) reinterpreted the Schroder et al. (1967) complexity theory into a creativity theory, and used a 2 X 2 design to test complexity (SCT) vs. the Remote Associates Test (Mednick, 1963), in a task calling for "creative information search." He found that complex subjects (a) exhibit greater breadth of information search, (b) search more evenly across and within domains, (c) are more willing to act upon and explore their environment, and (d) maintain better differentiation among classes of information. The RAT was not able to produce similar effects. Karlins argued that the primary difference between the SCT and the RAT is the "integrative" vs. "combinatory" mechanism underlying the two theories.

Adams, Harvey, and Heslin (1966) selected subjects on the TIB test for

Systems 1 through 4. The remaining subjects (where possible) were hypnotized and instructed that they had experienced past histories leading to (according to Systems theory) development toward specific system type functioning. After the history had been hypnotically induced, subjects responded to a number of scales. Induced System 1 subjects were less flexible than System 2 or 3 subjects, who were less flexible than System 4 subjects. In evaluative ratings, induced System 1 (as compared with 2 and 4) subjects indicated greater favorability toward the American way of life and religion, and less favorability toward Castroism and the Black Muslims. The authors view their hypotheses as generally confirmed, indicating that specific past histories do produce outcomes that are described in Systems theory as specific stages of behavior.

Scott (1962a) had subjects respond to his measure of structural complexity [H-Sc (N)], and then asked them to resort the nations under instructions, in order to obtain an indicant of flexibility. He found that complex subjects are more likely to (a) expand groups of nations (sorts) when asked to do so, and (b) tend to gain information by this process (i.e., gain dimensional complexity). In other words, complex subjects are more flexible, and gain additional complexity via their flexible behavior.

Tendency toward Extreme Judgments

Several writers have suggested that the multidimensionality of complex subjects is likely to produce an "averaging" of dimensionally based responses, leaving the unidimensional simple persons to respond more often with more extreme scores on single salient scales. White and Harvey (1965) found that the frequency of extreme scores on 11-point Hardy judgment scales is greater for simple than for complex subjects. Similar results were not obtained for high vs. low scorers on the F or the Dogmatism Scale.

Larsen (1971) obtained opposite results. Testing Mormon students on dogmatism and complexity (Rep), he obtained ratings of three concepts of differential importance (negative) to the Mormon Church. While differences were obtained for extreme judgments based on the dogmatism scale, the results based on the complexity measure were not significant. [Both sets of data suggest little relationship between dogmatism (Rokeach, 1960) and complexity. While some experimenters have reported a negative correlation (Franklin & Carr, 1971), others have demonstrated that these results are due to extraneous effects (Feather, 1973). Differentiation in this research was measured by counting the number of arguments pro and con on an issue of concern to subjects.]

Sawatzky and Zingle (1971) selected subjects on the ITI and had them respond on a 7-point judgment scale measuring self-perception. Simple subjects produced more extreme scores than complex subjects.

Nidorf and Argabrite (1970) argued for a theoretical point of view which is diametrically opposed to that stated above. Complex persons should be more confident, resulting in more extreme judgments. Using a test which apparently has some similarity to a simplified RCQ, the subjects were asked to judge a number of concepts on a number of 12-point semantic differential scales. The obtained data supported their hypothesis: Complex persons made more extreme judgments. In considering their results, caution appears necessary because of the test the authors utilized.

Brown (1972) found differences between college drug-users and non-drug-users on integration (PCT) and differentiation (Rep), but these differences were not statistically significant.

The rather inconsistent results in this category may be due to a subject selection/measurement problem. The results indicating greater extremity for simple subjects were obtained using measures derived from Systems theory, which are potentially greatly influenced by the "content" definitions of some of the systems. "Simple" subjects (i.e., Stage 1) are, for example, also defined as generally authoritarian. It may well be that the "dogmatic-authoritarian-rigid" overtones of System 1 (and to some extent System 2) produce these results. On the other hand, the results indicating more extreme judgments for complex subjects, based on a category count measure of the RCQ-type may again be an effect of the measure. Persons with stronger feelings may indeed be more verbally aggressive, e.g., may produce more categories and more extreme judgments. Neither result may directly relate to complexity proper.

Decision Making

There have been two kinds of decision-making research as a function of complexity theory. Both have been generated by the Interactive Complexity theories and their antecedents. The first set of studies is concerned with the effects of complexity under conditions of varied response uncertainty. Sieber (1964) and Sieber and Lanzetta (1964) had become interested in individual difference variables to explain some of the error variance in their work on decision making under conditions of uncertainty. They found that complex subjects (SCT) differ from simple subjects in several response characteristics when exposed to a stimulus which is not clearly recognizable and presented tachistoscopically. It was found that complex subjects engaged in more information search, and presented more facts when their decisions (identification of the stimulus) had been made. Further, they gave more information which was relevant but not directly observable from the problem. Sieber and Lanzetta (1966) considered that these findings might be due to motivational differences between complex and simple persons or, alternatively, they might be produced by a differential ability for discriminating or encoding information, resulting in the production of controlled associates to the differentiated problem components.

Using an operant conditioning procedure, they replicated their previous findings concerned with differences in information search (prior to decision making). Again, complex persons expressed greater uncertainty about the correctness of their decisions. In addition, Sieber and Lanzetta found that reinforcement training of simple subjects produced more complex responding: Structurally simple subjects who received prior training displayed a level of predecision information acquisition, information output when stating their decisions, awareness of other alternatives, and uncertainty about the correctness of their decisions which was greater than that of control simple subjects and not different from that of untrained structurally complex subjects (Sieber & Lanzetta, 1966). These findings, associated with the fact that not only the directly reinforced responses but also associated (unreinforced) responses were modified by the Sieber and Lanzetta procedure, appear to be an argument for considering complexity to be a "style" (rather than a preference or ability)— suggesting that at least domain-specific complex responding may be increased by training.

In a research program designed to test the various components of Interactive Complexity theory simultaneously, Streufert and associates selected complex and simple subjects on the SCT and placed them into a complex experimental decision-making simulation. Subjects acted as (2- or 4-man, equal-rank) decision-making teams, and were exposed to a range of environmental manipulations. Streufert and Schroder (1965) varied information load (quantity of information per unit time) and found that subjects produced more differentiation and integration in decision making under conditions of intermediate information load (1 item of information per 3 minute period). Lower and higher information loads reduced differentiation and integration, and reduced the discrepancies between groups of simple and complex subjects (which are maximal at optimal load levels). Similar optimal levels and their parallel effects were found for decision making under failure (Streufert, Streufert, & Castore, 1969). Optimal failure levels (i.e., associated with highest general differentiation and integration) and maximal discrepancy between simple and complex persons occurred when failure to nonfailure information proportions were 3/7 to 4/7. Variations in success levels again had similar effects (Streufert, 1970). Parallel results (SCT) were also obtained by Kennedy (1971), using a stock market game. Stager (1967) used the simulation environment developed by Streufert to study the effects of group composition on differentiation and integration in decision making. He found that the flexibility with which decisions were made [and absence of role centrality

(Hutte, 1965)] increased in linear function with the number of complex (SCT) group members in a 4-man decision-making group. A similar analysis of decision making by Turney (1970) produced the same results. Turney suggested, however, that some members who are simple might be useful in a group, particularly if the performance criteria set for the group include some structured tasks.

Leadership

Several theorists (Bass, Fiedler, & Krueger, 1964; Bieri, 1961; Schroder et al., 1967) have suggested that complexity would likely relate to leadership, particularly to Fiedler's (1958) Least-Preferred Coworker (LPC) scale. An analysis of that relationship was reported by Mitchell (1970). Using Scott's measure of complexity (H-Sc for groups, with leadership relevance) applied to a domain-specific area, he obtained a correlation of +.51 with the LPC scale. No relationship was obtained between H-Sc(N) and LPC. Mitchell then predicted from the LPC scale to a number of characteristics usually associated with complexity. He found that high LPC persons differentiate more between task and interpersonal characteristics of both persons and situations, high LPC persons are more complex about utilizing information about various task situations, and high LPC persons are less dependent on interpersonal cues. Mitchell emphasized that this is the first time any psychological scale has shown meaningful relationships to LPC.

Larson and Rowland (1974), on the other hand, were unable to support the hypothesis that high LPC scores are positively related to complexity (Rep and Mitchell's modification of Scott's H-Sc). Further, Evans and Dermer (1974) obtained data indicating that the low end of the LPC scale may be associated with complexity while high LPC scores are not necessarily positively related to complexity. However, these authors used measures assumed by them to be correlated with complexity (tolerance for ambiguity, dogmatism, desire for certainty) rather than complexity measures *per se*.

In another study, Mitchell (1971) found that performance of groups with complex leaders was better than performance of groups with simple leaders. Using a reinforcement paradigm, Nydegger (1971) was able to train complex persons (SCT) so that they would rate themselves higher (and be rated higher by group members) on a sociometric measure. Training had no effects on simple subjects. Nydegger (1975) found that while both complex and simple subjects were affected by reinforcement, complex subjects made more use of feedback cues than simple subjects, and were rated higher on leadership by themselves and by others. Finally, Streufert, Streufert, and Castore (1968) related the behavior of complex and simple (SCT) leaders to Stogdill's (1962) leadership categories (via ratings by both group members and observers).

Complex leaders differed considerably from simple leaders. While simple leaders emphasized initiation of structure, production emphasis, and demands of reconciliation, complex leaders were rated higher on tolerance for uncertainty, persuasiveness, consideration, and predictive accuracy.

Affect and Clinical Applications

A number of studies have been concerned with complexity and affective arousal. Bryson and Driver (1969) found that, in response to a given stimulus, complex subjects manifest a higher arousal level than simple subjects, as measured by GSR. Reich and Farr (1973) determined that subjects who felt high involvement in statements about God were less complex (H-statistic) in their judgments than low involved subjects.

Studies of the relationship between complexity and the repression-sensitization factor (e.g., Ogilvie, 1971) have shown ambiguous results. A clear correlation between measures of the two variables has not been demonstrated. Thomas (1969) found that males high in Seeman's measure of personality integration were higher in cognitive levels of integration than low personality integration males.

Finally, in a study comparing creative, schizophrenic, and normal subjects, Cropley and Sikand (1973) found that schizophrenics were significantly lower than the two other groups of subjects on four "style" variables (general complexity, flexible complexity, flexibility, and differentiation on Driver and Streufert's complexity self-description test).

Some Final Comments

We have seen that the diversity of complexity theory, of complexity measurement, and of complexity research continues to exist. So far, the suggestions of Wiggins (1968) and Zajonc (1968) that complexity theories need "integration" have not been heeded extensively. This chapter represents a first attempt to discuss the various views via a "common language" by translating the various formulations into a common terminology. However, the definitions are hardly sufficient for a coherent theoretical approach. The next step in the integration process for complexity must necessarily be an integrated theory which (a) accounts for the various views and methodologies of the complexity theorists, and (b) provides a more uniform base for theoretical prediction and data interpretation.

The most striking aspect of complexity as a "phenomenon" in psychology is the inconsistency among the various measurement techniques, yet the similarity of experimental results. While different researchers have made similar predictions, they have used widely diverse (and uncorrelated) measures of complexity as a personality characteristic. Nonetheless, they have typically obtained identical results. For example, the need for consistency has been shown as higher for simple than for complex subjects, no matter on what measure the subjects had been selected. These results could be due to a number of reasons. First, of course, common artifacts might have been introduced. It is unlikely that this interpretation is correct, since the measurement techniques used have been so diverse in nature and administration (e.g., objective vs. subjective). Secondly, it may be that the measures are geared toward separate and different components of complexity, and that *each* of these components is likely to produce the expected differences in perceptions or behavior. Finally, the problem may be less severe than one might assume after reading factor analytic studies of complexity measures (e.g., Vannoy, 1965).

The measures of cognitive complexity may not relate to each other in strictly linear fashion and, consequently, may produce low or insignificant correlations. For example, the sentence (paragraph) completion measure places differentiation at an intermediate score (3) on a 7-point (1-7) scale from cognitive simplicity (no differentiation or integration) to complexity (integration). The Rep test, on the other hand, assigns the highest score for complexity to differentiation. An integrator would obtain a low score. Correlations (if linearity is assumed) between the two scales would consequently be near zero, unless the sentence completion test were scored for differentiation only. If, as all theories would suggest, both differentiators and integrators are likely to be low in need for consistency, then (considering the lower incidence of integrators in the population) both measures should select persons who would behave according to the theoretical predictions. Similar nonlinear relationships among other measures of complexity and associated data characteristics can be postulated as well.

Which of these three interpretations will hold remains to be tested in future research which is specifically designed to determine the communalities and differences among various complexity approaches. It is obvious that research of this kind is needed.

REFERENCES

Adams, D. K., Harvey, O. J., & Heslin, R. E. Variation in flexibility and creativity as a function of hypnotically-induced past histories. In O. J. Harvey (Ed.), *Experience, structure and adaptability*. New York: Springer, 1966.

Adams-Webber, J. R. An analysis of the discriminant validity of several repertory grid indices. *British Journal of Psychology*, 1970, **61**, 83-90.

Adams-Webber, J. R. The complexity of the target as a factor in interpersonal judgment. *Social Behavior and Personality,* 1973, **1,** 35-38.

Alker, H. A. Is personality situationally specific or intrapsychically consistent? *Journal of Personality,* 1972, **40,** 1-16.

Anderson, N. H., & Barrios, A. A. Primacy effects in personality impression formation. *Journal of Abnormal and Social Psychology,* 1961, **63,** 346-350.

Asch, S. E. Forming impressions of personality. *Journal of Abnormal and Social Psychology,* 1946, **41,** 258-290.

Attneave, F. *Applications of information theory to psychology.* New York: Holt, 1959.

Bailey, S. T. Independence and factor structure of self-concept meta-dimensions. *Journal of Counseling Psychology,* 1970, **17,** 425-430.

Baldwin, B. A. Change in interpersonal cognitive complexity as a function of a training group experience. *Psychological Reports,* 1972, **30,** 935-940.

Bass, A. R., Fiedler, F. E., & Krueger, S. Personality correlates of Assumed Similarity (ASo) and related scores. Urbana: University of Illinois, Group Effectiveness Laboratory, 1964.

Bem, D. J. Constructing cross-situational consistencies in behavior: Some thoughts on Alker's critique of Mischel. *Journal of Personality,* 1972, **40,** 17-26.

Bieri, J. Cognitive complexity-simplicity and predictive behavior. *Journal of Abnormal and Social Psychology,* 1955, **51,** 263-268.

Bieri, J. Complexity-simplicity as a personality variable in cognitive and preferential behavior. In D. W. Fiske & S. R. Maddi (Eds.), *Functions of varied experience.* Homewood, Ill.: Dorsey, 1961.

Bieri, J. Cognitive complexity and personality development. In O. J. Harvey (Ed.), *Experience, structure, and adaptability.* New York: Springer, 1966.

Bieri, J. Cognitive complexity and judgment of inconsistent information. In R. P. Abelson, E. Aronson, W. J. McGuire, T. M. Newcomb, M. J. Rosenberg, & P. H. Tannenbaum (Eds.), *Theories of cognitive consistency.* Chicago: Rand McNally, 1968.

Bieri, J. Category width as a measure of discrimination. *Journal of Personality,* 1969, **37,** 513-521.

Bieri, J., Atkins, A. L., Briar, S., Leaman, R. L., Miller, H., & Tripodi, T. *Clinical and social judgment: The discrimination of behavioral information.* New York: Wiley, 1966.

Bieri, J., & Blacker, E. The generality of cognitive complexity in the perception of people and inkblots. *Journal of Abnormal and Social Psychology,* 1956, **53,** 112-117.

Bieri, J., Bradburn, W. M., & Galinsky, M. D. Sex differences in perceptual behavior. *Journal of Personality,* 1958, **26,** 1-12.

Bieri, J., & Messerley, S. Differences in perceptual and cognitive behavior as a function of experience type. *Journal of Consulting Psychology,* 1957, **21**, 217-221.

Black, H. K. *The relationship of cognitive complexity-simplicity and affective stimuli in interpersonal attraction and differentiation.* Unpublished doctoral dissertation, Pennsylvania State University, 1971.

Bottenberg, E. H. Kognitive Attituden und Intelligenz. *Psychologische Beiträge,* 1970, **12**, 415-446.

Brown, L. B. *A cognitive functioning approach to the differentiation of college drug-users and non-users.* Unpublished doctoral dissertation, University of Utah, 1972.

Bruner, J. S., Goodnow, J. J., & Austin, G. A. *A study of thinking.* New York: Wiley, 1956.

Bruner, J. S., & Tajfel, H. Cognitive risk and environmental change. *Journal of Abnormal and Social Psychology,* 1961, **62**, 231-241.

Bruner, J. S., & Tajfel, H. A rejoinder. *Journal of Personality and Social Psychology,* 1965, **2**, 267-268. (a)

Bruner, J. S. & Tajfel, H. Width of category and concept differentiation: A note on some comments by Gardner and Schoen. *Journal of Personality and Social Psychology,* 1965, **2**, 261-264. (b)

Bryson, J. B., & Driver, M. J. Conceptual complexity and internal arousal. *Psychonomic Science,* 1969, **17**, 71-72.

Bryson, J. B., & Driver, M. J. Cognitive complexity, introversion, and preference for complexity. *Journal of Personality and Social Psychology,* 1972, **23**, 320-327.

Byrne, D. *The attraction paradigm.* New York: Academic Press, 1971.

Campbell, D. T., & Fiske, D. W. Convergent and discriminant validation by the multi-trait, multi-method matrix. *Psychological Bulletin,* 1959, **56**, 81-105.

Campbell, V. N. *Assumed similarity, perceived sociometric balance and social influence.* Unpublished doctoral dissertation, University of Colorado, 1960.

Carr, J. E. Cognitive complexity: Construct descriptive terms vs. cognitive process. *Psychological Reports,* 1965, **16**, 133-134. (a)

Carr, J. E. The role of conceptual organization in interpersonal discrimination. *Journal of Psychology,* 1965, **59**, 159-176. (b)

Carr, J. E. Differentiation as a function of source characteristics and judge's conceptual structure. *Journal of Personality,* 1969, **37**, 378-386.

Claunch, N. C. *Cognitive and motivational characteristics associated with concrete and abstract levels of cognitive complexity.* Unpublished doctoral dissertation, Princeton University, 1964.

Cohen, H. S., & Feldman, J. M. On the domain specificity of cognitive complexity: An alternative approach. *Proceedings of the Annual Convention of the American Psychological Association,* 1975.

Corfield, V. K. The role of arousal and cognitive complexity in susceptibility to social influence. *Journal of Personality*, 1969, **37**, 554-566.

Cox, G. B. *Cognitive structure: A comparison of two theories and measures of integrative complexity.* Unpublished doctoral dissertation, Duke University, 1971.

Crano, W. D., & Schroder, H. M. Complexity of attitude structure and processes of conflict reduction. *Journal of Personality and Social Psychology*, 1967, **5**, 110-114.

Crockett, W. H. Cognitive complexity and impression formation. In B. A. Maher (Ed.), *Progress in experimental personality research* (Vol. 2). New York: Academic Press, 1965.

Crockett, W. H., Gonyea, A. H., & Delia, J. G. Cognitive complexity and the formation of impression from abstract qualities or from concrete behaviors. *Proceedings of the Annual Convention of the American Psychological Association,* 1970, **5**, 375-376.

Crockett, W. H., Mahood, S., & Press, A. N. Impressions of a speaker as a function of set to understand or to evaluate, of cognitive complexity, and of prior attitudes. *Journal of Personality,* 1975, **43**, 168-178.

Cropley, A. J., & Sikand, J. S. Creativity and schizophrenia. *Journal of Consulting and Clinical Psychology,* 1973, **40**, 462-468.

Cross, H. J. The relation of parental training conditions to conceptual level in adolescent boys. *Journal of Personality,* 1966, **34**, 348-365.

Crouse, B., Karlins, M., & Schroder, H. M. Conceptual complexity and marital happiness. *Journal of Marriage and the Family,* 1968, **30**, 643-646.

Driver, M. J. *Conceptual structure and group processes in an internation simulation. Part One: The perception of simulated nations.* Princeton, N.J.: Princeton University and Educational Testing Service, ONR Tech. Rep. No. 9, NR 171-055 and AF Tech. Rep. AF 49(638)-742, and Res. Rep. NIMH Grant M 4186, 1962.

Driver, M. J., & Mock, T. J. *Human information processing, decision style theory and accounting information systems* (Working Paper No. 39). Graduate School of Business, University of Southern California, May, 1974.

Driver, M. J., & Streufert, S. *Group composition, input load and group information processing* (Institute Paper, 142). Institute for Research in the Behavioral, Economic and Management Sciences, Purdue University, 1966.

Driver, M. J., & Streufert, S. Integrative complexity: An approach to individuals and groups as information processing systems. *Administrative Science Quarterly,* 1969, **14**, 272-285.

Emmerich, W., Goldman, K. S., & Shore, R. E. Differentiation and development of social norms. *Journal of Personality and Social Psychology,* 1971, **18**, 323-353.

Epting, F. R. The stability of cognitive complexity in construing social issues.

British Journal of Social and Clinical Psychology, 1972, **11**, 122-125.

Epting, F. R., & Wilkins, G. Comparison of cognitive structural measures for predicting person perception. *Perceptual and Motor Skills,* 1974, **38**, 727-730.

Evans, M. G., & Dermer, J. What does the Least Preferred Co-Worker Scale really measure? A cognitive interpretation. *Journal of Applied Psychology,* 1974, **59**, 202-206.

Feather, N. T. Cognitive differentiation, cognitive isolation, and dogmatism: Rejoinder and further analysis. *Sociometry,* 1973, **36**, 221-236.

Feldman, J. M., & Hilterman, R. J. Stereotype attribution revisited: The role of stimulus characteristics, racial attitude and cognitive differentiation. *Journal of Personality and Social Psychology,* 1975, **31**, 1177-1188.

Felknor, C., & Harvey, O. J. *Parent child relations as an antecedent to conceptual functioning* (Conference Paper). University of Miami, Ohio, 1968.

Fertig, E. S., & Mayo, C. Impression formation as a function of trait consistency and cognitive complexity. *Journal of Experimental Research in Personality,* 1970, **4**, 190-197.

Fiedler, F. E. *Leader attitudes and group effectiveness.* Urbana: University of Illinois Press, 1958.

Flynn, J. C. *Cognitive complexity and construct constellatoriness as antecedent conditions of role variability.* Unpublished master's thesis, Ohio State University, 1959.

Foa, U. G., & Turner, J. L. Psychology in the year 2000: Going structural? *American Psychologist,* 1970, **25**, 244-247.

Franklin, B. J., & Carr, R. A. Cognitive differentiation, cognitive isolation and dogmatism. *Sociometry,* 1971, **34**, 230-237.

Freud, S. [*Basic writings*] (A. A. Brill, trans.). New York: Modern Library, 1938.

Freud, S. *An outline of psychoanalysis.* New York: Norton, 1949.

Gardiner, G. S. Complexity training and prejudice reduction. *Journal of Applied Social Psychology,* 1972, **2**, 326-342.

Gardiner, G. S., & Schroder, H. M. Reliability and validity of the Paragraph Completion Test: Theoretical and empirical notes. *Psychological Reports,* 1972, **31**, 959-962.

Gardner, R. W. Cognitive styles in categorizing behavior. *Journal of Personality,* 1953, **22**, 214-233.

Gardner, R. W., Holzman, P. S., Klein, G. S., Linton, H. B., & Spence, D. P. Cognitive control: A study of individual consistencies in cognitive behavior. *Psychological Issues,* 1959, **1** (Whole No. 8).

Gardner, R. W., Jackson, D. N., & Messick, S. Personality organization in cognitive controls and intellectual abilities. *Psychological Issues,* 1960, **2** (Whole No. 8).

Gardner, R. W., & Schoen, R. A. Differentiation and abstraction in concept formation. *Psychological Monographs,* 1962, **76**, (41, Whole No. 560).

Gardner, R. W., & Schoen, R. A. Reply to the note by Bruner and Tajfel. *Journal of Personality and Social Psychology,* 1965, **2**, 264-267.

Goldstein, K., & Scheerer, M. Abstract and concrete behavior: An experimental study with special tests. *Psychological Monographs,* 1941, **53**, (2, Whole No. 239).

Gourd, E. W. *Cognitive complexity-simplicity and information processing in theatre audiences: An experimental study.* Unpublished doctoral dissertation, Bowling Green State University, 1973.

Greaves, G. Conceptual system functioning and selective recall of information. *Journal of Personality and Social Psychology,* 1972, **21**, 327-332.

Guetzkow, H. A use of simulation in the study of international relations. *Behavioral Science,* 1959, **4**, 183-191.

Harvey, O. J. Some cognitive determinants of influencibility. *Sociometry,* 1964, **27**, 208-221.

Harvey, O. J. Some situational and cognitive determinants of dissonance resolution. *Journal of Personality and Social Psychology,* 1965, **1**, 349-355.

Harvey, O. J. System structure, flexibility and creativity. In O. J. Harvey (Ed.), *Experience, structure and adaptability.* New York: Springer, 1966.

Harvey, O. J. Conceptual systems and attitude change. In C. W. Sherif & M. Sherif (Eds.), *Attitude, ego involvement and change.* New York: Wiley, 1967.

Harvey, O. J. *Beliefs and behavior: Some implications for education.* Paper presented at the NSTA Annual Meeting, 1970. (a)

Harvey, O. J. Belief systems and education: Some implications for change. In J. Crawford (Ed.), *The affective domain.* Washington, D. C.: Communication Service Corporation, 1970. (b)

Harvey, O. J., Hunt, D. E., & Schroder, H. M. *Conceptual systems and personality organization.* New York: Wiley, 1961.

Harvey, O. J., Prather, M. S., White, B. J., & Hoffmeister, J. K. Teachers' beliefs, classroom atmosphere and student behavior. *American Educational Research Journal,* 1968, **5**, 151-166.

Harvey, O. J., Reich, J. W., & Wyer, R. S. Effects of attitude direction, attitude intensity and structure of beliefs upon differentiation. *Journal of Personality and Social Psychology,* 1968, **10**, 472-478.

Harvey, O. J., & Schroder, H. M. Conceptual organization and group structure. In O. J. Harvey (Ed.), *Motivation and social interaction.* New York: Ronald Press, 1963.

Harvey, O. J., & Ware, R. Personality differences in dissonance resolution. *Journal of Personality and Social Psychology,* 1967, **2**, 227-230.

Harvey, O. J., White, B. J., Prather, M. S., Alter, R. D., & Hoffmeister, J. K. Teachers' belief systems and preschool atmospheres. *Journal of Educational*

Psychology, 1966, **57**, 373-381.

Heider, F. Attitudes and cognitive organization. *Journal of Psychology*, 1946, **21**, 107-112.

Heslin, R., & Streufert, S. Task familiarity and reliance on the environment in decision making. *Psychological Record*, 1968, **18**, 629-637.

Hill, K., & Kuiken, D. Conceptual complexity and concept learning of painting styles. *Journal of Personality and Social Psychology*, 1975, **32**, 154-159.

Holzman, P. S. Scanning: A principle of reality contact. *Perceptual and Motor Skills*, 1966, **23**, 835-844.

Hovland, C. I. *The order of presentation in persuasion.* New Haven: Yale University Press, 1957.

Hunt, D. E. *Modification of conceptual development.* Paper presented at a symposium of the Society for Research in Child Development meeting, 1961.

Hunt, D. E. A conceptual systems change model and its application to education. In O. J. Harvey (Ed.), *Experience, structure, and adaptability.* New York: Springer, 1966. (a)

Hunt, D. E. A model for analyzing the training of training agents. *Merrill-Palmer Quarterly of Behavior and Development*, 1966, **12**, 137-156. (b)

Hunt, D. E. Adaptability in interpersonal communication among training agents. *Merrill-Palmer Quarterly of Behavior and Development*, 1970, **16**, 325-344. (a)

Hunt, D. E. *Data banks for analyzing and implementing student-directed learning.* Paper presented at the conference of the OISE, Toronto, 1970. (b)

Hunt, D. E. Matching models and moral training. In C. Beck, B. Crittenden, & E. Sullivan (Eds.), *Moral education: Interdisciplinary approaches.* Toronto: University of Toronto Press, 1971.

Hunt, D. E. Person-environment interaction: A challenge found wanting before it was tried. *Review of Educational Research*, 1975, **2**, 209-230.

Hunt, D. E., & Dopyera, J. Personality variation in lower-class children. *Journal of Psychology*, 1966, **62**, 47-54.

Hunt, D. E., & Halverson, C. F. *Manual for scoring sentence completion responses for adolescents.* Unpublished manuscript, Syracuse University, 1964.

Hunt, D. E., & Hardt, R. H. Developmental stage, delinquency, and differential treatment. *Journal of Research in Crime and Delinquency*, 1965, January, 20-31.

Hunt, D. E., & Hardt, R. H. *The role of conceptual level and program structure in summer Upward Bound programs.* Paper presented at the Convention of the Eastern Psychological Association, 1967.

Hunt, D. E., & Joyce, B. R. Teacher trainee personality and initial teaching style. *American Educational Research Journal*, 1967, **4**, 253-259.

Hunt, D. E., Kingsley, R. C., Massari, D. J., Shore, R. E., & Sweet, J. S. *Conceptual level scoring from paragraph completions in adolescents*. Unpublished manuscript, Syracuse University, 1967.

Hunt, D. E., & Sullivan, E. V. *Between psychology and education*. Hinsdale, Ill.: Dryden, 1974.

Hutte, H. Decision making in a management game. *Human Relations*, 1965, **18**, 5-20.

Irwin, M., Tripodi, T., & Bieri, J. Affective stimulus value and cognitive complexity. *Journal of Personality and Social Psychology*, 1967, **5**, 444-448.

Janicki, W. P. Effects of disposition on resolution of incongruity. *Journal of Abnormal and Social Psychology*, 1964, **69**, 575-584.

Jaspars, J. M. Individual cognitive structures. *Proceedings of the 17th International Congress of Psychology*, Amsterdam, 1964.

Jaspars, J. M., Van de Geer, J. P., & Tajfel, H. On the development of national attitudes in children. *European Journal of Social Psychology*, 1972, **2**, 347-369.

Jensen, A. R., & Rohwer, W. D., Jr. The Stroop Color-Word Test: A review. *Acta Psychologia*, 1966, **25**, 36-93.

Johnston, S., & Centers, R. Cognitive systemization and interpersonal attraction. *Journal of Social Psychology*, 1973, **90**, 95-103.

Karlins, M. Conceptual complexity and remote associate proficiency as creativity variables in a complex problem solving task. *Journal of Personality and Social Psychology*, 1967, **6**, 264-278.

Karlins, M., & Lamm, H. Information search as a function of conceptual structure in a complex problem-solving task. *Journal of Personality and Social Psychology*, 1967, **5**, 456-459.

Karlins, M., Coffman, T., Lamm, H., & Schroder, H. M. The effect of conceptual complexity on information search in a complex problem-solving task. *Psychonomic Science*, 1967, **7**, 137-138.

Kelly, G. A. *The psychology of personal constructs*. Vol. 1: *A theory of personality*. New York: W. W. Norton, 1955.

Kennedy, J. L. The systems approach: A preliminary exploratory study of the relation between team composition and financial performance in business games. *Journal of Applied Psychology*, 1971, **55**, 46-49.

Klein, G. S. Need and regulation. In M. R. Jones (Ed.), *Nebraska symposium on motivation*. Lincoln: University of Nebraska Press, 1954.

Krohne, H. W. *Der Einfluss von Umweltkomplexität, Angstabwehr und konzeptuellem Niveau auf die Informations-verarbeitung* (Doctoral dissertation). Marburg/Lahn: Philipps-Universität, 1971.

Krohne, H. W. Untersuchungen zur kognitiven Komplexität. In G. Reinert (Ed.), *Bericht über den 27. Kongress der Deutschen Gesellschaft für*

Psychologie in Kiel 1970. Göttingen: Verlag für Psychologie, 1973, pp. 564-573.

Krohne, H. W., & Schroder, H. M. Anxiety defense and complex information processing. *Archiv für Psychologie,* 1972, **124,** 50-61.

Kuusinen, J., & Nystedt, L. Individual versus provided constructs, cognitive complexity, and extremity of ratings in person perception. University of Stockholm: *Reports from the Psychological Laboratories,* 1972, No. 365.

Larsen, K. S. Affectivity, cognitive style and social judgment. *Journal of Personality and Social Psychology,* 1971, **19,** 119-123.

Larson, L. L., & Rowland, K. M. Leadership style and cognitive complexity. *Academy of Management Journal,* 1974, **17,** 37-45.

Lawlis, G. F., & Crawford, J. D. Cognitive differentiation in women and pioneer-traditonal vocational choices. *Journal of Vocational Behavior,* 1975, **6,** 263-267.

Leventhal, H. S. Cognitive processes and interpersonal prediction. *Journal of Abnormal and Social Psychology,* 1957, **55,** 176-180.

Leventhal, H. S. The effects of set discrepancy on impression change. *Journal of Personality,* 1962, **30,** 1-15.

Leventhal, H. S., & Singer, D. L. Cognitive complexity, impression formation and impression change. *Journal of Personality,* 1964, **32,** 210-216.

Lewin, K. *Principles of topological psychology.* New York: McGraw-Hill, 1936.

Lewin, K. *Field theory in social science.* New York: Harper, 1951.

Lilli, W. Active and passive preference of complex stimuli depending on cognitive differentiation of judgment. *Psychologische Beiträge,* 1973, **15,** 291-300.

Little, B. R. Sex differences and comparability of three measures of cognitive complexity. *Psychological Reports,* 1969, **24,** 607-609.

Luchins, A. S. Experimental attempts to minimize the impact of first impressions. In C. I. Hovland (Ed.), *The order of presentation in persuasion.* New Haven: Yale University Press, 1957, pp. 62-75. (a)

Luchins, A. S. Primacy-recency in impression formation. In C. I. Hovland (Ed.), *The order of presentation in persuasion.* New Haven: Yale University Press, 1957, pp. 33-61. (b)

Luchins, A. S. Definitiveness of impressions and primacy-recency in communications. *Journal of Social Psychology,* 1958, **48,** 275-290.

MacNeil, L. W. Cognitive complexity: A brief synthesis of theoretical approaches and a concept attainment task analogue to cognitive structure. *Psychological Reports,* 1974, **34,** 3-11.

MacNeil, L. W., & Rule, B. G. Effects of conceptual structure on information preference under sensory deprivation conditions. *Journal of Personality and Social Psychology,* 1970, **16,** 530-535.

Mayo, C. *The effect of cognitive complexity on conflict resolution in impression formation.* Paper presented at the meeting of the Eastern Psychological Association, Atlantic City, 1959.

Mayo, C., & Crockett, W. H. Cognitive complexity and primacy-recency effects in impression formation. *Journal of Abnormal and Social Psychology*, 1964, **68**, 335-338.

McLachlan, J. F. C., & Hunt, D. E. Differential effects of discovery learning as a function of student conceptual level. *Canadian Journal of Behavioral Science*, 1973, **5**, 152-160.

Mead, G. H. *Self, mind and society.* Chicago: University of Chicago Press, 1934.

Mednick, S. A. The associative basis of the creative process. In M. T. Mednick & S. A. Mednick (Eds.), *Research in personality.* New York: Holt, Rinehart & Winston, 1963.

Meltzer, B., Crockett, W. H., & Rosenkrantz, P. S. Cognitive complexity, value congruity, and the integration of potentially incompatible information in impressions of other. *Journal of Personality and Social Psychology*, 1966, **4**, 338-343.

Metcalfe, R. J. Own vs. provided constructs in a Rep test measure of cognitive complexity. *Psychological Reports*, 1974, **35**, 1305-1306.

Miller, A. G. Amount of information and stimulus valence as determinants of cognitive complexity. *Journal of Personality*, 1969, **37**, 141-157.

Miller, H., & Bieri, J. An informational analysis of clinical judgment. *Journal of Abnormal and Social Psychology*, 1963, **67**, 317-325.

Miller, H., & Bieri, J. Cognitive complexity as a function of the significance of the stimulus objects being judged. *Psychological Reports*, 1965, **16**, 1203-1204.

Mitchell, T. R. Leader complexity and leadership style. *Journal of Personality and Social Psychology*, 1970, **16**, 166-174.

Mitchell, T. R. Cognitive complexity and group performance. *Journal of Social Psychology*, 1971, **86**, 35-43.

Moerdyk, A. P. Cognitive complexity and school achievement in arts and science. *Journal of Behavioral Science*, 1973, **1**, 315-318.

Nidorf, L. J. *Individual differences in impression formation.* Unpublished doctoral dissertation, Clark University, 1961.

Nidorf, L. J., & Argabrite, A. H. Cognitive complexity and the tendency to make extreme judgments. *Perceptual and Motor Skills*, 1970, **31**, 478.

Nidorf, L. J., & Crockett, W. H. Cognitive complexity and the integration of conflicting information in written impressions. *Journal of Social Psychology*, 1965, **66**, 165-169.

Nydegger, R. V. Leadership status and verbal behavior in small groups as a function of schedule of reinforcement and level of information processing complexity. *Proceedings of the Annual Convention of the American Psychological Association*, 1971, **6**, 293-294.

Nydegger, R. V. Information processing complexity and leadership status. *Journal of Experimental Social Psychology*, 1975, **11**, 317-328.

Ogilvie, L. P. *The relationship between repression-sensitization and complexity-simplicity.* Unpublished doctoral dissertation, University of Arizona, 1971.

Oltman, P. K., Goodenough, D. R., Witkin, H. A., Freedman, N., & Friedman, F. Psychological differentiation as a factor in conflict resolution. *Journal of Personality and Social Psychology,* 1975, **32,** 730-736.

Oppenheimer, R. Analogy in science. *American Psychologist,* 1956, **11,** 127-135.

Osgood, C. E., & Tannenbaum, P. H. The principle of congruity in the prediction of attitude change. *Psychological Review,* 1955, **62,** 42-55.

Osofsky, J. D., & Hunt, D. E. *Dispositional correlates of parental teaching behavior.* Paper presented at the meeting of the Society for Research in Child Development, 1969.

Peterson, C., & Scott, W. A. *Generality and topic specificity of cognitive styles.* Unpublished manuscript, University of Colorado, 1974.

Petronko, M. R., & Perin, C. T. A consideration of cognitive complexity and primacy-recency effects in impression formation. *Journal of Personality and Social Psychology,* 1970, **15,** 151-157.

Pettigrew, T. F. The measurement and correlates of category width as a cognitive variable. *Journal of Personality,* 1958, **26,** 532-544.

Piaget, J. *The origins of intelligence in children.* New York: International Universities Press, 1952.

Posthuma, A. B., & Carr, J. E. Differentiation matching in school desegregation workships. *Journal of Applied Social Psychology,* 1974, **4,** 36-46.

Press, A. N., Crockett, W. H., & Delia, J. G. Effects of cognitive complexity and of perceiver's set upon the organization of impressions. *Journal of Personality and Social Psychology,* 1975, **32,** 865-872.

Press, A. N., Crockett, W. H., & Rosenkrantz, P. S. Cognitive complexity and the learning of balanced and unbalanced social structures. *Journal of Personality,* 1969, **37,** 541-553.

Pribram, K. H. Some dimensions of remembering: Steps toward a neuro-psychological model of memory. In J. Gaito (Ed.), *Macromolecules and behavior.* New York: Academic Press, 1966.

Reed, S. C. *Some relationships between conceptual complexity and mental abilities* (Research Bulletin RB-66-33). Princeton, N.J.: Educational Testing Service, 1966.

Reich, J. W., & Farr, S. P. Dimensional responding and affective involvement effects on categorization complexity. *Journal of Personality and Social Psychology,* 1973, **26,** 48-53.

Reynolds, R. J. Classroom verbal interaction patterns as a function of instructor cognitive complexity. *Journal of Teacher Education,* 1970, **21,** 59-64.

Richardson, L., & Soucar, E. Comparison of cognitive complexity with achievement and adjustment: A convergent-discriminant study. *Psychological Reports,* 1971, **29,** 1087-1090.

Rokeach, M. *The open and closed mind.* New York: Basic Books, 1960.

Rosenkrantz, P. S., & Crockett, W. H. Some factors influencing the assimilation of disparate information in impression formation. *Journal of Personality and Social Psychology,* 1965, **2,** 397-402.

Sawatzky, D. D., & Zingle, H. W. Level of conceptual functioning and polarization of judgments. *Perceptual and Motor Skills,* 1971, **33,** 358.

Schachtel, E. G. *Metamorphosis.* New York: Basic Books, 1959.

Schneider, G. A., & Giambra, L. M. Performance in concept identification as a function of cognitive complexity. *Journal of Personality and Social Psychology,* 1971, **19,** 261-273.

Schroder, H. M. Conceptual complexity and personality organization. In H. M. Schroder & P. Suedfeld (Eds.), *Personality theory and information processing.* New York: Ronald Press, 1971. (a)

Schroder, H. M. The measurement and development of information processing systems. *Management Information Systems,* 1971, **14,** 811-829. (b)

Schroder, H. M., Driver, M. J., & Streufert, S. *Human information processing.* New York: Holt, Rinehart & Winston, 1967.

Schroder, H. M., & Harvey, O. J. Conceptual organization and group structure. In O. J. Harvey (Ed.), *Motivation and social interaction.* New York: Ronald Press, 1963.

Schroder, H. M., & Hunt, D. E. Failure avoidance in situational interpretation and problem solving. *Psychological Monographs,* 1957, **71** (Whole No. 432).

Schroder, H. M., & Hunt, D. E.:Dispositional effects upon conformity at different levels of discrepancy. *Journal of Personality,* 1958, **26,** 243-258.

Schroder, H. M., Karlins, M., & Phares, J. O. *Education for freedom.* New York: Wiley, in press.

Schroder, H. M., & Streufert, S. *The measurement of four systems of personality structure varying in level of abstractness: Sentence completion method* (ONR Tech. Rep. No. 11). Princeton, N.J.: Princeton University, 1962.

Scott, W. A. Cognitive consistency, response reinforcement and attitude change. *Sociometry,* 1959, **22,** 219-229.

Scott, W. A. Cognitive complexity and cognitive flexibility. *Sociometry,* 1962, **25,** 405-414. (a)

Scott, W. A. Cognitive consistency, response reinforcement and attitude change. In N. F. Washburne (Ed.), *Decisions, values and groups.* New York: Pergamon Press, 1962. (b)

Scott, W. A. Cognitive structure and social structure: Some concepts and relationships. In N. F. Washburne (Ed.), *Decisions, values and groups.* New York: Pergamon Press, 1962. (c)

Scott, W. A. Cognitive complexity and cognitive balance. *Sociometry,* 1963, **26**, 66–74. (a)

Scott, W. A. Conceptualizing and measuring structural properties of cognition. In O. J. Harvey (Ed.), *Motivation and social interaction.* New York: Ronald Press, 1963. (b)

Scott, W. A. Brief report: Measures of cognitive structure. *Multivariate Behavioral Research,* 1966, **1**, 391–395.

Scott, W. A. Structure of natural cognitions. *Journal of Personality and Social Psychology,* 1969, **12**, 261–278.

Scott, W. A. Varieties of cognitive integration. *Journal of Personality and Social Psychology,* 1974, **30**, 563–578.

Sechrest, L., & Jackson, D. N. Social intelligence and accuracy of interpersonal predictions. *Journal of Personality,* 1961, **29**, 167–182.

Shrauger, S. Cognitive differentiation and the impression formation process. *Journal of Personality,* 1967, **35**, 402–414.

Shrauger, S., & Altrocchi, J. The personality of the perceiver as a factor in person perception. *Psychological Bulletin,* 1964, **62**, 289–308.

Sieber, J. E. Problem solving behavior of teachers as a function of conceptual structure. *Journal of Research in School Teaching,* 1964, **2**, 64–68.

Sieber, J. E., & Lanzetta, J. T. Conflict and conceptual structure as determinants of decision-making behavior. *Journal of Personality,* 1964, **32**, 622–641.

Sieber, J. E., & Lanzetta, J. T. Some determinants of individual differences in predecision information processing behavior. *Journal of Personality,* 1966, **4**, 561–571.

Signell, K. A. Cognitive complexity in person perception: A developmental approach. *Journal of Personality,* 1966, **34**, 517–537.

Smith, S., & Leach, C. A hierarchical measure of cognitive complexity. *British Journal of Psychology,* 1972, **63**, 561–568.

Soucar, E. Students' perception of liked and disliked teachers. *Perceptual and Motor Skills,* 1970, **31**, 19–24.

Soucar, E., & DuCette, J. Cognitive complexity and political preference. *Psychological Reports,* 1971, **29**, 373–374.

Stager, P. Conceptual level as a composition variable in small group decision making. *Journal of Personality and Social Psychology,* 1967, **5**, 152–161.

Stogdill, R. M. New leader behavior description subscales. *Journal of Psychology,* 1962, **54**, 259–269.

Streufert, S. Communicator importance and interpersonal attitudes toward conforming and deviant group members. *Journal of Personality and Social Psychology,* 1965, **2**, 242–246.

Streufert, S. Conceptual structure, communicator importance and interpersonal attitudes toward deviant and conforming group members. *Journal of Personality and Social Psychology,* 1966, **4**, 100–103.

Streufert, S. Increasing failure and response rate in complex decision making. *Journal of Experimental Social Psychology,* 1969, **5**, 310-323.

Streufert, S. Complexity and complex decision making: Convergences between differentiation and integration approaches to the prediction of task performance. *Journal of Experimental Social Psychology,* 1970, **6**, 494-509.

Streufert, S. Success and response rate in complex decision making. *Journal of Experimental Social Psychology,* 1972, **8**, 389-403.

Streufert, S., Bushinsky, R. G., & Castore, C. H. Conceptual structure and social choice: A replication under modified conditions. *Psychonomic Science,* 1967, **9**, 227-228.

Streufert, S., & Castore, C. H. Information search and the effects of failure: A test of complexity theory. *Journal of Experimental Social Psychology,* 1971, 7, 125-143.

Streufert, S., Castore, C. H., Kliger, S. C., & Driver, M. J. *Conceptual structure and interpersonal attraction* (ONR Tech. Rep. No. 3). New Brunswick, N.J.: Rutgers University, 1967.

Streufert, S., & Driver, M. J. Conceptual structure, information load and perceptual complexity. *Psychonomic Science,* 1965, **3**, 249-250.

Streufert, S., & Driver, M. J. Impression formation as a measure of the complexity of conceptual structure. *Educational and Psychological Measurement,* 1967, **27**, 1025-1039.

Streufert, S., & Fromkin, H. L. Complexity and social influence. In J. Tedeschi (Ed.), *Social influence processes.* Chicago: Aldine, 1972.

Streufert, S., & Nogami, G. Y. The value of human life: An initial analysis. Purdue University: ONR Tech. Rep. No. 27, 1970.

Streufert, S., & Schroder, H. M. *The measurement of four systems of personality structure varying in the level of abstractness: Impression formation method* (ONR Tech. Rep.). Princeton, N.J.: Princeton University, 1963.

Streufert, S., & Schroder, H. M. Conceptual structure, environmental complexity and task performance. *Journal of Experimental Research in Personality,* 1965, **1**, 132-137.

Streufert, S., & Streufert, S. C. Effects of conceptual structure, failure and success on attribution of causality and interpersonal attitudes. *Journal of Personality and Social Psychology,* 1969, **11**, 138-147.

Streufert, S., & Streufert, S. C. The development of internation conflict. In W. Austin & S. Worchel (Eds.), *The social psychology of intergroup relations.* Belmont, Cal.: Brooks/Cole, 1978.

Streufert, S., Streufert, S. C., & Castore, C. H. Leadership in negotiations and the complexity of conceptual structure. *Journal of Applied Psychology,* 1968, **52**, 218-223.

Streufert, S., Streufert, S. C., & Castore, C. H. Complexity, increasing failure and decision making. *Journal of Experimental Research in Personality*, 1969, **3**, 293-300.

Streufert, S., Suedfeld, P., & Driver, M. J. Conceptual structure, information search and information utilization. *Journal of Personality and Social Psychology*, 1965, **2**, 736-740.

Suedfeld, P. Attitude manipulation in restricted environments: I. Conceptual structure and response to propaganda. *Journal of Abnormal and Social Psychology*, 1964, **68**, 242-247. (a)

Suedfeld, P. Conceptual structure and subjective stress in sensory deprivation. *Perceptual and Motor Skills*, 1964, **19**, 896-898. (b)

Suedfeld, P. Verbal indices of conceptual complexity: Manipulation by instruction. *Psychonomic Science*, 1968, **12**, 377.

Suedfeld, P. Characteristics of decision-making as a function of the environment. In B. King, S. Streufert, & F. Fiedler (Eds.), *Managerial control and organizational democracy*. Washington, D.C.: V. H. Winston & Sons, 1978.

Suedfeld, P., & Epstein, Y. M. Attitudes, values and ascription of responsibility: The Calley case. *Journal of Social Issues*, 1973, **29**, 63-71.

Suedfeld, P., & Hagen, R. L. Measurement of information complexity: I. Conceptual structure and information pattern as factors in information processing. *Journal of Personality and Social Psychology*, 1966, **4**, 233-236.

Suedfeld, P., & Rank, A. D. Revolutionary leaders: Long-term success as a function of changes in conceptual complexity. *Journal of Personality and Social Psychology*, 1976, **34**, 169-178.

Suedfeld, P., & Streufert, S. Information search as a function of conceptual and environmental complexity. *Psychonomic Science*, 1966, **4**, 351-352.

Suedfeld, P., Tomkins, S. S., & Tucker, W. H. On relations among perceptual and cognitive measures of information processing. *Perception and Psychophysics*, 1969, **6**, 45-46.

Suedfeld, P., & Vernon, J. Attitude manipulation in restricted environments: II. Conceptual structure and the internalization of propaganda received as a reward for compliance. *Journal of Personality and Social Psychology*, 1966, **3**, 586-589.

Thomas, M. M. *Personality integration and cognitive processes*. Unpublished doctoral dissertation, George Peabody College for Teachers, 1969.

Todd, F. J., & Rappoport, L. A cognitive structure approach to person perception: A comparison of two models, *Journal of Abnormal and Social Psychology*, 1964, **68**, 469-478.

Tomlinson, P. D., & Hunt, D. E. Differential effects of rule-example order as a function of learner conceptual level. *Canadian Journal of Behavioral Science*, 1971, **3**, 237-245.

Townes, B. D., & Carr, J. E. Differentiation matching versus level of differentiation in students' judgments of teacher effectiveness. *Journal of Applied Social Psychology,* 1973, **3**, 73-83.

Tripodi, T., & Bieri, J. Cognitive complexity as a function of own and provided constructs. *Psychological Reports,* 1963, **13**, 26.

Tripodi, T., & Bieri, J. Information transmission in clinical judgments as a function of stimulus dimensionality and cognitive complexity. *Journal of Personality,* 1964, **32**, 119-137.

Tripodi, T., & Bieri, J. Cognitive complexity, perceived conflict, and certainty. *Journal of Personality,* 1966, **34**, 144-153.

Tuckman, B. W. Personality structure, group composition and group functioning. *Sociometry,* 1964, **27**, 469-487.

Tuckman, B. W. Integrative complexity: Its measurement and relation to creativity. *Educational and Psychological Measurement,* 1966, **26**, 369-382. (a)

Tuckman, B. W. Interpersonal probing and revealing and systems of integrative complexity. *Journal of Personality and Social Psychology,* 1966, **3**, 655-664. (b)

Tuckman, B. W. Group composition and group performance on structured and unstructured tasks. *Journal of Experimental Social Psychology,* 1967, **3**, 25-40.

Turney, J. R. The cognitive complexity of group members, group structure and group effectiveness. *Cornell Journal of Social Relations,* 1970, **5**, 152-165.

Uhlman, F. W., & Saltz, E. Retention of anxiety material as a function of cognitive differentiation. *Journal of Personality and Social Psychology,* 1965, **1**, 55-62.

Vannoy, J. S. Generality of cognitive complexity-simplicity as a personality construct. *Journal of Personality and Social Psychology,* 1965, **2**, 385-396.

Ware, R., & Harvey, O. J. A cognitive determinant of impression formation. *Journal of Personality and Social Psychology,* 1967, **1**, 38-44.

Watson, S. R. *Counselor complexity and the process of hypothesizing about a client: An exploratory study of counselors' information processing.* Unpublished doctoral dissertation, University of California, 1976.

Werner, H. *Comparative psychology of mental development.* New York: International Universities Press, 1957.

White, B. J., & Harvey, O. J. Effects of personality and own stand on judgment and production of statements about a central issue. *Journal of Experimental Social Psychology,* 1965, **1**, 334-347.

Wiggins, J. S. Personality structure. *Annual Review of Psychology,* 1968, **19**, 293-350.

Witkin, H. A. Perception of the upright when the direction of force acting on the body is changed. *Journal of Experimental Psychology,* 1950, **40**, 93-106.

Witkin, H. A. Origins of cognitive style. In C. Scheerer (Ed.), *Cognition: Theory, research, promise.* New York: Harper & Row, 1964.

Witkin, H. A. Psychological differentiation and forms of pathology. *Journal of Abnormal Psychology,* 1965, **70**, 317-336.

Witkin, H. A. A cognitive-style perspective on evaluation and guidance. *Proceedings of the Invitational Conference on Testing Problems,* 1973, 21-27.

Witkin, H. A., & Asch, S. E. Studies in space orientation III and IV. *Journal of Experimental Psychology,* 1948, **38**, 603-614, 762-782.

Witkin, H. A., & Berry, J. W. Psychological differentiation in cross-cultural perspective. *Journal of Cross-Cultural Psychology,* 1975, **6**, 4-87.

Witkin, H. A., Dyk, R. B., Faterson, H. F., Goodenough, D. R., & Karp, S. A. *Psychological differentiation: Studies of development.* New York: Wiley, 1962.

Witkin, H. A., Goodenough, D. R., & Karp, S. A. Stability of cognitive style from childhood to young adulthood. *Journal of Personality and Social Psychology,* 1967, **7**, 291-300.

Witkin, H. A., Lewis, H. B., Hertzman, M., Machover, K., Meissner, P. B., & Wapner, S. *Perception through personality.* New York: Harper, 1954.

Wolfe, R. The role of conceptual systems in cognitive functioning at varying levels of age and intelligence. *Journal of Personality,* 1963, **31**, 108-123.

Wyer, R. S. Assessment and correlates of cognitive differentiation and integration. *Journal of Personality,* 1964, **32**, 395-509.

Zajonc, R. B. The process of cognitive tuning in communication. *Journal of Abnormal and Social Psychology,* 1960, **61**, 159-167.

Zajonc, R. B. Cognitive theories in social psychology. In G. Lindzey & E. Aronson (Eds.), *The handbook of social psychology* (2nd ed.) (Vol. 1, 320-411). Reading, Mass.: Addison-Wesley, 1968.

Zimring, R. M. Cognitive simplicity–complexity: Evidence for disparate processes. *Journal of Personality,* 1971, **39**, 1-9.

CHAPTER 3

AN INTERACTIVE
COMPLEXITY THEORY

INTRODUCTION

The complexity theories have used terminology in quite divergent ways (Chap. 2). Sometimes identical or near-identical terms have been applied to disparate phenomena in various theories, or even within the same theory. To avoid confusions of this nature, the terminology used in this and following chapters is defined: Because of the wide use of the terms "complex" and "complexity," we will not replace them with new terminology; the reader is, however, asked to focus on their specific meaning in this context.

Complexity theory: A theory of structural, usually dimensional, differences among persons in cognitive information processing.
Interactive complexity theory: A theory which makes predictions of structural dimensional information processing on the basis of the complexity of the individual and the characteristics of the environment to which he is exposed.

Complexity (also cognitive complexity): The utilization of several dimensions of cognition in the placement of stimuli. Complexity can be either differentiative or differentiative and integrative.

Dimensionality: The dimensions used by a person to place perceived stimuli or cognitive units. Dimensions, unless otherwise stated, are assumed to be independent, i.e., orthogonal or near-orthogonal.

Multidimensionality: The use of several dimensions to place perceived stimuli or cognitive units.

Unidimensionality: The use of one (or few) dimensions to place perceived stimuli or cognitive units.

Discrimination: Same as basic terminology introduced in Chapter 2.

Differentiation: Same as basic terminology introduced in Chapter 2.

Integration: Same as basic terminology introduced in Chapter 2.

Differentiative multidimensionality: Same as differentiation.

Integrative multidimensionality: Same as integration.

More unidimensional: Applied to a person who processes stimulus information by placing stimuli on one or few dimensions.

More multidimensional: Applied to a person who processes stimulus information by placing stimuli on several dimensions.

Area of complexity: The specific realm in which the multidimensional capacity of differentiation or integration is likely present in a person (e.g., perceptual social complexity or executive nonsocial complexity, etc.).

Cognitive domain: The specific situation in which multidimensional or unidimensional characteristics of a person are likely utilized, resulting in domain-specific multidimensionality or domain-specific unidimensionality (e.g., perception of home life vs. the work situation or perception of the scientific vs. the historical literature).

Hierarchical complexity: A multidimensionality in which the placement of stimuli on dimensions is fixed and unchangeable, and where the relationships among dimensions (if any) are also fixed.

Flexible complexity: A multidimensionality in which the placement of stimuli on dimensions is not necessarily constant, and where the relationships among dimensions are modifiable. Modifications are produced by cognitive operations and by the effects of novel or changed stimulus characteristics.

Information load: The number and kind of external stimuli impinging on the organism within a specific limited time period. Information load contains all (except affective) characteristics of stimuli (affect is likely to be produced internally in response to loading stimuli, but may "add" to effective load). It is not assumed that semantic stimulation from the environment is already dimensional in characteristic. It merely provides—if appropriate—the opportunity for dimensional placement of the stimulus configuration.

Complex environment (or complex real-world): In contrast to previous definitions in other theories, this term implies merely that the *environment contains a multitude of stimuli.* The characteristics of the stimuli and their potential placement on dimensions by the receiver are not implied. However, it is assumed that stimuli from a complex environment may be—if appropriate—placeable on a number of dimensions by a person with the appropriate capacity in the relevant domain, something that is less likely for stimuli from a simple environment. In other words, dimensional complexity is viewed *only* as a characteristic of the person processing the information, not as a characteristic of his environment. In this and the following chapter, we shall—to avoid confusion—*not* refer, as other theorists have done, to multidimensional persons as "complex" and unidimensional persons as "simple."

A number of other definitions which either are of less relevance for this chapter or are defined identically or similarly by all theorists are provided in Chapter 2.

CONTENT AND STRUCTURE

Before talking about dimensionality as such, we should remind the reader (cf. Chap. 2) that we are concerned with the structure of dimensions, not with their content. We are not interested in whether some stimulus is labeled good or bad (dimensional content), or how far to the right or left on any particular scale (dimension) it is placed. Rather, we are concerned with (1) how many independent dimensions a person brings to bear in his perceptions and his behavior (i.e., on how many dimensions he places a particular stimulus or stimulus configuration), i.e., differentiation, and (2) how these dimensions relate to each other with regard to that particular stimulus or stimulus configuration, i.e., integration. Certainly, the content of dimensions is and should be of interest to psychologists. Whether an attitude toward some person, object, or event is favorable has a good amount of importance. Whether a businessman views a certain action as having or not having utility for him or his company is also important. But it is not the *only* important phenomenon, as much recent research has shown. We have already pointed out (see Chap. 1) and we will clarify further (cf. Chap. 6) that content information based on one dimension alone is often insufficient to predict behavior. Frequently the content characteristics from two or more dimensions (e.g., from cognitive as well as affective as well as conative attitudes) are necessary to make predictions for behavior in the complex world. The present chapter deals with predictions based on structural (dimensional) characteristics. It does not intend to replace or modify the predictions of psychological theories dealing with content. Rather, it intends to add the "other" necessary ingredient for hopefully more accurate predictions of human behavior in response to complex situations.

WHAT IS DIMENSIONALITY?

People use dimensions every day in their lives. We deal with objects in terms of their length, width, and height. We view colors in terms of hue, brightness, and saturation. We can easily distinguish between the volume and the pitch of a tone. But these are "physical" dimensions. Several dimensions can, and at least for some people do, exist as well in the realm of semantic concepts. How do we utilize such dimensions, how do we perceive them, find them, apply them? Are we born with the capacity to perceive multi-dimensionally? Apparently we are, when we consider physical dimensions. *Everyone* can see color in terms of hue, brightness, and saturation—everyone except those born with a severe physical handicap: If there is no color vision (e.g., via disintegration or absence of cones), then the dimensionality of color perception is drastically reduced.

We may then conclude that at least the perception of physical di-mensionality probably involves an inborn ability. Some people may have the ability to a greater degree, others to a lesser. Probably the same would hold for semantic dimensionality. Research, including some of our own, suggests that one can "learn" to be multidimensional. Some people find it rather easy to absorb and utilize dimensions that are provided for them by others. Some people find it impossible. Consequently, we would propose that the capacity to perceive, store, and utilize information in a multidimensional fashion represents an interaction between an innate ability and a learned style.

What this innate ability is, remains unknown. It may be some form of "intelligence" (not touched on by extant intelligence tests—see below), or it may be a completely independent ability (one should note that intelligence measures and measures of multidimensionality do not correlate for persons of normal or high intelligence). Some researchers state that they have discovered a difference in EEG patterns for multidimensional as opposed to uni-dimensional individuals. Whether this finding holds up under extensive tests is yet to be seen. In any case, it would still have to be questioned whether these supposed EEG differences are innate or acquired.

Even though we are far from being able to know what kind of "ability" component is involved in cognitive multidimensionality, we can say much more about its "style" component. The next section will deal with the development of a more multidimensional (and of a more unidimensional) cognitive style. We may then state that:

3.1 Complexity is an interactive product of ability and style.

DEVELOPMENT OF COMPLEXITY

Readers should be reminded that we want to talk about the development of semantic dimensionality. We assume that various forms of dimensionality in the domain of physical perception are developed—even though at discrepant rates and to discrepant levels—by nearly all persons (cf. the research and theory of Piaget, 1954 and associates).

Effects of Training

Let us assume, for the moment, that the necessary ability of a particular person to develop cognitive complexity (at least all innate components of that ability) is given. The style of complexity can then be trained, even though this training may be a *slow and tedious process*. We can distinguish between two kinds of dimensionality training to which a child might be exposed: direct training and indirect training.

Direct training again can be achieved by two different means. Possibly the easier of the two is to repeatedly suggest to the child to "take another person's point of view" and to point out to him *how* this other person thinks (in addition to *what* he thinks). Then let the child explore that point of view, let him develop it further for himself. In effect, this is training in structural empathy. The child learns to perceive the world the way another person does. He learns that he can switch the perceptions back and forth between his own views and the views of another. He learns, in effect, that there is more than one dimension, that stimuli can be ordered differently on different dimensions,[1] depending on one's focusing point: He learns to differentiate.

Another training method is a little more subtle—and a little more difficult to work with. Here the child is taught to interpret the behavior of others on dimensions that are not his own, and he learns to reinterpret his own behavior from a different point of view—in other words, on other dimensions. In effect, the dimensions for this process, at least initially, must be provided, i.e., explained and practiced, externally. The problem with this approach is the potential threat and stress it provides. Particularly, training in reperceiving

[1] A subsequent effect allows the child to even learn differential placement of stimuli on a single dimension, e.g., by referring the dimension to divergent situations, demands, etc.

(alternate perceptions) one's own behavior can be exceedingly threatening and may result in loss of security. Insecurity and threat, in addition to their unpleasantness, however, are likely to *reduce* multidimensionality—in other words, close the person to alternate perceptual activity.

Indirect training is less certain in its results and much slower in developing multidimensional perceptions. Here the experience with different kinds of people, different events and different phenomena, which cannot easily be ordered on available dimension(s), tends to generate new dimensions. However, the experience should not be excessive if it is to be effective. Experience with too many unfamiliar events in too short a period of time is likely to produce overload due to too much incongruity (see Chap. 5). Overload, again, tends to reduce dimensionality of perception. On the other hand, too little incongruity of experience is also a likely producer of unidimensional perceptions. In other words, multidimensionality is indirectly raised by a *moderate* (i.e., less than threatening) level of novelty, a level that is only moderately incongruous. It is quite possible that this phenomenon accounts for the differences we have found in the dimensionality among various population groups in the U.S. (unpublished data). The highest proportion of more multidimensional persons in several studies was obtained in groups of children of the lower middle class who had been protected, but not overprotected (e.g., both parents had spent some time away from home, working). These were children who had not been forced to "fend for themselves" too often. The least number of more multidimensional children were found in the lower classes, where the children often did have to fend for themselves, and in many cases were overexposed to a level of incongruity they could by no means handle. Equally low was the number of more multidimensional children from the upper upper class, where the children had often been overprotected and shielded from incongruity (cf. the discussions of the relationship between incongruity and complexity in a subsequent chapter).

The reader may have noticed that, so far, we have spoken only about the dimensionality of perception. Except in some instances (see below), perceptual dimensionality should be learned (particularly in the case of children) before executive dimensionality is learned. If the child has no opportunity for experience with executive dimensions (e.g., via decision making), only his perceptions can become multidimensional. On the other hand, only executive multidimensionality may be present if the child is consistently provided with externally given perceptual dimensions that have been satisfactorily worked out by someone else (see below).

We may then state that:

3.2 Training for complexity can be achieved via direct and indirect methods. Direct training can proceed via an "empathy" method, assuming that the dimensions of the "other" are discrepant from one's own existing dimensions in their ordering of stimuli. Similarly, direct training can proceed via the reperception of the self and of others on novel dimensions (even though this method has some drawbacks). Indirect training can be produced via exposing the the person to moderate levels of experience with novel and incongruent stimuli that can only be satisfactorily ordered on novel dimension(s).

Are There Stages of Development?

Most views of development talk about stages: The child grows from one stage to another, reaches plateaus, and may even become arrested at a plateau. Previous complexity theories do not make an exception to this rule. We do not subscribe to such a fixed viewpoint, at least not as far as multi-dimensionality is concerned. Certainly—again with some exceptions—a person must learn to differentiate before he can learn to integrate. One simply cannot integrate if differentiated dimensions do not exist. However, it is not necessary to have a great number of dimensions to integrate them. For that matter, it should be considerably easier to integrate two dimensions than to integrate a much larger number. The effort of integrating many dimensions, particularly for the inexperienced, can be excessive and make the task impossible. In other words, we believe that the processes of differentiation and integration of dimensions can (and, for optimal usage in the child, probably should) be learned nearly simultaneously. One can hardly speak of a stage of differentiation, followed by another of integration, after an initial stage of unidimensionality. For that matter, the process of development may run first from unidimensionality to differentiation and possibly integration, and then return to unidimensionality. That, also, we shall discuss below.

We may then state that:

3.3 Some differentiation has to precede integration. However, high levels of differentiation are not necessary to allow for integration, and may even be detrimental.

3.4 Integration can, but need not, be learned nearly simultaneously with differentiation.

Areas of Complexity

The development of multidimensionality may occur simultaneously or independently within a number of cognitive areas. We have already mentioned the distinction between perceptual complexity and executive complexity. Here we assume that, in most cases, perceptual multidimensionality comes first. But there are further areas. One can, for example, distinguish between social complexity (perception and decision making in the interpersonal realm) and nonsocial complexity (dealing multidimensionally with objects, ideas, nonsocial events). For that matter—in the sense of the Sentence Completion Test as it has been used by Streufert and associates—one might divide dimensionality into a 2 X 2 matrix: perceptual social, perceptual nonsocial, executive social, and executive nonsocial complexity.

These areas of dimensional structure in human cognition are not intended to be exhaustive. One could probably divide dimensionality finer, possibly even (perhaps on the basis of individual differences) differently. Nonetheless, the divisions into social vs. nonsocial and perceptual vs. executive areas appear to be quite useful in explaining observed differences in behavior.

It is not at all unusual that someone who is relatively high in nonsocial complexity may be low in social complexity, or vice versa. One might assume that social multidimensionality would be acquired first, since the initial interactions of the child are probably more often with persons than with objects, events, etc. One might also argue that social interactions are more important for the young child, leading to initial acquisition of social multidimensionality. It appears, however, that frequently this is not the case. Maybe the affect-arousing qualities of the early social surrounding for many (but not all) children (dependence on mother and father, rivalry with siblings, etc.) are too great to allow the somewhat "playful" or "trial and error" approach that appears useful in the development of social complexity.

On the other hand, the child's interaction with objects, for example toys, more easily allows for the "playful" orientation. And parents might even aid the child in the development of alternate perceptions for the world of toys. In the process, they permit the development of alternate perceptions and, subsequently, alternate actions on a dimensional basis. As a result, one tends to find more adults who are complex in their interaction with their nonsocial world than in their (particularly immediate) interpersonal environment.

As already suggested above, one could also make differential predictions for the development of perceptual complexity in comparison to executive complexity. The prediction appears obvious: Since people are exposed to stimuli which might be multidimensionally perceived before they can be multidimensionally utilized, perceptual multidimensional capacity should develop before executive multidimensionality does. In other words, the person should be able to understand the diverse meanings of dimensions before he can use them in his actions, in his decisions, etc. Most likely that is the more "typical" pattern, but it may not be exclusive. After all, we can find persons who are more multidimensional in their executive functioning, but are more unidimensional in their perceptual functioning. Of course, they may once have been more multidimensional here as well, and may have lost that capacity over time. Alternatively, however, they may *only* have developed executive complexity, i.e., would have developed this form of multidimensionality first. This might come about when the person is repeatedly *provided* by other persons with an analysis of the stimuli to which he is exposed, an analysis which is (and is clearly communicated to be) in multidimensional terms. As a result, the receiver of these communications may never learn the capacity to place stimuli multidimensionally himself, but may (since he receives less or no help in this area) learn to utilize these dimensions by locating executive cognitive (e.g., decision) operations on these dimensions.

We may then state that:

3.5 Complexity may differ for various areas of perception and behavior. While not exhaustive, it may be useful to distinguish between social and nonsocial areas of complexity and between perceptual and executive areas of complexity. It is likely, but not necessary, that perceptual complexity is learned before executive complexity. It is likely, but not necessary, that nonsocial complexity is learned before social complexity, and that nonsocial complexity remains higher for the life-span of the person, particularly with regard to the social complexity related to "significant others."

Acquisition and Utilization of Dimensions

How does the child acquire the use of dimensions? If we assume that only the *potential* for acquiring and utilizing multidimensionality is given as a genetic phenomenon, then the style of such utilization has to be developed by the acquisition of dimensions in some fashion. We believe that there are at least three processes of dimension acquisition:

(1) Dimensions may be defined and provided by others. Initially, it is likely some other person in the child's environment who points out that alternate semantic dimensions for perception (or, more rarely, for action) do exist. "Look at it in this way," the parent might say, or "What Aunt Edythe means is . . . ," and then tells the child how one can view the observed stimuli in a new and divergent way. Usually the adult also *labels* the different dimensional view. As a result, a new dimension may be born in the cognition of the child. Or is it? In many cases, the labels may, in effect, merely replace (or temporarily replace) labels on some already existing dimension, so that the ordering of stimuli need not be changed. In that case, it may appear as though a new dimension was formed; in effect, an old one was relabeled for that stimulus situation. An illustration might be useful. Let us say the child has an electric train set. He likes one of his train engines particularly. It is beautiful to him and it can pull a lot of cars uphill. It is a good engine (highly positive on the good-bad scale). One day the parent says, "Some of your trains are fast, others are slow." The child understands. "Yes, they are," he states, "and

this one is the fastest. That is why I like it so much." Fast toy trains mean good toy trains. Slow equals bad. The apparent new dimension slow–fast is perfectly correlated with the old dimension good-bad. In effect, there is no new dimension for the perceptual domain of toy trains.

Alternatively, the child may re-learn to apply the term "good." The parent may have said, "This train is unrealistically fast. No real train can run that fast." The child might then learn to re-order the train engines independently according to a good–bad dimension *and* according to a slow–fast dimension. In that case, he is now differentiating. But, he may merely have re-ordered his engines on his previous good–bad dimension. If some trains run unrealistically fast, that must mean that those which are too fast are not good. Only those that run at scale speed are good. So the favorite beautiful engine, which may also have been the fastest, cannot be so good anymore. Now the one that runs at the right speed is the good one, the one that runs at the most unrealistic speed is the worst one. In this case, a re-ordering of stimuli on the previously available dimension rather than differentiation has occurred.

(2) Utilization of existing dimensions. Of course, any individual may bring all those dimensions to his experience which he has already developed. These may or may not realistically fit the present stimulus configurations. Just as the more unidimensional person may have to distort the stimulus configuration to fit his single dimension, so multidimensional persons may also have to distort, if they cannot change their dimensionality to match the stimulus information (cf. the discussion of flexible vs. hierarchical complexity below). True, with several dimensions it is more likely that a better fit can be achieved than with one or few dimensions, even without change in existing dimensionality. But there is no *certainty* that the fit will be a good one.

(3) Discovery of dimensions. Semantic dimensions do not exist in the world around us (except in the cognitions and communications of the people in this world). Only stimuli exist. The dimensions are in the "mind of the beholder." But he can gain new insights about potential new dimensions through his experience with stimuli. From the work of Piaget we know that children at some point in their development learn to understand new physical dimensions. They suddenly "discover" that something is going on that they did not previously realize: e.g., the object moving behind another object has not ceased to exist, it is merely hidden. In the same way, one can discover dimensions that are not visually but semantically stored. Another illustration might be useful. A child has learned that it is good not to cheat. So he doesn't. But he has a teacher with whom he continuously gets into trouble. The teacher demands more than the child can handle. One day, in desperation, he cheats and he gains the teacher's praise for doing good work for the first time. There are a number

of potentially learned effects: He might change his view that cheating is bad to "cheating is good." As before, he still operates on only one dimension. Or he may say cheating is bad and stop doing it, or continue to do it and feel very guilty. Still there is only one dimension. Finally, he may acquire a "utility" dimension in addition to the "evaluative" dimension. He might state (or think) that cheating is bad, but sometimes it is useful and necessary. The cue determining which dimension is to be chosen for action at a particular time or in a particular situation (executive dimensionality) may depend on a single clue: the characteristics of the particular teacher, or how well he is doing in a particular class. That does not mean that the other dimension has been made inapplicable, i.e., he still views cheating as bad when he does it (in classes where he does poorly) and still views cheating as useful (but does not do it in classes where he does well). In any case, the child has developed an additional and different ordering of stimulus points on a second dimension: a dimension of "utility" in contrast to the already existing dimension of evaluation.

Developmental Stages

Many child psychologists have argued that stages of development can be ascertained: Because of an attained level of maturity, the child is able to discover new aspects of, or facts about, his environment (e.g., the work of Piaget). Complexity theorists have also frequently talked about "stages" (e.g., Harvey et al., 1961). The reader may have noted that we have avoided speaking of developmental stages. In the realm of multidimensionality they appear to be merely "labels" of the dimensionality of information processing. We do not believe that a development from unidimensionality to multi-dimensionality necessarily follows a standard pattern. Surely one must attain the ability to differentiate before one can integrate the differentiated dimensions. But the cognitive domain in which differentiation and integration occurs, the number of dimensions involved, the level of differentiation and integration, the pervasiveness of multidimensionality across cognitive domains, and so on are likely to differ from one person to another, and are likely to differ progressively and regressively over the "developmental" life-span of the individual himself. Further, similar levels of multidimensionality in parallel areas may develop in different persons at quite different ages. As a result, we favor a more continuous view of multidimensional development rather than a "stage" oriented view. More useful might be the concept of "critical periods" in the development of multidimensionality. But even these critical periods can, in most cases, be ascribed to standard "stimulus patterns" that hold for a particular society: e.g., the effects of the school experience on the development or reduction of multidimensionality (see below).

Flexibility and Openness

Certainly, one cannot attain the use of new dimensions if one is not open to novel perceptual orderings of stimuli. For that matter, one might propose that the development of any kind of multidimensionality is made impossible by a closed cognitive framework. Rokeach's (1960) concept of the open and closed mind was intended as a structural concept, and, in one way, it is indeed part of structural activity. Openness is necessary to realize that stimuli cannot fit on the previously attained dimension(s). Openness is also necessary to reorder stimuli on a new dimension and to organize dimensions into a new dimensional structure (see the section on integration below). On the other hand, openness does not necessarily lead to multidimensionality.

Openness is also a basis for flexibility. In its simplest form, flexibility can express itself in the willingness to use—even if only to try it out—the dimension of another person in order to examine the world from his point of view (empathy). Even more, flexibility might be necessary to reorganize (playfully or seriously) one's own dimensional structure in the face of more or less unplaceable stimuli. And flexibility becomes even more important when we deal with "integration" (see below).

We might then state that:

3.6 Complexity can be learned more easily for an area if it already exists for a related cognitive area.

3.7 Acquisition of new dimensions can occur via communication by others, discovery, or by transfer of an already existing dimension to new stimuli.

3.8 Complexity cannot be acquired unless openness to novel stimuli and to reorganization of stimuli along dimensional structures is given. Openness is also a requirement for the flexibility that is necessary to permit the restructuring (i.e., changing the previous integrations) of dimensions.

We might add that excessive openness can be detrimental. It is not unusual to observe excessively open multidimensional integrators or differentiators who find it impossible to act on stimulation (or cognition) since they cannot close long enough to select one dimension or one integration of several dimensions for a decision.

IS IT "GOOD" OR "BAD" TO BE MULTIDIMENSIONAL?

We have already talked about complexity and how it can be produced. To most readers, that may suggest it is a "good thing" to be multidimensional in one's orientation. For that matter, several complexity theorists have discussed the value of dimensional complexity in adjustment, in education, etc. They tend to view multidimensionality as inherently good.

We would emphatically warn the reader of such views. Particularly, theorists who deal with multidimensionality should not think unidimensionally by identifying the dimension unidimensional-multidimensional with the dimension bad-good. They *are* quite different dimensions. But let us not only differentiate; let us also integrate: It appears that multidimensionality has value specifically in those *situations* where it produces useful results, i.e., situations where behavior has to proceed in a potentially playful way, where a large number of stimuli must be taken into account, and where various alternatives have to be considered while looking at various overlapping groups of stimuli in various ways. On the other hand, unidimensionality would be an advantage where decisions have to be made according to a clear criterion, where rapidity of action is required, where alternative interpretations of the same set of stimuli would be viewed as superfluous and possibly as reflecting wishy-washyness. A complex (multidimensional) person living on a farm in some small community of an underdeveloped country, with a relatively fixed and stable culture, would probably be exceedingly maladapted if he developed the kind of multidimensionality that would be of value in a cosmopolitan city. Even in our complex western or westernized societies, those people who know what is "bad" as opposed to "good" (whatever that may be) or who know what is right as opposed to wrong, are often better off than those who can come to too many alternate conclusions, depending on which dimensional organization they happen to apply to the current stimulus configuration. Most successful in coping with the environment, however, might be those who are either able to change their dimensionality with the demands of the environment at will, or who can quickly "learn" a different and "currently more useful" dimensional style [e.g., the successful revolutionaly leaders discussed by Suedfeld and Rank, (1976)].

THE REDUCTION OF DIMENSIONALITY

So far we have discussed how multidimensional perception is generated. But there are many (very many?) instances of the opposite process. Sandra Koslin (personal communication) tells of an experiment comparing younger children with children who had already spent some years in school. She asked the children to place toys representing persons into a miniature room. These persons had different characteristics (e.g., adult, child, different skin colors, etc.). The dimensionality of the children was calculated via measuring the physical distance between the placed persons. It turned out that the children with less school experience employed more dimensions than those with more school experience. One might ask why.

School is a place where one learns. One learns to distinguish the right answers from the wrong ones, and one learns that some behavior is good and the opposite is bad. Everything is typically placed on the evaluative dimension. Other dimensions are either not supported or not even permitted. The frequent complaint that school is the killer of creativity in children has its basis, in part, in this phenomenon (see the statement on dimensionality and creativity below). In any case, it appears to us that the excessive emphasis on rightness vs. wrongness in the learning environment is likely to reduce previously established multidimensionality. Reduction of dimensionality to few or a single dimension would likely occur at any time when a person has to cope with a relatively simple, structured, and purposive environment. Purposiveness alone (except in rare circumstances) would not allow for the "playfulness" that is often the basis for multidimensionality. In such an environment, the dimensionality likely will be reduced to the most salient or most externally emphasized dimension. In school settings and many other situations in western culture, this dimension is most likely the evaluative one. But not in all settings will evaluation be most salient. Driver (1965), for example, has shown a reduction to a single alliance dimension in internation conflict.

Whether one views a decrease in multidimensionality produced by societal institutions, for instance via school experience, as useful or not should depend on one's view of society, on the number of multidimensional persons one feels are needed by society, and on the situation to which one believes the children of today will be exposed tomorrow.

One may question whether the dimensions the child used before his school experiences are lost forever. They might be. On the other hand, the observed reduction of dimensionality in the school situation may reflect a quite different process. It may reflect *dimensional habituation* occurring over time and over experience with a stimulus array.

In their propositions, complexity theorists have typically spoken of the exposure of persons to somewhat novel stimulus arrays. Many complexity researchers have employed somewhat novel stimulus situations to observe multidimensional behavior. Under those conditions, the subject must search within his store of dimensions for those that appear appropriate to the present stimulus array. A number of dimensions may be relevant, resulting in multidimensionality of perception and possibly of behavior. If, on the other hand, the person were to be repeatedly exposed to the same (or a very similar) stimulus array over time, he is likely to find which dimensions are the most "appropriate" to the situation, i.e., which responses based on which dimensions are likely positively reinforced, which provide the desired outcome, etc. Responses based on nonreinforced dimensional judgments may then start to drop out of the repertoire of behavior.

Let us return to the child described above. He may indeed have lost the capacity to use the dimensions he employed at a younger age. Or the additional dimensions may have dropped out of his behavior repertoire because in the setting of school they were less than useful. He has spent quite a bit of time in the school situation where his responses were repeatedly evaluated by adults. He has learned the basis on which these evaluations were made: His perceptions, responses, and behavior were either viewed as good or bad, either as right or wrong. For the school setting, an evaluative orientation has obviously become the most useful, the most appropriate. Consequently, he has learned to perceive stimuli and to respond to stimuli from this setting on the evaluative dimension only. However, the other "dormant" dimensions may not have been lost. Whether and to what degree they might be regenerated by the older child, when it is once more presented with a somewhat unfamiliar stimulus array in a somewhat unfamiliar situation (where habituation to lower dimensionality has not yet taken place), is currently not known.

We do not want to imply, however, that habituation to lower dimensionality is a phenomenon only found in children. Rather, it appears that the phenomenon is general: Familiarity with situations and their stimulus arrays would likely result in habituations to a lower number of dimensions (if reinforced, etc.) for persons of all ages.

We may then state that:

3.9 Multidimensionality in children may be reduced by training them in the application of fewer or of one dimension to both recurrent stimuli and novel stimuli.

3.10 Multidimensionality is likely reduced through habituation in repeated exposures to identical or similar situations and their stimulus arrays.

TRAINING DIMENSIONALITY IN THE ADULT

We have already said that the development of dimensionality is a long and tedious process. We were referring to children who have their first experience with the reordering of stimuli on various new dimensions. How difficult would it be to train an adult in multidimensional perception or behavior?

If the adult is already more multidimensional in some area(s), and has gained his multidimensionality in his childhood or teenage development, it should not be too difficult to extend this dimensionality into other areas, unless other phenomena (cf. the discussion of salience and affect below) would prevent it. On the other hand, if there is little or no multi-dimensionality present in *any* area, training may be much more difficult and effects may be variable. Structurally, the adult *tends* to be a "finished product." He often no longer has the time nor the inclination to approach the world in the "playful" way that allows the child to expose himself to an amount of incongruent novelty that may lead to increased multidimensionality (cf. Streufert, in press). In addition, he has—in contrast to the child's playfulness—often (but not necessarily) become more "rigid" in his approach to stimuli. Through his past reinforcement history he has learned to cope with stimulation in some particular way. Positive reinforcement for unidimensional problem solving and decision making likely has aided in maintaining the more unidimensional approach (in many areas, unidimensionality may well be the best, and consequently, the positively reinforced solution to problems). On the other hand, negative reinforcement for unidimensional behavior—since it cannot be understood (except in its content characteristics) by the more unidimensional person—is likely to get him to try even harder, and may consequently aid the persistence of unidimensionality. In other words, training a new style of multidimensionality in the adult is possible but very difficult. At best, one can select an area in which multidimensionality is desirable, and attempt to train it specifically for that area. What are the likely results?

Certainly, it is helpful if the person is "flexible" rather than "dogmatic" even if more unidimensional in his approach to stimuli. The salience of any single dimension which a person used with regard to the relevant stimuli should not be so high that he would be unable to cope with a multi-dimensional approach (see below). If flexibility and low salience are given, it should be possible to train him in multidimensionality within a specific limited domain by *providing* the needed dimensions and demonstrating how specific expected stimuli would fit on these dimensions. It would be con-siderably easier to train the person to differentiate these dimensions; much more difficult to train him to both differentiate and integrate. His dimen-sionality in this domain would likely be structured hierarchically, i.e., it could not change in and of itself without further direct training. As already stated, this hierarchical approach to multidimensionality would also remain domain specific. Obviously his response would look rigid, and he would likely have to use *all* the learned dimensions simultaneously. Even (except under stress conditions) the previous more unidimensional response may no longer be possible (he has, after all, learned that it was the "wrong" response).

If it is suggested to him that the multidimensional process he has learned in one domain is usable in other domains as well, he should be able to apply it there *only* if the dimensions of that domain are potentially identical and if the received stimuli fit on these dimensions in the same fashion. He should not be able to generate new dimensions for the additional domain. Of course, additional training in this new area (if it should differ in dimensionality) may provide him with the potential of (rigidly) dealing with multidimensional approaches to stimuli there as well.

We do not intend to say that it is impossible for a more unidimensional adult (where little or no multidimensionality is present in any semantic perceptions or semantic behaviors) to learn flexible multidimensionality across various domains. But we suggest that it is an exceedingly difficult, and probably an exceedingly frustrating and stressful, process.

We may then propose:

3.11 Training complexity (multidimensionality) in adults who operate more unidimensionally in all domains tends to be quite difficult. Training has to be domain specific.

3.12 Training a more unidimensional adult in a specific domain is more likely to produce differentiation than both differentiation and integration.

3.13 Trained complexity in the more unidimensional adult in one domain is not likely to spontaneously generalize to other domains. Retraining is most likely necessary for each domain within which complexity is deemed desirable.

HIERARCHICAL VS. FLEXIBLE COMPLEXITY

We have suggested that an adult who has not attained multidimensional capacity during his developmental period is likely to be only hierarchically complex. In other words, the number of dimensions he can utilize, the placement of stimuli on those dimensions, and the potential interrelationships among those dimensions are likely fixed.

But not only adults can be hierarchically complex. It is quite possible that a child attains only this kind of multidimensionality. Often this occurs when a child has (often flexible) multidimensional but authoritarian parents who do not permit the child to explore his world on his own, who prevent the playful approach to dealing with semantic concepts and the alternate placement of stimuli on conceptual dimensions. Some parents assure that their children will "copy" their dimensions. While the parents might have attained these dimensions themselves via trial and error, via playfulness (i.e., via *flexible* differentiative and integrative processes), the child is only allowed to learn those dimensions and their interrelationships which are provided by the parents. The child himself has little or no experience with flexibility in either differentiation or integration. As a result, he may develop a hierarchical multidimensional structure in one or more domains. In attempting to transfer his dimensional capacity from one (multidimensional) to another (yet unidimensional) domain, he should experience the same difficulty as the adult who is exposed to learning multidimensionality for the first time.

One other characteristic of hierarchical complexity should be considered. Since the pattern of differentiation is fixed, stimuli are placed at constant points on the dimensions on repeated exposure, so that the effect of the same stimulus configuration across time would not change. This means, in effect, that the dimensional structure of the person is reducible to single determinants. In other words—as in the case of the more unidimensional person who uses several labels for a stimulus pattern which, however, have identical meaning (high correlation)—there is some question whether one can legitimately view the hierarchically multidimensional person as truly multidimensional. Particularly if he has been trained to be a hierarchical integrator, his supposedly separate dimensions can often be reduced to one overall (only apparently integrated) determining dimension.

COMPLEXITY AND ENVIRONMENT

The theory proposed here is an interactive theory. It assumes that the stimulus effects of the environment interact with the real or potential complexity of the receiver to produce the dimensionality with which the information is processed. Of course, we cannot enter an information processor's brain and observe how his dimensions go into operation. We can only observe his responses to some set of stimuli. Consequently, we will initially state our predictions in terms of stimulus–response characteristics. The dimensional characteristics of the individual information processor and their effects will be dealt with later.

But before we analyze the effects of stimuli on responses, let us make one assumption about the person whose behavior we are trying to predict: *Let us assume that he is motivated to attend to the stimuli* and *let us assume that he is motivated to respond* in some meaningful fashion to the situation of which the stimuli are a part.

Effects of Information[2]

Information characteristics are important to complexity theory since stimulus information provides one basis for the utilization of dimensionality in

---

[2] It may be necessary to clarify the meaning of the term information in the present context. While many researchers have successfully used the term in the sense of information theory (one bit of information reduces uncertainty by one-half), this otherwise useful aid cannot be applied in the present context. While information may reduce uncertainty on one dimension, it might increase it on another. In other words, the information theory definition of information is too restrictive in the current context. We will use the term in the sense of Driver and Streufert (1969), who defined information as an external stimulus that has the tendency to "alter subjective (or objective) probabilities or *utilities.*" In other words, one might say that information is likely to produce the potential for a response from the person receiving the information.

persons exposed to the information. Past forms of complexity theory have viewed information in various ways. The most extensive statement in this regard probably was that of Schroder, Driver, and Streufert (1969). Here a distinction was made between information load (the quantity of information per unit time), eucity (the success component of information), and noxity (the failure component of information). Later research (Streufert, 1973) has shown that additional variables would have to be added, for example, relevance. We intend to make this view more parsimonious. It appears (excluding separate affect effects, with which we will deal later) that the different variables considered by Schroder, Driver, and Streufert can be included in the information load concept. Where noxity requires taking an action over again, thereby increasing current load by adding action requirements, eucity is likely to decrease load. Irrelevant information will be equivalent to load only with regard to some of the activities in which a person is engaging at the present time (see below).

We will use the term information load here as well. But the meaning will be more extensive: Information load will include all environmental stimulus effects that generate some form of action by the person. Information load will represent the *"amount" of information that has to be processed.* As we shall see later, secondary affective effects associated with information load (e.g., from success or failure experience) can also be viewed as further reductions or increases in information load.

But let us return to information provided by the stimulus situation. For the person involved, task relevant stimulation can vary from extremely low levels, where it is absent, to extremely high levels, where it is (theoretically) infinite. Extreme load levels of this nature are relatively rare, and occur only under special conditions (cf. Suedfeld, 1978). Normal task environments also provide *divergent information loads that tend to be less extreme in variability. In the following statements, we are referring to environments of this kind.* Their range of stimulation represents a variation of information load from relatively minimal to relatively maximal levels for the relevant situation.

We would predict that:

3.14 In the relative absence of information, relevant information will be sought, or (if relevant information is not available) irrelevant information will be sought, or information (often also irrelevant) will be internally generated by a person as a basis for his perceptions and responses.

We refer to relevant information as stimuli that are useful in responding to a current task or intent, and to irrelevant information as stimuli that are not useful for this purpose.

The level of active responses of a person (e.g., communications, decisions, etc.) to self-sought and self-generated information is not likely to be high. This form of responding should decrease as externally provided information increases (cf. Fig. 3.1). Most of the responses are likely to appear random and will not fit any particular pattern.

In most cases, though, a sufficient degree of external information is present in a stimulus situation. However, a good deal of the externally provided information may be less than useful (relevant) for the perceiver's current intents. How will he respond if considerable information, whether relevant or not, is provided? We know (cf. the research of Brock and of Streufert) that information has considerable value in Western society. Even when already too much information is provided for inclusion in a person's information processing activities, he is likely to ask for more information. Rather than selecting the relevant information that is already provided for action, the individual is likely to request additional information and to utilize the additional information

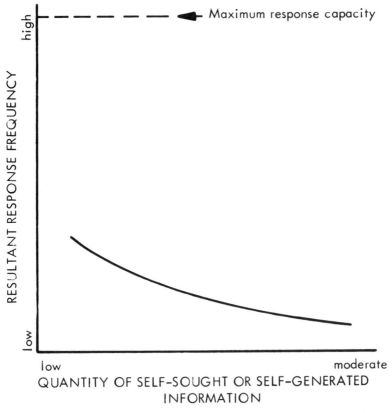

Fig. 3.1. Effects of self-sought or self-generated information on behavior.

(at least in part) as well, even if it is irrelevant. He will also likely utilize some irrelevant information that is externally provided. We would suggest that:

3.15 In the presence of information, persons tend to respond to that information, whether it is relevant or not relevant.

This does not mean that obviously relevant information will not have a larger effect on behavior than obviously irrelevant information. However, particularly in situations where the amount of available relevant information is limited, the effect of irrelevant information grows considerably. But even when considerable amounts of relevant information are provided, the irrelevant information retains some effect. Often people feel that the very presence of some information item must make it meaningful for the situation with which they are dealing.

Behavioral Difference

While one can describe human behavior in a number of ways, one particular description appears particularly useful from the view of interactive complexity theory:

3.16 Information processing and resulting behavior in response to information proceeds along specific curves relating stimulus characteristics to response frequencies. Three response types may occur separately or in combination with each other. The response types represent simple one-to-one responding, differentiative responding, and integrative responding.

In simple one-to-one responding, information input is directly translated into a (usually single) behavioral output. In decision making research, this kind of response has become known as "respondent decision making." It occurs with particular frequency for persons of more unidimensional structure and, in general, under environmental conditions that are less then optimal (see below for a discussion of "optimality").

In differentiated responding, a stimulus is placed on a number of different dimensions, and calls forth a response on several of these dimensions simultaneously (or subsequently) within a limited period of time. The various responses, however, are typically not related to each other via some form of plan or strategy. This kind of response occurs with particular frequency for persons who are more multidimensional differentiators, and it occurs, in general, at moderate (optimal) and higher levels of relevant information load (see below).

Integrated responding implies that a number of responses based on various dimensions are made (as in the last example above) but the responses relate to each other in a planned or strategic fashion. This kind of response is most often observed for persons who are multidimensional integrators, and occurs with greatest frequency under moderate (optimal) information load conditions (see below).

Given a specified limited time within which responses must be made, there should be a maximum response level that can be reached by any particular organism, although this maximum is likely to vary among organisms. The maximum level should be higher for respondent behavior than for differentiated behavior. The maximum level for integrative behavior should be lowest, since integration is likely to require the greatest cognitive effort, and since a larger number of information items may be "used up" in integrated responses which are made to a greater number of information items simultaneously.

Certainly there are other kinds of responses that do not fall into the integration, differentiation, and one-to-one respondent categories. Possibly the most important represents a kind of general irrelevant (unintegrated and undifferentiated) response which shows little relationship to information (if any) that has been recently received by the organism. We have already stated that—in the *absence* of information—the organism tends to seek information, or is likely to generate it himself. Of course, as the research of Suedfeld and associates has shown, information provided under excessively low load conditions may have particularly strong behavioral effects. Most likely such information would lead to strong one-to-one responses.[3] Beyond this information, however, the organism is still left to its own devices, e.g., the generation of general irrelevant behavior often based on self-generated cognitions or information.

A somewhat different but similar phenomenon apparently occurs at *excessively high* load levels: In some cases, the information present at high load levels may be rejected by some individuals, since all of it cannot be dealt with anyway. Instead of responding to the provided information, the organism may respond in what often appears to be a random fashion to internally generated cognitions. As high levels of information load increase further, this kind of responding would also increase. For Figure 3.1, one would then obtain a U-shaped function. This curve and the relationship of the previously discussed response types as a function of information load are shown in Figure 3.2.

The maximum levels under time constraints for each response type has been entered in that figure. As stated previously, this maximum is likely to vary from person to person; in other words, it is not viewed as a fixed entity

---

[3] It may well be that the overly strong response is here due to a situationally-produced inability to appropriately recognize information relevance.

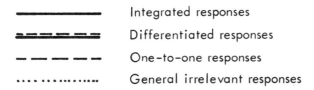

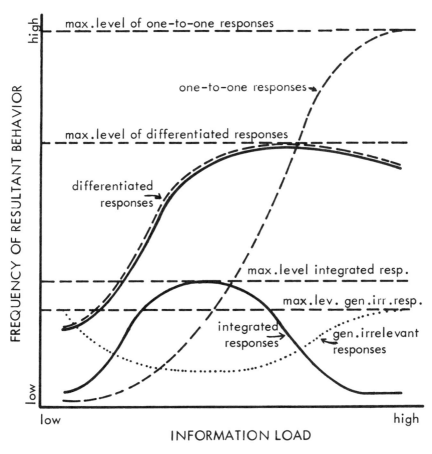

Fig. 3.2. Effects of information load on four kinds of response frequency.

across persons. However, a common *shape* of the curve across all persons is assumed. This means that an *"optimal" quantity* of each kind of behavior should be definable at more or less specific points on the information load dimension. Optimal here means "most conducive" to the production of a specific behavior. It does not necessarily refer to "habitual or accustomed" responding or to preferred levels of stimulation and/or responding. The latter shall be dealt with in the section on complexity and affect (below).

The concept of the optimum information load has resulted in considerable research and discussion among complexity theorists and researchers in recent years. For instance, Streufert and associates have repeatedly demonstrated optimal integrative perception and decision making for information load levels representing one item of information per 3-minute time period in complex decision making tasks. Other experimenters using the same or similar tasks have confirmed this finding. On the other hand, some researchers have attempted to extend the optimum concept to other perceptual and behavioral characteristics. For example, Cummings, O'Connell, and Huber (1978) used the experimental method developed by Streufert to measure the effects of information load on task satisfaction. The results were disappointing. Variables other than load proper appeared to affect satisfaction.

Results of this kind suggest that a general optimum may not exist. Suedfeld (1978) writes: "One problem of much of the research in this area has been the attempt to establish *general* levels of underload, overload, and optimal load. This is an attempt that I think is doomed to failure." We would agree. One should, however, be able to establish optimal load levels for specific response characteristics, e.g., one-to-one responding, integrated responding, differentiative responding, etc. But, one should not be able to extend the relevant optima for these response characteristics to such affective characteristics as "task satisfaction." And one must be careful to assure that the situations in which the optima are measured are relevant to the kind of response under study. For example, a stimulus situation that does not allow for integrative responding because it does not allow for multidimensionality is not likely to produce any point of optimum integration.

It has also been argued (e.g., Suedfeld, 1978) that optima should vary with characteristics of individuals, including their preferences and abilities, their current states of health, mood, fatigue, etc. It appears to us that these differences may affect the *level of responding* more than the optimum point for that responding. Our research over the years has shown that at least for differentiative and integrative responding the optima tend to be quite constant across individuals and even across interacting groups of various sizes. It may well be that optima (at least in the areas of multidimensional information processing) are produced by some physiological limiting mechanism, similar to the "magic number seven plus or minus two" in perception (Miller, 1956).

This assumption might be quite reasonable if one considers that optima have been demonstrated for a number of physiological responses, ranging from cells (e.g., Granit & Philips, 1965) to the individual (e.g., Quastler & Wulff, 1955). Nonetheless, we would like to remind the reader that he should not expect a *general* optimum that holds *across all tasks, all responses,* and *all persons.* Rather, one should be able to expect optima in relevant tasks for specific response types, and one should be able to expect these optima to be relatively constant across persons. The level of response frequencies that is obtained at the optimum points, however, should differ widely from person to person and from group to group.

With these restrictions in mind, and *all other things being equal,* we may state that:

3.17 A maximum amount of integrated behavior (in both perception and performance) should occur at moderate relevant information load levels.

3.18 A maximum amount of differentiative behavior should occur at moderate and moderately high relevant information load levels.

3.19 A maximum amount of one-to-one respondent behavior should occur at high information load levels.

3.20 A maximum amount of general irrelevant behavior should occur at low and high information load levels.

We want to again emphasize that in defining behavioral effects of relevant information load, we are not considering *extremely* low or high loads. The effects of sensory deprivation (extremely low information load conditions) have been discussed in detail by Suedfeld (e.g., Suedfeld, 1964, 1966) in various publications. They are not included here. Less is known about the effect of excessively high loads; yet one can probably assume that the "escape" or "freeze" response so often observed under these conditions, for both animals and people, would prevent *any* multidimensionality from affecting behavioral outcomes.

We have now stated those conditions under which we expect the maximum levels of various kinds of behavior (under the typical time constraints of real-world information processing) to occur. If one wants to produce an optimal quantity of some specific kind of behavior, one should be able to vary information load appropriately. Optimal integrative behavior would be predicted for intermediate relevant information loads, optimal differentiation for the same and somewhat higher levels. Since we are here primarily concerned with multidimensionality, we are considering intermediate relevant information loads as optimal. However, a warning is necessary. As already indicated, what behavior is most appropriate depends on the situation or the task. For many tasks and situations, multidimensional behavior is not desirable, and quick one-to-one responding is most appropriate. Consider another example: If a missile officer is sitting on board a ship somewhere at sea, and an enemy plane approaches and fires a missile at the ship, he should respond immediately. Let us say that the opposing missile is guided by the plane, and that the plane could be shot down before the enemy missile would hit the ship. To do that, the missile officer has to initiate the appropriate action against the enemy plane at once. However, he notices, through the information he received from his computer, that the enemy missile is traveling at a speed unusual and "unknown" to the intelligence operations of his country. That is additional information which could be integrated into a modified decision. That integration, however, would take some time. Maybe it would not take much time, but more than our missile officer can afford to lose. If he integrates, he loses his life. Obviously, integration is inappropriate for that situation. One-to-one responding, on the other hand, is likely appropriate: The integration (if any) can still occur after the immediate danger has been averted.

We may then suggest that *optimal* levels can be proposed for a number of behaviors and their informational determinants. These optima would be as legitimate as the optimum relevant information load we are employing with regard to multidimensional responding. The reader should, if possible, keep this in mind when he reads the word "optimum" relevant load in this work; "optimal load" specifically refers *only* to those load conditions which produce the maximum number of multidimensional (differentiation and integration) responses.

Effects of Relevance

It has already been stated that persons tend to respond to both relevant and irrelevant information (cf. proposition 3.15). Obviously, responses to irrelevant information are likely to be less appropriate to the requirements of the task or situation with which a person must cope. But there are additional effects.

In discussing the relationship between information load and differentiation/ integration, we have spoken consistently of *"relevant" information load*. The reason for this additional word lies in the necessity for information to be relevant if differentiation and integration are to be achieved. Relevant informative stimuli—assuming they allow for multidimensional responding— result in interested cognitive activity by the receiver of the information. On the other hand, irrelevant information tends to have two drawbacks: (1) irrelevant information typically does not "hang together," and (2) even if it does, the receiver typically may not attend to it sufficiently to generate differentiative and integrative cognitions. Rather, he typically uses the information in a unidimensional fashion: He may respond to it in a one-to-one fashion, he may be puzzled and use it to search for additional information ("It appears irrelevant, but may not be. I'm going to find out."), or he may ignore it altogether. Neither of these processes necessitate or even allow a multidimensional approach. Consequently, we propose that:

3.21 Multidimensional responses to information (e.g., differentiation and integration) vary (as predicted) with relevant information load.

3.22 Unidimensional responses (e.g., information search, one-to-one respondent behavior, general irrelevant behavior) vary (as predicted) with both relevant and irrelevant information load.

INTERACTIVE COMPLEXITY THEORY

We have proposed earlier that individual differences in dimensional information processing, i.e., in the capacity to differentiate and integrate, exist on the basis of an innate ability and a learned style. We propose that these individual differences in dimensional characteristics interact with the environmental effects proposed in the last segment of this chapter. Very few, if any, diverse effects on dimensional information processing characteristics would be predicted for conditions representing very low and very high information loads. However, maximum levels of differentiation and integration predicted for optimal relevant information loads should differ between more multidimensional and more unidimensional persons. We would propose that:

3.23 Integrators should exceed differentiators and differentiators should exceed more unidimensional persons (in a specific domain where these descriptions apply) in the number of integrated responses at moderate relevant information load levels.

3.24 Differentiators should exceed integrators and integrators should exceed more unidimensional persons (in a specific domain where these descriptions apply) in the number of differentiated responses at moderate and moderately high relevant information load levels.

3.25 More unidimensional persons should exceed differentiators and integrators in the number of one-to-one respondent behaviors at moderately low, moderate, and moderately high information load levels (particularly if the information load is relevant in nature).

These predictions are presented in graphic form in Figures 3.3, 3.4, and 3.5.

The reader may note that we have again made the distinction between relevant and irrelevant load for predictions of more multidimensional and more unidimensional behavior. But, we may ascribe relevance to individual difference effects as well.

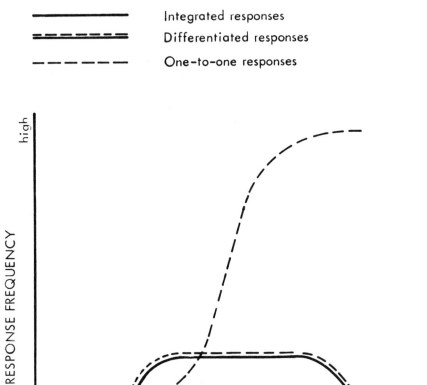

Fig. 3.3. Responses to information by more unidimensional persons.

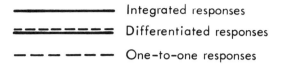

Integrated responses
Differentiated responses
One-to-one responses

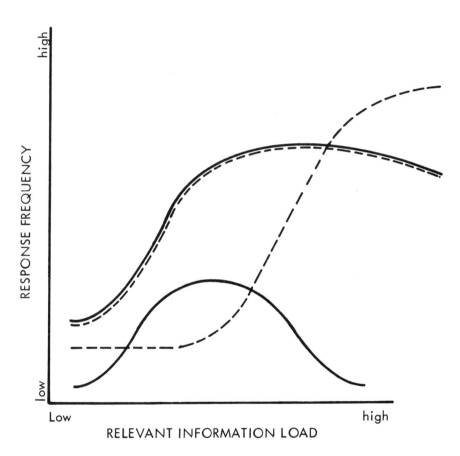

Fig. 3.4. Responses to information by differentiators.

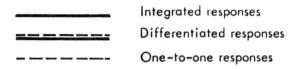

Integrated responses
Differentiated responses
One-to-one responses

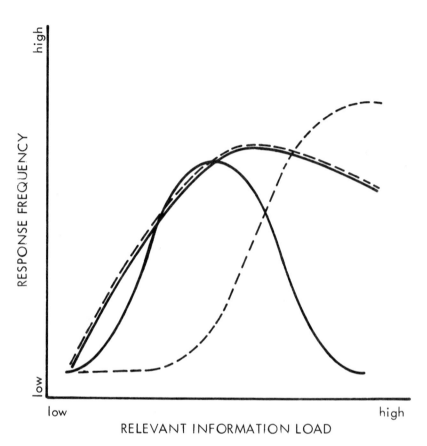

Fig. 3.5. Responses to information by more multidimensional integrators.

3.26 Differentiators and integrators are more likely to discover marginal levels of relevance inherent in information than more unidimensional persons would (whether or not the discovered relevance is meaningful).

We have not made specific individual difference predictions for general unresponsive behaviors. Since the maximal levels of these responses are located in load areas where differences between multidimensional and unidimensional persons tend to become minimal, we would not view differences in this response type across persons of diverse complexity as very likely or—if present—as very large.

Another look at information search should, however, be meaningful. We have already said that multidimensional persons are more likely to find relevance in marginally relevant information. In other words, they may—even with relatively irrelevant information—find some ways of differentiating and integrating some stimulus components of the information. On the other hand, they should have greater *need* for additional information that is required by them for their processes of differentiation and integration. This should affect their information search characteristics:

3.27 As information load increase, information search should decrease.

3.28 As information load (relevant and irrelevant) increases, the information search behavior of more multidimensional persons (differentiators and integrators) should decrease less than the information search behavior of more unidimensional persons.

3.29 At low information load levels, the information search activity of more unidimensional persons should exceed that of more multidimensional persons (differentiators and integrators). At high information load levels, the information search activity of more multidimensional persons should exceed that of more unidimensional persons.

Note that we are specifically speaking of information search *activity*. The wish for information is socially desirable in many societies, so that asking people how much more information they want tends to produce a distorted picture of interest in information. The predictions for information search activity are presented in graphic form in Figure 3.6.

COMPLEXITY AND AFFECT

Complexity theories have been so-called "cold cognitive theories" as a whole, because they have rarely attempted to take affect into account. We shall not remove ourselves very far from this viewpoint. We are dealing with the way verbal dimensions are utilized in information processing, certainly a cognitive phenomenon. Nonetheless, the fact that affective processes co-vary with cognitive processes cannot be ignored. Certainly deprivation and overload of information are likely to have affective concomitants. How would affect interact with cognitive processes to affect the phenomena we have proposed for interactive complexity theory?

Because of previously established characteristics in the cognitions of the individual, certain information is likely to be more salient than other

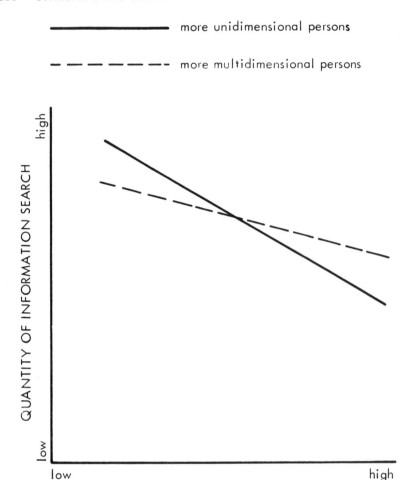

more unidimensional persons

more multidimensional persons

Fig. 3.6. Effects of information load on information search.

information. As a rule, such salience characteristics will call forth emotional, in addition to cognitive, responses. Certainly this emotionality should have major effects on information processing:

3.30 Salient information is likely processed at a lower level of dimensionality than nonsalient information.

3.31 More unidimensional persons are likely more severely affected by salience of information than more multidimensional persons.

3.32 For more unidimensional persons, and to some degree for differentiators, the salient dimension should be the one which is chosen for action (if more than one dimension is potentially present).

Of course, there is also salient information content. For example, a stimulus person might be placed at some specific very high or very low point on the evaluative dimension when there are affective associations with that person. That kind of salience, however, is of little interest to us here. We are specifically concerned with *dimensional salience,* i.e., what dimensions have affective connotations, or, what dimensions are more likely selected for perception, cognition, or action.

Affect and Information

One might view conditions of relative overload and conditions of relative deprivation of information as stressful. Under stress a person is unable to respond in a way he may consider appropriate. Stress is associated with negative affect. On the other hand (in the absence of specific success or failure), moderate information load levels should provide the person with the opportunity to apply a number of different kinds of responses (multidimensional as well as unidimensional). At this point, the person in effect has his maximal "freedom" of behavior. Load produced stress is reduced or absent. As a result, there is a greater potential for positive affect to occur. However, the occurrence of affect is likely associated with a number of other variables as well, even to a much greater degree. We might then propose that:

3.33 All other things being equal, affect should be positive at moderate relevant information load levels and negative at excessively high and excessively low information load levels.

In other words, more unidimensional behavior—irrelevant of the dimensionality of the behaving person—tends to be associated with negative affect; more multidimensional behavior (where it occurs), appears to be associated with more positive affect. In other words, positive affect seems to be relatively high under conditions where both more unidimensional persons and more multidimensional persons (although at different levels) reach their optimal multidimensionality. We should, though, emphasize once more that the predicted relationship between affect and complexity is merely a small part of the affect phenomenon. Other psychological events (reinforcements, mastery, achievement, task success or failure, etc.) are likely to have a much greater effect on expressed affect. Further, we cannot be certain that (in general or for specific individuals) peak optimality of multidimensional responding coincides *precisely* with highest positive affect. It may well be that they relate via an optimal and/or preferred incongruity mechanism which will be discussed in Chapters 5 and 8.

Affect and Responding

Affect is not only generated by the information a person receives, but also by the responses he makes (and their effects). One might propose that affect would be positive when a person feels that his environment is conducive to his "best" levels of perception and action. Similarly, affect might be negative when a person feels that the environment is hindering his perceptual and behavioral capacity. In many cases, this would mean that "optimal" environments would, again, gain the advantage of positive affect. But, that need not be so. In some cases, people develop a "style" of dimensional responding that may or may not be appropriate to the task or situation at hand. Even though these persons may realize that the specific style (e.g., differentiative responding or integrative responding) is inappropriate in the present situation or task, they find it difficult to change their style. Take, for example, persons who are excessive differentiators. These people tend to place stimuli on an inordinately large number of independent dimensions, but are (in part, because of the excessive cognitive effort that would be necessary to integrate all of these dimensions) unable to make a choice upon which dimension(s) to base a certain response at this particular time. As a result, they tend to vascillate, are unable to make decisions, and are typically unable to communicate their dilemma to other people. Others—who themselves are not excessive integrators—tend to respond by asking the person in difficulty to "finally make a decision," something they cannot do. Obviously, this is an inappropriate response—moreover, one that the person is quite aware of himself. He is likely to generate quite a bit of negative affect about his response (or the absence of a response), but since it is a style, it is very difficult for him to change.

One might assume that the negative reinforcement associated with inappropriate responding would, in time, eliminate this kind of response. Apparently that is not the case. In the first place, no one particular response is always inappropriate, so that all responses tend to gain a mixed positive and negative reinforcement history (cf. Pavlovian neurosis induction) which might, in effect, strengthen the response. But even if the reinforcement would be only negative, the resultant effect would be exceedingly slow, since *structural styles tend to be highly resistant to extinction.* Should some extinction occur, it would likely not be effective beyond the cognitive domain within which the negative reinforcement has been experienced.

3.34 Style determined responses of an individual in terms of cognitive dimensionality are not necessarily his preferred responses.

3.35 Internally provided or external negative reinforcement for a dimensional style of responding tends to have only small effects in changing dimensionality characteristics. If changes do occur, they are likely limited to the specific cognitive domain within which the reinforcement has taken place.

THE MEASUREMENT OF DIMENSIONALITY

Test Characteristics

Measuring the dimensionality of subjects and its effects has been a considerable problem of the "complexity theories." The previous chapter has pointed out some of these problems in detail. Certainly, measurement of structural characteristics must be more difficult than the measurement of content characteristics. Nonetheless, we should be able to say what requirements a (future—since it does not yet exist) test of structural dimensionality should fulfill.

Measurement techniques of behavioral multidimensionality or of perceptual multidimensionality must contain a least the minimal amount of dimensionality necessary to allow for the appropriate behavior of the person whose characteristics are measured. This means that (a) the stimulus component of the measure must permit potential multidimensional placement, and (b) the response component of the measure must allow for multidimensional responding. Some of the response formats should allow only for differentiation responses (similar to the Rep test, categorization in the SCT, etc.), others must allow for integration at various levels (similar to the SCT or the IFT tests).

To avoid problems that necessarily occur with subjective measures of dimensionality (i.e., that the evaluation of dimensionality of the responses hinges on the dimensionality of the scorer), measures of dimensionality should be objective, possibly similar to the multidimensional scaling approaches for the measurement of dimensionality.

An ideal measure of cognitive multidimensionality would then have the following characteristics:

(1) Objective measurement.

(2) Potential multidimensional placement of stimuli.

(3) Allow responses ranging from unidimensionality through levels of differentiation through levels of integration at maximum possible levels of each.

(4) Responses in the various areas of complexity (e.g., social vs. nonsocial and perceptual vs. executive) should be obtained separately. In its ideal form, the test should even obtain information on dimensionality in various cognitive domains.

(5) Specific measurement of behavior at various dimensional levels should not allow for higher level responding which could "hide" lower level responses.

The Dimensionality of Complexity

Considerable past research has shown that the various complexity tests concerned with cognitive dimensionality are not comparable with each other. Different groups of tests tend to produce different factors on a factor analysis of subjects' responses. The question has been repeatedly raised whether complexity is a unitary phenomenon or consists of a number of "unrelated" characteristics. The answer provided has often been disappointing, suggesting to several authors that complexity is indeed an "unfinished" product of scientific thought. But, the problem may lie more with the question than with the answer. The question whether complexity is a unitary phenomenon suggests that multidimensionality is *supposed* to be a unidimensional phenomenon, something it is by no means (and should not be). The various measures of complexity may only tap one of its dimensions (e.g., differentiation or integration, social multidimensionality or nonsocial dimensionality, etc.).

Ideally, one should devise a measure of cognitive dimensionality that would tap *all* the dimensions of complexity. These individual dimensions should be obtained as factors (similar to those on the intelligence measures) which might correlate with each other at low to moderate positive levels.

Of course, if one considers that dimensionality may not only be area specific (e.g., perceptual social complexity) but also domain specific (e.g., perceptual social complexity with regard to politicians), we have to expect an additional amount of error variance in the data we are obtaining.

Specific Problems of Previous Measurement Techniques

In many cases, investigators have believed that structural differences might be obtained via some content reflection of structure. In other words, they have assumed that persons with more multidimensional characteristics would necessarily have different attitudes, opinions, strategies, etc. than persons of more unidimensional characteristics. The measurement of these tendencies should reflect their dimensional structure. Certainly, simple objective tests could be derived to fulfill such a purpose. However, there are serious problems with this approach. Since, as stated, one cannot expect that the various dimensions at any level of complexity would be the same from person to person, it would be highly unlikely that any reflection of dimensionality into content variables would be equivalent across persons. If one wants to compare persons of disparate experience (e.g., across cultural subgroups or even across cultures), these problems would become excessively severe. In other words, content reflection tests of dimensional structure are not very useful.

But, can one not select certain dimensions which people might be likely to employ and measure the typical response of subjects on them, checking on the independence or correlation of their dimensions? In this case, we would again be able to use our familiar content measures; we would merely use a number of them and employ some statistical comparison technique (e.g., correlate the supposed dimensional responses to check for identity). Unfortunately, this approach, already tried by a number of people, also tends to fail. The approach has typically been employed in nomothetic fashion. The experimenter selects the dimensions that seem relevant and useful to him and measures the responses of his subjects on these dimensions. He then picks out those subjects who seem to respond on independent dimensions (if he finds any) and compares them with those subjects who don't.

There are at least two serious problems with this approach. First of all, there is no certainty that the experimenter can predetermine which relevant dimensions the subjects are likely to employ. Secondly, there is little likelihood that all subjects will employ the *same* dimensions. The result is usually a great amount of noise in the data, often suggesting that multidimensionality does not exist (or is, at best, a very limited and useless concept). As Bem (1972) has suggested, with regard to the use of molecular measures in attribution research, such measurement can only be valid if the set of possible factors (in this case, causes) which the experimenter assumes, matches that of the subject. Problematic, of course, is the fact that there is no way to determine or assume that this match will occur. Another problem with this approach is that subjects *might* be able to utilize the dimensions selected by the experimenter, even though they are not at all representative of their own typical thought processes. In that case, we would have a measure that does not represent subjects' actual structure, and prediction of behavior based on this measure would be in vain.

Another difficulty encountered by researchers in the past is the overly simple distinction between unidimensional and multidimensional persons. One should consider that there are structural distinctions at various levels of dimensional information processing that do not allow for the construction of a simple unidimensional scale running from unidimensionality to multidimensionality. The various factor analytic studies in the literature (see Chap. 2) of "complexity measures" have probably encountered difficulty because of this phenomenon. It should be noted that both unidimensional persons and multidimensional integrators often produce what looks like a simple unidimensional semantic space, while differentiators clearly produce responses on a number of independent dimensions. However, the response of the integrator is the effect of a number of already integrated dimensions, while the response of the unidimensional person never has been differentiated. No wonder that measures of differentiation and integration don't correlate. To determine the level of differentiative multidimensionality as compared to unidimensionality, one merely needs to obtain the number of dimensions in the repertoire of the person. To determine the level of integrative multidimensionality, one must devise measurement techniques that observe the subject *in the process* of differentiation and reintegration of received information via his structural dimensionality. In other words, the multidimensional integrator must be allowed to proceed via differentiated dimensions to one (or few) integrated dimensions. Linear factor analytic procedures comparing measures of complexity, then, should have been adjusted by entering one additional score on complexity measures of integration that would provide a low score for unidimensionality and multidimensional integration and would provide a high score for differentiation. With that score, a common factor of integrative and differentiative measures of complexity should be obtainable.

We have seen that although the "perfect" test can be described, it has not yet been devised. Because of the inherent difficulties in devising such a test, we may have yet to wait some time until the appropriate technique is developed. In the meantime, however, it may be useful to extend the available tests so that they are able to measure more than one kind of multidimensionality, allowing for better comparison of dimensionality measures on each of their own dimensions. Despite its limitations, the (unfortunately subjective) version of the Sentence Completion Test of Schroder and Streufert (1962), as revised by Streufert, fulfills at least some of these functions. It allows for scoring of perceptual social, perceptual nonsocial, executive social, and executive nonsocial complexity at unidimensional, multidimensional differentiative, and multidimensional integrative levels.

COMPLEXITY, PERSONALITY AND ABILITY

There have been a number of attempts to find commonalities in complexity and related approaches (Chap. 2). The employed tests often were not only tests of structural characteristics, but other personality and ability tests as well. Should one expect relationships between such variables and cognitive complexity (multidimensionality)?

Ability Variables

The question about a relationship between complexity and ability, most often intelligence, has been frequently raised. Research has shown that the relationship is limited to the lower range of the IQ scale: Persons of very low intelligence are not likely to be multidimensional. Whether this is due to some physiological mechanism, or whether persons of very low intelligence do not have the opportunity to learn a multidimensional style, is not known, but the former seems more likely than the latter. As a matter of fact, one could argue that the capacity to learn multidimensional cognitive operations is some form of intelligence not measured on current intelligence scales. If that were so, it should not be surprising that the correlation between multidimensionality and intelligence is low and restricted to part of the scales. Such relationships hold among certain subtests of intelligence as well.

Personality Variables

The vast majority of personality tests are content oriented. They should not, and do not, correlate with measures of complexity. Correlations can be expected only with tests which either are measures of structural multidimensionality or relate to some specific structural characteristics. However, the correlation with the latter tests should be relatively low.

A few examples of tests measuring characteristics relating to structure might be in order. We have already mentioned the Dogmatism test of Rokeach (1960) (nondogmatic persons tend to be more flexible), which tends to correlate with multidimensionality, in some instances (represented by the Sentence Completion or the Impression Formation tests) at approximately $-.2$ (cf., however, Feather, 1969). As stated above, flexibility is a component of structural differentiation and integration. At times, relationships between dimensionality measures and personality tests are more remote. A correlation of approximately $-.1$ is often obtained between measures of complexity (multidimensionality) and authoritarianism. Certainly, the conservative–liberal dimension inherent in the F test is purely content oriented and should not relate to dimensionality. On the other hand, the acquiescent response set tendency also inherent in the F measure has implications for structure. Persons who are yea- and nay-sayers are not as likely to process information in a multidimensional fashion, since they are focused outside of themselves with considerable salience. They could, at best, absorb multidimensionality from others, but, even if they did, would probably become hierarchical in their orientation (cf. earlier discussions).

COMPLEXITY AND CREATIVITY

Several authors have suggested that a relationship between complexity and creativity should exist. To investigate that proposition, a closer look should first be taken at the creativity phenomenon. There have been a number of definitions of the criterion for creativity. As a result, there have been varied measures which tend toward low correlations (if any) with each other. The consequence has been confusion—and disinterest from all but the most devoted followers of the creativity concept. An area, which in the mid-1960s seemed most promising, has become less than attractive to many researchers.

Could it be that creativity is "too complex" for the typical approach to a psychological variable? It may well be. Jackson and Messick (1965) have tried to point out some of the problems, suggesting that several processes seem to be part of creative behavior. Unfortunately, their statement has not found the appropriate echo. Moreover, two of their processes appear to be characteristics of multidimensional perception and/or behavior. Can one then say that creativity is in part complexity? Take a somewhat closer look at the proposals of Jackson and Messick (1965).

The Components of Creativity

Several authors have viewed creativity as some kind of intelligence. Jackson and Messick (1965) discuss this issue in some detail. They point out that a "correct" response, even in the context of Mednick's (1963) Remote Associates Test, is probably not creative. A creative response, so they say, must be *unusual.* And it cannot be "correct"; rather it must be "good." As we know the term "good," it implies evaluation, and indeed Jackson and Messick suggest that something creative must not be unusual in the sense of bizarre or odd, but rather it must be unusual in the sense of *appropriate.* What, however, is appropriate? Probably all would agree that the Parthenon is appropriate, or the Venus de Milo, or Beethoven's Kreuzer Sonata, or Hemingway's *Old Man and the Sea.* On the other hand, what about the *Garden of Earthly Delights* by Bosch, Gaudi's "Sagrada Familia" church, or certain expressionistic poems? The implication here is that society makes the evaluative (content!) judgment. Society may sometimes be represented by the general populus, sometimes by learned experts. Is this judgment justified? Can the noncreative understand the creative? (To put it into more popular terms, can the critic understand the writer, the composer, the conductor, musician, painter, or actor?)

Jackson and Messick are quite aware of this problem. The creator, they say, might be more aware of the requirements upon which his creation is based and may, therefore, disagree with the critic. Consequently, we have a *dual standard* for the evaluation of creativity: A work is creative if it is deemed so by the creator, but *also* by the viewer. With this conclusion, psychologists have gotten into the same bind that has tied their hands in defining the "genius." A genius must be intelligent (by definition) but he also must have contributed to society (as judged by society). If one were to accept these arguments, then one would conclude that Socrates was a genius only after he had taken the hemlock, and that the canonization procedure of the

Catholic Church is justified. Also in these terms, Van Gogh would have become creative only after he had died.

As members of society or even as "post hoc" social philosophers, we may well implicitly agree with this point of view. As psychologists, however, we must express some major reservations. If we want to distinguish between creativity as a *capacity* and as a *product,* if we want to use the concept of creativity to predict a certain kind of behavior, or if we intend to train someone to be creative, then we must measure a personal creativity in addition to a societal one. We would agree with Jackson and Messick to a point: A creative response is unusual, but it cannot be chaotic or meaningless. As Maddi (1965) suggests, it should be valuable. But valuable to whom? Also it should not be correct, not even in the sense of one of a number of alternatives (to some the term "appropriate" may imply just that). We propose that the creative response should have *utility.* Utility is not necessarily socially or normatively defined; it could be based either on the creative person himself or could be understood relative to the creator's specific reference group. Utility implies that the creation is useful for the creator (e.g., as an antedecent to a further response or as a means to an end) *or* to the society of which he is part, or both.

Up to this point, our creative person has provided us with a response which is unusual and utilitarian. We are in agreement with Jackson and Messick that such a response might yet be limited in its creativity. We are asking far more from our creators than to present us simply with novelty. Their creative work should have greater implications: It should, if possible, contain new concepts or new relationships among concepts. Jackson and Messick call this "transcedence of restraint" a *transformation.* They propose that this transformation should imply a revision of the world, that it should consist of a reorganization of perceptions in the creator, who communicates this reorganization to the viewer. To be specific and to be psychological in terminology, we are asking our creator to differentiate and reintegrate in a novel (i.e., flexible) fashion. Is differentiation sufficient for creativity, or must both differentiation and integration occur? The term differentiation implies the placing of stimuli from some stimulus configuration on two or more dimensions which are functionally unique. This is an analytic ability and hardly creative. It does, however, at least in many cases, provide the basis for the next or parallel step: integration. As stated in Chapter 2, points of views about the meaning of "integration" have differed; some authors (Lewin, 1951; Werner, 1957) have considered integration as a fixed organization of conceptual dimensions; others have seen a flexible organization of dimensions (Harvey, Hunt, & Schroder, 1961; Murphy, 1947; Schroder, Driver, & Streufert, 1967). It is without doubt that both fixed and flexible integrative processes do occur (see above); yet only flexible integration has meaning for the creativity concept.

Jackson and Messick (1965) also suggest that transformation (here integration) calls for flexibility. They believe that breaking a set (the Luchins water jar experiment), open-mindedness (Rokeach, 1960), and allocentric perception (Schachtel, 1959) may be good examples of this flexibility. This seems reasonable, yet we might add that flexibility alone may still be insufficient. Flexibility can occur without dimensional reorganization; in other words, it may occur by reordering some elements within a dimension or in terms of alternate uses of various established dimensions (differentiation). We are consequently looking for an approach to creativity which serves to combine integration and flexibility.

Jackson and Messick add yet another creative process. To be called creative, in the highest sense of the word, the creator must fulfill one more requirement: "condensation." Condensation, they say, is a quality which accentuates unusualness, appropriateness (in our terms, social or personal utility), and transformation (in our terms, flexible integration). In addition, Jackson and Messick suggest that each exposure to a creative work which entails condensation would deepen satisfaction, provide more surprise as *more* unusual elements are discovered, and would enrich stimulation. What are the implications of this reaction in the viewer? Take Goethe's *Faust,* for example. On repeated exposure, more and more meanings are discovered and more and more relationships between meanings. Indeed, unusualness, utility, and conceptual integration continue to appear in new relationships, and as Jackson and Messick say, the reader "savors" the experience.

In effect, it appears that the creator-critic problem is recurring. The level of creation is so high—in other words, the integration of cognitive dimensions is so complex—that the critic is unable to comprehend the interrelationships among the dimensions on a single exposure. Each partial relationship, as it is understood, results in renewed surprise, insight, and—to use Jackson and Messick's term—savoring. In conclusion, then, condensation can be conceived of as what complexity theorists have called "high level flexible integration and reintegration."

We conclude that creativity as a generally applicable concept (i.e., not some limited creativity in a specific limited area) would in part consist of the ability to deal with stimuli and previously stored information in a flexible integrative fashion at various levels of integration. In other words, we propose an *overlap* between what some scientists have called creativity and what other scientists have called complexity or multidimensionality. They are not the same. Neither can one state that all multidimensional persons are creative (it takes certain content characteristics as well) or that all creative persons are complex (for some specific kinds of creativity, structural multidimensional integration appears unnecessary). For that matter, there may be a relationship between multidimensionality and creativity that is akin to the relationship between intelligence and creativity, although we believe that the former is considerably closer than the latter: Integrative multidimensionality provides one of the necessary ingredients for an overall creativity phenomenon.

We may then propose that:

3.36 Creativity has a number of components consisting of content characteristics (e.g., evaluative quality as well as utility of the creative activity) and dimensional integrative characteristics (e.g., flexible integrative reorganizing and combining of perceptual and behavioral dimensions).

REFERENCES

Bem, D. J. Self-perception theory. In L. Berkowitz (Ed.), *Advances in experimental social psychology* (Vol. 6). New York: Academic Press, 1972.

Cummings, L. L., O'Connell, M. J., & Huber, G. P. Informational and structural determinants of decision-maker satisfaction. In B. King, S. Streufert, & F. Fiedler (Eds.), *Managerial control and industrial democracy.* Washington, D.C.: V. H. Winston & Sons, 1978.

Driver, M. J. *A structural analysis of aggression, stress and personality in an internation simulation.* Purdue University: Institute for Research in the Behavioral, Economic and Management Sciences, Institute Paper No. 97, 1965.

Driver, M. J., & Streufert, S. Integrative complexity: An approach to individuals and groups as information processing systems. *Administrative Science Quarterly,* 1969, **14**, 272-285.

Feather, N. T. Cognitive differentiation, attitude strength, and dogmatism. *Journal of Personality,* 1969, **37**, 111-126.

Granit, R., & Philips, C. G. Excitatory and inhibitory processes acting upon individual purkinje cells in cats. *Journal of Physiology,* 1965, **133**, 520-547.

Harvey, O. J., Hunt, D. E., & Schroder, H. M. *Conceptual systems and personality organization,* New York: Wiley, 1961.

Jackson, P. W., & Messick, S. The person, the product and the response: Conceptual problems in the assessment of creativity. *Journal of Personality,* 1965, **33**, 309-329.

Lewin, K. *Field theory in social science.* New York: Harper, 1951.

Maddi, S. R. Motivational aspects of creativity. *Journal of Personality,* 1965, **33**, 330-347.

Mednick, S. A. The associative basis of the creative process. In M. T. Mednick & S. A. Mednick (Eds.), *Research in personality.* New York: Holt, Rinehart & Winston, 1963.

Miller, G. A. The magical number seven plus or minus two: Some limits on our capacity to process information. *Psychological Review,* 1956, **63,** 81-97.

Murphy, G. *Personality: A biosocial approach to opinions and structure.* New York: Harper, 1947.

Piaget, J. *The construction of reality in the child.* New York: Basic Books, 1954.

Quastler, H., & Wulff, V. J. Report #R-62, Control Systems Laboratory. Urbana, Ill.: University of Illinois, 1955.

Rokeach, M. *The open and closed mind.* New York: Basic Books, 1960.

Schachtel, E. G. *Metamorphosis.* New York: Basic Books, 1959.

Schroder, H. M., Driver, M. J., & Streufert, S. *Human information processing.* New York: Holt, Rinehart, & Winston, 1967.

Schroder, H. M., & Streufert, S. *The measurement of four systems of personality structure varying in the level of abstractness: Sentence completion method* (ONR Tech. Rep. No. 11). Princeton, N.J.: Princeton University, 1962.

Streufert, S. Komplexitätstheorie und Kongruitätstheorie. In H. Mandl & G. L. Huber (Eds.), *Kognitive Strukturiertheit.* Stuttgart: Klett, in press.

Streufert, S. C. Effects of information relevance on decision making in complex environments. *Memory and Cognition,* 1973, **1,** 224-228.

Suedfeld, P. Attitude manipulation in restricted environments: I. Conceptual structure and response to propaganda. *Journal of Abnormal and Social Psychology,* 1964, **68,** 242-247.

Suedfeld, P. Attitude manipulation in restricted environments: II. Conceptual structure and internalization of propaganda received as reward for compliance. *Journal of Personality and Social Psychology,* 1966, **3,** 586-589.

Suedfeld, P. Characteristics of decision-making as a function of the environment. In B. King, S. Streufert, & F. Fiedler (Eds.), *Managerial control and organizational democracy.* Washington, D.C.: V. H. Winston & Sons, 1978.

Suedfeld, P., & Rank, A. D. Revolutionary leaders: Long-term success as a function of changes in conceptual complexity. *Journal of Personality and Social Psychology,* 1976, **34,** 169-178.

Werner, H. *Comparative psychology of mental development.* New York: International Universities Press, 1957.

CHAPTER 4

CONSISTENCY[1] AND MOTIVATION

Social psychologists and researchers in related areas have repeatedly demonstrated that people like their world to be consistent and sufficiently familiar. It seems disturbing when the world becomes too complex, too unpredictable, or too unexplainable. Inconsistencies in their environment appear to motivate people from all cultures to search for explanations and simplifications of the events around them, even if the explanations turn out to be contrived and inaccurate. Consistency, so it seems, is not just the hobgoblin of little minds: Everyone seems to be motivated to attain it under some conditions.

[1] In the past, a number of terms have been used nearly interchangeably with the term "consistency." For example, theorists have spoken of "balance," "congruity," and "consonance." With only slight discrepancies, the meanings of these terms have been rather similar.

In Chapter 5 we propose a change in meaning for the term "consistency" and leave the meaning of the other terms as they were previously. We shall use the term "congruity" (and associated with it the terms "balance" and "consonance") to indicate that no cognitive modifications are necessary to place recently received information on existing dimensions of judgment. Incongruity will imply the necessity to modify previous

To understand and to predict the search for consistency, a number of theories have been proposed. For some time it was assumed that a great proportion of human behavior could be explained via consistency motivation and would fall into the realm of consistency theories. Yet, there are major exceptions to the search for consistency and familiarity, suggesting that the analysis of behavior in our complex world requires more than a reductionistic approach. In this and the following chapters a theory is developed that considers more than one dimension in the motivational processes that underly the interaction of the human mind with external information. This chapter reviews consistency theory to date from a motivational vantage point. A general review appears unnecessary, since a number of writers have extensively dealt with the state of the theory as such (e.g., Abelson, Aronson, McGuire, Newcomb, Rosenberg, & Tannenbaum, 1968). Chapter 5 develops the current theory itself.

The theory we intend to propose will maintain the motivational framework in the prediction of behavior. A number of other current theories have, unfortunately, neglected motivation as an explanatory or predictive construct (e.g., with notable exceptions, the attribution theories currently in vogue). We believe that the inclusion of motivational components is necessary if a theory is to have meaning beyond the confines of the experimental laboratory (cf. the view expressed by Kiesler, 1974).

It should be noted that the discussions of theories here and the GIAL theory proposed in the next chapter are not new developments. In earlier form, the GIAL theory was proposed by Driver and Streufert (1965) and revised and extended at a later date (Streufert & Driver, 1970). Both studies have previously been available only in the form of technical reports or institute papers. The current chapters represent a further refinement of these views.

---

cognitions or the meaning of information or certain actions as predicted for "dissonance reduction," "restoration of balance," etc. The meaning of these terms is not changed.

The meaning of the term "consistency" is modified in the next chapter. As McGuire (1968) pointed out, the consistent should be something that one has expected. In contrast, the inconsistent is something that is unexpected. We shall propose that organisms do not only expect congruous information, but will also expect some amount of incongruous information. We shall propose that inconsistency occurs when the level of incongruity to which the organism is exposed *departs in either direction from the expected*, i.e., toward greater congruity or toward greater incongruity. To avoid confusion for the reader, we use the terms congruity in this chapter to indicate what all consistency terms have indicated in past writings. We use the term need for consistency as representative of motivation that includes, but is not limited, to the need for congruity. For more detail, see Chapter 5.

HISTORICAL BACKGROUND

The short history of systematic psychology as an independent discipline, and particularly the even shorter history of social psychology, seem to have been marked by repeated changes in focus. McGuire (1969), for instance, points out that an initial strong interest in attitudes gave way to concern with social groups, only to be replaced by another new approach to attitudes. This latter approach to attitude theory and attitude research has primarily centered on consistency theory views of attitude change. The return to an interest in attitudes, even though in a different style of dress, has been variously explained. Pepitone (1966) views the emergence of consistency approaches as the consequence of an unproductive theoretical situation that marked social psychology in the 1940s. Berkowitz (1969) suggests that theorists had become uncomfortable with assigning all human motivation to a few basic drives, and attempted to find explanations that would take man's complicated central nervous system and his language ability into account. Singer (1966) proposes that the emergence of consistency theories was a logical outgrowth of Gestalt psychology (e.g., Heider, 1946). There are still other interpretations. All of these views are probably accurate at least in part. It appears that the time was ripe for new theory, and particularly for the kind of theory that the consistency approaches were presenting. When several consistency views were nearly simultaneously presented by a number of social psychologists, they gained quick acceptance as a major theoretical breakthrough. However, the flurry of interest in consistency theory seems to have come to an end as well, giving way to research on "attributions," even though a number of researchers have shown that some phenomena are better explained by consistency views than by attribution views. As we shall attempt to show later, the downfall of consistency may not be its supposed inaccuracy but rather the simplicity with which the phenomenon is viewed. The same fate will likely befall attribution theory, unless it is viewed in a more complex form. But, let us return to consistency theory for the time being.

Some of the initially proposed consistency theories are briefly considered in the following pages. Unfortunately, there is insufficient space in a volume of this nature to consider the *nonmotivational* components of all the consistency theories, particularly of the newer, often more sophisticated, models. The interested reader is referred to the sourcebook on consistency edited by Abelson et al. (1968) and to the volumes by Feldman (1966) and Zimbardo (1969). We are here primarily concerned with the initial models and with the relationship of consistency to motivational constructs. Later consistency models will be discussed only if they propose a novel and different motivational basis for the behavior that they attempt to explain or predict.

One may propose (following the above-mentioned view of Berkowitz, 1969) that consistency theory became possible when social psychologists were willing to accept divergent views of human motivation. The primary emphasis on motivational derivates of learning theory had seemed very promising in earlier years, but later appeared insufficient to explain much human behavior in any *selective* way (cf. Pepitone, 1966). Reference to secondary reinforcement (including some forms of classical conditioning and related social psychological concepts as Gordon Allport's [1967] "functional autonomy") was of little more use than the "instincts"had been several years earlier: Secondary reinforcement could be used to describe just about every form of social behavior. Further, learning theory derivates were often difficult to put to a final test because of their universality. As a result social psychologists were frequently not able to generate interesting alternatives from learning theories.

Proposing a different motivational basis for much social behavior, and constructing theoretical predictions based on a novel motivational view, had a number of clear advantages: (1) It freed theoretical man from being "just like" the animals; (2) it potentially avoided universality of prediction, and consequently permitted research designs that would determine both whether and when the new theory would hold; and (3) it permitted one theory to be experimentally pitted against another theory, e.g., different and opposing predictions could be developed from reinforcement and consistency viewpoints.

What could become a viable alternative to a learning theory approach to human motivation? Here we may follow the suggestion made by the historical analyses of both Berkowitz and Singer. If as a theorist one were interested in "trusting" the special talents of man, both inborn (his complex CNS) and learned (language), then some of the Gestaltist notions about human behavior could provide a beginning point. The Gestaltists had already discovered that humans seemed to have a need for closing gaps; for instance, a series of dots arranged in circular order were often perceived as a circle, not as dots. Yet the perceptually-oriented Gestalt theory did not provide a sufficient answer; experimental subjects would follow the predictions of that theory only some of the time. Further, the theory (in its basic form) was not able to explain human *behavior*, e.g., the frequent occurrence of the "sour grapes" excuses, the kind of information search in which humans engage after they make a decision, or for that matter some forms of attitude change when new information becomes available. However, if one were to impose a Gestalt prediction on the *cognitive* system rather than on the *perceptual* system of human intellectual functioning, then the obtained predictions might be more general and more useful. For instance, one might suggest that there should be a single Gestalt of thoughts, attitudes, information, people, or whatever. Or, at least, one might propose that there should be a single consistent Gestalt in any one of these areas, or at least for those elements in an area that are cognitively associated with each other. Such a theory was proposed by Fritz Heider, the first of the major consistency theorists. Other theories, using different terminology and specifying divergent operations, followed in quick succession. All the theories have much in common; yet substantial differences, particularly in the stated or implied motivational basis for the theoretical superstructure, can be found. The following section outlines some of the "general" propositions of the early consistency theories. Differences among the various views will be discussed later on.

THE BASIC MODEL

Consistency theory, in its basic form, has a homeostatic view of man. A state of consistency within an individual's cognitive system could be described as a condition implying zero motivation. As soon as some internal or external agent disturbs the state of cognitive consistency, a motive emerges with the sole purpose of returning the organism to its original consistent state. Depending on the specific characteristic of each theory, however, a consistent cognitive system is variously viewed: It may be interpersonal (represent the communicative interactions of two or more persons with similar attitudes about some object), or it may be limited to agreement among the cognitions within the thought processes of a single individual (representing the inter-action of existing attitudes with corresponding information). Which of these (either or both) is emphasized depends on the respective theorist. In any case, the motive resulting from an inconsistency (among the views of two persons about an object or between existing attitudes and discrepant information) is explicitly or implicitly associated with a "discomfort." This discomfort, once experienced by a person, should lead to activity directed toward restoration of comfort (i.e., restoration of consistency within the cognitive system). Just as the "kind" (e.g., interpersonal attitudes vs. elements in a person's cognitive system) of units that are assumed to produce consistency or inconsistency are differentially described by the various theorists, so also the proposed kind of activity that is employed to restore consistency differs.

Another major difference among the views of the diverse consistency theorists is their approaches to the concept of motivation. Before the specific differences among the theorists are discussed, it may be of value to consider what kind of divergent approaches to consistency motivation are possible. Certainly, one might disregard the question of motivation altogether. If one does make motivational assumptions, then one might distinguish between two levels at which motivational constructs can be proposed: a molar level and a molecular level. At the molar level, it may be sufficient to suggest a human motivational system designed specifically to maintain or achieve consistency. Where, however, does that motivation come from? Is it a built-in (physiological) tendency of the organism to seek consistency? Is consistency seeking learned? Is the proposed consistency seeking activity based on primary or secondary motivation? Answers to questions such as these have potentially quite divergent implications, e.g., the consistency motive may or may not be universal for all persons, may or may not be subject to extinction, or may or may not hold for all situations in which a person operates.

The earlier consistency theories appear to be in agreement with each other as far as the molar approach to motivation is concerned. All of them postulate, in one way or another, that organisms seek to achieve and maintain a state of consistency. However, there is great variation in the kind of underlying (molecular) motivational basis to which the consistency motive can be ascribed. In some of the theories, any discussion of the underlying motivation is entirely absent. Two explanations for the lack of statements about underlying motivational principles come to mind. Consistency theorists may have been sure of their molecular motivational basis, or may have been happy with the Gestalt notions implied in Heider's view. Alternately, the unresolved mystery of the underlying motivational construct may have been uncomfortable enough to cause the issue to be disregarded. After all, one can settle for a molar approach to motivation by merely postulating some universal drive toward consistency.

In light of the increasingly strong rejection of the Gestalt view during the time consistency theories were originally proposed, and in light of the fact that some of the consistency theorists in their later writings backed away from the earlier molecular motivational assumptions of their theories (see below), the first of the explanations we suggested (a view that molecular explanations are superfluous) appears less tenable. Many of the consistency theorists probably avoided the issue of underlying motivation because it was more expedient merely to talk about molar motivation. Nonetheless, one may (post hoc) ascribe a tentative motivational basis to each of the theories by carefully evaluating the statements of the authors. Surprisingly, there appear to be wide differences among these inferred molecular motivational assumptions.

Part of the differences in the motivational bases for the various consistency views may be a direct function of the kind of things that the specific theories consider as (molar) causes for and solutions of the "discomfort" experienced by a person who finds himself with incongruent cognitions. A useful distinction, which may also help to unravel the basis of the different motivational assumptions of the theoretical approaches, has been proposed by Singer (1966). He divided consistency models into theories of cognitive style vs. cognitive process, and again divided the same models into multiobject general systems vs. single object special systems. This division yields a 2 X 2 matrix into which most of the original theories (but not all) can be comfortably placed. Multiobject general systems deal with an individual's cognitions about a social grouping, e.g., about his position and communications within a group of liked and disliked associates. Single object special systems "remain within the person's head"; they deal only with the consistency of a person's cognitions about some object. Theories that are concerned with multiobject general systems would require motivational constructs that permit explanation of conformity behavior as well as consistency seeking proper, while the noninterpersonal single object special systems need not be concerned with such concepts.

Theories that emphasize cognitive style approaches discuss consistency as a means of scanning and storing information that is received by a person who already has a wealth of stored information. The person is viewed as a responsive information processing system. His "style" determines how, when, and where information is absorbed, potentially modified (distorted because it is incongruent with existing stored information), and stored. In contrast, theories that are specifically concerned with process permit change and adjustment of existing attitudes, as well as distortion of incoming information, to arrive at a new set of congruent cognitions. In their simplest forms, style theories imply that an organism is static and merely responsive, while process theories imply activity and imply greater flexibility of the means by which consistency is achieved. Implied motivation is potentially quite different. Process theories require and often suggest much more complicated motivational systems which may or may not have been acquired by the consistency seekers via some past experience.

To what degree the consistency theorists have been influenced in their motivational postulates or implications by the characteristic emphasis of their respective theories remains, of course, questionable. The reader may find it noteworthy, however, that some relationship between the theories discussed below and their position in Singer's matrix can be easily drawn.

THE ORIGINAL THEORIES AND THEIR MOLECULAR MOTIVATIONAL ASSUMPTIONS

Heider's Balance Theory

The first major consistency theory to be published (although other researchers and theorists were at work on their own models at the same time) was Heider's (1946) discussion of attitudes and cognitive organization. Heider was concerned with the triad: He suggested that if a person "p" likes another person "o," then their attitudes toward a specific object "x" are likely to be similar. In other words, either both "p" and "o" will like "x" or neither will. If one were to place plus or minus signs to indicate the relationship between p, o, and x, then a "balanced" (Heider's term for what we are calling "congruent") triangular system would include either two or no minus signs. An uneven number of minus signs (one or three) in the triad would suggest an "imbalance" (incongruent) state, and there should be cognitive pressure toward the resolution of this imbalance. This cognitive pressure represents a molar motivational postulate.

What kind of underlying motivational systems or processes produce the molar motivation is not considered to a great extent by Heider. It appears that balanced systems are conceived as a satisfactory "Gestalt" while the Gestalt of triangular systems with unequal numbers of minus signs is unsatisfactory. A bad Gestalt would provide a "Pregnanz" to achieve a good Gestalt through achievement of balance. If, as some Gestalt psychologists have at times suggested, there is an underlying physiological process in the CNS that attempts to complete any incomplete system, then a motivational system responsible for the removal of the incomplete, inconsistent relationship among cognitive parts might qualify as a physiological molecular motivational construct. However, the postulated physiological basis for the propositions of Gestalt psychology has never been established, and the Gestalist view itself has come into disfavor because it was unable to predict or even explain many of the results that have been obtained in relevant perception experiments. If a physiological basis for the Gestalt view is not given, then any usefulness of its motivational constructs as explanations for molecular motivation toward congruence is negated. As Singer (1966) points out, the nonoperational statement of balance theory in a Gestalt framework merely restates the basic paradigm in different words.

An offshoot of the Heider system is the work of Cartwright and Harary (1956). These theorists extended the Heider paradigm from a 3-element system to a multielement system, employing a graphic approach to solve for degrees of balance. In the interest of conserving space, we shall not discuss this approach in greater detail, particularly since the Cartwright and Harary modifications and elaborations of Heider's model, no matter how useful otherwise, do not take major steps in the direction of a more extensive molecular definition of motivation.

Newcomb's ABX Model

A theory that is also quite similar to that of Heider's was proposed by Newcomb (1953, 1956). Newcomb employs the same basic triad setting, but applies it to communicative acts. For instance, one may view the following situation: Person A (Heider called him "p") likes person B (in Heider's system, "o"). Person A also likes object X and assumes that person B would feel likewise. However, person B communicates to A that he indeed dislikes X. That act of communication creates an imbalance in the interpersonal system: one minus sign in the triadic ABX relationship. That imbalance triggers (via molar motivation) additional communications designed to either remove the minus sign between B and X or to produce an additional minus sign, either between A and B or between A and X. In other words, person A would either come to dislike person B, or one of the two (either A or B) would persuade the other to change his mind about X.

Newcomb's motivational concept is somewhat different than that of Heider; the effect of learning is considered as an antecedent to the consistency motive. Positive (balanced) relationships among persons are seen as rewarding (Newcomb, 1963). In the same way, dislike could be furthered by reciprocal punishments among negatively associated persons who hold divergent attitudes, beliefs, etc. (cf. Byrne, 1962; Newcomb, 1960). Motivation toward consistency can here be defined as a *derived* motive based on the "reward minus cost" principle employed in social exchange theory (Homans, 1961; Thibaut and Kelley, 1959). This approach eliminates the need for proposing a molecular consistency motivation on which a more molar consistency motive is based.

Osgood and Tannenbaum's Incongruity Theory

Osgood and Tannenbaum (1955) used the semantic differential (Osgood, Suci, & Tannenbaum, 1957) as their basis for predicting the resolution of inconsistency. If we utilize their basic evaluative scale, running from good to bad, then cognitions that object (or person) A is good and person B is bad are not congruent with information that person A is like (or likes) person B. The further A and B are apart from each other on opposite ends of the scale at the point when their positive association becomes known, the greater the incongruence and the greater the pressure to decrease the incongruence in the system (molar motivation toward congruence). However, the further the person's cognitions about A or B represent the endpoints of that person's evaluative cognitive scale, the less he is able to change their position on the scale. This proposition would be in contradiction to the first were it not for the concept of "incredulity." Two concepts with strong opposite evaluations that are positively associated, or two concepts with strong evaluations on the same scale end that are negatively associated, produce disbelief which subtracts from the impact of the information communicating their association.

Osgood and Tannenbaum's consistency theory is distinguished from others primarily through the quantification of the relationship among the cognitions on the evaluative scale, and secondarily through the introduction of polarity, through the incredulity correction, and through an assertion constant. The system also differs in its motivational assumptions. Molar motivation is different in that it produces restructuring of cognitions *toward* a more congruent attitude organization. The theory does not necessarily propose complete removal of incongruence among cognitions. On the molecular motivational level, Osgood and Tannenbaum do not directly discuss the nature of an underlying motivational force. They merely suggest that the system will tend toward simplicity in information storage: the least effort principle. Their constructs, including the least effort principle, as well as some of the algebraic formulations (suggested for calculating the amount of attitude change) seem to hint at an acceptance of learning theory formulations as an underlying motivational principle. If previously acquired cognitions (e.g., attitudes) can be conceived as higher on a learning curve if they are closer to scale endpoints, then the attitude change predictions from Osgood and Tannenbaum's theory are in agreement with predictions that might be based on the shape of the learning curve after a specific level of habit acquisition. Viewed in this way, then, Osgood and Tannenbaum's theory considers both molar and molecular motivation characteristics.

A refinement of the congruity principle proposed by Tannenbaum (1968) suggests that separate predictions should be made for congruity as an attitude change model (e.g., a concern with the cognitions of the individual) and for congruity as a cognitive interaction model (e.g., a concern with the interactions among persons based on their respective cognitions). Even though that approach clears up some problems that have been encountered by those wishing to use the theory for predictive purposes, it adds little to the previously proposed motivational components of congruity theory.

Festinger's Dissonance Theory

The most "popular" consistency theory is probably Festinger's theory of cognitive dissonance. It is that theory that has not only been the most discussed, applauded, rejected, questioned [e.g., Bem (1967); Chapanis & Chapanis (1964); Rosenberg (1966)], and revised [e.g., Irle (1976); Kiesler (1974)], it is also the theory that has generated the most research. Festinger (1957) lists a good number of conditions that produce "dissonance" (Festinger's term for what we are calling incongruence) as well as three ways in which dissonance can be reduced: (1) changing one of the elements involved in dissonant relations, (2) adding new cognitive elements that are already consonant with existing cognitions, and (3) decreasing the importance of elements in dissonant relations. Much research has supported Festinger's theory (see, for instance, the discussion by Aronson, 1968, 1969; Brehm & Cohen, 1962).

In discussing the basis of dissonance and motivation toward consonance, Festinger (1957) likens dissonance to hunger: Dissonance is seen as an antecedent condition leading to activity (dissonance reduction) just like hunger leads to search for food. He considers reduction of dissonance to be a "basic process" that occurs in humans, no matter whether they are operating as individuals, in small groups, in large groups, etc. As such, the dissonance reduction motive should occur for internal (cognitive) as well as for external (interpersonal) contexts.

It is not quite clear whether Festinger (1957) is postulating a physiological consonance motive. He does clearly describe the motive to reduce dissonance in standard drive-like terminology. If the motive to reduce dissonance is, indeed, physiologically determined, then Festinger's view would satisfy the requirements for stating both molar and molecular motivational principles. Yet, Festinger does not operationalize the origin of a drive for consonance. The fact that dissonance can be reduced, that it does evoke a tension system, and that one can define operations that reduce dissonance, suggests a drive-like state, but Festinger does not discuss its antecedents nor does he elucidate its motivational characteristics. Moreover, postulating a basic drive toward consonance has not found much applause among those researchers who are familiar with physiologically-based drives, as the response to the book by Lawrence and Festinger (1962) demonstrated.

In subsequent writings, Festinger has been more tentative about the "drive property" assumption for his dissonance theory. For instance, he has suggested that the motivational force underlying dissonance reduction may be viewed as a construct open to validation (Festinger, 1958). In this fashion, he has avoided dealing further with the underlying molecular motivational concepts.

Festinger, in other words, appears to have retracted his initial commitment to a molecular motivational concept somewhat, while other theorists have either sparsely dealt with it or have avoided discussing it altogether. The omission of reference to basic motivational constructs is certainly seductive for the theorist; it is easier to emphasize molar motivation and to disregard all other questions about molecular motivation as irrelevant. As Singer (1966) puts it, the authors might say that anyone can see that incongruence is motivating. Examining the motivational basis of incongruence reduction may be viewed as belaboring the obvious. Difficulties arise with this approach when exceptions to the consistency paradigms appear; If it is "obvious" that incongruence produces a *basic* motivation toward congruence, then exceptions to the rule have to be explained away.

A rather "elegant" solution has been proposed by Kiesler (1974). He proposed that reduction of incongruity itself is *not* rewarding, rather the reduction of associated arousal states serves as a reinforcer.[2] For "dissonance reduction" to occur, the subject must first become aware of the incongruity involved in dissonant relationships. Kiesler points out that many dissonance experiments focused the attention of subjects on their *own* behavior, something that is usually not observed. Kiesler believes that nearly any own behavior of a person can serve as an incongruous stimulus, when the person's attention is focused on it. This behavior must then be explained to the self and the results of this "explanation process" are observed in dissonance experiments.

Through the change in the motivational emphasis and the different explanation of dissonance reduction behavior, Kiesler (1974) can explain a number of experimental findings that are not in agreement with previous consistency theory. He further eliminates some of the need for replacing consistency views with attribution views. Nonetheless, Kiesler's standpoint cannot account for many cases of experimentally obtained *search* for *incongruent* information. What happens if some subject placed in some experimental condition should seek incongruence rather than avoid or reduce it? What happens if someone would even "enjoy" some degree of incongruence under some conditions? If that were the case, then the argument about the "self-evidence" of congruence motivation would collapse, and some more basic (molecular) motivations might have to be called upon to permit reexamination of the entire consistency approach. Some findings of this kind are examined below.

LATER REVISIONS OF CONSISTENCY THEORIES

Consistency theory, particularly Festinger's theory of cognitive dissonance, has produced volumes of research. Large quantities of research, in turn, tend to quickly pinpoint shortcomings of the theory they are testing. Certainly, enough reported data have supported dissonance theory to keep it viable. Yet, some other work has proven to be somewhat embarrassing since results have been diametrically opposed to predictions made from the theories (e.g., Freedman, 1965; Fromkin, 1968; Price, Harburg, & Newcomb, 1966). Attempts to "explain away" unexpected results have only been partially successful. Some discrepant findings that have not supported consistency theory as originally stated have resulted in theory modification. One of the revisions of dissonance theory, for instance, deals with the concept of utility.

---

[2] Kiesler reviews a number of experiments, particularly those of Pallak and associates, to support his views.

Mills, Aronson, and Robinson (1959) demonstrated that people frequently do *not* avoid dissonant information *if* that information is useful to them. Canon (1964) and Aronson and Ross (1966) have shown that higher levels of utility combined with lower levels of dissonance result in search for the useful, even though somewhat dissonant, information.[3] On the other hand, low levels of utility for dissonant information combined with high levels of dissonance did result in the expected dissonance avoidance. Findings of this kind suggested the inclusion of the utility concept into dissonance theory. Even though not specifically "utility" oriented, Irle's (1976) dissonance theory, based on Festinger, also allows for search motivation.

In a revision of his propositions, Festinger (1964) suggests that an individual may seek dissonant information if two conditions obtain: (1) The dissonant information must be useful, and (2) he must be certain that subsequent dissonance resulting from exposure to that information can be reduced. The first of these statements is a clear modification of the original theory. The second is a restatement of the original (now not as persuasive) molar motivational principle. It appears that Festinger clearly maintains his view that dissonance is aversive. Yet, the change in theory suggests that motivation toward congruence is not the *only*, or not the basic, motive operating in an individual under these conditions, neither need it be the strongest motive. For that matter, the approach motive toward useful information may, at times, outscore the supposedly "drive-like" avoidance motivation that is designed to remove the person from dissonance. Festinger, through his second principle (dissonant information will be sought only if the person is certain that he can reduce subsequent dissonance), attempts to make the utility motive subordinate to the consonance motive. One may question why two different behaviors (reducing dissonance or search for dissonant information) that appear to be motivationally diametrically opposed need to be explained via only one of those motives. One might as well consider the two motives independent, but additive, as some of the adaptation level theories have done. Indeed, that kind of treatment of the obtained research data would be no less parsimonious and may appear less contrived. It would, however, begin to place considerable doubt upon the view that considers consonance (congruence) motivation to be basic and/or self-evident.

Festinger, however, is not the only theorist who would have us believe that incongruence seeking is secondary or subordinate to congruence seeking. Canon (1964) proposes a notion similar to that suggested in Festinger's revision: Persons might seek for dissonant information if the utility of that information outweighs its negative dissonance effects. Lowin (1965) remains

---

[3] One might explain this phenomenon via multidimensional approaches to information inherent in complexity theory (cf. Chap. 3).

even closer to the original Festinger view when he suggests that people may search for dissonant information because the refutation of that information would produce a state of consonance. Even the original dissonance theory had allowed search for dissonant information in the service of the consonance motive; Festinger (1957) argued that dissonant information might be sought, but only so that the organism might experience enough dissonance to produce action to reduce dissonance. This notion suggests that all dissonance (like all hunger) is unpleasant, but a little dissonance is not enough to initiate immediate action. Viewed in one way, this proposition suggests that dissonance might even be worse than hunger: We usually wait to eat until we are moderately hungry, but we might increase dissonance immediately to a moderate amount so that we can get rid of it right away.

Berlyne (1960) agrees that people find incongruence unpleasant. His view, however, is not quite as absolute. He also speaks of the unpleasantness of a *total* state of congruence, but maintains (1957, 1963, 1968) that tension reduction is the *basic* principle of motivation. He argues that exploratory behavior (seeking incongruent information) does indeed occur, but he sees it as devoid of positive affect. Rather, behavior, like exploration, manipulation, etc., supposedly serves to gain familiarity with previously unfamiliar stimulus fields. This familiarity would serve the congruence motive: More effective familiarity permits incongruence reduction. Berlyne suggests that many of the research results that would not have been predicted by the original consistency theories can be explained in this fashion (e.g., Berlyne, 1960, 1963, 1966; Berlyne, Salapatek, Gelman, & Zener, 1964; Harrington & Linder, 1962; Stevenson & Odem, 1964).

The problems encountered by views that attempt to explain away all seeking of incongruent information by making it subordinate to congruence seeking are not unlike those that were discussed above with reference to the Festinger revision. Some additional shortcomings are also pointed out by Maddi (1968) (see below).

Some of the more recent approaches to the consistency problem have avoided the problems discussed above in a number of ways. Pepitone (1964), for instance, suggests that the cognitive consistency models are too general. He proposes that consistency effects can be decomposed into effects of social motivation, particularly into status and security needs, as well as a cognitive motivation to form and maintain a veridical cognitive structure.

McGuire's consistency theory proposed least-square solutions for discrepancies among beliefs and desires inherent in each of a number of cognitive elements. That, of course, complicates things and permits a wider range of predicted behaviors. In addition, McGuire (1960a, 1960b, 1960c) postulates interaction effects produced by situational and salience characteristics.

Feather (1967b) suggests that congruence motivation is related to the expectations people develop as a function of experiences in past situations. He proposes that the final explanation of congruence seeking is likely to be very complex and that it must take into account variations in congruence seeking behavior for a single person across situations and variations among persons across the same situation. In a discussion of the characteristics of information search (Feather, 1967a), he postulates that persons seek for information that produces congruence, avoid information that produces incongruence, but also seek information (irrelevant of its consistency characteristics) for extrinsic reasons.

MADDI'S VARIETY MOTIVE

Maddi (1968), at least to some degree supported by McGuire (1968), recognizes the coexistence of congruence seeking and incongruence seeking. In a restatement and elaboration of some points previously presented by Fiske and Maddi (1961), he proposes a variety motive which would produce such behaviors as the pursuit of novelty, unexpectedness, change, and complexity. By definition, this variety motive (at the molar level) would be motivation in the direction of incongruence. Maddi, however, by no means rejects the congruence motive. He believes that both have their own place in human cognition. Sufficient research has demonstrated that a congruence motive exists and operates under certain conditions and for certain stimulus patterns. Maddi (1968) calls on research reported by Welker (1961), Dember (1961), Maddi (1961b), Berlyne (1950, 1955) and on the formulations of Hebb (1955), Harlow (1953), Dember and Earl (1957), White (1959), Montgomery (1954), Duffy (1963), as well as his own collaborative work with Fiske (1961), to support the view of a variety motive which is *independent* of the congruity motive. It should be noted that not all of the work cited by Maddi tests human congruence vs. incongruence behavior. A good deal of it, as a matter of fact, is concerned with much more molecular motivational behavior. This approach probably strengthens rather than weakens Maddi's point: The motivation in the direction of variety appears to be rather pervasive.

If two independent motives, one for congruence seeking and one for incongruence seeking (variety), do exist, how can they operate within the same person? How do they interact with each other or counterbalance each other? Maddi (1968) reviews a number of possibilities. He initially considers the previously discussed suggestions of Berlyne (1957, 1963, 1968) which subsume exploration behavior under congruence motivation. Maddi rejects that view because it "explains away" rather than resolves the incompatibility of the two motives. Further, he suggests that Berlyne's position cannot account for the finding (often obtained in interviews) that people "enjoy" variety, when according to Berlyne's theory they should find it aversive (cf. Maddi, 1961c; Maddi & Andrews, 1966; Platt, 1961). Maddi also criticizes that Berlyne's view collapses the distinction between approach and avoidance behavior. He cites work by Welker (1959), whose animals when faced with a novel environment demonstrated initial avoidance and subsequent exploration. Berlyne's theory would predict the inverse sequence of behaviors.

Maddi's second suggestion as to how a congruence and a variety motive might be brought under one roof restates the Fiske and Maddi (1961) theory. In this view, persons have both congruence and variety motives. Which one is called to the fore would depend on an interaction of situational and personality factors. Fiske and Maddi propose an activation level at which a person is *both* most comfortable and most effective. If the person finds himself below that activation level, he will increase activation via the variety motive; if he finds himself above that level, he will attempt to decrease activation via the congruence motive. What level of activation is best is determined by an individual difference variable. But there is another, possibly more important, determinant of which motive is aroused: the environment. Different tasks require different activation levels. For instance, if a person's current activation level is higher than is necessary for optimal performance, he will likely decrease activation, e.g., seek consistency. The opposite is true if his level of activation is less than necessary for optimal performance.

How can the organism operate so effectively with so many things (internal as well as external to the organism) affecting its activation level, and for that matter, how can it work well with so many different kinds of activation (and associated arousal) levels? Fiske and Maddi take us back to the propositions of Hebb (1955) for an explanation. The work is done by a postulated excitation mechanism in a postulated center of the brain, probably in the reticular formation. With this proposition, Fiske and Maddi, and later Maddi, certainly propose a molecular basis for their interactive molar congruity and variety motives. Unfortunately, it is impossible to operationally define how this system actually does its work. If the activation levels (and associated arousal levels) are divergent for each task and, moreover, for each individual operating within the confines of that task, then the number of potential responses is effectively infinite, and only very general experimental predictions can be advanced.

The third potential way of describing the relationship between congruence motivation and variety motivation that is considered by Maddi (1968) actually implies no relationship at all. The congruence motive and the variety motive might merely coexist. Either some persons might be congruence seekers while others are variety seekers, or the same person might be a congruence seeker in one cognitive area and a variety seeker in another. This approach is not very satisfactory as long as one favors the view of human motivation as a generally *interrelated* interactive system. Such interrelationships across cognitive areas or cognitive domains would, however, not argue against different degrees of "average" congruity or variety seeking in these areas or domains (cf. the GIAL theory in the next chapter).

Finally, Maddi (1968) considers the possibility that an interaction of the congruence motive and the variety motive might produce the greatest "satisfaction." While variety is entertaining, and congruence is reassuring, some combination of the two might be ideal. This last view hints at a potential interaction between the unspecified motives, but it does not define the basis of the motives nor does it indicate the forms interactions might take. Again, without further elaboration, this view appears not very satisfactory.

McGuire (1968) agrees that the opposing forces of motivation toward congruence and incongruence (variety) might coexist and produce some form of "dynamic equilibrium, moreover an equilibrium that has evolutionary survival value." However, how does that equilibrium work?

Argyris (1969) has suggested that Maddi's data need not be explained by an equilibrium at all, but merely might be due to previously learned situational requirements for norm-related behavior. Under normal conditions, congruence-oriented behavior might be expected. Once societal norms are removed (e.g., after considerable *T* group experience or in a creative task that an individual does by himself), variety-oriented behavior might emerge. Research that has obtained results supporting consistency theories has tended to utilize social situations where norms and pressures were easily invoked. Research that has supported Maddi's suggestions has often come from less constrained research settings. Argyris' suggestion holds some similarity to the previously discussed social learning views of Newcomb (1963) and of social exchange theory.

One of the major efforts to relate motivation toward congruence with data suggesting that organisms frequently engage in behavior that may be identified as incongruence seeking has been made by Hunt (1963). Hunt initially attempts to bring goal attainment and consistency theory together, and to add a touch of "warm affect" to what is usually called "cold cognition." In addition, he considers motivation carefully both at the molar and the molecular levels.

GOAL ATTAINMENT AND CONSISTENCY SEEKING

Hunt (1963) reviewed the data on exploration and manipulation with the familiar conclusion that drive or affect based theories cannot account sufficiently for the information search characteristics of the mammalian cortex. He postulates a need for "motivation inherent in information processing," i.e., for a physiologically-based motive that is intrinsic to cognitive operation. Hunt selects the tendency to reduce incongruity as the *basic* cognitive motive.

Hunt developed his position from the analysis of brain organization postulated by Pribram. He noted that both the frontal intrinsic sector of the brain (which mediates plans, decisions, and goal setting) and the posterior intrinsic sector (which mediates perception and evaluates) appear to involve elaborate feedback mechanisms. He maintains that the motive underlying all feedback systems is the reduction of incongruity between some standard and the incoming stimuli. In the posterior perceptual realm, this motive would underlie phenomena such as the reduction in incongruity between evaluations measured by Osgood and Tannenbaum (1955), the tendency toward consistency among concepts studied by McGuire (1960), and the strain to eliminate dissonance between acts and beliefs investigated by Festinger (1957). Hunt referred to incongruities involving standards (i.e., beliefs, attitudes) developed over a period of time as *long-term incongruity*. By attributing all long-term incongruity reduction to one basic motive, Hunt has attempted to unite the diverse consistency theories.

Hunt pursued his integrative course by postulating that the incongruity reduction motive also operates behind momentary adjustment of cognitive functioning, described by Russian research as the "orienting reflex" (Razran, 1961). Any sudden or unexpected departure from a current pattern of stimulation (e.g., surprise) apparently arouses the complex information-seeking orienting reflex, which operates until the discrepancy is resolved or assimilated. Clearly, the orienting reflex can be viewed as a means of reducing incongruity by attaining more information about a novel input. Hunt terms this variant of his master motive "*short-term incongruity* resolution." This form of incongruity motive might account for processes such as momentary changes in adaptation level or assimilation-contrast effects in perception. These processes could represent short-term resolutions of incongruity via changes in standards, inputs, or both.

Hunt next explained the executive operation of the frontal intrinsic sector of the brain in terms of the incongruity motive. He described at least two kinds of executive, decision-making functions which can be viewed as feedback systems operating on an incongruity reduction basis. The clearest case is the continuous matching between plans or goals with input (information) concerning ongoing events. Incongruity, in this case, is equivalent with frustration. A second decision-making function is the matching of goals with plans. At times, several plans or strategies may seem relevant to a goal, yet they may be mutually exclusive. This state of incongruity is frequently termed conflict. Hunt has suggested that the intrinsic congruity motive can explain the basic tendency to attain goals, and thus he has integrated goal-setting and congruity seeking as cognitive motives.

CONGRUITY, COGNITION AND AFFECT

While Hunt argued for intrinsic cognitive motives, he did not view them as devoid of affect. He maintained that the incongruity mechanism arouses affect in addition to its main function of energizing cortical activity. Affective response is viewed as a very frequent and important, but not an essential, result of congruity seeking. Hunt cited considerable evidence that incongruity of every type noted above can lead to affect arousal. This evidence ranges from Yoshii and Tsukiyama's (1952) finding that rats at a choice point (i.e., in a state of conflict or incongruity in the frontal intrinsic sector of the brain) display EEG patterns typical of emotional arousal, to Vinogradova's (1958) report that the absence of an expected conditioned fear arouser (i.e., a short-term incongruity in the posterior intrinsic sector) can result in emotional arousal.

Hunt's case for affect involvement in incongruity is quite clear. It reiterates the suggestion found in Tomkins' (1962) data on affect that while affect is very important in cognitive activity (particularly in more complex activity), it is not essential. However, when Hunt examined the direction or valence (i.e., positive or negative) of affect aroused in cognitive functioning, his model is not so clear. Research stemming from Festinger's view supports the idea that negative affect and aversive behavior are aroused by incongruity and novelty (which is always a kind of incongruity, by definition). However, a large body of evidence implies that incongruity or novelty can arouse positive affect and approach tendencies. For instance, Hebb and Mahut (1955) found that hungry rats preferred a long, incongruous path to food over a short "boring" one. This might indicate that the positive valence of incongruity can attenuate drive motivation. Hunt dismissed the argument that incongruity seeking occurs only in service of drives by citing studies such as those of Hebb and Mahut or Montgomery and Segall (1955), which showed that rats would endure heightened drive or fear to attain incongruity.[4] Hunt also discussed studies which indicated that incongruity seeking is not related to hypothetical needs for activity (Montgomery & Zimbardo, 1957) or stimulation (Kivy, Earl, & Walker, 1956).

Hunt concluded that incongruity can arouse both positive and negative affect. This postulate is supported by Welker's (1956) finding that given moderately novel toys, chimpanzees are at first afraid, then show increasingly positive interest, and finally display negative boredom. A similar temporal pattern is noted by Hebb (1949) in reviewing Chandler's (1934) analysis of

[4] The reader will also recall that high drive intensity lowers novelty seeking (e.g., Chapman & Levy, 1957).

reactions to dissonant music. Hunt proposes that such findings are comprehensible if one postulates an optimum of "something . . . which divides pleasure and attraction from displeasure and repulsion" (p. 73).

OPTIMAL INCONGRUITY CONCEPTS

In his search for an optimum, Hunt first considered a variant on Helson's (1959) adaptation level. McClelland (1955) and Haber (1958) have postulated that in each area of stimulation (e.g., visual brightness) specific adaptation levels (ALs) are developed. The relationship between an AL and subsequent stimuli is shown in Figure 4.1. In general, the expected pattern is that stimuli congruent with the AL produce no affect; stimuli somewhat divergent from the AL induce positive affect; and extremely divergent stimuli produce negative affect. The AL itself can change as a function of changing patterns of stimulation so that affective reactions to identical stimuli can shift. Hunt saw this formulation as relevant to some short-term incongruity mediation. One could say that ALs concerned with incongruity (as opposed to sheer stimulation intensity[5]) are formed in the manner described by McClelland et al. and by Haber.

However, some problems arise with this view. The short-term ALs fail to account for long-term incongruity systems. There is no specific provision for operationally defining the optimal discrepancy points in this view. And, finally, the curve shown by Haber (Fig. 4.1) fails to account for inputs which, despite varied prior exposure, regularly produce only positive or negative affects (e.g., Hunt & Quay, 1961). This last problem can be dealt with, however, by postulating stimulus-specific variance in the height and breadth of the positive affect portion of the curve in Figure 4.1. As limiting cases, one can imagine ALs for which either the positive or the negative parts of the curve vanish (Fig. 4.1–dotted line). Despite the short-run perspective and vagueness in definitions of optima in the AL view, its basic assumptions of bilateral symmetry and of an optimal incongruity which produces maximal positive affect are highly suggestive (see below).

Hunt next considered the optimal arousal view as proposed by Hebb (1955) and Leuba (1955). Hebb and Leuba argued that cognitive operations such as motor responses or cue discrimination operate most efficiently at

---

[5] It is quite possible that separate ALs for intensity and novelty–complexity or incongruity exist. Some physiological data suggest that parts of the thalamic reticular system mediate novelty–complexity ALs, while the brain stem reticular system may be related to intensity ALs (see Tomkins, 1962). An intriguing proposition is that a tradeoff may exist, such that where intensity ALs are high, novelty ALs are low, and vice versa.

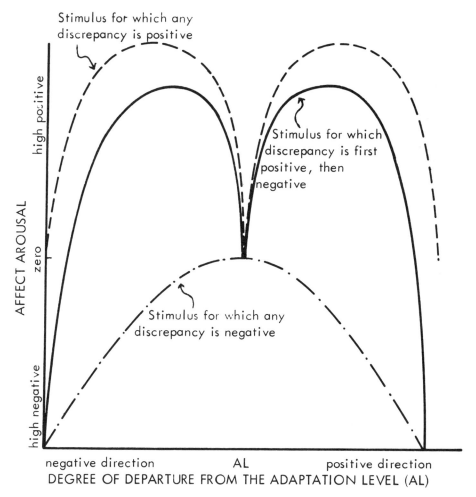

FIG. 4.1. Curves depicting three theoretical patterns of affective reactions to discrepancies from the adaptation level of a stimulus.

some moderate, "optimum" degree of cortical arousal. As arousal approaches this optimum, affects are positive; beyond it, they are negative. Incongruity which produces optimal arousal is itself optimal, in this view. When input is below the optimal arousal point, greater incongruity (or affect, drive, etc.) is sought; while when input is above optimal, less incongruity is sought (Fig. 4.2).

One comment on this view may be in order. It is possible to see Hebb's view of incongruity largely in terms of drive and arousal theory. However,

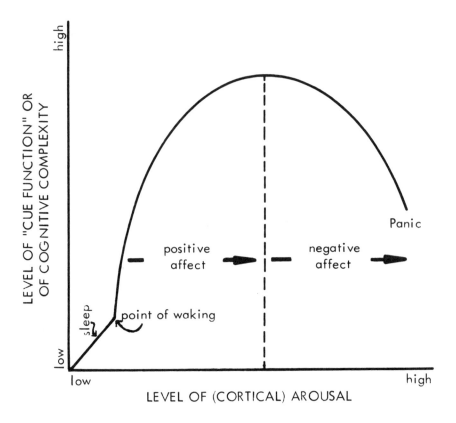

FIG. 4.2. Optimum arousal level model (after Hebb, with modifications).

although Hebb has clearly made arousal an essential step in relating in-congruity to behavior, he has not made incongruity unimportant nor has he based *all* cognitive motivation on external drives or affects (see Cofer and Appley, 1964, p. 409). There is no reason to believe that Hebb has abandoned a view that moderate incongruity is as essential in explaining variations in arousal level as any drive or affect. Furthermore, Hebb (1955) noted that the cortex seems capable of originating its own arousal via reticular processes. Thus, one could see in Hebb's views how incongruity per se could produce cortical "arousal" without any necessary affective arousal. With this in mind, the differences between Hebb's view and those of Hunt and Berlyne do not seem so severe.

Finally, Hunt revealed his own choice for an optimum which is based on the position of Berlyne (1960). He noted that Berlyne's "collative variables" (novelty, complexity, change) relate to the amount of incongruity in the environment[6]; hence, Berlyne and Hunt concur in relating arousal to incongruity, as shown in Figure 4.3. As with Hebb, Hunt postulated that as incongruity increases toward optimal, affect is positive; and that beyond optimal, it is negative. However, unlike Hebb, Hunt and Berlyne saw intensity of arousal as declining toward the optimum and rising toward extremes of congruity (boredom) or incongruity (panic). By arousal Hunt apparently meant general emotional arousal, not the cortical arousal employed by Hebb.

Furthermore, Hunt implied that one can directly relate input incongruity

[6] Berlyne's "collative variables" may reflect conditions other than incongruity. Complexity, for example, may imply stimuli which are congruent with current stored plans or ideas but which nevertheless change probabilities or linkages in the cortex. Thus "collative variables" might better be related to what Schroder, Driver, & Streufert (1967) term information load (cf. Streufert & Driver, 1965, 1967; Streufert, Driver, & Haun, 1967; Streufert & Schroder, 1965; Streufert, 1970).

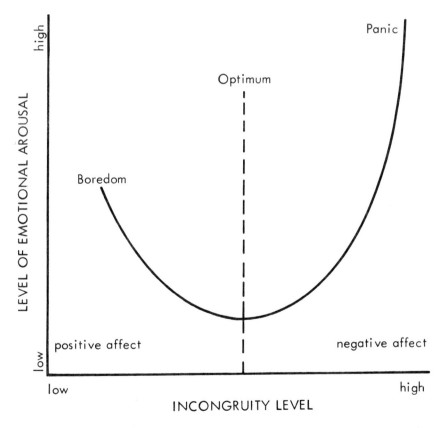

FIG. 4.3. Optimum incongruity level model (after Hunt, with modifications).

to cognitive activation (e.g., novelty seeking) without any reference to affective arousal. A study by Haywood and Hunt (1963) suggests that adrenalin injections had little effect on novelty-seeking behavior. However, this study is not crucial to a comparison of the views of Hebb and Hunt. As noted above, Hebb could agree with Hunt that cognitive behavior can be aroused via incongruity with no affect involved at all. In addition to nonaffective arousal, however, Hebb argued that affects and drives can contribute to general arousal of the cortex and, thus, affect incongruity reactions. Furthermore, the idea of increasing affect (e.g., boredom, panic) under nonoptimal incongruity is not necessarily opposed to Hebb's view, since one can argue that high affect arousal involved low cortical arousal (and low cognitive activation). For instance, one can argue (as do Schroder et al., 1967) that too much noxity or eucity (i.e., negative or positive affect) actually decreases cognitive activity levels. This is not to say that Hunt and Hebb are in agreement on all points, but it should be noted that the differences are not insurmountable.

QUESTIONS RAISED BY HUNT'S INTEGRATION

Hunt's integrative effort is valuable because it has indicated how the general motive of incongruity reduction might subsume diverse areas of consistency theory and goal-attainment theory. Hunt has also brought the interaction of affect and cognitive theory into sharper focus. But, perhaps the most important contribution of this work is that it recasts several venerable problems and raises several new issues.

One vital issue concerns the possibility of attaining maximum parsimony by explaining the congruity motive, as well as the incongruity motive, in a single model: via an expanded consistency theory. Such a theory will be proposed in the next chapter. Another issue concerns the development of a clearer delineation of the relationship between affect and optimal incongruity. For instance, if the optimal is viewed as dividing positive approach from negative withdrawal, how can one account for extreme negative reactions on *either* side of the optimum, e.g., the negative feelings of boredom on one side and fear on the other? Furthermore, Berlyne has now conceded that moderate *arousal* can be optimal, hence the zero arousal optimum view of Hunt is no longer in accord with Berlyne.

In our view, incongruity would produce both arousal and affect, somewhat along the lines suggested by Haber (Fig. 4.1). However, the mechanism which focuses incongruity seeking at a certain level (AL) can be explained without reference to affective or arousal "side effects." As one resolution to the disagreements among the various theories, and as an incorporation of affect and complexity views with consistency theory, we will propose a general incongruity adaptation level (GIAL) in the following chapter.

SUMMARY: THE CONGRUITY-INCONGRUITY MOTIVE CONFUSION

Motivation has been viewed in this chapter from two vantage points: molar motivation and molecular motivation. Theorists and researchers concerned with human cognitive behavior seem to have only one major disagreement about molar motivation: Does an independent (but potentially interactive) motivation toward incongruity exist, or does it not. It appears that everyone agrees on the existence of congruity motivation. Incongruity motivation, on the other hand, is viewed as either (1) nonexistent; (2) existent in the service of the congruity motive, and, consequently, part of the congruity motivation; (3) existent independent of, and noninteractive with, congruity motivation; and (4) existent independent of, but in various ways interactive with, the congruity motive.

The confusion about molecular motivation is still greater. Even the consistency theories, which are rather similar at the molar motivation levels, appear to assume different underlying molecular motivational principles. In other cases, the molecular motivation issue is entirely avoided by the theorists. Several positions make passing reference to some generally unspecified physiological mechanism and to past experience of the organism (his reinforcement history).

It appears that the future will probably see much more complex models of cognition (cf. McGuire, 1968) and that the answer to our current dilemmas will be found in a choice between theories that are primarily proposing a congruity motive (e.g., dissonance theory) and those that are suggesting some kind of *optimal* congruity level (e.g., Maddi, 1968). While it is currently impossible to submit the motivational bases (molecular motivation) of the various theories to experimental test (until the bases are more clearly defined), it is at least possible to design critical experiments that compare standard congruity models with adaptation level theory. For example, such experiments might expose subjects who are overloaded with incongruity vs. subjects who have been deprived of incongruity to standard dissonance reduction designs or to manipulations that in the past have resulted in incongruity search. One may hope that such comparisons might be as fruitful tests of theory as tests of congruity theory have been. We would not be at all surprised if experimenters would obtain complex interactions among the various variables and levels of these experiments. After all, the incompatible results that have been obtained by experimenters investigating congruity and variety views of human cognition may well suggest that we have not yet determined all the cognitive or affective components which underlie human behavior in a complex environment.

REFERENCES

Abelson, R. P., Aronson, E., McGuire, W. J. Newcomb, T. M., Rosenberg, M. J., & Tannenbaum, P. H. (Eds.), *Theories of cognitive consistency: A source book.* Chicago: Rand McNally, 1968.
Allport, G. *Personality.* New York: Holt, 1967.
Argyris, C. The incompleteness of social psychological theory: Examples from small group, cognitive consistency and attribution research. *American Psychologist,* 1969, **24**, 893-908.
Aronson, E. Dissonance theory: Progress and problems. In R. P. Abelson, E. Aronson, W. J. McGuire, T. M. Newcomb, M. J. Rosenberg, & P. H. Tannenbaum (Eds.), *Theories of cognitive consistency: A sourcebook.* Chicago: Rand McNally, 1968.
Aronson, E. The theory of cognitive dissonance: A current perspective. In L. Berkowitz (Ed.), *Advances in experimental social psychology* (Vol. 4). New York: Academic Press, 1969.
Aronson, E., & Ross, A. *The effect of support and criticism on interpersonal attractiveness.* Unpublished data, 1966.
Bem, D. J. Self-perception: An alternative interpretation of cognitive dissonance phenomena. *Psychological Review,* 1967, **74**, 183-200.
Berkowitz, L. Social motivation. In G. Lindzey & E. Aronson (Eds.), *The handbook of social psychology* (2nd ed.) (Vol. 3). Reading, Mass.: Addison Wesley, 1969.
Berlyne, D. E. Novelty and curiosity as determinants of exploratory behavior. *British Journal of Psychology,* 1950, **41**, 68-80.
Berlyne, D. E. The arousal and satiation of perceptual curiosity in the rat. *Journal of Comparative and Physiological Psychology,* 1955, **48**, 238-246.
Berlyne, D. E. Uncertainty and conflict: A point of contact between information theory and behavior theory. *Psychological Review,* 1957, **64**, 329-339.
Berlyne, D. E. *Conflict, arousal, and curiosity.* New York: McGraw-Hill, 1960.
Berlyne, D. E. Motivational problems raised by exploratory and epistemic behavior. In S. Koch (Ed.), *Psychology: A study of a science* (Vol. 5). New York: McGraw-Hill, 1963.
Berlyne, D. E. Curiosity and exploration. *Science,* 1966, **153**, 25-33.
Berlyne, D. E. The motivational significance of collative variables and conflict. In R. P. Abelson, E. Aronson, W. J. McGuire, T. M. Newcomb, M. J. Rosenberg, & P. H. Tannenbaum (Eds.), *Theories of cognitive consistency: A sourcebook.* Chicago: Rand McNally, 1968.

Berlyne, D. E., Salapatek, P. H., Gelman, R. S., & Zener, S. L. Is light increment really rewarding the rat? *Journal of Comparative and Physiological Psychology,* 1964, **58,** 148-151.

Brehm, J. W., & Cohen, A. R. *Explorations in cognitive dissonance.* New York: Wiley, 1962.

Byrne, D. Response to attitude similarity-dissimilarity as a function of affiliation need. *Journal of Personality,* 1962, **30,** 164-177.

Canon, L. Self-confidence and selective exposure to information. In L. Festinger (Ed.), *Conflict, decision, and dissonance.* Stanford, Calif.: Stanford University Press, 1964.

Cartwright, D., & Harary, F. Structural balance: A generalization of Heider's theory. *Psychological Review,* 1956, **63,** 277-293.

Chandler, A. R. *Beauty and human nature.* New York: Appleton-Century, 1934.

Chapanis, N. P., & Chapanis, A. Cognitive dissonance: Five years later. *Psychological Bulletin,* 1964, **61,** 1-22.

Chapman, R. M., & Levy, N. Hunger drive and reinforcing effect of novel stimuli. *Journal of Comparative and Physiological Psychology,* 1957, **50,** 233-238.

Cofer, C. N., & Appley, M. H. *Motivation: Theory and research.* New York: Wiley, 1964.

Dember, W. N. Alternative behavior. In D. W. Fiske & S. R. Maddi (Eds.), *Functions of varied experience.* Homewood, Ill.: Dorsey Press, 1961.

Dember, W. N., & Earl, R. W. Analysis of exploratory, manipulatory and curiosity behaviors. *Psychological Review,* 1957, **64,** 91-96.

Driver, M. J., & Streufert, S. *The "general incongruity adaptation level" (GIAL) hypothesis: An analysis and integration of cognitive approaches to motivation* (Institute Paper 114). Lafayette, Ind.: Purdue University, Institute for Research in the Behavioral, Economic and Management Sciences, 1965.

Duffy, E. *Activation and behavior.* New York: Wiley, 1963.

Feather, N. T. An expectancy value model of information-seeking behavior. *Psychological Review,* 1967, **74,** 342-360. (a)

Feather, N. T. A structural balance approach to the analysis of communication effects. In L. Berkowitz (Ed.), *Advances in experimental social psychology* (Vol. 3). New York: Academic Press, 1967. (b)

Feldman, S. (Ed.). *Cognitive consistency.* New York: Academic Press, 1966.

Festinger, L. *A theory of cognitive dissonance.* Evanston, Ill.: Row, Peterson, 1957.

Festinger, L. The motivating effect of cognitive dissonance. In G. Lindzey (Ed.), *Assessment of human motives.* New York: Grove Press, 1958.

Festinger, L. *Conflict, decision and dissonance.* Stanford, Calif.: Stanford University Press, 1964.

Fiske, D. W., & Maddi, S. (Eds.). *Functions of varied experience.* Homewood, Ill.: Dorsey Press, 1961.

Freedman, J. L. Preference for dissonant information. *Journal of Personality and Social Psychology,* 1965, **2**, 287-289.

Fromkin, H. L. Reinforcement and effort expenditure: Predictions of "reinforcement theory" vs. predictions of "dissonance theory." *Journal of Personality and Social Psychology,* 1968, **9**, 347-352.

Haber, R. N. Discrepancy from adaptation level as a source of affect. *Journal of Experimental Psychology,* 1958, **56**, 370-375.

Harlow, H. R. Mice, monkeys, men, and motives. *Psychological Review,* 1953, **60**, 23-32.

Harrington, G. M., & Linder, W. K. A positive reinforcing effect of electrical stimulation. *Journal of Comparative and Physiological Psychology,* 1962, **55**, 1014-1015.

Haywood, H. C., & Hunt, J. McV. Effects of epinephrine on novelty preference and arousal. *Journal of Abnormal and Social Psychology,* 1963, **67**, 206-213.

Hebb, D. O. *The organization of behavior.* New York: Wiley, 1949.

Hebb, D. O. Drives and the C.N.S. *Psychological Review,* 1955, **62**, 243-254.

Hebb, D. O., & Mahut, H. Motivation et récherche du changement perceptif chez le rat et chez l'homme. *Journal de Psychologie Normale et Pathologique,* 1955, **48**, 209-220.

Heider, F. Attitudes and cognitive organization. *Journal of Psychology,* 1946, **21**, 107-112.

Helson, H. Adaptation level theory. In S. Koch (Ed.), *Psychology: A study of a science* (Vol. 1). New York: McGraw-Hill, 1959.

Homans, G. C. *Social behavior: Its elementary forms.* New York: Harcourt Brace, 1961.

Hunt, J. McV. Motivation inherent in information processing and action. In O. J. Harvey (Ed.), *Motivation and social interaction: Cognitive determinants.* New York: Ronald Press, 1963.

Hunt, J. McV., & Quay, H. C. Early vibratory experience and the question of innate reinforcement value of vibration and other stimuli: A limitation on the discrepancy (burnt soup) principle in motivation. *Psychological Review,* 1961, **68**, 149-156.

Irle, M. *Lehrbuch der Sozialpsychologie.* Göttingen: Hogrefe, 1976.

Kiesler, C. A. *A motivational theory of stimulus incongruity with application for such phenomena as dissonance and self attribution.* Paper presented at the American Psychological Association Convention, New Orleans, 1974.

Kivy, P. N., Earl, R. W., & Walker, E. L. Stimulus context and satiation. *Journal of Comparative and Physiological Psychology,* 1956, **44**, 90-92.

Lawrence, D. H., & Festinger, L. *Deterrents and reinforcements: The psychology of insufficient reward.* Stanford, Calif.: Standford University Press, 1962.

Leuba, C. Toward some integration of learning theories: The concept of optimal stimulation. *Psychological Reports,* 1955, **1,** 27–33.

Lowin, A. *Information selectivity as a function of agreement with message and ease of message refutation.* Unpublished doctoral dissertation, Columbia University, 1965.

Maddi, S. R. Affective tone during environmental regularity and change. *Journal of Abnormal and Social Psychology,* 1961, **62,** 338–345. (a)

Maddi, S. R. Exploratory behavior and variation-seeking in man. In D. W. Fiske & S. R. Maddi (Eds.), *Functions of varied experience.* Homewood, Ill.: Dorsey Press, 1961. (b)

Maddi, S. R. Unexpectedness, affective tone, and behavior. In D. W. Fiske & S. R. Maddi (Eds.), *Functions of varied experience.* Homewood, Ill.: Dorsey Press, 1961. (c)

Maddi, S. R. The pursuit of consistency and variety. In R. P. Abelson, E. Aronson, W. J. McGuire, T. M. Newcomb, M. J. Rosenberg, & P. H. Tannenbaum (Eds.), *Theories of cognitive consistency: A sourcebook.* Chicago, Rand McNally, 1968.

Maddi, S. R., & Andrews, S. L. The need for variety in fantasy and self-description. *Journal of Personality,* 1966, **34,** 610–626.

McClelland, D. C. *Studies in motivation.* New York: Appleton-Century-Crofts, 1955.

McGuire, W. J. Cognitive consistency and attitude change. *Journal of Abnormal and Social Psychology,* 1960, **60,** 345–353. (a)

McGuire, W. J. Direct and indirect persuasive effects of dissonance producing messages. *Journal of Abnormal and Social Psychology,* 1960, **60,** 354–358. (b)

McGuire, W. J. A syllogistic analysis of cognitive relationships. In C. I. Hovland & M. J. Rosenberg (Eds.), *Attitude organization and change.* New Haven, Conn.: Yale University Press, 1960. (c)

McGuire, W. J. Résumé and response from the consistency theory viewpoint. In R. P. Abelson, E. Aronson, W. J. McGuire, T. M. Newcomb, M. J. Rosenberg, & P. H. Tannenbaum (Eds.), *Theories of cognitive consistency: A sourcebook.* Chicago: Rand McNally, 1968.

McGuire, W. J. The nature of attitudes and attitude change. In G. Lindzey & E. Aronson (Eds.), *The handbook of social psychology* (2nd ed.) (Vol. 3). Reading, Mass.: Addison Wesley, 1969.

Mills, J., Aronson, E., & Robinson, H. Selectivity in exposure to information. *Journal of Abnormal and Social Psychology,* 1959, **59,** 250–253.

Montgomery, K. C. The role of exploratory drive in learning. *Journal of Comparative and Physiological Psychology,* 1954, **47,** 60–64.

Montgomery, K. C., & Segall, M. Discrimination learning based upon the exploratory drive. *Journal of Comparative and Physiological Psychology,* 1955, **46**, 225-228.

Montgomery, K. C., & Zimbardo, P. G. The effect of sensory and behavioral deprivation upon exploratory behavior in the rat. *Perceptual and Motor Skills,* 1957, **7**, 223-229.

Newcomb, T. M. An approach to the study of communicative acts. *Psychological Review,* 1953, **60**, 393-404.

Newcomb, T. M. The prediction of interpersonal attraction. *American Psychologist,* 1956, **11**, 575-586.

Newcomb, T. M. Varieties of interpersonal attraction. In D. Cartwright & A. Zander (Eds.), *Group dynamics: Research and theory* (2nd ed.) New York: Harper & Row, 1960.

Newcomb, T. M. Stabilities underlying changes in interpersonal attraction. *Journal of Abnormal and Social Psychology,* 1963, **66**, 376-386.

Osgood, C. E., Suci, G. J., & Tannenbaum, P. H. *The measurement of meaning.* Urbana, Ill.: University of Illinois Press, 1957.

Osgood, C. E., & Tannenbaum, P. H. The principle of congruity in the prediction of attitude change. *Psychological Review,* 1955, **62**, 42-55.

Pepitone, A. *Attraction and hostility.* New York: Atherton Press, 1964.

Pepitone, A. Some conceptual and empirical problems of consistency models. In S. Feldman (Ed.), *Cognitive consistency.* New York: Academic Press, 1966.

Platt, J. R. Beauty: Pattern and change. In D. W. Fiske and S. R. Maddi (Eds.), *Functions of varied experience.* Homewood, Ill.: Dorsey Press, 1961.

Price, K. O., Harburg, E., & Newcomb, T. M. Psychological balance in situations of negative interpersonal attitudes. *Journal of Personality and Social Psychology,* 1966, **3**, 265-270.

Razran, G. The observable unconscious and the inferrable conscious in current Soviet psychophysiology: Introceptive conditioning, semantic conditioning and the orienting reflex. *Psychological Review,* 1961, **68**, 81-147.

Rosenberg, M. J. Some limits of dissonance: Toward a differentiated view of counterattitudinal performance. In S. Feldman (Ed.), *Cognitive consistency.* New York: Academic Press, 1966.

Schroder, H. M., Driver, M. J., & Streufert, S. *Human information processing.* New York: Holt, Rinehart & Winston, 1967.

Singer, J. E. Motivation for consistency. In S. Feldman (Ed.), *Cognitive consistency.* New York: Academic Press, 1966.

Stevenson, M. W., & Odem, R. D. Visual reinforcement with children. *Journal of Experimental Child Psychology,* 1964, **1**, 248-255.

Streufert, S. Complexity and complex decision making. *Journal of Experimental Social Psychology,* 1970, **6,** 494-509.

Streufert, S., & Driver, M. J. Conceptual structure, information load and perceptual complexity. *Psychonomic Science,* 1965, **3,** 249-250.

Streufert, S., & Driver, M. J. Impression formation as a measure of the complexity of conceptual structure. *Educational and Psychological Measurement,* 1967, **27,** 1025-1039.

Streufert, S., & Driver, M. J. The general incongruity adaptation level (GIAL). Purdue University: Office of Naval Research Tech. Rep. No. 32, 1970.

Streufert, S., Driver, M. J., & Haun, K. H. Components of response rate in complex decision making. *Journal of Experimental Social Psychology,* 1967, **3,** 286-295.

Streufert, S., & Schroder, H. M. Conceptual structure, environmental complexity, and task performance. *Journal of Experimental Research in Personality,* 1965, **1,** 132-137.

Tannenbaum, P. H. The congruity principle: Restrospective reflections and recent research. In R. P. Abelson, E. Aronson, W. J. McGuire, T. M. Newcomb, M. Rosenberg, & P. H. Tannenbaum (Eds.), *Theories of cognitive consistency: A sourcebook.* Chicago: Rand McNally, 1968.

Thibaut, J. W., & Kelley, H. H. *The social psychology of groups.* New York: Wiley, 1959.

Tomkins, S. S. *Affect—imagery—consciousness* (Vol. 1). New York: Springer, 1962.

Vinogradova, O. S. On the dynamics of the orienting reflex in the formation of conditioned connections. In L. G. Voronin, A. Leontijev, A. R. Luria, E. N. Sokolov, & O. S. Vinogradova (Eds.), *The orienting reflex and orienting investigatory activity.* Moscow: Akad. Pedag. Nauk, RSFSR, 1958.

Welker, W. I. Effects of age and experience on play and exploration of young chimpanzees. *Journal of Comparative and Physiological Psychology,* 1956, **49,** 223-226.

Welker, W. I. Escape, exploratory, and food-seeking responses of rats in a novel situation. *Journal of Comparative and Physiological Psychology,* 1959, **52,** 96-111.

Welker, W. I. An analysis of exploratory and play behavior in animals. In D. W. Fiske & S. R. Maddi (Eds.), *Functions of varied experience.* Homewood, Ill.: Dorsey Press, 1961.

White, R. W. Motivation reconsidered: The concept of competence. *Psychological Review,* 1959, **66,** 297-333.

Yoshii, N. K., & Tsukiyama, K. EEG studies of conditioned behavior of the white rat. *Japanese Journal of Physiology,* 1952, **2,** 186-193.

Zimbardo, P. G. (Ed.). *The cognitive control of motivation.* Glenview, Ill.: Scott Foresman, 1969.

CHAPTER 5

THE GENERAL INCONGRUITY ADAPTATION LEVEL (GIAL):

A theory developed in cooperation with Michael J. Driver

THE NATURE OF THE OPTIMAL INCONGRUITY MECHANISM

The formulation of an optimal incongruity hypothesis by Hunt (1963) can be viewed as an effort to integrate the various cognitive theories of motivation and an effort to relate them to affect arousal (see discussion in previous chapter). Hunt's work has advanced cognitive motivation theory considerably, yet some findings and theoretical positions still remain to be integrated. We already suggested in the preceding chapter that some questions about the relationship between affect and cognition are still unanswered.

Different Meanings of "Incongruity" and "Congruity"

A second problem concerns the distinction between the meaning of "congruity" and "incongruity" as proposed by Osgood and Tannenbaum versus the meaning of these terms in the discussions of Hunt. For Osgood and Tannenbaum (1955), complete congruity would imply that information received by the organism permits simplicity of storage: The evaluative *meaning* of the received information (even if it is "new" information) is identical to the evaluation (for the object considered in the information) already present (stored) in the person's frame of reference. To Osgood and Tannenbaum, a state of congruity (identity of incoming information with stored concepts) should be desirable for the organism. Hunt (1963) would consider a state of complete congruity undesirable and would suggest that the organism would show little, if any, interest in repetitive information. Osgood and Tannenbaum would suggest that incongruity implies information which is not in agreement with a person's preestablished concepts, producing an aversive state and motivation in the direction of greater congruity (with polarity assumed). For Hunt, incongruity need not be aversive. An optimal level of incongruity would produce no desire (or action) toward change in the incongruity level [even though via the TOTE (Miller, Galanter, and Pribram's, 1960, Test-Operate-Test-Exit) system congruity may be sought for a specific operation]. Too little incongruity would produce motivation to seek (or focus on) information that would increase the incongruity experienced by the organism, and too much incongruity would produce motivation that would decrease the experienced incongruity (or would modify the adaptation level). In only one particular case would Osgood's and Hunt's uses of the term incongruity be operationally similar, though not identical. If one observed an organism who is exposed to information that is *highly* discrepant from his stored concepts, then both Hunt's and Osgood's position would predict behavior that may look somewhat like Festinger's dissonance reduction. Both would term this behavior congruity seeking and consider an environment with that level of incongruity as aversive. However, under conditions of greater agreement of information with the organism's stored concepts, the theories would predict diverse behaviors in the service of the congruity mechanism (Osgood and Tannenbaum) and the optimum incongruity construct (Hunt). Osgood's organism would not seek changes, while Hunt's organism would engage in search for (or focus on) novel (e.g., dissonant, imbalanced) information.

It appears, then, that the meaning of the "incongruity" positions of these two theories are quite divergent. Although both agree that congruity is sought (and desirable) for any specific set of incoming information that is not in agreement with stored concepts, Osgood and Tannenbaum leave it at that, while Hunt proposes an additional mechanism that provides continued search for, openness to, and focusing on, different moderately incongruent information across a number of informational areas.

One might suggest that a general informational departure from Hunt's optimum incongruity level is, in and of itself, incongruous (in Osgood and Tannenbaum's terminology). Some of the predictions made by the congruity theory of Osgood and Tannenbaum (1955) and of Tannenbaum (1968) can be easily reconciled with such a position. However, that view encounters another serious problem. Depending on the quantitative values that one might attach to the respective motivational levels experienced by the organism [as a function of departures from the adaptation level in either direction (Hunt) and as a function of the *in*congruity experienced by that departure (Osgood and Tannenbaum)], either the Hunt or the Osgood view will emerge as superfluous as long as one conceives of motivations as *additive* in some fashion. Let us explain this view by assuming the simplest case: We shall view the two congruity motives as parallel linear or parallel curvilinear functions. In other words, they are additive but do not intersect. The values of the two motivational systems toward congruity may now "sum" in three different ways: (1) At information incongruity levels beyond Hunt's adaptation level, the incongruity motivations in the direction of congruity would add; (2) if departure from the adaptation level toward greater congruity would produce congruity motivation (Osgood and Tannenbaum) and incongruity motivation (Hunt), then the two motives would subtract; (3) if the organism found information that is placed at the organism's adaptation level, then only congruity motivation (Osgood and Tannenbaum) would be present.

One might assume that either identical or divergent "values" (motive strength) could be attached to the Osgood and Tannenbaum motives. Let us view their effects.

(a) When the organism is exposed to information incongruity beyond Hunt's adaptation level [as in (1) above], then the values of the motivational systems are irrelevant since they would add to bring the organism back toward greater incongruity—either to the adaptation level or beyond.

(b) If the quantitative values attached to the two motivations were identical, then the organism should be relatively comfortable in all information incongruity levels between congruity and the adaptation level (since the pull is equal in both directions). Among the varied experimental evidence produced by consistency researchers and those who have supported a variety motive, there seems to be little support for such a view (cf. the discussions in Abelson, Aronson, McGuire, Newcomb, Rosenberg, & Tannenbaum, 1968).

(c) If, on the other hand, the motivation produced by the incongruity of departing from the adaptation level toward greater congruity (Osgood) were greater in quantity than the motivation to reachieve the adaptation level (Hunt), then the organism would continue to seek for congruity and would finally come to rest (but possibly not comfortably) at a total congruity point. That prediction would not differ greatly from one made by the early consistency theories of Festinger, Heider, Newcomb, and others.

(d) If motivation produced by the incongruity of departing from the adaptation level toward greater congruity (Osgood) were smaller in quantity than the motivation to reachieve the adaptation level (Hunt) then the organism would gravitate toward Hunt's incongruity adaptation level, and only the total motivational force would be affected (superoptimal incongruity would be more aversive than suboptimal incongruity).

These simple additions and subtractions of two separate motivational forces certainly are not parsimonious, unless some specific intersection of the two potential motivations is demonstrated. A more efficient formulation might be to view Osgood and Tannenbaum's congruity model as operating only on one side of Hunt's adaptation level (where incongruity is superoptimal).

Hunt's Model and Complexity Theory

An additional problem that has not been touched by the Hunt work is the relationship between congruity and complexity. It will be remembered that complexity is viewed by the present authors as the dimensionality (including the relationships among dimensions) of human information processing, not as used by McGuire (1968) who at times has assigned this term to theories that attempt to deal with seeking and avoiding of incongruity.[1] Similarly, we are not concerned with preferences for pattern complexity (e.g., the work of Barron, 1953). Preference for pattern complexity has at least in some research been related to preference for symmetry, a concept that may well have its roots in a need for congruity.

Theorists who have discussed dimensional complexity (e.g., Bieri, Witkin, Harvey, Schroder, Streufert, and others) have as a rule shown little interest in incongruity. Exceptions to this rule are Driver and Streufert (1965, 1966), Scott (1962, 1963a, 1963b, 1969), and Streufert (1970). Driver and Streufert pointed out that more complex (potentially multidimensional) information *potentially* contains more incongruity than simple information that allows placement of the stimulation on only a single dimension. The incidence of informational complexity tends to be positively correlated with the incidence of incongruity. However, the two are *not necessarily* related. Complex information can (although it does not do so frequently) merely represent congruent information on a number of separate dimensions.[2] Only when the information on one or more of the dimensions is novel, unexpected, or changed, or when the

---

[1] McGuire (1968) may not necessarily exclude dimensionality from his view of complexity theory. He has persuasively argued that consistency theories should take a more structural approach in the mapping of human cognitive systems, rather than emphasize the study of the consistency need in its own right.

[2] Maddi's (1968) variety motive includes the pursuit of novelty, unexpectedness, change, and complexity. One might persuasively argue that the first three produce

combination of informational dimensions or their relationships among each other are novel, unexpected, or changed, can complexity be said to produce incongruity. Because of the number of elements involved in complex information, occurrence of incongruity would certainly be more likely than it would be for simpler information.

Complexity, however, may provide the key mechanism through which Hunt's adaptation level system and his use of the Miller et al. (1960) TOTE system interaction can be explained. In fact, a complex multidimensional system would correspond much more easily with Hunt's motivational construct than with those of the early consistency theorists. If one considers only one item of information on one dimension, then there is no need to postulate an adaptation level. Both Osgood and Tannenbaum (and other early consistency theorists) and Hunt describe the reduction of some specific incongruity toward a zero level. For Osgood, that is the end of the operation, until new incongruity happens to appear in the environment. Hunt, however, suggests active incongruity search by the organism; his attention shifts to another different source of information that contains the "right" level of incongruity. *It appears unlikely that the organism could continue to reduce incongruity on the same dimension over and over again.* More likely, the attention shift would call forth (or focus on) a different dimension in the person's cognitive structure, particularly if it is necessary to continue to work on the same "object" in the environment. The more multidimensional[3] the organism is, and the more diverse the available information received from an object is, the more likely one can assume that Hunt's shift from currently congruous to still incongruous information would employ divergent dimensionality.

If one introduces individual differences in complexity, one might even suggest that more multidimensional individuals would be able to simultaneously hold several informational dimensions in mind, so that any decrease

---

modifications in the environment that are not familiar, or not expected, and consequently can be safely viewed as inducers of incongruity. Complexity, however, need not produce incongruity, even though one may call on it to produce variety. The only cogent argument that would indicate that complexity always produces incongruity might suggest that multidimensionality of information (as perceived) is itself incongruent (as viewed by Osgood and Tannenbaum) and consequently unpleasant, and would produce a motivation toward greater unidimensionality. This view would be in contradiction of theory and research on complexity, and would not permit the individual difference characteristics in preference for (and use of) the multidimensionality that complexity researchers of various bents have amply demonstrated. One might then suggest that complexity seeking may or may not be part of an incongruity oriented variety motive.

[3] Complexity as an individual difference variable is useful as an explanatory and predictive concept in this regard. However, there is no need to necessarily postulate individual differences in the service of a congruity–incongruity motivation theory.

in the incongruity along one dimension can result in equivalent increases in focus on dimensions that contain higher levels of incongruity. Implications of complexity theory for incongruity theory of this kind will be considered in a subsequent chapter.

Optimal Incongruity

Let us return to the theoretical structure proposed by Hunt. He states that motivation is based on an incongruity between current inputs into the organism and an established standard that exists in the organism. According to Hunt, that standard would either be learned *or* innately structured. Hunt does not specify which of the two might be more powerful or occur more frequently. Hunt also does not commit himself to a view about the motivational characteristics of his optimum. He proposes that approach or avoidance of incongruous stimuli is based on past experience with either arousal *or* incongruity, and refers the answer to these alternatives to future research. In other words, Hunt does not make clear whether he views his optimal incongruity mechanism as a molar or molecular motivational construct, and does not locate the origin of the mechanism. He refers to learning as resulting in potential changes in the adaptation level, and refers to centers in the CNS as basic to a need for information processing. However, is this a genetic mechanism inherent in the mammalian cortex? Is it learned, and consequently merely an epiphenomenon of another more basic (molecular) motivational system? Is it some specific combination of physiological motives and effects of the organism's past experience (learning)?

A number of propositions attempting to explain the kind of motivation that may account for optimal incongruity could be advanced. For instance, one could argue that organisms may seek an "optimal" incongruity because at that point emotional arousal is optimal. Hunt recognized this view but also cited evidence which indicated that emotional arousal has no effect on novelty (i.e., incongruity) seeking (Haywood & Hunt, 1963). Another view might be that organisms seek an "optimal" incongruity because at this point cognitive processes achieve either their maximal efficiency (as in Hebb or Leuba) or their maximal functional complexity. The latter position suggests that incongruity phenomena might be integrated via organismic complexity theory. For instance, in the views of Walker or of Schroder et al., optimal complexity would be maintained in part by "optimal" incongruity of information input and in part by optimal emotional arousal and congruent information input. In such a view, the amount of incongruity which is optimal would be a function of the current values of all other determinants of complexity. Although this view would comfortably account for the data of Streufert and Castore (1971) and Streufert, Driver, and Haun (1967) on information search (above) and would not be in disagreement with other experimental results, it would be hard put to account for much of the research that has been reported by consistency researchers. What appears to be needed is a theoretical structure that can account for (1) consistency seeking, (2) inconsistency seeking, including search for novelty, complexity, and all concepts contained in Maddi's variety motive, (3) the interaction between consistency and inconsistency seeking, (4) a molecular motivational basis (instead of, or in addition to, the molar motivational construct) for consistency-inconsistency seeking, (5) clarification of the process underlying the motivated behavior toward consistency-inconsistency (e.g., can the behavior be viewed as style or preference based), and (6) clarification of individual and cultural differences, if any, in congruity-incongruity motivation. Such a theory is proposed in this chapter. First, however, it seems necessary to return to the "consistency" concept.

CONSISTENCY THEORY RECONSIDERED: CONSISTENCY AS AN EXPANDED CONCEPT—A REDEFINITION

In Chapter 4 and in previous statements in the present chapter, we have spoken of consistency theory as a set of theoretical views with common predictions: the view that organisms prefer to manipulate information that is in disagreement with stored concepts for the purpose of decreasing the disagreement between information and frame of reference. We used the terms congruence and incongruence to describe the degrees of departure in information received by the organism from stored information. *We shall, at this point, propose differential definitions of congruity and consistency.*

Congruity-Incongruity Defined

It may be useful to initially repeat our view of congruity-incongruity. Congruity occurs when the information received by an organism does not in any way depart from his frame of reference for that information. The information contains zero novelty and (in Osgood and Tannenbaum's terms) permits utter simplicity of storage. Incongruence occurs when information received by an organism is in disagreement with one or more stored concepts of the organism and requires manipulation of the information or of the stored concepts or both before congruence can occur. These definitions do not differ substantially from the views of Osgood and Tannenbaum.

Consistency-Inconsistency Defined

Now turn to the concepts of "consistency" and "inconsistency." It is rather difficult to find a definition of these terms in the psychological literature. The concepts were extensively discussed by McGuire, and we shall look to his writings for some insight into the meaning of the *terms aside* from their operational definition in volumes of psychological res. .n. McGuire (1968) writes that consistency theory has a classic Apollonian view: It regards the organism as oriented toward the familiar and toward the confirmation of the expected. That would leave us to ask: and what does the organism expect? What is he familiar with? Does he indeed expect complete congruity? Hunt, Maddi, and Driver and Streufert would probably deny such an expectation, and even Berlyne might disagree with that notion. For that matter, McGuire (1968) suggests that a dynamic equilibrium between variety needs and congruity needs is not only conceivable, but is frequently indicated by data and can be seen to have evolutionary survival value. It appears that an organism that expects complete congruity in his environment may be as poorly adapted to the world as an organism that expects complete chaos.

Most psychologists, when asked what consistency is, would answer: what consistency researchers do. Consistency researchers use a "tour de force," or, as McGuire puts it, they depict man in situations of rather "deadly serious-ness." Most research by experimenters seeking to obtain responses from subjects that can be viewed as incongruity reduction tends to place subjects into situations of rather high levels of incongruity and makes sure that subjects are clearly aware of the incongruity. If one wants to demonstrate the validity of the theoretical concept, that is precisely the ideal way to do it. Kiesler (1974) would say the experimenter assures that an arousal state in association with the incongruity is created. No man wants to live in a world that is extremely inconsistent with his expectations, in other words, a world that is chaotic or Kafkaesque. Consequently, the expected reduction of incongruity does occur. However, in other, more playful situations, novel and unexpected information appears to have the exact opposite effect on be-havior: Exposure to novelty produces more search for novelty, produces exploration, etc. These findings (see discussion of the work by Berlyne and Maddi in the previous chapter) are diametrically opposed to the classical formulation of consistency theory. Yet they need not be, if we accept an adaptation level concept of some kind.

One might suggest that adult organisms exposed to the environment within which they exist would consequently experience specific degrees of congruity and incongruity. How much congruity or incongruity is experienced would be a specific function of their characteristic environment and of their previous experience with their environment. When they become familiar with their environment, they will also become familiar with the typical incongruity levels inherent in their environment, and they will come to *expect* that level of incongruity. As McGuire suggests, such an equilibrium may well have survival value.[4] Too little incongruity and too much incongruity may well serve as danger signals, requiring action to restore the *consistency of the organism's expectations with his perceptions.* We propose that *consistency is achieved when the expected and familiar incongruity level is reached.*

Viewed in this fashion, the meaning of inconsistency is changed. *Inconsistency now refers to deviations from expectancy either in the direction of excessive incongruity or in the direction of excessive congruity.* Viewed in this fashion, the consistency motive can account for the wealth of data that have been collected by consistency theorists (all of whom have used highly incongruent relationships among informational and/or stored elements of cognition), and the data collected by those arguing for a variety (or a similar) motive. *Subsequent use of the term inconsistent in this book will consequently imply deviation of information from the expected in either an incongruent or a congruent direction.* The meanings of the terms incongruence and congruence are not changed.

Consistency and Congruity vs. Incongruity Seeking

Defining "consistency" as different from, and more inclusive than, such concepts as "congruity," "balance," and "consonance" resolves one problem discussed above. The reader may remember that the only way to integrate the two divergent uses of the term "incongruity" by Hunt and by Osgood and Tannenbaum would have required a dual motivational system which turned out to be of relatively little use. Proposing a single consistency motive that encompasses both congruity seeking and incongruity seeking, and their interaction via an adaptation level, seems a useful and parsimonious step since it eliminates the need for "dual" motivation systems and corresponding interpretations. Moreover, this view permits a clearer conceptualization (and operationalization) of individual differences in consistency motivation. Previous discussions of these differences have usually merely alluded to the existence of differences among individuals (e.g., Brehm & Cohen, 1962) but have rarely treated them theoretically or experimentally (e.g., Feather, 1967). Individual differences now merely need to be defined by the location of an adaptation level on a dimension running from very low to very high incongruity levels, i.e., by the specific points on the incongruity dimension

---

[4] McGuire, however, does view such an equilibrium as attended by considerable tension, which can be seen as testimony to his standard consistency position.

where consistency seeking behavior for the purpose of reducing vs. seeking incongruity is initiated.

The optimal adaptation level that must be proposed to take account of a modified consistency theory is necessarily divergent from the view proposed by Hunt. Other modifications, e.g., those that serve to integrate complexity theory and certain affect characteristics, require even more divergences. It appears useful at this point to introduce the theoretical structure underlying our views and to discuss its relationship to complexity, affect, and other concepts subsequently.

THE GENERAL INCONGRUITY ADAPTATION LEVEL (GIAL) HYPOTHESIS

To begin with, consider the idea of an adaptation level (AL) as it was developed by Helson (1959). Helson and others have shown how ALs develop among the many perceptual and evaluative concepts in what Pribram terms the posterior intrinsic sector of the brain (Chap. 4). Atkinson (1957) and others have demonstrated how levels of aspiration (which may be viewed as a type of AL) are developed in the frontal intrinsic sector. In both cases, past experience dictates current ALs.

Functions of the GIAL

In the operation of each specific AL (e.g., a light intensity AL), a feedback mechanism can be postulated in which any departures from the AL (i.e., any inconsistency) sets up a cognitive activation which persists until the stimulus input or the perception of that input matches the AL or the AL itself changes. This proposition differs from Hunt's use of the TOTE (Miller et al., 1960) system merely in the level to which incongruity is reduced. (Hunt postulates that *all* incongruity is removed for a specific incongruent input into the organism.) Normally, the stimulus or its perception is altered to fit the AL; however, when a non-AL stimulus value persists over time, alteration in the AL can be expected (see Helson, 1959). The brain can be viewed as possessing a very large number of specific ALs, each sensitized to detect a specific kind of inconsistency (i.e., deviation from an AL), for example, change in light intensities, the appearance of other organisms or divergent evaluative positions.

In each area where a specific AL occurs, the organism has experienced a particular overall amount of incongruity in the past. *One could hypothesize that organisms form expectations concerning the probable amount of incongruity they will encounter* in each area, based on their past experience with incongruity in that area. That quantity will, in the future, be perceived as consistent with expectation. However, it is a well-known tendency of mammalian brains to abstract and generalize. Therefore, one can hypothesize that *organisms could pool or average their experiences of incongruity in specific areas into a more global general incongruity experience.* By "general incongruity" is meant the total amount of novelty, ambiguity, surprise, imbalance, dissonance, disagreement, failure, conflict, etc. which an organism typically encounters, averaged over all specific ALs (SIALs).

Organisms could average their prior general incongruity experience over time and thus develop general expectations concerning the "normal" (consistent!) amount of general incongruity to expect in their environment. This expectation concerning general incongruity can be termed the General Incongruity Adaptation Level (GIAL).[5] Organisms with past experience rich in general incongruity would develop high GIALs, and those with relatively constant pasts would evolve low GIALs. Both would define points or ranges where the incongruity to which they may be exposed would be experienced as consistent.

The GIAL would define the optimal incongruity level for an organism. Like any other AL, *the GIAL would motivate cognitive activity whenever the general incongruity currently being experienced by the organism departs from the expected value, i.e., whenever inconsistency is experienced.* The GIAL would be the joint effect of all SIALs. Incongruity would be perceived through the incongruity mechanism of the specific adaptation levels. Reduction of incongruity operations and search for incongruent information to reattain the GIAL would operate via the cognitive or motor mechanisms served by the SIALs. For the sake of simplicity, the GIAL can, for the time being, be viewed as a point, a specific value of expected general summed or averaged incongruity, rather than as a range of expected values (this view will be modified somewhat later in this chapter). Thus, any departure from the GIAL value would excite some cognitive activity and only attainment of the GIAL would produce consistency and a consequent cessation of activity. It may be that the *amount* of cortical excitation varies in a linear or more complex fashion as inconsistency occurs in either direction from the GIAL, but this phenomenon of vigor of activation should be carefully distinguished from the fact of activation vs. quiescence.

When the functioning of the GIAL is considered in connection with the operation of specific ALs (such as the ALs monitoring light intensity or

---

[5] The use of the AL concept in this book is not exactly parallel to Helson's usage. Note in particular that the mathematical nature of the GIAL pooling mechanism might be better conceptualized as an arithmetic average rather than the geometric average. Experimentation should suggest the best quantitative formulation for the GIAL.

disagreement from other persons), a most interesting, dynamic motivational cycle can be described. In Hunt's view, each SIAL operates to reduce incongruity within its domain. If all cognitive mechanisms operated on this principle, cognitive activity should be reductionistic, i.e., tend toward a quiescent "total congruity" as a terminal condition. In the absence of new input, this state of terminal congruity should ultimately occur. However, with a GIAL in operation, the picture is altered. It is proposed that all specific incongruity adaptation levels (SIALs) sum (or average) to the GIAL. The general incongruity level (in reference to the GIAL) then would be the sum of all specific incongruity levels. The GIAL would operate via the inclusion of incongruity information (whether obtained from outside or from inside the organism) contained in all of the specific IALs. It would operate to restore the general adaptation level via increasing or decreasing incongruity with regard to specific information areas served by specific IALs.[6] Whenever the general incongruity over all SIALs (i.e., all perceptual dimensions, plans, concepts) is not consistent with the GIAL, cognitive activation should occur until general incongruity is consistent with the GIAL or until the GIAL is itself altered. This process would most likely occur via incongruity search or reduction for those incongruity level(s) that is (are) most discrepant from the SIAL(s).

When general incongruity is *less* than the GIAL, cognitive activation may take the form of an environmental exploration for more input or an internal search of stored concepts[7] in order to find new incongruities relevant to one or more SIALs where incongruity is currently particularly low. In other words, to attain consistency with the GIAL, *incongruity must be actively sought.* The incongruity-seeking operations raised by the GIAL may go still further. For instance, activity initiated by the GIAL might inhibit or halt congruity-seeking tendencies of specific ALs when general incongruity is below the GIAL optimum value. For example, an organism in a condition of suboptimal incongruity (i.e., boredom) might delay or halt completion of a task it normally would regularly finish; or such an organism might seek to prolong an argument over a matter it would usually try to settle quickly.

As long as the current general incongruity is above the GIAL value, cognitive activation would take the form of efforts to reduce incongruity, e.g., via relating divergent material to resolving problems, or possibly even via excluding incongruous material by devices such as escape, perceptual

---

[6] Singer (1966) has argued against adaptation level theories as merely "responsive" to environments but inactive within themselves. The view that the organism may search for incongruity internally eliminates that problem.

[7] An alternate interpretation of GIAL functioning would permit the GIAL to function as other ALs do: It may activate *nonspecific incongruity search* directly *without* necessarily operating via *search in specific (SIAL) areas.*

distortion, or "logic tight" compartmentalization. Furthermore, the GIAL in an "overload" condition might facilitate or enhance the normal tendency of specific ALs to attain greater congruity. For example, when general incongruity exceeds the GIAL value, a person's normal tendency to pressure others for conformity, or to seek quick answers to problems, might be intensified with an impetus from the GIAL mechanism. From these dynamic properties of the GIAL one can see that this concept is not a mere "tolerance for ambiguity" or "frustration tolerance" in a new guise. It is proposed as an *active*, cognitive process which maintains a certain expected level of general incongruity in a cognitive system.[8]

Development of the GIAL

Although the more normal result of an inconsistency between a current level of incongruity and the GIAL would produce motivation to restore consistency by returning the organism to the GIAL, a change in the GIAL itself (through repeated inconsistency) is possible. The GIAL is viewed as a product of past experience. Consequently, the GIAL may change as an organism's cumulative experience with incongruity changes. At present, only some tentative suggestions about the development of the GIAL can be presented. Initially, all incongruity experienced by a young organism would be inconsistent, since all incongruity (and probably all information) is unfamiliar. Continuous exposure to novelty would suggest that the young organism is living in a highly incongruent environment. In the process of inconsistency reduction, the organism organizes this complex environmental information into categories which allow for the formulation of primitive relationships. However, each new relationship and its associated stimuli would serve to increase the amount of incongruity even further. For instance, after the young child learns that a particular face means "father," he is suddenly faced with the fact that there are lots of fathers. Consequently, the GIAL should initially show a steady—possibly stepwise—rise toward some temporary maximum.

At some point, depending on the environment to which the organism is exposed, he might reach a plateau where the environment is now sufficiently predictable, and sufficient categories for sorting and organizing new information are given. Up to that point, inconsistency has been experienced only as an incongruity level beyond the GIAL. For the first time now the

[8] This view has implications for research designs: Some constant preexperimental exposure to the same environment would decrease variable error due to other GIAL modifiers during a preexperimental period. This method, however, would not serve to equate individual differences in GIAL which are based on much longer periods of exposure.

experienced level of incongruity might regularly fall below the GIAL, producing a new and different kind of inconsistency for the organism. To overcome this inconsistency, the young organism may now explore further the relationships and components inherent in his environment. The best known example for this "new" kind of search for consistency may be the incessant question "why?", a question which, at this stage of development, rarely produces more congruent relationships among objects. Rather, the question appears to facilitate the child's search for more incongruent (novel) information so that he can again achieve consistency with familiar expectations, i.e., in order to maintain his GIAL.

In these early years of an organism, the GIAL would be subject to somewhat radical shifts as the environment's incongruity varies. This is because the GIAL is based on relatively little experience as yet. However, due to the mechanism of averaging over time, a more stable GIAL value should gradually emerge, even in a widely varying environment. As an increased understanding of stimuli from the environment develops, and as variations in environmental stimulation and incongruity become less surprising and more expected, the GIAL is likely to stabilize at a sufficiently high level to allow the child to have a better and more reality based "understanding" of his world. As time passes, a change in the GIAL's value should require increasingly longer exposures to a deviant level of general incongruity to offset accumulating support for the current GIAL value. During this phase of resistance to change, the GIAL should primarily activate cognitions and behaviors that serve to attain the optimum (achieve consistency). As the period over which a deviant incongruity value must persist increases, the probability of its being altered by cognitive operations increases. A derivation from this view is that changes in the GIAL should become increasingly infrequent with advancing age. Individual differences in GIAL-determined motivation toward (AL) consistency should consequently become relatively stable and measurable (see below).

Individual Differences in Incongruity Adaptation

It is evident that GIALs can vary considerably between individuals as well as over time. A limiting case would be a GIAL whose value is set at or near complete congruity. This case could occur only in a very static, simple world and would closely approximate an organism for which all inconsistency activates only congruity-seeking tendencies (as Festinger originally postulated). For this organism, inconsistency (as defined in this chapter) would be equivalent to incongruity. But in more dynamic environments, the organism would come to expect some degree of incongruity and a more complex motivational cycle would likely emerge. This cycle consists of search for incongruent information to attain the GIAL, comparison, and, where possible, integration of that information with stored concepts, inconsistency reduction due to the departure of the incongruity now in the system from a specific or from the general adaptation level, and finally more information (incongruence) intake as soon as the GIAL or a relevant specific adaptation level sinks below the optimum. The pace and complexity of this cycle would be a function of the organism's specific GIAL value.

The incongruity adaptation levels may vary systematically with the centrality of plans or concepts involved. For example, one might expect or prefer rather high degrees of incongruity in more peripheral plans and concepts (peripheral SIALs) as compared with more central plans and concepts (central SIALs). This pattern might explain why in some task areas great uncertainty activates maximum activity while in others it has no such effect.

A preliminary objective paper-and-pencil measure of individual differences in GIAL has been developed by Driver and Streufert (1966). A midwestern sample of college students produced a sample mean of approximately 50 on a 100-point scale. A recent administration of the measure on the campus of one of the California state colleges produced a sample mean near 60, with a quite similar standard deviation as the midwestern sample had shown. (Standard deviations have generally varied between 10 and 15 on this measure.) Perhaps these differences in sample means indicate how persons with different incongruity experience produced by divergent geographic areas differ in their GIAL levels. Similar effects might be produced by changes in cultures over time.

The theoretical structure we have proposed makes rather simple and straightforward motivational assumptions, and, moreover, assumptions that are experimentally testable. We assume that to survive, a mammalian (and probably many simpler) species had to be able to adapt to various incongruity levels in its environment. By selection, the *potential* for an incongruity adaptation level would therefore be physiologically given. The degree to which a member of a given species uses his AL potential is, however, assumed to be primarily learned. Activation produced by the motive to restore the consistency with an adaptation level can produce learning about "to be expected" incongruity levels initially in very simple settings for the small child and later in much more complex settings for, let us say, an advanced graduate student. If tested *at their respective levels,* the graduate student with his much wider store of learned information should find it much more difficult to change his adaptation level than the small child. This theory, then, refers a molecular motivational construct to principles of activation and learning.

As a product of direct past experience (i.e., learning), with congruous and incongruous stimulation, the GIAL represents a style theory rather than a preference theory. (Preferences may emerge not only as a function of incongruity experience, but for many other reasons as well, e.g., communication with others about incongruity experiences, etc.) An organism may well attain a GIAL level at which he is not completely comfortable, since he might "prefer" less incongruity or more incongruity. Nearly everyone has experienced people who are bored, yet are unable to do anything to entertain themselves, or, vice versa, people who are overly excited and active and continue to wish that they could slow down. It may well be that McGuire's reference to the "tension" that occurs with a "dynamic equilibrium" refers to this phenomenon. We would suggest that the person has *learned* to expect a particular level of incongruity and, like it or not, is stuck with his equivalent GIAL for the time being, unless he is forced into an environment that he cannot modify to coincide with his GIAL.

Individual or cultural differences in the GIAL would be a function of the specific organism's past experience. A person who grows up in a culture or a family–school setting that provides little incongruity would come to expect little incongruity and, consequently, would develop a lower GIAL.[9] A person growing up in a very incongruent environment would expect high levels of incongruity and would develop a high GIAL. Cultural differences (e.g., across nations) would reflect average differences in the incongruity inherent in those cultures, their physical environments, their child-rearing techniques, etc.

THE GIAL AND AFFECT

The GIAL hypothesis can lead to a clearer position on the relationship between affect and optimal incongruity. It will be recalled that a problem, in Hunt's view, was that suboptimal incongruity was described as a source of both positive and negative affect. Taken in its simplest form, the GIAL hypothesis suggests one solution to this dilemma. The GIAL has so far been viewed as a general expectation, devoid of affect. This view suggests that affect arousal at optimal incongruity (i.e., the GIAL value) is equal to zero. As incongruity departs from the GIAL value in either direction (i.e., as inconsistency increases), either one of two patterns of affect arousal might occur (cf. Chap. 4): (a) an initial rise and fall of positive affect followed by increasing negative affect as distance from the GIAL increases; (b) a general increase in negative affect as distance from the GIAL increases (cf. Fromkin, 1970).

---

[9] The terms "high" and "low" incongruity are used in a general sense and do not refer to some specific measured level of incongruity. Obviously, absolute high or low levels cannot be specified in a purely theoretical statement. The development of incongruity measures is not yet sufficiently advanced to allow us to specify absolute values of incongruity.

Either of these patterns might prove viable under experimental analysis, but existing data suggest still a third pattern: that affect is *positive* rather than zero at the GIAL value and that it gets less positive and increasingly negative as distance from the GIAL increases. How does this model affect the GIAL hypothesis? It might suggest that the GIAL could possibly be conceived as a preference rather than as an expectancy. (One would assume that an organism would prefer positive over negative affect states.) However, such a change of conception of the GIAL is not essential since organisms might not consciously desire the GIAL and yet might react to its attainment with characteristic positive affect. One might also suggest that the consistency with expectations at the GIAL "feels better" to the organism, a view that would generally agree with the motivational implications of previous consistency theories (see Chap. 4). When asked, a person might merely state that he "prefers to feel good," a feeling that is obtained at the expected (consistent) incongruity level of the GIAL. The connections between affect and the GIAL, as well as the connections between the GIAL and cognition, are obviously quite diverse. Some of these issues will be broadened in detail below.

AFFECTIVE CONCOMITANTS OF INCONGRUITY MOTIVATION

We will consider what emotions are aroused by various states of incongruity. This problem is significant for a number of reasons. First, it is theoretically important to determine whether any regular causative pattern exists between cognitive incongruity and emotional states. At least one theorist (Tomkins, 1962) has proposed that informational states relating to degrees of incongruity may trigger various emotions. Any theory of affect arousal must consider what role incongruity states might play. Another reason for concern with the emotional concomitants of incongruity is the possible dependency of cognitive motives on affect arousal. It could be that cognitive motives cannot differentially energize behavior without affect arousal, but would merely serve a cue function—i.e., by directing the focus of effort toward more or less incongruity. Conversely, it could be that incongruity motivation would energize behavior and that this effect might be either amplified or diminished by concomitant emotion. Finally, incongruity motives may be entirely unaffected by what may be merely epiphenomenal emotional "side reactions."

In this section, several possible incongruity-affect models will be examined. These models should be viewed as suggestions for research hypotheses. It is also hoped that this discussion will stimulate a reexamination of existing data which may lead to reformulations of these models and consequently to better hypotheses.

Models of Berlyne and Hunt and Some Modifications

The degree and quality of emotion which accompanies and possibly amplifies or attenuates various degrees of incongruity are problems which have yet to be satisfactorily resolved. Experimental data on this topic are very scarce and theory tends to be somewhat ambiguous. Hunt's (1963) treatment of this area is exemplary; it is one of the first efforts to analytically explore the emotional "warmth" which may underlie so-called "cold" cognitive theories.

Hunt marshals enough data to indicate that both positive and negative emotions sometimes accompany incongruity (cf. also Kiesler, 1974). The assertion that information processing per se has intrinsic affect arousing capacity is quite challenging (see also Tomkins, 1962). Hunt's further use of affect data to postulate an optimal incongruity hypothesis also seems a useful step. However, when Hunt specifies a model describing how affect relates to optimal incongruity, some problems are encountered. Consider Hunt's adaptation of Berlyne's (1960) "arousal potential" model (Fig. 5.1). At this point, the term "arousal" need not be specified too closely. Arousal can be taken to mean positive or negative emotional and/or drive state. The critical features of this model (Fig. 5.1) are: (a) zero or near-zero affect (drive) at optimal incongruity; (b) no positive affect at all; and (c) increasing negative affect (drive) as distance from optimal incongruity increases.

The relationship of this model to Hunt's subsequent view of the matter presents some difficulty. Having presented the above model, Hunt states that an optimum of incongruity determines the division of pleasant approach from unpleasant withdrawal (pp. 79-80). In effect, Hunt seems to be reiterating Hebb's seminal view that up to a certain point, lack of correspondence between expectancy and perception may simply have a stimulating (or pleasurable) effect, beyond this point, a disruptive (or unpleasant) effect (p. 149, 1949). This second model is depicted in Figure 5.2. If we try to combine the models in Figures 5.1 and 5.2, the left-hand side (low incongruity) of the picture is unclear. The Berlyne-Hunt model suggests that low incongruity produces only increasingly negative boredom, whereas the Hebb-Hunt model argues for "positive approach" in suboptimal incongruity situations. Are we to assume that negative boredom affect arousal (Fig. 5.1) gradually overcomes or competes with the "positive approach" in Figure 5.2? The experimental data cited by Hunt support the Hebb view that the arousal of positive affect has to be included in any final model. Yet the data on boredom (e.g., Heron, Doane, & Scott, 1956) support the Berlyne view that extremely low incongruity arouses negative affect.

Possibly the apparent conflict can be resolved as shown in Figure 5.3.

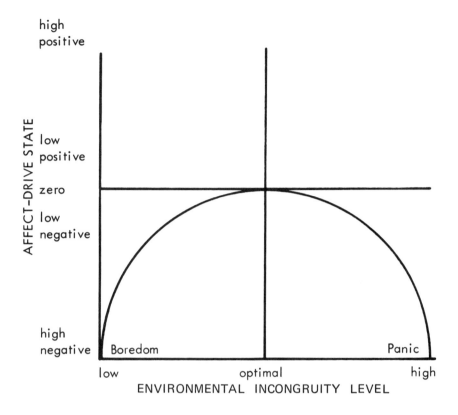

FIG. 5.1. Berlyne-Hunt model relating level of cognitive incongruity to affect-drive state (after Hunt with modifications).

Essentially, this model (Model 1) combines the dichotomous Hebb-Hunt view with the "all negative" Berlyne-Hunt model. It departs from the latter view in two ways: (a) A second (suboptimal) zero affect point is indicated (point "X" in Fig. 5.3); (b) affect does not universally become more negative as one departs from the optimal incongruity level, that level of incongruity which the individual is attempting to maintain. On this latter point, note in Figure 5.3 that as incongruity increases toward the optimum, positive affect at first increases, then decreases. This pattern is in accord with experimental data indicating that more incongruity is preferred to less incongruity, i.e., greater positive affect appears to be associated with increased incongruity [e.g., Butler's (1954) monkeys peeking more often at more complex scenes; Montgomery's (1952) rats preferring more novel goal boxes; and Hebb & Mahut's (1955) rats preferring longer, more incongruous routes to food].

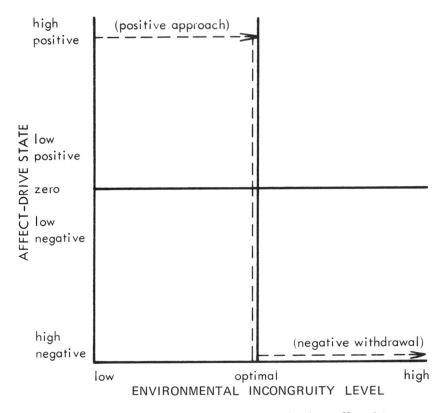

FIG. 5.2. Hebb-Hunt model relating incongruity level to affect-drive state.

After a consideration of Model 1, one might reasonably inquire why a particular direction of incongruity change, i.e., in the suboptimal direction, involves positive affect arousal, whereas in the superoptimal direction one finds only negative affect. Would it not be just as reasonable to postulate that *slight* superoptimal incongruity also arouses positive affect—i.e., a "challenge." In other words, could one not attribute to the incongruity optimum a "butterfly" model as described for specific concept adaptation levels by Haber (1958)? This model (Model 2) is presented in Figure 5.4.

Model 2 retains the Berlyne-Hunt idea that optimal incongruity is related to zero arousal and allows for a symmetric arousal of positive affect before plunging into negative arousal. However, Model 2 is also rather cumbersome and seems out of touch with actual events. For instance, Welker (1956) described a sequence in which chimpanzees at first display "fear" at very novel toys, then gradually show increasing "attraction" and "interest" climaxed by "intense fascination," and finally they show increasing "bore-dom." There appears to be no zero affect midpoint or butterfly pattern. Similarly, Hebb (1949) describes Chandler's early (1934) analyses of reactions to dissonant music. At first, such music is harsh and unpleasant, then it becomes quite pleasant as incongruity decreases, and finally, the music becomes dull and boring (Hebb, 1949, p. 233). These results seem to favor Model 1 over a butterfly view. However, these data also challenge Model 1.

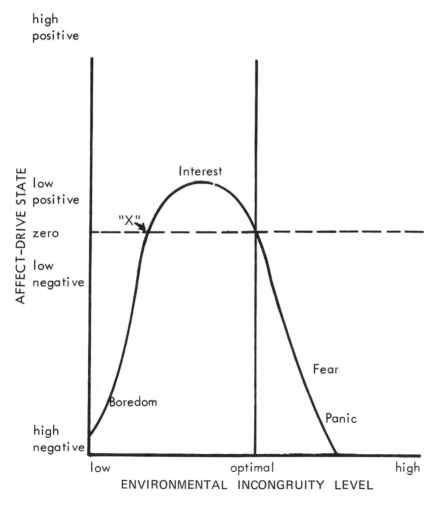

FIG. 5.3. Affect Model 1: A zero-affect optimal model of affect–drive states associated with incongruity levels.

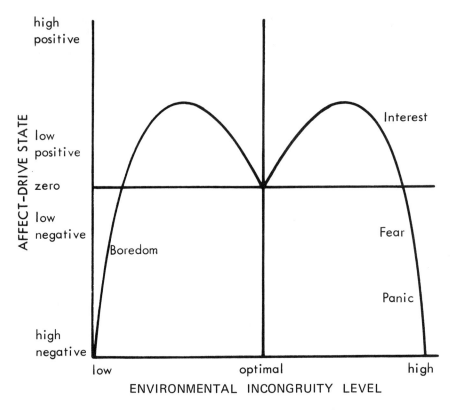

FIG. 5.4. Affect Model 2: A "butterfly" model of affect–drive states associated with incongruity levels.

One must ask how the positive affect peak of Model 1 is associated with optimal incongruity. Is it really at some point below the optimum? An alternative view is in Model 3 (shown in Fig. 5.5), which differs from Model 1 in Figure 5.3 by a simple shift of the incongruity optimum to the center of the positive affect arousal curve.

The Views of Tomkins, Some Problems, and Some Modifications

Model 3 possesses many interesting properties. It retains the Berlyne–Hunt idea that negative affect arousal occurs at extremes. It also retains the Berlyne–Hunt view that an approach to the optimum from either direction increases *relative* positiveness of the affect, while leaving the optimal decreases the relative positiveness of affect. The model also agrees with sequential data such as Welker's or Chandler's. In addition, the model corresponds in several ways with the very interesting and seminal affect theory presented by Tomkins (1962). Tomkins argues that the positive affect of interest accompanies any fairly moderate increase in the density of neural input from external and/or internal sources (i.e., any moderately incongruous input).

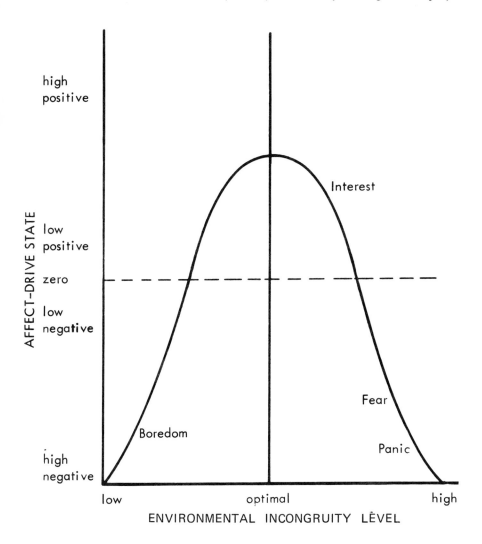

FIG. 5.5. Affect Model 3: A positive affect optimal model of affect–drive states associated with incongruity levels.

Tomkins also maintains that a more rapid increase in input produces fear. Finally, he postulates that very intense input can induce the total "freeze" of startle. The correspondence between Tomkins' view and Model 3 is not exact, since he maintains that rapid decreases in neural firing (i.e., attainment of congruity or recognition of stimuli) produces a positive increasing joy affect. This would not seem to accord with the totally negative boredom aspect of our models.[10] However, there are a number of ways in which this conflict might be theoretically resolved.

In one solution, a joy reaction can be inserted into the general affective reaction to incongruity. With the supposed change toward congruous input that (according to Tomkins) produces joy in the organism, joy may be aroused first, but if congruity persists, boredom might take over. Time, then, may affect the emotional response to constant stimulation: Too much of a good thing is not a good thing. This view attributes a rather complex and ambiguous affect reaction pattern to the optimum incongruity mechanism. Although there are no data that would contradict such a view, it appears to be somewhat unparsimonious.

Another way to include Tomkins' joy reaction is to theoretically allow it to occur only when the general incongruity level to which the organism is exposed is superoptimal. A congruent input in the realm of some specific incongruity adaptation level would reduce the general incongruity toward that required by GIAL (the summed effects of all adaptation levels). Although a joy-producing input in the realm of a *specific* adaptation level may be entirely congruent, it should also produce a relief effect by reducing *general* incongruity. Joy, then, may be relief (a sudden drop in a superoptimal general incongruity toward the GIAL). This argument would assume that joy cannot occur when the organism is bored, in other words, when total input incongruity is already suboptimal. An example might illustrate that point: For a child who has only one puzzle left to put together, the achievement of that last feat—when all parts suddenly fall together into the expected picture (congruence)—usually produces more negative affect ("Now what do I do?") than joy.

A third solution is to take another look at the concept of "joy" itself. Is it really produced by congruity? Probably both yes and no. Joy is usually associated with the *sudden* occurrence of the *familiar* (a decrease in neural firing), in other words with the unexpected occurrence of the expected. It may well be that an input that results in a joy reaction contains reestablished

---

[10]We will not deal with the problem of how incongruity is represented in the CNS via neural input. Certainly, both increases *and* decreases in neural firing could be incongruous. We will take the view of Tomkins "with a grain of salt," viewing—for the present purpose—his increases of input merely as increases in *incongruous* input.

congruence as well as remnant incongruence simultaneously, which may average at or near the general incongruity input level at or near the GIAL (and consequently produce positive affect). In support of this position, one may point to the short life of "joy" feelings: The positive affect produced by the change in input exists only as long as the surprise element lasts. Subsequently, the organism likely experiences boredom unless it finds new incongruence in the information input.

Finally, in departing from the view of Tomkins, one may argue that joy is not at all produced by changes in inputs that lead toward the completely congruent, but rather by information inputs that are "consistent"; in other words, inputs which contain information with incongruence levels at or near the person's GIAL or a specific incongruity AL. This argument is probably not different from the previous one that considers the combination of "surprise" and "familiarity" as long as the effect is produced by the GIAL mechanism; in other words, by the summed effects of incongruity inputs at all operative SIALs. If this argument were made for any SIAL, however, the mechanism would have to be different: The input would have to occur at or near the adaptation level itself. However, we argued earlier that the "familiar" is not necessarily congruent and that the organism learns to view both excessive incongruence *or* congruence as "unfamiliar" and "inconsistent." A joy reaction with its short-lived high levels of positive affect may well be adaptive if *familiar* levels of *in*congruity return; the organism can again orient itself (therefore "joy") but must quickly become able to handle expected incongruence levels, something he might find rather difficult to do were the positive affect of "joy" to remain with him for some time.

A further problem concerns changes in specific ALs or the GIAL itself. This problem may primarily be a question of the duration of an incongruity state, since in this model unacceptably incongruous input conditions initially produce corrective action plus some affective reaction; however, if the incongruity persists, the GIAL itself slowly changes and hence the basis for affect would change. For example, a situation which had been in a boredom range may gradually become interesting if the GIAL drops low enough under continuous pressure. Similarly, specific ALs may shift average expectations so that what had been incongruous is no longer so. Clearly, much research is needed in which both specific ALs, the GIAL, and affects are analyzed over varied time intervals.

Affect Models and the GIAL

While there are many problems inherent in the models presented above, several questions in particular deserve some attention. One is how these models affect the GIAL hypothesis. If one adopts Model 1 or 2 (Figs. 5.3

and 5.4), which postulate zero affect at optimum incongruity, it is possible to consider the GIAL a purely cognitive expectation level. However, if one prefers a model which attributes positive affect to the optimum, can an expectation interpretation of the GIAL be retained? Shouldn't the GIAL be classed as a form of preference or utility? This might empirically prove to be the case, but it need not be demanded on logical grounds alone. Complexity, novelty, or incongruity preferences, as measured in some paper-and-pencil test, might not relate linearly to physiological affect reactions. A person might not necessarily be aware of any preference in regard to incongruity, yet still display signs of positive affect arousal upon attainment of expected incongruity. An individual might even think he prefers more or less incongruity than the amount of incongruity which arouses maximum positive affect, as measured in experiments. Thus, these affect models do not preclude any particular interpretation of the GIAL and vice versa.

A second question can be briefly dealt with. Do the affect models imply that cognitive motives are really affect motives? The answer requires a closer examination of the pattern of cognitive motivation. If it can be shown that activation of cognitive operations is largely a function of incongruity and that any affects recruited only produce secondary perturbations in the general effect, then a cognitive flavor still remains uppermost.

Although Model 3 (Fig. 5.5) represents rather generally applicable first approximations to the affect problem, the ultimate shape of the solution must await detailed empirical analysis. Fortunately, the problem is very amenable to testing. One can construct laboratory tasks in which general and specific incongruity is varied systematically. In such environments, affect arousal coming from other sources can be minimized and arousal stemming from incongruity per se can be measured in several ways (e.g., physiological measures: heart rate, heart volume, respiration, etc.; plus introspective measures: self-report rating scales; or observational ratings of affect intensities in the conversation of groups).[11] Individual differences in GIALs and other relevant variables could also be analyzed through the use of preliminary tests. Such procedures could reveal whether the shape of the incongruity affect reaction is simply curvilinear (as in Figs. 5.3 or 5.5) or more complex (as in Fig. 5.4). However, even when the curve shape is known, the optimal point still requires identification. Affects will not serve as criteria because the same basic curve could support an optimal zero-affect model (Fig. 5.3) and an optimal positive affect model (Fig. 5.5).

What is required is some *extrinsic* criterion for optimal incongruity. One

---

[11] Both physiological and introspective measures may be simultaneously necessary to overcome some of the so far undecipherable similarities of physiological responses to diverse affects.

solution would be to utilize the subjects' stated GIAL as measured by a standard test. The GIAL could be located on the incongruity axis of a graph and affect reactions plotted on the ordinate, as incongruity is experimentally modified over a range on either side of the GIAL. With this approach, one would expect the GIAL to correspond either to the point of maximal positive arousal (Fig. 5.5) or to a point of zero affect (Fig. 5.4). This solution is somewhat unsatisfactory, since it deals with subjective estimates of GIAL and affect arousal only. It does not directly touch the heart of the entire problem—cognitive activation. While any departure from congruity may activate cognition, one may ask when this activation is maximal. Another view is that the optimal incongruity point is likely reached when the subject is not motivated to perform any cognitive behavior (either search or incongruity reduction).[12] The relation between cognitive functioning and incongruity will be considered in more detail below, but before leaving affect, one final point requires explanation.

This discussion has only dealt with affect that is directly produced by information processing activities of the brain. However, as was noted by Hunt for specific ALs, there are times when drive and affect are aroused by the positive or negative nature of input—i.e., the content as opposed to the incongruity of input. Information concerning a food deficit or threat is likely to arouse strong negative affect, whether congruent or not. An example of this is Van Ostrand's (1960) finding that devaluation of self by others results in negative affect whether congruent with self-perception or not.

Harvey and Clapp (1965) have confirmed the finding that negative evaluations of a person, although congruent with his views, can produce negative affect. However, some caution must attend these results since Deutsch and Solomon (1959) obtained the opposite results: Incongruent positive evaluations were not well received while congruent negative evaluations were. The "positivity effect" and the "congruence effect" are hardly in agreement with each other. These contradictory findings well illustrate the potential value of the GIAL concept. It may be that Harvey and Clapp's subjects had either (a) a higher average GIAL than Deutsch and Solomon's subjects, or (b) experienced too little incongruity relative to their GIAL just before the experiment, whereas Deutsch and Solomon's subjects may have experienced an overload of incongruity before entering the experiment. These points suggest that experiments on incongruity response should, if possible, control for GIAL *and* particularly for comparability of incongruity in experience just prior to experiments.

Still another point concerns the specific AL or concept in any study. It is

---

[12] As will be seen below, this argument may hold more for specific incongruity adaptation levels, but not for the GIAL.

of crucial importance to determine just what frame of reference a subject will use. For instance, in self-concept studies, it is unclear whether self-relevant input is incongruous with one's "actual self-concept," one's "ideal self-concept," or one's concept of what others should tell one. For instance, an input incongruous with an "ideal self" may be congruous with "actual self" concept. Thus, it is not sufficient to assume that an input is incongruous. All relevant specific ALs should be assessed and the input's subjective relationship to each AL—as well as its "overall" incongruity—should be determined, if clear tests of the role of incongruity in affect arousal are to be achieved.

While these remarks raise some issues concerning current empirical tests of the affective response to incongruity, they should not obscure the primary point that incongruity is not likely to be the sole cause of emotional response in man. Total affect is probably a function of both content and incongruity of input. Where content is largely neutral or incongruity is very salient, one of the incongruity recruited affect models described above should illustrate the affect aroused. When content is laden with positive or negative import or incongruity is not salient, genetically-based or learned affect reactions to input content may largely determine affect arousal and direction.

SOME SPECULATIONS ABOUT RELATIONSHIPS BETWEEN THE GIAL AND INFORMATION SEARCH

The last sections have attempted to present a theory of cognitive motivation designed to integrate several opposing viewpoints. As an integrative theory, the GIAL must cope with all of the theoretical concepts and the research findings with which these concepts have dealt. For instance, the GIAL theory modified the definition of the term "consistency" and, as such, must demonstrate that, in the long run, an organism's expectation (or at least its preference) is for incongruity at some level beyond the zero point if the theory is to remain viable. Similarly, the theory will have to deal with the sticky problem of affect, a problem that one might rather ignore because of the limiting measurement difficulties. In the next section, an attempt is made to relate the GIAL theory to some of the concepts that have been encountered by previous theories and that have provided problems which many of these approaches found difficult or impossible to deal with in their entirety. A number of alternate ways in which these concepts may be integrated with (or related to) GIAL theory will be presented.

Information Search Behavior:
Cognitive Theory

An optimal incongruity mechanism may affect cognition in at least two ways: (a) It may energize specific cognitive functions, such as external information seeking or introspective analyses; (b) it may affect the operation of more general cognitive structures, i.e., the intensity of general motivation toward "balance" or the degree of integrative complexity in information processing systems.

Many theorists have stressed largely the former aspect. Specifically, they have sought to relate the degree of information search to an optimal incongruity concept. Perhaps the simplest model relating search activity to incongruity is the linear pattern depicted in Figure 5.6. The idea is that as

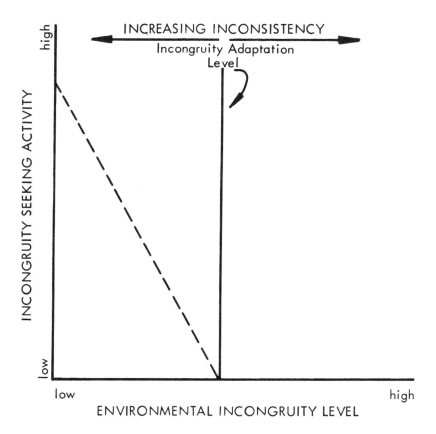

FIG. 5.6. A linear model relating search for incongruity to incongruity provided by the present environment.

incongruity increases, search decreases. The optimal incongruity concept can be introduced by postulating that the incongruity level—at which search ceases—be defined as the incongruity adaptation point (as shown in Fig. 5.6).

A possible objection to this model lies in the claim that activity appears to be maximally motivated as one departs in *either* direction from the GIAL. For instance, some kind of information search activity has been demonstrated at moderately high levels of incongruity (Streufert & Castore, 1971). This objection can be dealt with by considering another aspect of the GIAL. The GIAL is defined as the point of transition between incongruity increasing activity and incongruity decreasing activity. The search referred to above is considered to serve an incongruity increasing function. However, as Festinger and others have pointed out, some forms of search behavior serve an incongruity reduction function. To illustrate, a person may request information that is likely to decrease incongruity (e.g., make sense out of confusion) or he may even search for somewhat incongruous information in order to resolve a still more incongruous problem. We will call this kind of incongruity-reducing search *"cloze search" activity* as opposed to *"complex search" activity,* which is designed to increase incongruity.

With these concepts in mind, a V-shaped model can now be presented (Fig. 5.7). This "V" model postulates that search decreases as one goes from congruity toward the incongruity adaptation level, and that cloze behavior increases as one goes to even higher levels of incongruity. The "V" model, however, runs into some further objections, which stem from known empirical findings regarding search, from affect-optimal incongruity models, and from other theories of cognitive functioning.

Consider the empirical problems first. Some data on group search (e.g., Streufert, Suedfeld, & Driver, 1965) show a simple linear decline in search behavior which might support a V-type model. However, there may be some doubt about the applicability of their design to the present concern with incongruity. Other data suggest a pattern which is exactly the inverse of the "V" model. One of the search patterns reported by Streufert et al. (1967) and by Streufert and Castore (1971) shows a curvilinear *inverted* V shape. Lanzetta (1963) reported an even more pronounced inverted V in human group search behavior. Using a different realm of information and information search (exploration rather than task oriented search), Chandler (1934) suggested that a piece of "dissonant" music is at first disliked, then sought and liked as it gets more familiar, and finally avoided as boring. Welker (1961) reports a similar curvilinear pattern of avoidance, then increasing manipulation, then bored apathy in the reactions of chimpanzees to novel stimuli.

These kinds of data, even though based on quite divergent orientations toward arriving information, cast doubt on the "V" model at it is stated above. However, there is one way of reconciling the data with this model. One

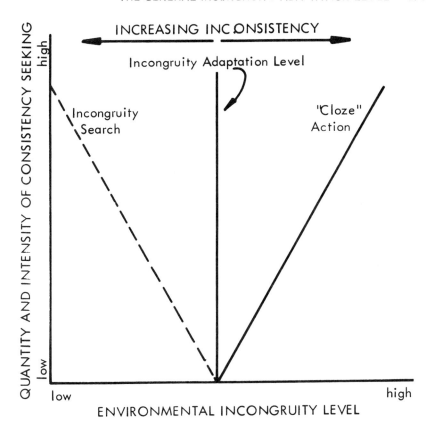

FIG. 5.7. The "V" model relating consistency seeking activity to incongruity provided by the present environment.

can postulate that any novel or incongruous stimulus induces a *specific response sequence*: On first encounter, the organism retreats from an object that is *highly* inconsistent with previously established concepts or ALs, in many cases even in tasks where one is supposed to be open to information (resulting in the "I just don't believe that" response). If the object later does not turn out to be, or ceases to be, too incongruous—i.e., relative to the relevant specific incongruity adaptation level (SIAL) for that class of objects and relative to the GIAL—then brief tentative exposures to the object may be made for the purpose of identifying it, i.e., for the purpose of reducing incongruity (decreasing inconsistency). If these efforts achieve any success, then the organism should increase this cloze type search very rapidly in order to eliminate any other uncertainties (inconsistencies) concerning the object.

Once the object presents no more excessive incongruity, the cloze action should decrease and the organism may ignore the object. This sequence would account for the pattern in the Chandler and Welker data.

The "V" model relating GIAL and search could operate with respect to this specific response sequence as follows. If the *general* state of incongruity is below the GIAL, there are two effects:

(a) The amount of cloze search relevant to a specific AL is amplified by search in service of incongruity arousal; the organism explores the highly incongruent object both to reduce incongruity in the particular concept involved and to increase general incongruity in service of the GIAL. This amplification may also result in a prolongation of search.

(b) The threshold for initiating search is lowered, i.e., stimuli which normally are so novel or incongruous that the organism usually avoids them totally now trigger the specific search sequence described above. This last GIAL state may, of course, be produced intentionally by the organism to permit exploration of, or response to, a specific highly incongruent event.

If the general level of incongruity is higher than the GIAL, the cloze search operation may be speeded up and intensified, and the threshold for initiating search may be raised—i.e., stimuli which normally evoke a specific search sequence would now produce avoidance. If the general incongruity is at or very near the GIAL, the "normal" specific cloze search sequence should occur as originally described above. Such a view would suggest that search should increase as incongruity decreases beyond the GIAL toward very low incongruity, while cloze action should increase from the GIAL toward high incongruity, as one would expect from the "V" model.

This reconciliation of the "V" model with other data, however, does not agree with the experimental results obtained by Lanzetta and by Streufert et al. Yet we cannot be entirely certain whether incongruity was indeed increased in these experiments with experimentally-induced changes in the complexity or quantity of information input. More appropriate to the concern we have here is the work of Streufert and Castore (1971), who held information quantity constant and exposed subjects to varying degrees of failure for a task in which failure was not expected. In other words, failure beyond an expected (acceptable) level could have been viewed as "incongruent" by the subjects.[13] Streufert and Castore found that subject-

---

[13] Nearly all subjects indeed expressed surprise and dismay at the failure information in post-experimental interviews. On rating scales that subjects completed periodically throughout the experiments, they continued to indicate lower expectations of failure than the levels of failure that they subsequently experienced.

initiated information search increased toward a maximum as failure increased (and as incongruity of the information received by the subjects increased), and that information search decreased when failure (incongruity) was increased further. These data then suggest that an inverse V relationship might be found, a relationship that also occurred in the data of Lanzetta and Streufert et al. (experiments which were earlier suggested not to be applicable but which appear more relevant once the data of Streufert and Castore are considered). How can one reconcile these findings with the "V" theory?

A closer look at the Streufert and Castore results suggests that the information search decisions which their subjects made consisted primarily or entirely of "cloze" actions. If it is true that the information received by the subjects became increasingly inconsistent with increasing failure (in this case inconsistency is produced by incongruity), then the first part of the data obtained by Streufert and Castore would be theoretically expected, but why would information search show a rapid decrease under conditions of incongruity levels that might be highly above the GIAL?

Other theorists, particularly those who are commonly known as consistency theorists, have already pointed out that information search in the service of greater (hoped for) congruity occurs only on some occasions, and that other "incongruity-reducing" mechanisms occur much more regularly. Particularly if one views dissonance experiments which McGuire said depict man in situations of deadly seriousness, there seems to be little evidence of *any* kind of information search, no matter whether in the service of a congruity motive or what Maddi has called a "variety" motive. One may then porpose that even "cloze" type information search reaches limits, once the environmental incongruity that is experienced by an organism exceeds its GIAL by a great amount. This kind of "super-incongruent" situation would much more likely produce behaviors that result in immediate reduction of incongruity toward the adaptation level, for instance, escape and/or distortion behavior. This kind of view is represented in Figures 5.8 and 5.9. Figure 5.8 illustrates this effect for a specific incongruity adaptation level relevant to a particular concept. If we assume that more than one specific incongruity adaptation level is operative simultaneously, then one may assume some amount of overlap of their incongruity-inducing and decreasing functions, producing both search *and* cloze action at both sides of (but near) the GIAL (cf. Fig. 5.9). Such a formulation would serve to explain continued activity at the GIAL, and permit some amount of specific (although summed) effects of specific incongruity ALs.[14]

---

[14] As indicated earlier, another view might suggest that the GIAL could have a direct access to activation without necessarily operating through seeking or reducing incongruity in areas served by specific IALs. Whether such a view would provide a useful alternative remains to be determined by future research.

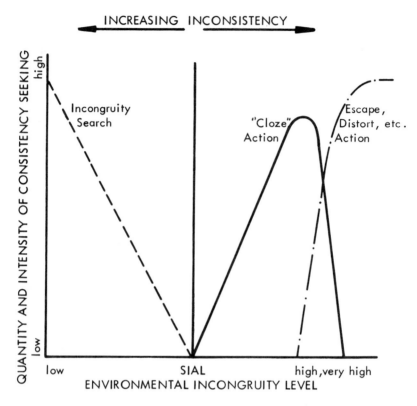

FIG. 5.8. A modified "V" model for a specific incongruity adaptation level, relating incongruity increasing (i.e., search) activity and incongruity decreasing (i.e., cloze and escape) activity to the incongruity provided by the present environment.

Information Search Behavior: Affect Theory

A consideration of most affect-incongruity models also suggests a need for search models that are more complex than a simple "V" theory. For instance, the Hebb–Hunt affect model which postulates "positive approach" up to the optimal incongruity point and avoidance thereafter, is not in accord with the simple "V" model. It is hard to reconcile *decreased* search as one approaches the GIAL in the "V" model with Hebb and Hunt's "positive approach" near the optimal; it is also hard to fit active cloze behavior with the negative withdrawal feature of the Hebb–Hunt model. For the other previously

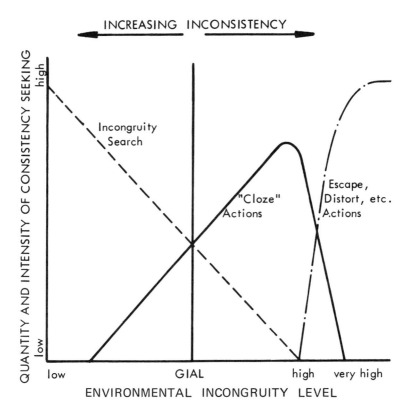

FIG. 5.9. A modified "V" model for the general incongruity adaptation level.

(Please note: The curve shapes in Figures 5.8 and 5.9 are not meant to be theoretically binding. The figures were drawn to demonstrate the authors' conceptualizations about the interrelationships among the "kinds" of activity that are represented. Whether the curves should best be represented as straight lines or whether they will turn out to be curvilinear remains to be investigated. Similarly, it is not known whether points of intersection of the curves with each other and with the GIAL are correctly represented.)

discussed affect models, there are even more serious discrepancies. All of these models imply increasing fear and panic with increasing incongruity beyond the optimum. Panic and calculated cloze-type search seem unlikely in one person at the same time. The affect models all specify intense boredom at extremely low general incongruity levels. As suggested by Welker's data, boredom likely is not related to *any* search activity, even the specific cloze search sequence. We don't mean to imply, however, that bored people do not perform some behaviors aimed at reducing that state. Yet, it seems unlikely that boredom produced by low general incongruity should generate intense search. Finally, many of the affect models postulate a zone of positive affect at or near the GIAL, which may suggest that increased cognitive activity should (according to those models) be found at or near the GIAL.

These considerations suggest an inverse V search model (Fig. 5.10). This model would agree with considerable data and with several affect models; but it seems to contradict our original definition of the GIAL as a transition area[15] between search and cloze action. The "inverted V" model also assumes correspondence between GIAL and the positive affect incongruity optimum, which may not always occur. Ultimately, only data will resolve these problems; however, further consideration of the issues may lead to some tentative convergence between these opposing models. First, note that the inverse V model only concerns search which arouses incongruity, not cloze action. If one adds increasing cloze action to the pattern proposed by the "inverted V" model (Fig. 5.10) and accepts our previous formulation of escape behavior, then the modified view (Fig. 5.9) merely fails to account for potential low levels of search under conditions of very low environmental incongruity levels. We shall add (below) a relevant function explaining that behavior.

One can carry the convergences among the various models even further. It can be argued that the GIAL is not a passive mechanism, even when the general incongruity matches the GIAL. In fact, it may be reasonable to suggest that the organism attempts to maintain the GIAL (within a region of positive affect) through constant search, either within the organism's environment or within the organism itself. Hence, even when the GIAL is

---

[15] In previous discussion, the GIAL has been defined as a point rather than as an area of transition. The "point" theory certainly should hold for any specific adaptation level; however, as indicated via the discrepancy between Figs. 5.8 and 5.9, the GIAL should display the interaction of several specific ALs, some of which are producing "cloze" action while others are producing search action under normal circumstances. The GIAL "point" should then lie within a range of transition from generally more cloze to generally more search action (with decreasing environmental incongruity), or within a range of transition from greater search action to greater cloze action (with increasing environmental incongruity).

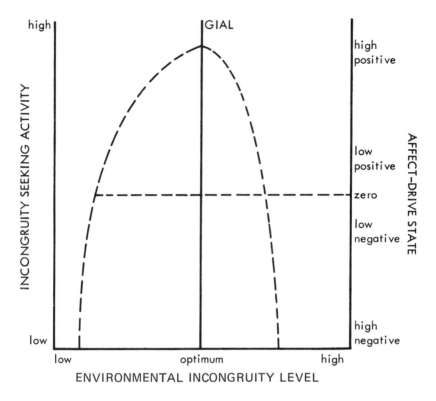

FIG. 5.10. An "inverted V" model relating the incongruity provided by the present environment to incongruity search and affect-drive state.

attained, one might expect that a maintenance search pattern would remain in operation. [This proposition would also overcome the criticism that Singer (1966) has leveled at adaptation level formulations: In this case, the organism is not merely a respondent puppet of its environment.] The pattern we have just proposed may be viewed in Figure 5.9 as the area of joint action for search and cloze activity, produced by the simultaneous operation of several specific incongruity adaptation levels. Such a formulation would greatly decrease the discrepancy between the various incongruity-search models and the GIAL model of consistency we have proposed.

The major remaining difference among the models concerns the pattern of search on the low incongruity side of the GIAL. The "V" model as well as the adaptation of that model proposed in Figure 5.9 call for increased search; the "inverted V" model calls for decreased search as incongruity decreases. To integrate these models and to tie them into the "boredom" formulations of other theorists, one might propose a mechanism that operates similarly to the "escape" mechanism shown in Figure 5.9, yet a mechanism that would function on the opposite side of the environmental incongruity level. For instance, one might distinguish between different kinds of "search" activity: simple search and complex search. Complex search may be defined as search originating from self-initiated behavior, resulting from the integration of many sources (and potentially dimensions) of information. Such search, of course, would only be possible as long as some amount of complex and/or incongruent information (environmental and/or stored) is available. Simple search would depend on external guidance and might involve very little integration of diverse information. Further, simple search may imply no directed *activity* at all (at most, some form of openness to information); rather, it may be viewed as a boredom-produced dependence on external information. As such, environmental incongruity levels where simple search would be the primary mechanism would be as aversive (negative affect producing) as incongruity levels that would primarily produce escape actions. Where simple search activity would be associated with boredom, escape activity would be associated with fear. By increasing or decreasing the information search and/or cloze activities of specific incongruity adaptation levels, the GIAL would attempt to maintain incongruity within positive affect areas (as close to the GIAL as possible).

Streufert et al. and Streufert and Castore have reported research that investigates both simple and complex search activity. While their data support an "inverted V" formulation for what we are now calling complex search behavior, their data for simple search (not corrected for social desirability) show that search decreases or remains relatively constant with increasing incongruous failure information or information quantity. One may assume that a correction for social desirability would produce an even more striking decrease in simple search with increasing incongruity. This proposition is included in Figure 5.11. This figure accounts for the divergent views presented by most or all of the theoretical and data-based statements discussed above.

This view still does not deal with possible discrepancies between a "preferred" incongruity adaptation level and an actual (stylistic) GIAL for any particular person. There is some tentative evidence suggesting that the two may not always be the same for all persons. The curves presented here would have to be made even more complicated to account for such differences. For the moment, however, we shall avoid complicating things even further.

THE GIAL AND EXPERIMENTAL PREDICTIONS

Some of the theoretical hypotheses we have advanced, as well as some of the curve forms and intersections in Figure 5.11, may be summarized in a

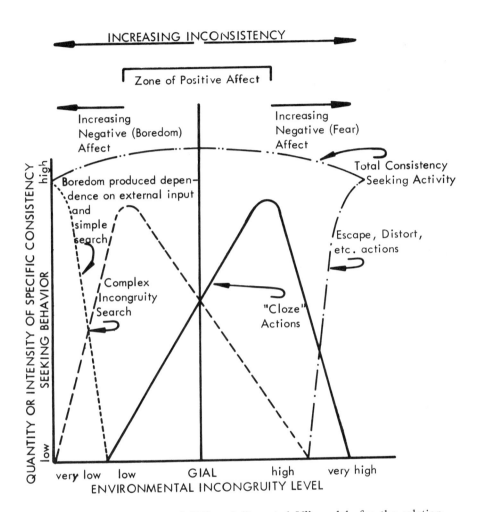

FIG. 5.11. An integration of "V" and "inverted V" models for the relationship between the incongruity provided by the present environment and consistency seeking.

number of statements that invite experimental testing. Although one may always argue that it is yet "too soon" to make hard and fast predictions, we believe it is of value to stick "one's theoretical neck" out somewhat, particularly if one hopes to learn where an initial theory may require revisions and additions. Researchers are invited to help us improve the theory or, for that matter, to find whether the theory should be supported or rejected as a whole. The statements below are not necessarily all of the hypotheses that may be derived from GIAL theory; for instance, they include concepts such as information avoidance only by implication. Yet they probably represent the major hypotheses that can be advanced.

Development

5.1 On the average, a person's GIAL should show a decelerating growth rate over the years of his development from infant to adult.

5.2 Persons in settings (e.g., jobs) that contain more incongruity should, on the average, possess—or should, on the average, develop—higher GIALs than persons in situations containing less incongruity.

5.3 Cultures containing more incongruity should, on the average, produce higher GIALs in their members than cultures containing less incongruity.

Personality Effects

5.4 Persons with high GIALs who are exposed to environments varying within average incongruity ranges should engage in more complex search activity than persons with low GIALs. Similarly, they should spend more time and/or effort on complex search activity.

5.5 Persons with high GIALs who are exposed to environments varying within average incongruity ranges should engage in less cloze type search activity than persons with low GIALs. Similarly, they should spend less time and/or effort on cloze search activity.

5.6 Persons with high GIALs should show simple search (including boredom and disinterest) sooner and escape and distortion actions later than persons with low GIALs.

Environment Effects

5.7 Highly incongruent (relevant to a person's GIAL) environments should produce activity directed toward the reduction of incongruence as usually described by the early consistency theories, including considerable escape activities, distortion of information, etc., but including less information search of any kind.

5.8 Moderately incongruent (relevant to a person's GIAL) environments should produce activity directed toward the reduction of incongruence as usually described by previous consistency theories, including considerable cloze type information search but including less distortion and escape activities, and including less complex information search.

5.9 Environments with incongruence levels at or near a person's GIAL should produce relatively similar amounts of cloze and complex information search activities, with these activities potentially governed by divergent SIALs. Little or no distortion-escape activities or simple search activities should occur.

5.10 Moderately congruent (relevant to a person's GIAL) environments should produce activity directed toward the increase of incongruence, similar to activities described by variety theory, including considerable complex search activity but including less simple or cloze search activity.

5.11 Highly congruent (relevant to a person's GIAL) environments should produce some openness to the increase of incongruence, including simple search and dependence on environmental stimulation but including less complex search or cloze search activities.

Interaction of Adaptation Levels

5.12 Specific incongruity adaptation levels (SIALs) should sum or average (in an, as yet, unspecified way) to produce a value for the GIAL. Under conditions of low general incongruity, certain SIALs may be maintained at superoptimally high levels and vice versa.

Affect

5.13 Environmental conditions at or near a person's GIAL should be associated with positive affect; conditions some distance from the GIAL on either side should be associated with negative affect. Very high levels of superoptimal incongruity should induce reactions of fear, panic, etc., while very high levels of suboptimal congruity should induce reactions of boredom, lack of interest, etc.

5.14 Increases in superoptimal incongruity within the negative affect range and increases in suboptimal congruity within the negative affect range should produce increases in negative affect.

Exploration and Search for Congruence

5.15 Objects and events that are moderately congruent should be explored primarily to provide novel incongruous stimulation. Objects and events that, in an organism's experience, have failed to provide information leading to greater incongruity (e.g., novelty) should be disregarded, particularly when the organism's current incongruity input is suboptimal.

5.16 Objects and events that are moderately incongruent should be explored primarily to provide cloze type information. Moderately incongruent objects and events that in the organism's experience have failed to provide cloze information leading to greater congruity (e.g., events that remain somewhat chaotic in spite of repeated cloze attempts of the organism) should be disregarded, particularly when the organism's current incongruity input is superoptimal.

5.17 Objects and events that are highly congruent should be generally disregarded, and should be explored only when the organism receives information that points toward potential incongruity in the object or event.

5.18 Objects and events that are highly incongruent should be generally avoided and/or distorted. They should be explored only when an organism is able to decrease its other current environmental incongruity inputs (via achieving low suboptimal levels on several SIALs, i.e., increasing his security) to a point where the SIAL concerned with the highly incongruent object or event adds to the current values of other SIALs to produce a normal GIAL.

REFERENCES

Abelson, R. P., Aronson, E., McGuire, W. J., Newcomb, T. M., Rosenberg, M. J., & Tannenbaum, P. H. *Theories of cognitive consistency: A sourcebook.* Chicago: Rand McNally, 1968.

Atkinson, J. W. Motivational determinants of risk taking behavior. *Psychological Review,* 1957, **64**, 359–372.

Barron, F. Complexity–simplicity as a personality dimension. *Journal of Abnormal and Social Psychology,* 1953, **48**, 163–172.

Berlyne, D. E. *Conflict, arousal, and curiosity.* New York: McGraw-Hill, 1960.

Brehm, J. W., & Cohen, A. R. *Explorations in cognitive dissonance.* New York: Wiley, 1962.

Butler, R. A. Incentive conditions which influence visual exploration motivation. *Journal of Experimental Psychology,* 1954, **48**, 19–23.

Chandler, A. R. *Beauty and human nature.* New York: Appleton-Century, 1934.

Deutsch, M., & Solomon, L. Reactions to evaluation by others as influenced by self-evaluations. *Sociometry,* 1959, **22**, 93–112.

Driver, M. J., & Streufert, S. *The general incongruity adaptation level (GIAL) hypothesis: An analysis and integration of cognitive approaches to motivation* (Institute Paper 114). Lafayette, Ind. Institute for Research in the Bahavioral, Economic and Management Sciences, Purdue University, 1965.

Driver, M. J., & Streufert, S. *The general incongruity adaptation level (GIAL) hypothesis: II. Incongruity motivation in relation to affect, cognition, and activation-arousal theory* (Institute Paper 148). Lafayette, Ind.: Institute for Research in the Behavioral, Economic and Management Sciences, Purdue University, 1966 (a).

Driver, M. J., & Streufert, S. *An objective measure of the general incongruity adaptation level.* Lafayette, Ind.: Purdue University (mimeo, copyrighted), 1966 (b).

Feather, N. T. An expectancy value model of information-seeking behavior. *Psychological Review,* 1967, **74**, 342-360.

Fromkin, H. L. *Feelings of interpersonal undistinctiveness: An unpleasant affective state* (Institute Paper 262). Lafayette, Ind.: Purdue University, Krannert School of Industrial Administration, 1970.

Haber, R. N. Discrepancy from adaptation level as a source of affect. *Journal of Experimental Psychology,* 1958, **56**, 370-375.

Harvey, O. J., & Clapp, W. Hope, expectancy and reaction to the unexpected. *Journal of Personality and Social Psychology,* 1965, **2**, 45-52.

Haywood, H. C., & Hunt, J. McV. Effects of epinephrine on novelty preference and arousal. *Journal of Abnormal and Social Psychology,* 1963, **67**, 206-213.

Hebb, D. O. *The organization of behavior.* New York: Wiley, 1949.

Hebb, D. O., & Mahut, H. Motivation et récherche du changement perceptif chez le rat et chez l'homme. *Journal de Psychologie Normale et Pathologique,* 1955, **48**, 209-220.

Helson, H. Adaptation level theory. In S. Koch (Ed.), *Psychology: A study of a science* (Vol. 1). New York: McGraw-Hill, 1959.

Heron, W., Doane, B., & Scott, T. H. Visual disturbance after prolonged perceptual isolation. *Canadian Journal of Psychology,* 1956, **10**, 13-18.

Hunt, J. McV. Motivation inherent in information processing and action. In O. J. Harvey (Ed.), *Motivation and social interaction: Cognitive determinants.* New York: Ronald Press, 1963.

Kiesler, C. A. *A motivational theory of stimulus incongruity with application for such phenomena as dissonance and self-attribution.* Paper presented at the convention of the American Psychological Association, New Orleans, 1974.

Lanzetta, J. T. Information acquisition in decision making. In O. J. Harvey (Ed.), *Motivation and social interaction: Cognitive determinants.* New York: Ronald Press, 1963.

Maddi, S. R. The pursuit of consistency and variety. In R. P. Abelson, E. Aronson, W. J. McGuire, T. M. Newcomb, M. J. Rosenberg, & P. H. Tannenbaum (Eds.), *Theories of cognitive consistency: A sourcebook.* Chicago: Rand McNally, 1968.

McGuire, W. J. Résumé and response from the consistency theory viewpoint. In R. P. Abelson, E. Aronson, W. J. McGuire, T. M. Newcomb, M. J. Rosenberg, & P. H. Tannenbaum (Eds.), *Theories of cognitive consistency: A sourcebook.* Chicago: Rand McNally, 1968.

Miller, G. A., Galanter, D., & Pribram, K. H. *Plans and the structure of behavior.* New York: Holt, 1960.

Montgomery, K. C. A test of two explanations of spontaneous alternation. *Journal of Comparative and Physiological Psychology,* 1952, **45**, 287-293.

Osgood, C. E., & Tannenbaum, P. H. The principle of congruity in the prediction of attitude change. *Psychological Review,* 1955, **62**, 42-55.

Scott, W. A. Cognitive complexity and cognitive flexibility. *Sociometry,* 1962, **25**, 405-414.

Scott, W. A. Cognitive complexity and cognitive balance. *Sociometry,* 1963, **26**, 66-74. (a)

Scott, W. A. Conceptualizing and measuring structural properties of cognition. In O. J. Harvey (Ed.), *Motivation and social interaction.* New York: Ronald Press, 1963. (b)

Scott, W. A. Structure of natural cognitions. *Journal of Personality and Social Psychology,* 1969, **12**, 261-278.

Singer, J. E. Motivation for consistency. In S. Feldman, (Ed.), *Cognitive consistency.* New York: Academic Press, 1966.

Streufert, S. Complexity and complex decision making. *Journal of Experimental Social Psychology,* 1970, **6**, 494-509.

Streufert, S., & Castore, C. H. Information search and the effects of failure: A test of complexity theory. *Journal of Experimental Social Psychology,* 1971, **7**, 125-143.

Streufert, S., Driver, M. J., & Haun, K. H. Components of response rate in complex decision making. *Journal of Experimental Social Psychology,* 1967, **3**, 286-295.

Streufert, S., Suedfeld, P., & Driver, M. J. Conceptual structure, information search and information utilization. *Journal of Personality and Social Psychology,* 1965, **2**, 736-740.

Tannenbaum, P. H. The congruity principle: Retrospective reflections and recent research. In R. P. Abelson, E. Aronson, W. J. McGuire, T. Newcomb, M. Rosenberg, & P. H. Tannenbaum (Eds.), *Theories of cognitive consistency: A sourcebook.* Chicago: Rand McNally, 1968.

Tomkins, S. S. *Affect–imagery–consciousness* (Vol. 1). New York: Springer, 1962.

Van Ostrand, D. *Reactions to positive and negative information about the self as a function of certain personality characteristics of the recipient.* Unpublished master's thesis, University of Colorado, 1960.

Welker, W. I. Effects of age and experience on play and exploration of young chimpanzees. *Journal of Comparative and Physiological Psychology,* 1956, **49**, 223-226.

Welker, W. I. An analysis of exploratory and play behavior in animals. In D. W. Fiske & S. Maddi (Eds.), *Functions of varied experience.* Homewood, Ill.: Dorsey Press, 1961.

CHAPTER 6

ATTITUDES, SOCIAL INFLUENCE AND INTERPERSONAL ATTRACTION[1]

Written in cooperation with Howard L. Fromkin

ATTITUDES

To most researchers who have not delved deeply into the literature, attitudes are the prime example of unidimensional concepts. After all, attitudes are typically measured on a single dimension, often the semantic differential scale good–bad, or an equivalent Likert scale. How one feels— favorably or unfavorably—toward an object, an event, or a person appears to the content of *the* evaluative dimension. And, if attitudes were only content, they should be of relatively little interest to those of us who are concerned with multidimensionality of human perception and performance.

But is attitude indeed unidimensional? And does it—even if there were no need for dividing attitudes into dimensional component scales—operate by itself to produce behavior in complex real-world situations? Or is it necessary

[1] Much of the material presented in the social influence section of this chapter was presented previously in somewhat different form by Streufert and Fromkin (1972). The material has been updated and extended.

207

to consider the attitudinal dimension (if there is *one*) in interaction with other dimensions when behavior outside of the lab is to be predicted?

We need not review the concept of attitude, as we have done for "complexity" and for "cognitive motivation," since there are excellent reviews in the literature (e.g., Kiesler & Munson, 1975; McGuire, 1969). Instead we will at once deal with the dimensionality of attitudes.

Are Attitudes Multidimensional?

Following the suggestions of philosophers, psychologists have—rather early in the development of their science—considered attitudes from three vantage points. They believed that attitudes could have cognitive, affective, and conative components. The *cognitive* component of the attitude involved the trait perception of the observed object, event, or person: how one views it, what stereotypes one has toward it. If one were to describe the object "rationally," one would probably describe it in a cognitive fashion. Again we can speak of "cold cognition." In other words, emotions are not likely to come into play.

Another component of attitudes is *affective*. Here we are concerned with the *feelings* toward the object of the attitude. The response is primarily an emotional one, often associated with some level of physiological arousal.

The third component of attitudes is *conative*. Does the attitude we have measured by some cognitive or affective measure result in action toward the object of the attitude? If it does, a conative component is involved.[2]

There have been many psychologists who have argued that the distinctions made by these three terms are valuable (e.g., Brown, 1965; Campbell, 1947; Kretch & Crutchfield, 1948; Kretch, Crutchfield, & Ballachey, 1962; Secord & Backman, 1964). Experimental attempts to demonstrate the validity or lack of validity of the distinction have often utilized a manipulation which has attempted to transform all three components onto the same scale, a procedure which might well have produced methodological artifacts (Campbell & Fiske, 1959). These results do not widely support the existence of three separate attitude components (Campbell, 1947; Kahn, 1951). McGuire (1969) concludes, on the basis of this evidence, that it is up to those who argue for a multicomponent attitude view to demonstrate the necessity for this partition of the attitude concept. Kiesler and Munson (1973) also favor a single

---

[2] One might go one step further and distinguish here between intent to act and actual resultant behavior. The latter is certainly affected by a host of additional variables (environmental restrictions, group norms and pressures, reinforcement contingencies, etc.). We are aware of these effects but will—for the sake of saving space—not dwell on them here. Researchers should, however, consider these effects when using our predictions in experiments where conative measurement occurs.

attitudinal dimension, but, referring to the work of Bickman (1972), appear a little less certain.

It appears to us that the multicomponent view of attitudes is well founded. If cognitive, affective, and conative components were similar, they should correlate and produce identical behavior. However, considerable research has shown that the relationship between measured (usually affective) attitude and (conative) behavior is a rather fragile one (e.g., Festinger, 1964; LaPiere, 1934; Mann, 1959; Saenger & Gilbert, 1950). One particularly popular analysis of the distinction involved the means-ends approach to attitudes. Rosenberg (1956), for example, demonstrated that an attitude consists of (1) the valence of the goal to which the attitude is relevant (somewhat similar to cognition or affect) and (2) the object's perceived instrumentality (somewhat similar to the conative component) toward that goal. Attitudes can be changed by *either* experimentally inducing changes in instrumentality *or* by changes in goal valence (we will here not join in the extensive discussion about whether these components average or add into the final attitude). The work of Rosenberg (1956, 1960a, 1960b) is paralleled by the investigations and theoretical views of a number of others (e.g., Carlson, 1956; Cartwright, 1949; Di Vesta & Mervin, 1960; Peak, 1955, 1958; Smith, 1949; Smith, Bruner, & White, 1956; Walker & Heynes, 1962; Zajonc, 1960). Especially persuasive, however, is the theoretical and experimental work of Fishbein and associates (e.g., Ajzen & Fishbein, 1973; Anderson & Fishbein, 1965; Fishbein, 1963; Fishbein & Hunter, 1964; Fishbein & Raven, 1962), which has clearly demonstrated that one needs at least a measure of intent to get from the attitude (as measured on some evaluative scale) to actual behavior (cf. also Rokeach & Kliejumas, 1972; Rosen & Komorita, 1971; Sample & Warland, 1973; Weinstein, 1972; Wicker, 1971).

It is more difficult to demonstrate the distinction between the cognitive and evaluative components of attitudes. But the measurement techniques that have been typically used might make the difference between the processes in which people engage clearer. While cognitive attitudes are often measured by adjective check lists, affective components are measured by "good to bad" or "like to dislike" scales. They tend to tap different human processes.

Even *within* each of the three components of attitudes, things may not be as unidimensional as one might think. McGuire (1969), for example, suggests that the evaluative component of the attitude should be unidimensional (while the cognitive might be multidimensional). Yet the example of the liked/disliked prostitute mentioned in Chapter 1 might imply that even evaluative attitudes may consist of more than one (even if differentiated) underlying dimension. McGuire's suggestion that cognitive attitudes could well be multidimensional is gladly accepted.

In any case, however, it appears that the attitudes some people hold can be described with at least three separate dimensions, which themselves might be divisible into yet further dimensions. Kothandapani (1971), using a multitrait-multimethod approach, demonstrated the three components of feeling, belief, and action intention with two factor analytic techniques. Why, then, did some researchers (e.g., Campbell, 1947; Kahn, 1951) obtain high correlations among these supposed dimensional components? One possibility has already been mentioned: the methodological artifact in the analysis described by Campbell and Fiske (1959). But there is an even more intriguing possibility. The data analysis (obtained over groups of persons and not through separate analysis of individuals) might have resulted in a statistical artifact as well, produced by averaging across people of different dimensionalities.

Individual Differences in Dimensionality and Attitudes

If we take a number of persons who (typically) respond on an evaluative attitudinal component as *one* of their dimensions, and in addition hold different numbers (from none to many *diverse*) of attitudinal dimensions, then any correlational or factor analysis *across* these subjects will turn their divergent dimensionality into noise in the statistical analysis, unless the experimenter is able to tap dimensions of different content on one single measure. This is rarely done. As a result, only the common dimension will show up, and others, across persons, will be correlated with the first. For example, if all persons are able to respond meaningfully to dimension A, but only a small subset responds meaningfully (and orthogonally) to dimension B, yet another subset to C, another to D, ... to X, and if for the remaining subjects there is no difference between A and B, or A and C, ... A and X, then a correlational procedure across subjects will result in a correlation of A with B, C, D...X, even though they are orthogonal for certain groups of subjects. Quite likely the results obtained by Osgood, Suci, and Tannenbaum (1957) as well as the results obtained by Campbell (1947) and Kahn (1951) may have come about in this fashion.

It appears that some subjects indeed may have only a single unidimensional attitude in any cognitive domain, including both the cognitive and affective, in some cases even the conative component. Other subjects would likely be able to differentiate these component dimensions. Still others would differentiate and reintegrate them, depending on environmental constraints, current needs, received communications, etc. As McGuire suggests, at least the cognitive aspect of the attitude might well be multidimensional, allowing the integrator a wide range of different responses.

But let us return to our more unidimensional respondent for the moment. He should not only employ a unitary attitude concept, his concept should also be pervasive across a number of areas. If he indeed *responds,* as well as thinks and feels along the same single dimension, then it would be likely that he also attributes, achieves, risks, and generally lives according to that single dimension. One might expect that his responses on the attitude scale (if we want to view that scale as the basic description of a unidimensional person's psychological orientation, for the moment) should be paralleled on other measures relevant to another person, object, or event, regardless of what these measures are. For example, as demonstrated in the research of Streufert and Streufert (1969), if we place this person into a group which achieves some level of success, then as success increases, his attributions of causality for the success to the group should increase and his evaluative attitudes toward the group should increase in like fashion. Other similar examples are easily found.

We might then propose:

6.1 Attitudes toward an object, person, or event can consist of at least three dimensions, which may be described as a cognitive, an affective, and a conative attitudinal component.

6.2 The greatest underlying dimensionality (subdimensions of an integrated superordinate dimension) can be expected for the cognitive attitude, the least for the evaluative attitude. Nonetheless, particularly in situations of ambivalent feelings toward an object (or person, or event), the evaluative attitude may be subdivided into further (at least differentiated) dimensional components as well.

6.3 It should be possible to demonstrate by appropriate measurement that individuals who respond more multidimensionally in other cognitive domains should typically respond with more attitudinal subdimensions in any cognitive domain under consideration than persons who typically respond unidimensionally.

6.4 Persons who hold a more unidimensional attitude should respond in the same fashion when their attitudes, as well as when other response characteristics (e.g., attributions), are measured.

In other words, we propose that the more unidimensional respondent is not likely to "average" or "add" attitudinal components into a final response, but that his response is determined by some *single* phenomenon. He also should respond to single events. Suppose, our respondent has no previous information about object, person, or event A. If he received information that associates A with something he considers either "good" or "bad," he should rate A in the same fashion. If he receives contradictory information later, then he should not be likely to change his previously established attitude as expressed in the rating, unless the new information by itself holds greater salience than the previous information. Consequently, a series of informative statements which are contradictory to the previously established attitude—where each information is slightly less salient than the original information—should not change that attitude at all, or very little. In contrast, persons who integrate information (particularly flexible multidimensional integrators) should either average or add the information, so that each additional item of information (even if less salient) should have some effect on the resultant attitudinal response.

We may then propose:

6.5 Persons with more multidimensional characteristics will be simultaneously and sequentially affected by each item of information relevant to an attitude, and will average or add the information to produce a joint effect. Further, they will weigh the resultant attitude by time and space relevance to themselves (including utilities and disutilities).

6.6 Persons with more unidimensional characteristics will base their attitudes on the single most salient information regarding the attitude object, person, or event and will not be widely affected by additional information unless that information by itself (or its source) has greater salience to them than previous information (or sources). If greater salience is given, then the attitude will be re-formed to a match with the value of the novel information.

SOCIAL INFLUENCE

The potential effects of individual differences in complexity on social influence have been previously described by Streufert and Fromkin (1972). The discussion, at this point, will conform to the arguments presented there to a great extent. Following a general discussion of social influence, we will consider how sources, messages, and targets are matched or mismatched on dimensionality and point out the effects for communications. Finally, we will discuss some of the previous research in the area and point out relevant effects of complexity variables.

To obtain a social influence situation, we need a source of information, a message containing the information, and a receiver (a target) of the information. The purpose of the message is to influence the target: to change his attitudes or opinions, or to persuade him to act in some specific fashion. Most research on the message in the area of social influence has been primarily concerned with "what" is being communicated, i.e., the *content* of the communication. For example, if the message states that "Mercedes Benz is a very safe car," the source of the message most likely wants the target to consider purchasing a Mercedes Benz. However, in all but the most sterile laboratory situations, there are additional messages beyond the intended one. In this case, the additional messages may be that the source wants to sell a

Mercedes, or is looking for validation of his own beliefs by getting his friends to make the same decision he has already made, etc. Additional message components might be the personality of the source, communications about his status, his seriousness, demand characteristics of source and setting, and the like. In other words, the message is hardly a single stimulus; most likely it represents a complex of stimulus configurations. Moreover, the complex of stimuli can be potentially located by the receiving target on a number of dimensions which may relate to each other in oblique or orthogonal fashion. Of course, this dimensionality can produce problems for the experimenter. If parallel experiments are designed by two experimenters, and different results are obtained, the discrepancy may be caused by the particular set of dimensions that occurred in each experiment *in addition* to the intended message. In the real world, which is much more complex than the laboratory, it is highly unlikely that any message is limited to a unidimensional characteristic, and any social influence is by necessity potentially multi-dimensional (we must say potentially, since not all subjects might perceive the potential dimensional components). In the real world, the communicator may build his own dimensionality into the message. Here, then, is the exception to the statement we made in Chapter 3 that dimensionality is only a target characteristic and not inherent in the message (there, stimulus configuration).

The message (the stimulus) then sets the upper limit of the dimensionality with which the target might perceive the information he is receiving. Whether he does view the message in a multidimensional fashion, what this specific multidimensionality looks like, including how many dimensions are perceived, would depend on the target's capacity for multidimensionality and on situational constraints. If, for some reason (either due to his own limited capacity for multidimensional perception or due to stressful situational characteristics), he does perceive the message unidimensionally, then he may or may not select the *intended* communication dimension. Rather, he may pick any dimension from the set of potential message dimensions, probably the one which, through his own needs or through some communication effect, appears to be the most salient. If, of course, the received dimension differs from the intended dimension, miscommunication ensues. The degree to which communication is successful (identical perceived and intended dimension(s)) or unsuccessful (divergent perceived and intended dimension(s)) would depend on (1) the number of potential perceivable dimensions in the message, (2) internally- or externally-produced stimuli for the target which are perceived simultaneously with the message, (3) content of the receiver's current cognitive and affective state, including such things as his attitudes, his degree of openness, etc.; and (4) the degree of his capacity to perceive multi-dimensionally, specifically on the communicated dimension(s). The effect a message has on the receiver would be an effect of the interaction between these environmental, social, physical (physiological), and personality factors.

It would be impossible, even in the laboratory, but particularly in the real world, to "know" the effects of the physiological state of a target receiver of a message. Nonetheless, we can increase our predictive capacity of communication success if we learn more about some others of these factors. Particularly, an estimate of the target's capacity to perceive a message multidimensionally might be useful. Such an estimate would allow us to achieve a better "matching" of source and target.

Matching Source and Target with Message Dimensionality

In line with the theory stated in Chapter 3, we are viewing the dimensionality potentially inherent in a message (i.e., the intended dimensions which a source places into a message as communication to the target) as interacting with the dimensionality in the cognition of the target receiver of the message. The number of relevant dimensions in the target's *perceptual* area of complexity is here of greatest importance. If the message allows for (is intended for) only unidimensional perception, then of course it can only be perceived unidimensionally, unless the receiver "adds" dimensions from his own cognitions, and consequently distorts the message content. If the source presents a message that contains a number of dimensions, then it can be perceived unidimensionally (again distorted) by a target person who has only one perceptual dimension in the relevant cognitive domain available to him, and it may be perceived multidimensionally by a person who is able to employ the relevant perceptual dimensions. If the message is constructed by the source to contain more dimensions and information than can be absorbed by the dimensionality of the target person, then the perception of more unidimensionally as well as more multidimensionally[3] operating persons should be depressed and become more or less unidimensional (see Fig. 6.1).

When potentially perceivable message dimensionality is intermediate—or one might say optimal—the differences between persons at various levels of perceptual dimensionality should be most apparent. At this level, the individual with more multidimensional capacity would utilize more dimensions than his more unidimensional counterpart and at the same time would utilize more dimensions in his perception of the message than he himself would, if

---

[3] It could be argued that multidimensional persons might "maintain" a high level of dimensionality in message perception even if the dimensionality of the message is greatly increased. However, one must consider that we are dealing with a "single" message in which the interrelationships of all dimensions are important to allow comprehension of the message dimensionality. If this perceptual process is hindered, dimensionality of perception must necessarily decrease.

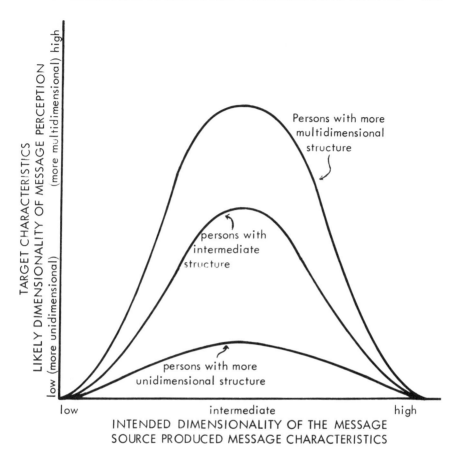

FIG. 6.1. Effects of intended message dimensionality and the target's dimensional structure on message perception.

message dimensionality were at a higher or lower level.

Research on information processing (Streufert, 1970) has suggested that interacting individuals and groups attempt to achieve message complexity levels which produce this "optimal" information processing. Particularly more multidimensional persons are not satisfied with receiving unidimensional information. They typically seek additional information by exploring their environment further to gain additional cues. Initially, the original source is likely approached with a request to provide further information. If this information is not forthcoming, or if the information does not allow for the desired multidimensionality of perception, they may continue to seek additional message sources to provide messages of the necessary dimensionality. Exactly the opposite process occurs when a more unidimensional person is the target of a multidimensional message. In this case, the message is either distorted by him to fit into his unidimensional perception, or the target person will (while rejecting the multidimensional person as "wishy-washy") look for a new source of information that would provide him with the desired unidimensional information. Often, multidimensional persons who are dissatisfied with the information they have received talk about "getting more points of view" on the subject. More unidimensional individuals, on the other hand, frequently state that they want "to find out the truth on the matter from someone who really knows." In other words, a unidimensional message is easily understood[4] and consequently can be easily accepted or easily rejected by the more unidimensional subject. A multidimensional message is not understood by him; it is distorted or rejected. On the other hand, a unidimensional message is typically understood but unsatisfying to the more multidimensional subject while a multidimensional message, assuming that the dimensionality is matching to his own, is typically well understood by him (see Fig. 6.2).

We have talked about the understanding or misunderstanding of messages. It should be made clear that "understanding" is not the same as "preference." Generally, one might propose that persons of similar structure would prefer to receive messages on more "involved" issues and subjects from each other, assuming they are currently exposed to similarly loading or incongruent environments, whether they agree with the content of the message or not.[5] In either case, it would be easier for them to handle the message content and to place it appropriately within their perceptual framework. Of course, in many instances communication consists of interaction between sources/targets of different dimensionality levels. In that case, one could assume that the intended content of the message of a more unidimensional source would be understood by both more unidimensional and more multidimensional targets, while the messages sent by more multidimensional sources (assuming they are

---

[4] When we speak about understanding or not understanding messages, we do not mean that the verbal content of the message is or is not understood. Such "understanding" would relate to the intelligence levels and not to complexity. Rather, we refer to the understanding of the source's placement of stimuli on the source's own dimensions by the target. If the target "understands" in this sense; he is able to (if temporarily) duplicate the dimensional structure and content placement on the source's dimensions (empathy).

[5] Of course, environmental demands or characteristics must be considered. For example, in an overloading emergency situation (e.g., a disaster) the unidimensional message from an expert would certainly be prefered to a multidimensional potentially "tentative" analysis of the situation, even by a multidimensional (but personally threatened) individual.

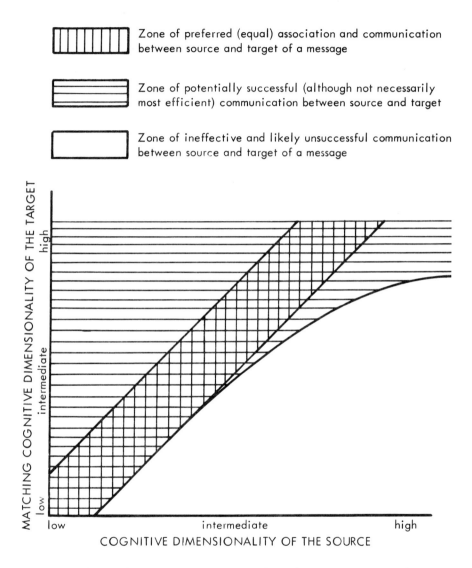

FIG. 6.2. Effects of the cognitive dimensionality of source and target of a message on the success of the communication.

intended to be multidimensional) can in their intent be understood only by more multidimensional targets.

Matching source and target to obtain "understandable" message characteristics merely aids in communication of the message. It does not necessarily provide the basis for effective or ineffective social influence. As shall be seen in the sections below, both message content and a number of structural effects must be considered if one intends to make specific influence predictions.

The Complexity of the Target and Social Influence

The success of the source in communicating to the target is, in good part, an effect of target characteristics *per se*. If one views the target from the standpoint of dimensionality, then its characteristics are even more important since it is the more unidimensional target that is unable to perceive a multidimensional message. We will view the target characteristics from three vantage points: (1) source effects on the target, (2) message effects on the target, and (3) target characteristics *per se*.

1. Source effects

A large amount of research on persuasion and attitude change has focused on change produced by differences in the message source. Most of the relevant literature can be subsumed under Kelman's (1958, 1961) analysis of source characteristics and the related dynamics of persuasive impact. According to Kelman's analysis, the persuasive impact of a message varies with three factors: (a) source credibility, (b) source attractiveness, and (c) source power. The changes in attitudes that are the result of these three classes of source characteristics are closely related to the psychological mechanisms of attitude change: internalization, identification, and compliance. When a person attempts to find a veridical position on some issue, then the attitude change in the direction which may be advocated by a credible source is viewed as "internalization." If a person is interested in making a positive impression on another, i.e., either initiate or maintain a favorable relationship, then the acceptance of the viewpoint advocated by an attractive source is viewed as "identification." The third mechanism ("compliance") involves the person's acceptance of the view which is advocated by a powerful source. In this case, he does not internally accept this position for himself, but espouses it externally. Let us first deal with credibility.

Hovland and associates (e.g., Hovland & Weiss, 1951; Kelman & Hovland, 1953) have been frequently cited as the first researchers on communicator credibility. They initially focused on the communicator's perceived expertise on an issue. For example, a world famous professor of international economics and trade would be a more "credible" communicator than a world famous professor of music on an issue such as "America should increase import duties." In the research of Hovland and Weiss (1951), college student subjects read excerpts from newspaper and magazine articles on a number of topics, such as the feasibility of an atomic powered submarine. The articles were experimentally attributed either to a highly credible source (e.g., a famous American nuclear physicist) or to sources which to the subjects (at that time) were low in credibility (e.g., the newspaper "Pravda.") The effect of the information was measured immediately and opinion change in the direction advocated by the message was greater for articles attributed to highly credible sources than for articles attributed to less credible sources. However, in later retests of the opinion change after a period of 4 weeks, there was almost no difference between the effect of the two sources. This result was produced through the decrease of attitude change produced by the high credible source toward the level that had been achieved by the low credible source.

In a study by Kelman and Hovland (1953), high school students listened to a tape recorded educational program presented by a speaker who was in favor of extreme leniency for juvenile delinquents. In the introduction statement before the program, the characteristics of the speaker were experimentally varied. In one case, it was stated that the speaker was a highly respected, honest, and well-informed judge, who had the public interest at heart. In the other case, the speaker was said to be of questionable character, and was chosen at random from the studio audience. In a third condition, a speaker was introduced as a person who had been chosen at random from the studio audience and no additional information was provided. The prerecorded speeches were, of course, identical and opinion change was measured immediately after the presentation of the speeches. It showed that the groups hearing the message presented by the credible positively evaluated source became more favorably disposed towards leniency than the groups receiving a message from a less credible negatively evaluated source. Groups who had been exposed to the neutral speaker responded more closely to the groups who had been introduced to a positive information source. Half of the subjects were presented 3 weeks later with the introduction used during the original program. The remaining subjects did not hear this introduction a second time. In the no reinstatement group, the difference in opinion between positive and negative source conditions had decreased considerably. However, if the introductions were replayed, the attitude change produced by the credible positively evaluated source and that produced by the negatively evaluated source remained relatively intact.

The decreasing effect of credibility, over time, that was found in the two studies we have discussed has been called the "sleeper effect" (cf. Cohen,

1964; Hovland, Janis, & Kelley, 1953) or the "discounting cue" effect (McGuire, 1969). These explanations suggest that high credibility produces two simultaneous effects. The first is an information effect due to the content of the message, i.e., the nature, number, and kind of the persuasive arguments. The second is the communicator effect. A highly credible and evaluatively positive source is presumed to increase the listener's desire to agree and to decrease the listener's desire to critically examine the information he has received. A less credible and evaluatively negative source is seen as decreasing the receiver's desire to agree and to increase the receiver's desire to critically examine the content of the information. As time passes, the memory of source characteristics diminishes, and the net effect of persuasion is that the value of the source itself loses its effect, no matter whether the value was positive or negative.

A number of criticisms have been leveled at this interpretation. It appears that a number of phenomena are interacting with the proposed cause of the sleeper effect. For example, the variations of source credibility in the two studies discussed above also include characteristics of communicator expertise (i.e., the communicator's knowledge of the facts about the issue) and characteristics of trustworthiness (i.e., his motivation for communicating the supposed facts in an unbiased manner) (cf. Hovland, Janis, & Kelley, 1953).

We agree that a number of phenomena (e.g., information discrepant from one's own position, source characteristics, trustworthiness of the communicator, intent of the communicator, credibility of the communicator) would have a joint effect on the attitudinal outcome. When a number of these factors produce high incongruity in the target of the communication, we would have to expect cloze activity, resulting more in "dissonance reduction" or other similar phenomena than in attitude change. When some of the incongruity over time has been resolved (through cloze activity) or forgotten, the effect would be the same as it occurred in the message involving less incongruity: Some attitude change is likely to occur.

Another group of studies have focused on the communicator's "intent to persuade" (cf. review by McGuire, 1966). Again, the results suggest several complications. It appears that communicator credibility is more than a simple phenomenon. A number of components may contribute to its effect. It is probable that these various components represent a number of independent dimensions (not to speak of the dimensionality inherent in the message characteristics that have arisen in this research area). For example, if one speaker is introduced as "having the public interest at heart" and a second speaker is merely introduced as "a person taken from the audience," then differences in the specific (and possibly the number of) dimensions applied by the audience to the situation will necessarily arise. We might add further that the prerecorded speeches which were used in these experiments were by no means controlled for dimensionality.

We have already stated that persons who operate primarily uni-dimensionally tend to respond to the salient stimuli in their environment. For that matter, their single or few dimension(s) *may* not even include very many shades of grey; they may produce bifurcated, good vs. bad, or correct vs. incorrect, or relevant vs. irrelevant judgments. As a result, we may propose that more unidimensional persons should respond either to the source of the message *or* to the message content, whichever happens to be more salient. They should not respond to both informative items unless both of them can be viewed as "identical." In other words, if a good source would originate a good message, response to both of them simultaneously would be possible. If the source of the message is most salient, then unidimensional persons should either agree with the message, assuming that they value the source positively, or they should disagree with the position advocated by the source, if they view the source negatively. They should do this without listening very carefully or without critically evaluating the content of the message. If that is so, then attitude measurement immediately following the message should result in a major effect, with considerable change in the direction advocated by the message when the source is positively evaluated and little or no change when it is negatively evaluated. If a disassociation of the source from the message content, or a fading recollection of the source itself, occurs with the passage of time, then a delayed retest of attitudes should produce lesser differences between positively and negatively valued sources, i.e., the sleeper effect. Alternatively, if (in the more rare case—see below) the message content is the most salient stimulus, more unidimensional subjects should not be more persuaded by positive sources than they are persuaded by negative sources, since the message content is identical in both situations. Furthermore, their response should not be changed over time.

More multidimensional persons tend to respond to several dimensions of stimulation simultaneously. They should also respond to various dimensions invoked by the source of the message and additional dimensions perceived by the target to be in the message. In other words, more multidimensional persons should evaluate and weigh *both* the source credibility and the dimensionality, i.e., the number and the content of dimensional arguments contained in the message. Further, although we might assume that the more multidimensional person would listen to and critically evaluate the message arguments, the persuasive impact of the message will be enhanced by its attribution to a positively valued source and diminished by attribution to a negatively valued source. Consequently, we would predict that the im-mediately tested persuasive impact of messages which are attributed to positive and negative sources will be at least the same as, or will be greater than, the difference which occurred for more unidimensional persons. To generate predictions about the effects of time-delayed measurement for more multidimensional persons, we will briefly consider the manner in which more multidimensional persons manipulate information (different from the mere "agreeing" or "disagreeing" response of more unidimensional persons).

More multidimensional persons should respond to information in at least three ways. First, they are likely to process information by placing it on the relevant dimensions present in the cognitive system (differentiation). Second, those who are multidimensional integrators would likely integrate the information with already stored information on relevant dimensions, potentially requiring some changes in their structural dimensionality. Third, the newly integrated information will be available for future integration with information received at a later time.

One characteristic of more multidimensional persons that has been observed in considerable research by Streufert and associates is that previously modified dimensions appear to produce increased openness to similar or relevant information for the area that is represented by these dimensions. Consequently, if a change in the multidimensional target is produced by a message, then the target is likely to be open to further message relevant information in the not too distant future. Given these arguments (and assuming that the message content, if examined, turns out to be veridical), the more multidimensional person might show further attitude change in the direction advocated by the source after some time delay. No change would be expected if no further information on the subject matter could be attained.

Everything else being equal, we might then propose:

6.6 More multidimensional persons should respond to a highly credible source with high opinion change. Given the opportunity to obtain additional corroborating information, the opinion change should remain constant or increase over time.

6.7 More multidimensional persons should respond to a low credible source with intermediate opinion change. With the opportunity to obtain additional corroborating information, the opinion change should increase over time.

6.8 More unidimensional persons should respond to a highly credible source with moderately high opinion change. The opinion change should decrease over time.

6.9 More unidimensional persons should respond to a low credible source with low opinion change. The opinion change should increase or remain stable over time.

We turn now to the second source factor, attractiveness. The target may find a source attractive for a number of reasons. Whatever these reasons may be, a positive attitude toward the source is likely to produce greater influence. On the other hand, a negative attitude should produce less social influence

(Berkowitz, 1957; Osgood & Tannenbaum, 1955). We would predict that the structural dimensionality of the target person should interact with source attractiveness in a similar fashion as it did with source credibility, to affect influence and attitudes. We would predict only slight to moderate differences between more unidimensional and more multidimensional persons when attitudes or influence are measured immediately after exposure to the usually unidimensional experimental situation. However, with time, the more multi-dimensional subject is likely to seek out additional dimensional information on the subject. Only when a number of additional dimensions are introduced would major differences between more unidimensional and more multi-dimensional persons be expected.

The predictions for effects of source power are somewhat more complex. A number of types of source power have been suggested in the psychological literature. Among these are coercive power (the ability of the source to punish the target if it refuses to accept the influence), reward power (the ability of the source to reward the target when the influence attempt is accepted), referent power (the ability of the source to present social rewards to the target), expert power (where the competence of the source in a task situation may aid the target in achieving a goal), and more (French & Raven, 1959). Considerable research has demonstrated that coercive, reward, and referent power do have strong effects, but that these effects are not always reliable (Berkowitz, 1962; Ring & Kelley, 1963; Solomon, 1964; Zander & Curtis, 1962; Zipf, 1960). Most likely, these various forms of power are producing specific unidimensional compliance which leaves little room for differences between unidimensional and multidimensional individuals. In some cases, reward power may be an exception. If a reward is more appropriate for more multidimensional persons, they may comply (but not internalize). If the reward is more appropriate (e.g., in dimensionality and possibly congruity) to more unidimensional persons, they may more likely comply (and internalize). A good example for this effect is the research of Suedfeld and Vernon (1966).

A somewhat different situation is produced by effects of expert power. An expert is a highly credible source of information: an authority source. We have already discussed the differential responses of more unidimensional and more multidimensional persons in response to a source of informational authority. Here, we are, however, dealing with a somewhat different kind of expertise. If a target of information is repeatedly exposed to messages from a source, he will sooner or later determine whether this information source is consistently accurate or whether it is consistently inaccurate. The research by Kennedy in the simulation of business and industrial games (SOBIG) laboratory at Princeton in the early '60s provides a good example. Kennedy exposed more unidimensional and more multidimensional subjects to four sources of predicted stock market quotations. One of the sources was consistently accurate, the others were inaccurate. More unidimensional subjects bought and sold their stocks on the simulated market entirely in line with the predictions made by the accurate source. More multidimensional subjects, on the other hand, who also discovered that only one source was accurate, were unwilling to rely on it extensively in more than the short run. They assumed that some element of truth should be contained in the remaining sources of information and attempted to combine (integrate) the predictions of two or more of the information sources in various ways. Since the information from three of the four sources was irrelevant to success in the simulated game, their efforts necessarily failed. The multidimensional approach to information put them at a disadvantage.

We might then predict that:

6.10 Differences between responses of more unidimensional and more multi-dimensional persons to coercive and referent powers are not expected. Different responses to reward power should occur only when rewards are specifically focused on the needs or preferences of more multidimensional vs. more unidimensional persons.

6.11 All other things being equal, more unidimensional subjects are more likely to place their trust in the single most salient expert, even if the information received from other experts also contains elements of truth. More multidimensional persons are more likely to place their trust in a number of experts, even if some of these experts are delivering messages which contain random information or are partially incorrect.

2. Message factors

In the discussion so far, we have been looking at characteristics of the source. We now turn to message characteristics. First of all, we will concern ourselves with a question that has been foremost in the discussion of communication engineers and their predecessors. One may ask whether it is more persuasive to allow an audience to draw its own conclusion, or whether one should make the desired conclusion explicit in a persuasion attempt. One experiment directly approached this question. Hovland and Mandell (1952) presented their subjects with messages on current economic issues. In one condition, the message began with simplified information on general economic principles followed by a description of the economic state of affairs (e.g., the precarious financial position of the United States of America). The provided principles and description of the economic situation produced an *unstated* logical conclusion (desirability or undesirability of devaluation of the American currency). In the second condition, this conclusion was explicity stated for the subjects. The finding of the Hovland and Mandell (1952) study, as well as a number of other studies (Cooper & Dinerman, 1951; Fine, 1957;

Hadley, 1953; Hovland, Lumsdaine, & Sheffield, 1949; Maier & Maier, 1957; McKeachie, 1954; Thistlewaite, deHaan, & Kamenetzky, 1955; Thistlewaite & Kamenetzky, 1955) indicated that the explicit statement had a greater persuasive impact. When the audience was left to draw its own conclusion, the effect was less strong.

A number of different explanations have been provided for this effect. Most of them argue that explicitly drawn conclusions should facilitate the audience's understanding of the message. In this view, the audience appears to be a passive receiver of the information. Members of the audience are either uninterested in drawing their own conclusion or are seen as less than sufficiently intelligent to come to the correct conclusion themselves. Therefore, when the conclusion is not contained in the message itself, the audience is viewed as "missing the point" (cf. McGuire, 1969, p. 209). On the other hand, indirect evidence would suggest that with the exception of the Hovland and Mandell (1952) study, when subjects are intelligent enough (Cooper & Dinerman, 1951; Thistlewaite, deHaan, & Kamenetzky, 1955), or are motivated enough (Marrow & French, 1945; Thistlewaite & Kamenetzky, 1955), or when the issues and arguments are familiar enough (cf. Cohen, 1964, p. 7), so that they can draw their own conclusions, then subjects who do draw their own conclusions appear to be more persuaded. One may find an intriguing extension of the ideas in McGuire's logical model of attitude organization (McGuire, 1960a, 1960b; cf. also Dillehay, Insko, & Smith, 1966).

It appears to us that the greater persuasive impact of conclusions which are drawn and presented explicitly would vary with the source characteristics, with the degree to which the issue is familiar and complex, and with the arguments, time factors, and individual differences that are present. One might also suggest that these variables will interact with each other to produce higher order interactions. Again, the multidimensional approach appears to become relevant. As suggested above, more unidimensional persons would likely search for the most salient information in their environment, so that they can identify the correct position on an issue.

It appears that certain *source* characteristics (e.g., credibility) and certain *message* characteristics may serve as the basis for selecting the salient attribute. A statement coming from a highly credible source is likely to produce opinion change with a fairly strong subsequent sleeper effect. As a rule, at least for highly valued sources, source salience might exceed message salience, even if message salience is present as well. But what would happen if information about a source is not given, i.e., when the source is unidentified or ambiguous? Here, the more unidimensional person would be unable to pick the salient cues from the source characteristic and would be forced to seek salience in the information presented in the message itself. He might find this difficult to do when a conclusion is not drawn for him. Complex information, if prepared by a more multidimensional source, is likely to be multi-dimensional and consequently too confusing. As a result, different more unidimensional persons would be likely to pick different cues from the information. Alternatively, more unidimensional persons may respond to extraneous cues in the message, which may be simpler to utilize, or they may turn the message off and not respond at all. As a result, one might expect that the message with implicit conclusions (unless the message is indeed unidimensional) which is presented without salient source characteristics would produce little or no opinion change in more unidimensional persons and, consequently, would also result in negligible sleeper effects.

In contrast to the more unidimensional person, the more multidimensional individuals are likely to respond to a number of components of the message. Where the source of the message remains unidentified or ambiguous, we may assume that the more multidimensional person would respond to each of the message components that he can accommodate in his structure. He would likely respond to these components to the same degree as or potentially even more than to the conclusion of the message. The conclusion, then, would not weigh as heavily as the sum of the message components presented. If we assume that the message components would be relevant and would be moderately compelling, then a message with an explicitly stated conclusion should have only a slight advantage, if any at all, over a message that does not draw any explicit conclusion. After some time delay, during which more multidimensional individuals might rehearse the information or might seek for or be open to additional information on the same topic, an increased effect of the message would again be expected, whether the conclusion was explicit or implicit. One might add that since a message with a stated conclusion contains, in effect, more information, it might maintain any advantage in terms of attitude change that it had immediately after the message was received by the target.

All else being equal, we might then conclude:

6.12 More multidimensional subjects who are exposed to a message with explicitly stated conclusions should show moderately high attitude change, given the opportunity to obtain additional corroborating information. The attitude change should remain constant or increase slightly over time.

6.13 More multidimensional subjects who are exposed to a message with an implicit conclusion should show moderate to moderately high attitude change, given the opportunity to obtain additional corroborating information. The attitude change should remain constant or increase slightly over time.

6.14 More unidimensional subjects who are exposed to a message with explicit conclusions should show moderately high attitude change. Due to a sleeper effect, this attitude change should decrease over time.

6.15 More unidimensional subjects who are exposed to a message with implicit conclusions should show little attitude change. Their attitudes should remain constant over time.

Another area in which much research has been presented is the effect of primacy over recency on attitude formation and attitude change. Here, we typically have two sources of social influence attempting to persuade the target to accept opposing points of view. In the experiment, subjects are presented first with one set of information about a person, object, or event, and then are presented with an opposing set of information. The question asked here is: Which will be more influential? Most researchers have obtained a primacy effect: The first message seems to produce more of an attitude change or a stronger attitude than the second message (e.g., Anderson, 1965; Anderson & Barrios, 1961; Asch, 1946; Luchins, 1957b; Stewart, 1965). This effect has been explained via learning theory (Hovland, Campbell, & Brock, 1957; Hovland & Mandell, 1957; Miller & Campbell, 1959) or via perceptual theory (Asch, 1946; Luchins, 1942). Based on these theoretical formulations, modified experiments have been designed which were able to produce the opposite effect: greater influence of the recent message (e.g., Anderson & Hubert, 1963; Luchins, 1957a; Stewart, 1965). All of these theories assume that either a primacy or a recency effect should occur. In most cases it has, although several experiments have shown a great deal of error variance. The multidimensional point of view is concerned with the explanation of this variance. It is presumed that more unidimensional subjects will again focus on the most salient attribute of the person, object, or event described; in other words, they will display either primacy effects or recency effects, depending on the manipulation characteristics of the experiment. On the other hand, more multidimensional subjects will tend to integrate the information from both messages, resulting in an intermediate or combined position between primacy and recency. Some experiments, e.g., Streufert and Driver (1967), have demonstrated these differences between more unidimensional and more multidimensional subjects. We are dealing with this phenomenon in greater detail on page 255 of the chapter on social perception.

Another area of interest has not been researched at all. We have already mentioned that the source might include its own dimensionality in the message, intending for those particular dimensions to be perceived by the target. As a result, sources of more multidimensional cognitive structure would potentially produce messages of greater multidimensionality than sources of more unidimensional cognitive structure. We need not again deal with the possibilities of mismatch or match between source and target via message characteristics. But, we may ask, when is a message likely to be most effective in producing attitude change?

Obviously, a message which matches source and target would have an advantage over a message that provides a mismatch. However, the relationship may not be quite that simple in all cases. The relationship may well hold—irrelevant of the content position of the message—for more multidimensional persons who are receiving a multidimensional message from a more multidimensional source. It may not hold for the equivalent information exchange among more unidimensional persons. Here, the content characteristics of the message would likely become important since additional dimensions on which (e.g., evaluative) discrepancies can be resolved are not available. Unless the target is currently below his GIAL, a message with a highly discrepant position on a single dimension would call forth cloze actions and produce the kind of rejection of the message (and the source) that has been observed in the boomerang effect (Hovland, Harvey, & Sherif, 1957) and in the work on latitude of rejection. On the other hand, the effected attitude change, if it occurs, is likely greater for more unidimensional targets than for more multidimensional targets, since integrative processes cannot diminish the intended effect of the message.

We might then state that:

6.16 Social influence is likely more effective for more multidimensional persons when source and target are matched via the dimensionality of the message.

6.17 If attitude change is produced by a message between matched source and target, that attitude change is likely greater when source, message, and target are unidimensional than when they are multidimensional.

6.18 Social influence between matched source and target with more unidimensional characteristics is likely effective only if the message content falls into the latitude of acceptance of the target.

3. Target characteristics

In the above discussions about the effects of source and message, we have (from time to time) spoken about dimensional differences within the target and their effects. Thus there is no need to return to an extensive discussion of these effects at this point. However, there is one area of target characteristics which has so far been omitted. Except for the work of Streufert and Fromkin (1972), complexity theorists have not dealt with dimensional effects on selective exposure.

The concept of selective exposure has been very important in the estimation of the effectiveness of mass communication (cf. Klapper, 1949, 1960) and has served as a core proposition of dissonance theory (Brehm & Cohen, 1962; Festinger, 1957, 1964). We all know now that voluntary exposure to information is highly selective. Apparently, people tend to seek out information which supports or reinforces previous beliefs and tend to avoid information that challenges their opinions (Freedman & Sears, 1965, p. 59). Two kinds of experimental methodology have been used to analyze the selective exposure principle. In free choice situations, subjects were selected on the basis of a previous action, for instance, the purchase of a new automobile (Ehrlich, Guttman, Schönbach, & Mills, 1957), or their belief in hereditary or environmental theories of child development (Adams, 1961), their preference among political candidates (Freedman & Sears, 1963), or their preference for a particular kind of examination (Mills, Aronson, & Robinson, 1959; Rosen, 1961). In the experiment, the subject was given a choice of exposing himself to literature which supported or did not support his initial position. As the dependent variable, subjects' interest level in reading the article and their ranking of their preferences were determined.

In the exposure experiments (Allyn & Festinger, 1961; Brodbeck, 1956; Davis & Jones, 1960; Jecker, 1964; Maccoby, Maccoby, Romney, & Adams, 1961; Mills & Ross, 1964), subjects were exposed to information which was either consistent or inconsistent with previous beliefs or behavior. In this case, the dependent variables tended to be measures of subjects' modes of reducing cognitive dissonance. The data suggest that voluntary selective exposure is based on at least two different mechanisms: (1) the seeking of supportive information and (2) the avoidance of nonsupportive information.

Some data has been reported suggesting that individuals do seek supportive information (cf. Adams, 1961; Ehrlich et al., 1957; Freedman & Sears, 1963; Rosen, 1961). With the exception of Festinger (1957, p. 162-176) and Cohen, Brehm, and Latané (1959), the avoidance postulate, however, has received mixed support (Feather, 1962, 1963; Mills, Aronson, & Robinson, 1959; Steiner, 1962) and theoretical supplementation (Brock, 1965). In toto, there appears to be no clear experimental evidence for a general tendency to avoid nonsupportive information and to seek supportive information (Freedman & Sears, 1965, p. 69). Several more recent experiments seem to demonstrate it is probably more fruitful to search for conditions that interact with the informational characteristics (i.e., supportive vs. nonsupportive) which might submerge or enhance the information avoidance tendency. Among these are individual difference variables, as differences in the person's GIAL (e.g., Driver, Streufert, & Nataupsky, 1969) and situational differences.

Festinger (1964) has hypothesized that seeking or avoiding discrepant information will greatly depend on how confident the person is that he is holding a correct position. If the individual is very confident, he should be able to reduce dissonance by seeking out opposing information. He should believe that he would be able to refute it. If he is not so confident, he should avoid opposing information and reduce potential dissonance by some other mode, e.g., by derogation of the information source (cf. the findings of Mills

& Ross, 1964; Sears, 1965; Sears & Freedman, 1965). Again, one might explain this phenomenon via GIAL theory. Opposing information, which necessarily is incongruent, is sought only when there is little other incongruity present, when "confidence" assures one of being "right" in the first place. When lack of confidence in one's own position produces an initial state of incongruity, then the additional incongruity (at least for lower GIAL persons) of opposing information produces cloze actions such as dissonance reduction.

One might assume that confidence of being correct, when it exists, should apply especially to more unidimensional persons, since a more multidimensional person is more rarely sure of the entire accuracy of his point of view, unless of course he is concerned with a relatively simple matter. On the surface, then, one could assume that more multidimensional individuals would avoid conflicting information because it could lead to even greater uncertainty. That, however, would be an oversimplification. As a matter of fact, multidimensionality (as we have seen earlier) only can come about via openness to conflicting (i.e., incongruous) information. Of course, more multidimensional persons are not perpetually (e.g., under conditions of incongruity overload) searching for conflicting information. In the absence of the salience for one or the other point of view, including salience of one's current point of view, more multidimensional persons should remain somewhat, although possibly not entirely, open to novel information. This openness to information should not be widely affected by confidence. For more unidimensional persons, however, the predictions of dissonance theory might well hold. Under conditions of high confidence, they may be open to opposing information, while under conditions of low confidence, they may be relatively closed to this information (cf. also Sieber & Lanzetta, 1964).

We may then propose that:

6.19 Under conditions of high confidence in their current position, unidimensional subjects should expose themselves to contradictory information. As confidence decreases, their exposure to contradictory information should decrease and the exposure to supportive information should increase.

6.20 Under conditions of high confidence in their current position (if it exists), more multidimensional subjects should expose themselves to a moderate amount of supportive and a moderate amount of contradictory information.

Another series of studies are concerned with the utility and novelty of information. Several writers on information receptivity agree that the novelty-familiarity dimension of information input could be a powerful determinant of voluntary selective exposure (Festinger, 1964; Freedman & Sears, 1965; Rhine, 1967; Sears, 1965). Based on these views, we could conclude that information seeking behavior reflects greater preference for *familiar*, non-supportive information as compared to novel, nonsupportive information. However, other studies (Brock & Balloun, 1967; Brock & Fromkin, 1968; Sears & Freedman, 1965) have not been able to support this finding. Brock, Albert, and Becker (1970) obtained results on several different dependent variables which indicated that supportive information is preferred by committed subjects when the information is unfamiliar.

Some success in accounting for information receptivity has been obtained with individual difference variables, such as educational level and socio-economic class (Lazarsfeld, Berelson, & Gaudet, 1948; Star & Hughes, 1950; Steiner, 1963) and complexity (e.g., Streufert and associates, as discussed in Chapter 2), and with situational variables, such as the individual's expected role in the communication process (Brock & Fromkin, 1968). Although no GIAL experiments were carried out in this field, the level of incongruity with resulting search and cloze, activities would be able to account for the data as well.

Not all of the problems in the field of selective exposure have been solved, however. Some modifications in theory have been proposed (Feather, 1967; Festinger, 1964), yet additional changes may be required, both in theory and method. Most of the difficulties in the field appear to relate to questions of motivation. One might ask when, why, and how in the absence of moderator variables, is an individual motivated to seek (or to selectively expose himself to) supportive (supposedly consistent) or nonsupportive (supposedly inconsistent) information. The General Incongruity Adaptation Level Theory (presented in Chapter 5) has some potential comments on this area. If, for example, lack of confidence would be a by-product of too much incongruence, then the seeking of supportive information appears very reasonable. If, on the other hand, (1) lack of confidence would be due to insufficient information on the issue, while (2) the incongruity experienced by the person is currently below the GIAL, one would predict that the subject should seek contradictory information.

How Does Dimensionality Relate to Selective Exposure?

As presented in Chapter 2, the earlier formulations of interactive complexity theory (e.g., Schroder, Driver, & Streufert, 1967) have suggested that a more multidimensional individual should be more open to information, including inconsistent and nonsupportive information. Later research by Streufert and associates (e.g., Streufert, Suedfeld, & Driver, 1965) has shown that the relationship between dimensional complexity and exposure is not that simple. It seems that the differences in openness to supportive and nonsupportive information are not as greatly affected by dimensionality as was previously expected. Rather, subject's dimensionality appears to determine *how* the received information is utilized in relating the message which is received by an individual to his current attitudes. Unfortunately, the selective exposure literature has not generally made a distinction between information reception and information processing, so that the two points of view do not fit neatly with each other. Nonetheless, one can say that both more multidimensional and more unidimensional persons seem to request and seek information that may not be consistent with their existing views (Streufert, Suedfeld, & Driver, 1965). But, one can also state that more multidimensional individuals appear to request more different *kinds* of information than more unidimensional individuals (Karlins & Lamm, 1967). This openness to more different kinds of information would increase the probability of exposure to inconsistent and nonsupportive information. After exposure to nonsupportive information, more unidimensional and more multidimensional individuals would likely use different resolution processes. Crano and Schroder (1967) have shown that more unidimensional individuals tend to use a single way of reducing the attitudinal conflict which had been induced by a nonsupportive message. More multidimensional individuals, on the other hand, tended to utilize several means of reducing conflict. Streufert (1966) found that exposure to counter-attitudinal messages tends to result in fixed (stable) attitudes in more unidimensional individuals, and in flexible attitudes in more multidimensional individuals.

We may then propose that:

6.21 While both more unidimensional and more multidimensional individuals seek inconsistent and novel information, the more multidimensional individuals will expose themselves to more different kinds of information than the more unidimensional persons.

6.22 Once exposed to inconsistent or counter-attitudinal information, more unidimensional persons will resolve their conflict by a single means, while more multidimensional individuals will use several means of resolving conflict, if they are available.

6.23 Attitudes resulting out of a resolution of counter-attitudinal information will be relatively stable in more unidimensional persons and relatively flexible in multidimensional persons.

To summarize, the predictions of dissonance theory should fit the more unidimensional subjects considerably better than the more multidimensional subjects. The familiar manipulations of dissonance theorists, which leave only one means of resolution open for a conflict, would increase the probability that more unidimensional subjects will follow the predictions of the theory and, to some degree, would help to decrease the divergent tendency of more multidimensional subjects. However, given the opportunity, the more multidimensional person should be able to cope with more inconsistent information (through integration) and should be able to "select" (after exposure) relevant information from a given information quantity. Consequently, he should not have to cope with as much total information. Research on complexity and information search by Karlins and Lamm (1967) provides a good example for this proposition. We do not mean to propose with this statement that the more multidimensional individual, by necessity, has a higher general incongruity adaptation level. Rather, the ability to integrate makes it possible for him to reduce inconsistency in his environment at a higher rate, and consequently reduce high levels of incongruity to which he might be exposed. Nonetheless, when overload conditions become extreme (when the amount of inconsistent, i.e., nonsupportive, information becomes exceedingly large) and could not possibly be utilized in an integrative fashion, one would expect no further differences between multidimensional and unidimensional individuals. Similarly, no great differences should be expected under conditions of extreme information deprivation (cf. research reported by Streufert & Driver, 1965; Streufert & Schroder, 1965). However, as soon as information conditions change toward less extreme overload conditions or less extreme deprivation conditions, the discrepancies between the more multidimensional and the more unidimensional individual should re-emerge (cf. Suedfeld, 1964).

We may then propose that:

6.24 Given the opportunity to integrate or re-integrate contradictory information, more multidimensional individuals should be more able to cope with nonsupportive information and may expose themselves to more of that information than more unidimensional individuals.

6.25 Under conditions of overload with discrepant information, or deprivation from information, differences between unidimensional and multidimensional individuals should cease to exist.

One additional thought might be added. It appears from the above predictions that most of the previous research which has not considered complexity variables seems to be in line with the predictions we have made for more unidimensional individuals. The reason for this is obvious: The majority of the population (somewhere between 70% and 80%) appears to be more unidimensional in most of their perceptions and behavior, at least in most of their cognitive domains. As a result, the data from more multidimensional individuals tend to be thrown into error variance, leaving enough common experimental variance from unidimensional subjects to obtain significant results. As we have stated previously, however, it remains very questionable whether one should simply discard 20% or 30% of the subjects who do not behave as other "normal" subjects do, and ignore the fact that under some experimental conditions most subjects do provide evidence of *some* multidimensionality. This, of course, means that under certain experimental conditions, leading to greater dimensionality on the part of all subjects, no meaningful results would be obtained.

ATTRACTION

Byrne (1971) and his associates have amply demonstrated that similarity leads to attraction, on attitude scales, in intentions and in behavior. Similarity is operationalized by Byrne primarily through matching on attitude scales between the subject and the "other"; attraction is often determined via the Interpersonal Judgment Scale (IJS). In most cases, the subjects do not previously know the other, so that they do form a "new" attitude about him or her. From the previous discussion on attitudes and on social influence, it should be clear that both more unidimensional and more multidimensional persons would respond favorably to a "similar" other. For the more unidimensional person, the "generalized" positive attitude (see prediction 6.4) toward a similar other should apply. For more multidimensional persons, too little dimensionality may be present in the Byrne design to allow them to respond multidimensionally (e.g., they cannot know how the specific attitude statements of the "other" have come about). Alternatively, they may simply assume that the attitude statements presented to them were generated via a dimensional structure similar to their own (they are, after all, only slightly discrepant from those of the subject). In either case, there is reason for acceptance of the other by the subject, even though one might suspect that the attraction expressed might be lower for more multidimensional than for more unidimensional persons (salience).

What, however, does similarity mean? It seems to us that similarity might well be seen as expected communication matching (in the social influence sense). If one is similar to the "other" (both in dimensional structure and in attitudinal content), then one can exchange ideas without experiencing very much incongruity. There is likely no threat involved, one is reinforced (including in the sense discussed by Byrne), one does not experience a level of incongruity very far from, at least not above, the GIAL. Affect would probably be positive. (If the similarity with the other would result in an incongruity level below the GIAL, complex search can always be initiated.)

If we view communication matching, i.e., matching of source and target, in the social influence sense, then the predictions of Byrne might have to be modified somewhat, particularly if one wants to predict attraction in the real world. For subjects of more unidimensional conceptual structure, Byrne's predictions may be allowed to stand. Similarity would produce congruence and positive affect, dissimilarity would produce incongruence and negative affect, i.e., disliking of the "other."[6] The situation for more multidimensional subjects, however, would be more complicated.

One might predict that differentiators—given the opportunity to place the attitudes of the "other" in perspective—would at times reject the dissimilar other, at times (when his characteristics appear irrelevant to present concerns) view him in a more neutral fashion. Integrators, on the other hand, might not reject him at all. Especially for the flexible integrator, someone with a different set of attitudes might be very "useful" as a stimulus for further differentiation and integration of one's own cognitive structure (as long as the integrator's GIAL has not reached higher levels than he can handle). After all, the discrepant placement of attitudinal content is often merely a reflection of structural differences in dimensionality.

We do not intend to say that the integrator is by necessity more fascinated with the information than subjects of lesser dimensionality. But, multidimensional integrators can and do at least handle the information better if it is multidimensional (cf. Karlins & Lamm, 1967), and they can receive greater benefits from it, since it has more (dimensional) usefulness for them. For that matter, their personal history may have provided more frequent positive reinforcement for exposure to "incongruent" information, *possibly* even resulting in a somewhat higher IAL for attitudinal discrepancies (since the process of integration tends to relieve higher incongruities more quickly). In other words, subjects who are primarily unidimensional in their orientation should find a similar other attractive if that similarity is content relevant (e.g., if they feel similarly about an object, person, or event). Persons of integrative multidimensionality should find each other attractive if they can communicate on a structural level (i.e., if they think the same way about an object, person, or event). This is not to say that similarity in both content *and* structure would not increase the attraction for multidimensional persons as well. In part, their preference may depend on their GIAL and the incongruity level to which they are currently exposed.

We may then state that:

6.26 Similarity can occur at a content (what one thinks or feels) and a structure (how one thinks or feels) level.

[6] One should consider that Byrne's research designs build some amount of incongruence into the experiment: (1) The similar or dissimilar other is a stranger, and (2) the experience of this new person occurs under the condition of a psychological experiment. With that relatively high level of incongruity, meeting a dissimilar other would rise beyond the IAL and tend to generate negative affect.

6.27 More unidimensional persons should be attracted to each other on the basis of content similarity.

6.28 Multidimensional differentiators should be attracted to each other on the basis of content similarity when the dimension on which content similarity is expressed is selected for perception or behavior because of its high salience.

6.29 Multidimensional integrators should primarily be affected by structural similarity, and only secondarily be affected by content similarity.

We should note again that these predictions are made for situations which are themselves complex, not for highly simplified lab situations that allow for communication and reception of only a single dimension. Under those conditions, no discrepancies can be expected.

If we place a number of persons of divergent dimensionality into a group and observe their interaction with each other over some time, we should find (1) several clusters of unidimensional persons (each similar in attitudes), (2) changing clusters of differentiators (depending on task requirements and relevant salience), and (3) one or several clusters of integrators who do not necessarily match each other in attitudinal content. We would *not* predict great amounts of voluntary interaction (based on attraction) among persons of discrepant dimensional structure. However, we might find some interaction among more multidimensional targets with more unidimensional sources of information. The communication would probably be successful in the sense that the message is "understood" (see above) as intended, even though it may not be satisfying to the target. Voluntary interaction in the opposite direction is less likely, unless the more multidimensional person is acting in a submissive or strategic role. He should find it difficult or useless and frustrating to communicate unidimensional information in a setting which he himself perceives as multidimensional, unless, of course, he is using his communication for strategic purposes (again Fig. 6.2 is relevant).

We may then state that:

6.30 Attraction between persons of discrepant dimensionality is likely to be low. Voluntary successful communication among persons of discrepant dimensionality should occur, if at all, between more unidimensional sources and more multidimensional targets. Communication in the other direction is likely more rare, often due to hierarchical association or manipulation, and if it occurs, is often misperceived or not understood (except in situations where the more multidimensional person communicates unidimensionally for strategic purposes).

REFERENCES

Adams, J. S. Reduction of cognitive dissonance by seeking consonant information. *Journal of Abnormal and Social Psychology*, 1961, **62**, 74-78.

Ajzen, I., & Fishbein, M. Attitudinal and normative variables as predictors of specific behaviors. *Journal of Personality and Social Psychology,* 1973, **27,** 41–57.

Allyn, J., & Festinger, L. The effectiveness of unanticipated persuasive communications. *Journal of Abnormal and Social Psychology,* 1961, **62,** 35–40.

Anderson, L. R., & Fishbein, M. Prediction of attitude from the number, strength, and evaluative aspects of belief about attitude objects: A comparison of summation and congruity theories. *Journal of Personality and Social Psychology,* 1965, **2,** 437–443.

Anderson, N. H. Primacy effects in personality impression using a generalized order effect paradigm. *Journal of Personality and Social Psychology,* 1965, **2,** 1–9.

Anderson, N. H., & Barrios, A. A. Primacy effects in personality impression formation. *Journal of Abnormal and Social Psychology,* 1961, **63,** 346–350.

Anderson, N. H., & Hubert, S. Effect of concomitant verbal recall on order effects in personality impression formation. *Journal of Verbal Learning and Verbal Behavior,* 1963, **2,** 379–391.

Asch, S. E. Forming impressions of personality. *Journal of Abnormal and Social Psychology,* 1946, **41,** 258–290.

Berkowitz, L. Leveling tendencies and the complexity-simplicity dimension. *Journal of Personality,* 1957, **25,** 743–751.

Berkowitz, L. *Aggression: A social psychological analysis.* New York: McGraw-Hill, 1962.

Bickman, L. Environmental attitudes and actions. *Journal of Social Psychology,* 1972, **87,** 323–324.

Brehm, J. W., & Cohen, A. R. *Explorations in cognitive dissonance.* New York: Wiley, 1962.

Brock, T. C. Commitment to exposure as a determinant of information receptivity. *Journal of Personality and Social Psychology,* 1965, **2,** 10–19.

Brock, T. C. Albert, S. M., & Becker, L. A. Familiarity, utility, and supportiveness as determinants of information receptivity. *Journal of Personality and Social Psychology,* 1970, **14,** 292–301.

Brock, T. C., & Balloun, J. L. Behavioral receptivity to dissonant information. *Journal of Personality and Social Psychology,* 1967, **6,** 413–428.

Brock, T. C., & Fromkin, H. L. Cognitive tuning set and behavioral receptivity to discrepant information. *Journal of Personality,* 1968, **36,** 108–125.

Brodbeck, M. The role of small groups in mediating propaganda. *Journal of Abnormal and Social Psychology,* 1956, **52,** 166–170.

Brown, R. *Social psychology.* New York: Free Press, 1965.

Byrne, D. *The attraction paradigm.* New York: Academic Press, 1971.

Campbell, D. T. *The generality of social attitudes.* Doctoral dissertation, University of California, Berkeley, 1947.

Campbell, D. T., & Fiske, D. W. Convergent and discriminant validation by the multi-trait, multi-method matrix. *Psychological Bulletin,* 1959, **56,** 81-105.

Carlson, E. R. Attitude change through modification of attitude structure. *Journal of Abnormal and Social Psychology,* 1956, **52,** 256-261.

Cartwright, D. Some principles of mass persuasion. *Human Relations,* 1949, **2,** 253-267.

Cohen, A. R. *Attitude change and social influence.* New York: Basic Books, 1964.

Cohen, A. R., Brehm, J. W., & Latane', B. Choice of strategy and voluntary exposure to information under public and private conditions. *Journal of Personality,* 1959, **27,** 63-73.

Cooper, E., & Dinerman, H. Analysis of the film "Don't be a sucker": A study in communication. *Public Opinion Quarterly,* 1951, **15,** 243-264.

Crano, W. D., & Schroder, H. M. Complexity of attitude structure and processes of conflict reduction. *Journal of Personality and Social Psychology,* 1967, **5,** 110-114.

Davis, K., & Jones, E. E. Changes in interpersonal perception as a means of reducing cognitive dissonance. *Journal of Abnormal and Social Psychology,* 1960, **61,** 402-410.

Dillehay, R. C., Insko, C. A., & Smith, M. B. Logical consistency and attitude change. *Journal of Personality and Social Psychology,* 1966, **3,** 646-654.

Di Vesta, F. J., & Mervin, J. C. Effects of need oriented communication on attitude change. *Journal of Abnormal and Social Psychology,* 1960, **60,** 80-85.

Driver, M. J., Streufert, S., & Nataupsky, M. Effects of immediate and remote incongruity experience on responses to dissonant information. *Proceedings of the 77th Annual Convention of the American Psychological Association,* 1969, **4,** 323-324.

Ehrlich, D., Guttman, I., Schönbach, P., & Mills, J. Post decision exposure to relevant information. *Journal of Abnormal and Social Psychology,* 1957, **54,** 98-102.

Feather, N. T. Cigarette smoking and lung cancer: A study of cognitive dissonance. *Australian Journal of Psychology,* 1962, **14,** 55-64.

Feather, N. T. Cognitive dissonance, sensitivity and evaluation. *Journal of Abnormal and Social Psychology,* 1963, **66,** 157-163.

Feather, N. T. An expectancy-value model of information-seeking behavior. *Psychological Review,* 1967, **74,** 342-360.

Festinger, L. *A theory of cognitive dissonance.* Evanston, Ill.: Row, Peterson, 1957.

Festinger, L. Behavioral support for opinion change. *Public Opinion Quarterly,* 1964, **28**, 404-417. (a)

Festinger, L. *Conflict, decision and dissonance.* Stanford, Cal.: Stanford University Press, 1964. (b)

Fine, B. J. Conclusion-drawing, communicator credibility and anxiety as factors in opinion change. *Journal of Abnormal and Social Psychology,* 1957, **54**, 369-374.

Fishbein, M. An investigation of the relationships between beliefs about an object and attitude toward that object. *Human Relations,* 1963, **16**, 233-239.

Fishbein, M., & Hunter, R. Summation versus balance in attitude organization and change. *Journal of Abnormal and Social Psychology,* 1964, **69**, 505-510.

Fishbein, M., & Raven, B. H. The AB scales: An operational definition of belief and attitude. *Human Relations,* 1962, **15**, 35-44.

Freedman, J. L., & Sears, D. O. Voters' preferences among types of information. *American Psychologist,* 1963, **18**, 375.

Freedman, J. L., & Sears, D. O. Selective exposure. In L. Berkowitz (Ed.), *Advances in experimental social psychology* (Vol. 2). New York: Academic Press, 1965.

French, J. R. P., & Raven, B. The bases of social power. In D. Cartwright (Ed.), *Studies in social power.* Ann Arbor: Institute for Social Research, 1959.

Hadley, H. D. The nondirective approach in advertising appeals. *Journal of Applied Psychology,* 1953, **37**, 496-498.

Hovland, C. I., Campbell, E. H., & Brock, T. The effect of commitment on opinion change following communication. In C. I. Hovland (Ed.), *The order of presentation in persuasion.* New Haven: Yale University Press, 1957.

Hovland, C. I., Harvey, O. J., & Sherif, M. Assimilation and contrast effects in communication and attitude change. *Journal of Abnormal and Social Psychology,* 1957, **55**, 242-252.

Hovland, C. I., Janis, I. L., & Kelley, H. H. *Communication and persuasion.* New Haven: Yale University Press, 1953.

Hovland, C. I., Lumsdaine, A. A., & Sheffield, F. D. *Experiments on mass communication.* Princeton, N.J.: Princeton University Press, 1949.

Hovland, C. I., & Mandell, W. An experimental comparison of conclusion-drawing by the communicator and by the audience. *Journal of Abnormal and Social Psychology,* 1952, **47**, 581-588.

Hovland, C. I., & Mandell, W. Is there a law of primacy in persuasion? In C. I. Hovland (Ed.), *The order of presentation in persuasion.* New Haven: Yale University Press, 1957.

Hovland, C. I., & Weiss, W. The influence of source credibility on communication effectiveness. *Public Opinion Quarterly,* 1951, **15**, 635-650.

Jecker, J. D. Selective exposure to new information. In L. Festinger (Ed.),

Conflict, decision and dissonance. Stanford, Cal.: Stanford University Press, 1964.

Kahn, L. A. The organization of attitudes toward the Negro as a function of education. *Psychological Monographs,* 1951, **65**(13, Whole No. 330).

Karlins, M., & Lamm, H. Information search as a function of conceptual structure in a complex problem-solving task. *Journal of Personality and Social Psychology,* 1967, **5**, 456–459.

Kelman, H. C. Compliance, identification and internalization. *Journal of Conflict Resolution,* 1958, **2**, 51–60.

Kelman, H. C. Processes of opinion change. *Public Opinion Quarterly,* 1961, **25**, 57–78.

Kelman, H. C., & Hovland, C. I. "Reinstatement" of the communicator in delayed measurements of opinion change. *Journal of Abnormal and Social Psychology,* 1953, **48**, 327–335.

Kiesler, C. A., & Munson, P. A. Attitudes and opinions. In M. R. Rosenzweig & L. W. Porter (Eds.), *Annual review of psychology.* Palo Alto, Cal.: Annual Reviews, 1975.

Klapper, J. T. *The effects of the mass media.* New York: Bureau of Applied Social Research, Columbia University, 1949.

Klapper, J. T. *Effects of mass communication.* Glencoe, Ill.: Free Press, 1960.

Kothandapani, V. Validation of feeling, belief and intention to act as three components of attitude and their contribution to prediction of contraceptive behavior. *Journal of Personality and Social Psychology,* 1971, **19**, 321–333.

Kretch, D., & Crutchfield, R. S. *Theory and problems in social psychology.* New York: McGraw-Hill, 1948.

Kretch, D., Crutchfield, R. S., & Ballachey, E. L. *Individual in society* (2nd ed.). New York: McGraw-Hill, 1962.

LaPiere, R. T. Attitudes versus actions. *Social Forces,* 1934, **13**, 230–237.

Lazarsfeld, P. F., Berelson, B., & Gaudet, H. *The people's choice* (2nd ed.). New York: Columbia University Press, 1948.

Luchins, A. S. Mechanization in problem solving: The effect of Einstellung. *Psychological Monographs,* 1942, **54**, No. 248.

Luchins, A. S. Experimental attempts to minimize the impact of first impressions. In C. I. Hovland, (Ed.), *The order of presentation in persuasion.* New Haven: Yale University Press, 1957. (a)

Luchins, A. S. Primacy–recency in impression formation. In C. I. Hovland (Ed.), *The order of presentation in persuasion.* New Haven: Yale University Press, 1957. (b)

Maccoby, E. E., Maccoby, N., Romney, A. K., & Adams, J. S. Social reinforcement in attitude change. *Journal of Abnormal and Social Psychology,* 1961, **63**, 109–115.

Maier, N. R. F., & Maier, R. A. An experimental test of the effects of "developmental" versus "free" discussion on the quality of group decisions. *Journal of Applied Psychology*, 1957, **41**, 320-323.

Mann, R. D. A review of the relationship between personality and performance in small groups. *Psychological Bulletin*, 1959, **56**, 241-270.

Marrow, A. J., & French, J. R. P. Changing a stereotype in industry. *Journal of Social Issues*, 1945, **1**, 33-37.

McGuire, W. J. Direct and indirect persuasive effects of dissonance producing messages. *Journal of Abnormal and Social Psychology*, 1960, **60**, 354-358. (a)

McGuire, W. J. A syllogistic analysis of cognitive relationships. In C. I. Hovland & M. J. Rosenberg (Eds.), *Attitude organization and change*. New Haven: Yale University Press, 1960. (b)

McGuire, W. J. Attitudes and opinions. In *Annual review of psychology*. Palo Alto, Cal.: Annual Reviews, Inc., 1966, **17**.

McGuire, W. J. The nature of attitudes and attitude change. In G. Lindzey & E. Aronson (Eds.), *The handbook of social psychology* (Vol. 3) (2nd Ed.). Reading, Mass.: Addison Wesley, 1969.

McKeachie, W. J. Individual conformity to the attitudes of classroom groups. *Journal of Abnormal and Social Psychology*, 1954, **49**, 282-289.

Miller, N., & Campbell, D. T. Recency and primacy in persuasion as a function of the timing of speeches and measurement. *Journal of Abnormal and Social Psychology*, 1959, **59**, 1-9.

Mills, J., Aronson, E., & Robinson, H. Selectivity in exposure to information. *Journal of Abnormal and Social Psychology*, 1959, **59**, 250-253.

Mills, J., & Ross, A. Effects of commitment and certainty upon interest in supporting information. *Journal of Abnormal and Social Psychology*, 1964, **68**, 552-555.

Osgood, C. E., Suci, G. T., & Tannenbaum, P. H. *The measurement of meaning*. Urbana: University of Illinois Press, 1957.

Osgood, C. E., & Tannenbaum, P. H. The principle of congruity in the prediction of attitude change. *Psychological Review*, 1955, **62**, 42-55.

Peak, H. Attitude and motivation. In M. R. Jones (Ed.), *Nebraska symposium on motivation*. Lincoln, Neb.: University of Nebraska Press, 1955.

Peak, H. Psychological structure and psychological activity. *Psychological Review*, 1958, **65**, 325-347.

Rhine, R. J. The 1964 presidential election and curves of information seeking and avoiding. *Journal of Personality and Social Psychology*, 1967, **5**, 416-423.

Ring, K., & Kelley, H. H. A comparison of augmentation and reduction as modes of influence. *Journal of Abnormal and Social Psychology*, 1963, **66**, 95-102.

Rokeach, M., & Kliejumas, P. Behavior as a function of attitude-toward-object and attitude-toward-situation. *Journal of Personality and Social Psychology,* 1972, **22**, 194–201.

Rosen, S. Post decision affinity for incompatible information. *Journal of Abnormal and Social Psychology,* 1961, **63**, 188–190.

Rosen, B., & Komorita, S. S. Attitudes and action: The effects of behavior intent and the perceived effectiveness of acts. *Journal of Personality,* 1971, **39**, 189–203.

Rosenberg, M. J. Cognitive structure and attitudinal effect. *Journal of Abnormal and Social Psychology,* 1956, **53**, 367–372.

Rosenberg, M. J. An analysis of affective-cognitive consistency. In C. I. Hovland & M. J. Rosenberg (Eds.), *Attitude organization and change.* New Haven: Yale University Press, 1960. (a)

Rosenberg, M. J. Cognitive reorganization in response to the hypnotic reversal of attitudinal affect. *Journal of Personality,* 1960, **28**, 39–63. (b)

Saenger, G., & Gilbert, E. Consumer reactions to the integration of Negro sales personnel. *International Journal of Opinion and Attitude Research,* 1950, **4**, 57–76.

Sample, J., & Warland, R. Attitude and the prediction of behavior. *Social Forces,* 1973, **51**, 292–304.

Schroder, H. M., Driver, M. J., & Streufert, S. *Human information processing.* New York: Holt, Rinehart & Winston, 1967.

Sears, D. O. Biased indoctrination and selectivity of exposure to new information. *Sociometry,* 1965, **28**, 363–376.

Sears, D. O., & Freedman, J. L. The effect of expected familiarity with arguments upon opinion change and selective exposure. *Journal of Personality and Social Psychology,* 1965, **3**, 420–426.

Secord, P. F., & Backman, C. W. *Social psychology.* New York: McGraw-Hill, 1964.

Sieber, J. E., & Lanzetta, J. T. Conflict and conceptual structure as determinants of decision-making behavior. *Journal of Personality,* 1964, **32**, 622–641.

Smith, M. B. Personal values as determinants of political attitude. *Journal of Psychology,* 1949, **28**, 477–486.

Smith, M. B., Bruner, J. S., & White, R. W. *Opinions and personality.* New York: Wiley, 1956.

Solomon, R. L. Punishment. *American Psychologist,* 1964, **19**, 239–253.

Star, S. A., & Hughes, H. M. Report on an educational campaign: The Cincinnati plan for the United Nations. *American Journal of Sociology,* 1950, **55**, 389–400.

Steiner, G. A. *The people look at television.* New York: A. Knopf, 1963.

Steiner, I. D. Receptivity to supportive versus nonsupportive communications. *Journal of Abnormal and Social Psychology,* 1962, **65**, 266–267.

Stewart, R. H. Effect of continuous responding on the order effect in personality impression formation. *Journal of Personality and Social Psychology*, 1965, 1, 161-165.

Streufert, S. Conceptual structure, communicator importance and interpersonal attitudes toward conforming and deviant group members. *Journal of Personality and Social Psychology*, 1966, 4, 100-103.

Streufert, S. Complexity and complex decision making: Convergences between differentiation and integration approaches to the prediction of task performance. *Journal of Experimental Social Psychology*, 1970, 6, 494-509.

Streufert, S., & Driver, M. J. Conceptual structure information load and perceptual complexity. *Psychonomic Science*, 1965, 3, 249-250.

Streufert, S., & Driver, M. J. Impression formation as a measure of the complexity of conceptual structure. *Educational and Psychological Measurement*, 1967, 27, 1025-1039.

Streufert, S., & Fromkin, H. L. Complexity and social influence. In J. Tedeschi (Ed.), *Social influence processes*. Chicago, Ill.: Aldine, 1972.

Streufert, S., & Schroder, H. M. Conceptual structure, environmental complexity and task performance. *Journal of Experimental Research in Personality*, 1965, 1, 132-137.

Streufert, S., & Streufert, S. C. Effects of conceptual structure, failure and success on attribution of causality and interpersonal attitudes. *Journal of Personality and Social Psychology*, 1969, 11, 138-147.

Streufert, S., Suedfeld, P., & Driver, M. J. Conceptual structure, information search and information utilization. *Journal of Personality and Social Psychology*, 1965, 2, 736-740.

Suedfeld, P. Attitude manipulation in restricted environments: I. Conceptual structure and response to propaganda. *Journal of Abnormal and Social Psychology*, 1964, 68, 242-247. (a)

Suedfeld, P. Conceptual structure and subjective stress in sensory deprivation. *Perceptual and Motor Skills*, 1964, 19, 896-898. (b)

Suedfeld, P., & Vernon, J. Attitude manipulation in restricted environments: II. Conceptual structure and the internalization of propaganda received as a reward for compliance. *Journal of Personality and Social Psychology*, 1966, 3, 586-589.

Thistlewaite, D. L., deHaan, H., & Kamenetzky, J. The effects of "directive" and "nondirective" communication procedures on attitudes. *Journal of Abnormal and Social Psychology*, 1955, 51, 107-113.

Thistlewaite, D. L., & Kamenetzky; J. Attitude change through refutation and elaboration of audience counterarguments. *Journal of Abnormal and Social Psychology*, 1955, 51, 3-9.

Walker, E. L., & Heynes, R. W. *An anatomy for conformity*. Englewood Cliffs, N.J.: Prentice-Hall, 1962.

Weinstein, A. G. Predicting behavior from attitudes. *Public Opinion Quarterly,* 1972, **36**, 355-360.

Wicker, A. W. An examination of the "other variables" explanation of attitude-behavior inconsistency. *Journal of Personality and Social Psychology,* 1971, **19**, 18-30.

Zajonc, R. B. The process of cognitive tuning in communication. *Journal of Abnormal and Social Psychology,* 1960, **61**, 159-167.

Zander, A., & Curtis, T. Effects of social power on aspiration setting and striving. *Journal of Abnormal and Social Psychology,* 1962, **64**, 63-74.

Zipf, S. G. Resistance and conformity under reward and punishment. *Journal of Abnormal and Social Psychology,* 1960, **61**, 102-109.

CHAPTER 7

SOCIAL PERCEPTION AND PERSON PERCEPTION

Written in cooperation with Glenda Y. Nogami

Psychologists have often attempted to keep human perceptions in the laboratory relatively simple. But even in the physiological realm, the visual information "color" contains the potential for dimensions which are typically perceived by the human mind (hue, brightness, and saturation). How many more potential dimensions might be perceived for even the simplest social interaction in the laboratory of the social psychologist? Tagiuri (1969) agrees that the perceptions and cognitions of persons are usually multifaceted, something which is maximized when each of two (or more) persons are objects of each others' perceptions as well as perceivers of each other. Speaking of the dimensions of perceptions in the dyad, Tagiuri suggests that we are probably dealing with a delicate relationship that interacts with the cognitive style of the perceiver and with the characteristics of the stimulus person, the situation, and the judgmental task. We would agree. The cognitive style to which Tagiuri refers contains, among other phenomena, also the complexity (dimensional characteristics which a person brings to the inter-action with others) of the perceiver.

Certainly we might assume that perceptions of inanimate objects or events, which occur in a social context (in the presence and during relevant interaction with other persons), might involve less application of dimen-sionality than perceptions of other persons. Nonetheless, even this kind of situation (social perceptions) can call for the use of multidimensionality. When we view the dimensionality of the human perceptual effort within the social context, we will have to focus (1) on the stimulus constellation in the environmental situation and (2) on the capacity of the perceiver to utilize various dimensions[1] (aspects of his cognitive style). This chapter shall not be organized along the lines of this distinction. Rather—for the sake of better communication—this chapter is subdivided along more classical lines. First, we will deal with perceptions of nonhuman objects in the social context. Next we shall turn to person perceptions, and finally we will deal with attributions. We neither intend to present a complete review of any of these areas, nor do we plan to exhaustively cover all those areas within the perceptual realms where dimensionality might contribute to a greater understanding of perceptual phenomena. We merely intend to point out *some* of the contributions that multidimensional approaches might make. When we deal with "attribution," we shall also attempt to show (with the use of an example from attributions of responsibility) how a multidimensional approach can solve problems created by contradictory experimental evidence.

PERCEPTIONS IN THE SOCIAL CONTEXT

As early as the beginning of this century, psychologists have shown interest in the effects of social situations on perceptions, primarily perceptions of physical phenomena (cf. review of Tajfel, 1969). A prominent example of this kind of work is the series of experiments by Asch and associates, where groups of subjects are, for example, exposed to stimuli (e.g., a number of clicks) and are asked to report the number of clicks they heard. Unknown to

[1] As stated in a previous chapter, dimensions are not typically inherent in stimulus material. Rather they are part of the perceiver's cognitive structure. Of course, the quantity and diversity of the stimulus configuration determines whether or not the stimuli may be placed by the perceiver on one or more (if available) cognitive dimensions. An exception is the potential intended dimensionality of a message by a communicator to the target perceiver. Here, a specific dimensionality may already (intentionally or unintentionally) be inherent in the message and may be perceivable by the target if the stimuli address dimensions available in his cognitive structure that match dimensions of the communicator (see below).

a single subject, all others present are confederates of the experimenter who report potentially incorrect counts. Since the 1940s and through the middle '60s, work on this problem greatly increased. Some of the theorists and researchers have approached this problem from a "rational" focus (often cognitive); others have shown a more affective bias. Both approaches have generated considerable research. But despite the multitude of data, Tajfel (1969) comes to the conclusion that the results cannot be explained by any single set of hypotheses. One might ask why.

As in other areas, social psychologists have attempted to find the single variable that would determine and explain the perceptual characteristics of their subjects. They were—as in so many other areas of social psychology—not successful. Again the "level of analysis" (to which we referred earlier) may have deceived the researchers. Tagiuri (1969) states, with reference to perceptions, that the vicarious functioning of cues, the coupling of person, and context and (most subtle of all) the sensitivity of the object person to the context—all demand the study of *higher order* variables. Indeed, perception, just like performance, is—in the social context—typically a multidimensional phenomenon. A *single* independent variable with exclusive effects on some observed perceptual phenomenon could only be found (in a multidimensional perceptual universe) if, for example, one of the following conditions prevailed:

(1) The experimenter is measuring the effects of a relatively pervasive low level informational variable and manages to hold the other variables constant. (His data may, however, be refuted by another experimenter with only slight variations in experimental design.)

(2) The experimenter is emphasizing the salience of his variable either by characteristics of his design or by specific instructions to the subjects. (Again, his data may be refuted by experimenters with only minimally divergent experimental designs.)

(3) The experimenter is manipulating his informational variable at a level where perceptual integration has already taken place, or where perceptual integration is allowed to take place before responding, so that a single integrated set of (lower level) variables enters into the perceptual outcome. (He may, however, find that his integrated perceptions are not stable, since changes in the design may result in different integration processes and different perceptual outcomes.)

In sum, the experimenter may have used a design that is "unconfounded" from the standpoint of excellence of experimental methodology, but he may have sacrificed reliability *and* applicability to "real world perceptual processes" (external validity) in doing so.

Assuming that the experimenter uses a design that does not *force* the subject into a more or less "unnatural" utilization of a single informational variable (or dimension), and assuming he does not measure previously integrated perceptual responses, what are the likely effects? Probably he will sometimes obtain separate, sometimes more integrated effects of the various informational stimuli, unless he specifically takes dimensional effects into account. In other words, measured perceptions may be disparate. If that is the case, we can hardly expect that a single set of hypotheses would account for the variety of data that have been reported in the literature, and could do so only if past experiments had considered the potential complexity of the perceptual situation and the dimensional capacity of their perceiving subjects. With some notable exceptions (e.g., Sieber & Lanzetta, 1964), this has not been done. Nonetheless, the data obtained in experiments at simple levels are informative about potential *components* of multidimensional perceptual processes.

The dimensionality of perceptions is, without question, a major factor, not only in social perceptions (see e.g., Streufert & Driver, 1967). Physical stimuli themselves, even in the absence of social information, can be perceived multidimensionally. We have already mentioned results of the experiment where subjects select and compare colors in a multidimensional scaling task. Without knowing that they are doing so, subjects sort color chips according to hue, brightness, and saturation, i.e., three distinctive dimensions for a non-social task situation. And there is ample evidence that social or societal situations modify the dimensions of perception for both social and physical stimuli (Hudson, 1960). In other words, information received from other persons in addition to information obtained from the physical environment is likely to add dimensionality to an already multidimensional perceptual situation. That holds as well for some experimental situations. Let us look at one example.

An Example of Perceptual Dimensionality: The Asch Task

Asch (1952, 1961) exposed his subjects to objective information from the physical environment and asked them to indicate how they had perceived the information. In this and other related experiments, one of a number of manipulations were utilized: e.g., subjects heard a number of clicks and were asked to state how many they had heard, subjects were asked to judge the length of lines or the distance between lights (but were exposed to different stimuli than comparison others), etc. Before subjects were able to report their perceptions, they had to listen to the perceptual reports of a group of (often confederate) others. All other group members (typically) gave an identical response that the subject found difficult to agree with. This placed the subject into an apparent dilemma. He could either respond correctly (but against the group) or could respond incorrectly (but in agreement with the group). In about one third of the cases, the subjects responded as the group did. The remaining subjects responded with their "true" perceptions. Moreover, when subjects from the former group were asked whether they knew that they had inaccurately conformed to the group, several subjects in a number of experiments denied that they had.

Several possible reasons for the conforming behavior and its denial were investigated. Did the subjects comply with or identify themselves with the group, or did they internalize the group norm? Was their perception indeed faulty? Were there some private reasons hidden away in the cognitive or emotional processes of the subjects that led them to conform and to lie about their conformity? Were the subjects themselves unaware that they departed from the physical truth?

Delving into the private experience of the individual subject to search for his motivation is more than uncomfortable for the experimental social psychologist. Brown (1965) described such a problem as an "epistemological nightmare." For the experimentally oriented social psychologist, this is in many cases a problem that must—if it cannot be resolved—be removed from the social psychological arena. Can that be achieved?

How can one view the perceptual process without letting the perceiving individual "interfere" with the data one wants to collect from him? The frequently heard answer to this question is not unusual: If one reduces the perceptual situation to its minimum, there will be fewer variables affecting subject's perceptions and consequently his responses. In other words, all extrinsic influences on, and all unnecessary internal response tendencies of, the perceiver must be eliminated. For the Asch task, both influence from the experimenter and influence from the group (except for the group's opinion) should be eliminated or reduced. The perceiver should be affected only by (a) the physical information he is receiving and (b) specific limited group-based social information. The effect of this procedure is obvious: Once more the researcher is attempting to eliminate all stimulus characteristics which are potentially translatable by the perceiver into multidimensionality that could affect his perceptual characteristics. Only the information of the experimental manipulation remains. In other words, only the dimension(s) the subject may use to judge the social information and the dimension(s) the subject may use to judge the physical information remain and are placed in direct conflict. From the current theoretical viewpoint, what is the effect on the subject in the Asch-type experiment?

Possibly for the first time in his life, our subject is confronted with limited directly contradictive "truths": the truth of his own perceptions vs. the truth of the group norm. On a potential single dimension running from "true" to "false," he must make opposing entries for the same phenomenon, and some solution must be forthcoming since he is required to commit himself. If the subject is (stylistically) more unidimensional in his perceptions, he has a serious problem. One of the "true" entries on his dimension must be false. He must make a choice: Either he or the group is incorrect. Should he have doubts about his competence (his eyesight might be bad and the task is visual), he might choose to go along with the group (and believe in the group's accuracy). Should he have a need for social approval, he might identify with the group and do the same. Should he feel that his own competence is high, or should the group not be valued by him, then he might refuse to conform. The more difficulty he might have in resolving the conflict between "truth" and "truth" at divergent points on the same dimension, the more emotional upheaval might be caused by the resolution.

More multidimensional subjects would have more resolution processes available to them than the more unidimensional subjects. Take first the differentiator, who is able to separate one "reality" from another. He has several options. For example, he might view his own judgment as accurate (on a reality dimension) but decide to conform specifically, to "comply" in Kelman's (1961) terms. In that case, he should be aware of his inaccurate response. Or, in some rare cases, he might even develop two divergent dimensions of physical reality. In any case, the response of the differentiator is likely to be made on the perceptual dimension that has the greatest salience to him. If the group norm appeared of greater importance, he would likely comply. If the experimenter intentionally increased the salience of that dimension, it would also increase the likelihood that differentiators would follow the implied suggestion. If the dimension on which his own judgment falls is of greater importance, he would not conform. In any case, no major affective stress should be expected from the differentiator placed into this conflict situation as long as the salience of the choice dimensions is sufficiently discrepant.

The integrator would likely lean toward a "restructuring" of the received information. The differentiator did not need to do this, he merely needed to make a "choice." The more unidimensional subject might appear to have restructured as well; in effect, however, his restructuring would merely have implied an absolute change in part of his perceptions (I was wrong, they were right, or the inverse). In contrast, the integrator would more likely seek out information or informational components that would serve to explain the discrepancies between his own perceptions and those of the group. He would likely, in his perceptual response, follow some restructured perceptual cognitions that would include components of his perceptions, of the group's perceptions, of the setting and components of the explanatory integration. As such, the choice might be to agree with the group, to remain at (or close to) his own perceptions, or to report some third (possibly even intermediate) outcome. In any case, the integrator should (if he has indeed integrated) show fewer (or no) stress effects than the more unidimensional perceiver.

Dimensional Effects of Discrepancies in Other Experiments

The Asch task certainly is not the only experiment where dimensional effects can be expected and observed. Let us look at some of the determinants of the perceiver's response. Faith of the perceiver in the group and the normative influence of the group appear as important considerations in social perceptions. Tajfel (1969) points out that group influences on individual perceptions appear to be governed by two major classes of variables. Both the relationship between the individual and the group, and the individual's faith in his own perceptions and his faith in the perceptions of the group, appear to be of major importance. Part of the relationship between the individual and the group is the control the group has over the individual, i.e., the normative influence of the group. In an analysis of that influence, Deutsch and Gerard (1955) have shown that individuals giving anonymous judgments did not conform as often with the group. Other experimenters (with few exceptions) have confirmed that finding. We might conclude on that basis that at least some of the subjects must be aware of their inaccurate responding, i.e., they are holding at least two dimensions of judgment: a social (possibly utility) dimension and a physical (i.e., truth) dimension. Under conditions of the possibility of normative control, they respond on one; under conditions of its absence, they respond on the other. Note that we are dealing here with dimensions, not just with choice points, since some research has shown that normative control will move the perceiver closer, but not to the point of, the group response.

An argument that only *one* dimension is present in *each* case appears unlikely. If that were so, anonymity should not increase accuracy of responding. Moreover, it appears that the salience of the group [i.e., length of interaction with it (Bovard, 1951); common goal orientation (Jackson & Saltzstein, 1958)] also increases the conformity of responding along a group-oriented rather than along a truth-oriented dimension. Both differentiators and integrators (through a somewhat different process) would likely respond in this fashion. As Tajfel (1969) points out, without normative influence (e.g., through anonymity of response) it is more likely that cognitive restructuring has taken place (when individuals converge in their judgment).

On the other hand, experimental manipulations that commit the subject to a particular view would necessarily decrease the need for both differentiation and integration, and should result in a reliable (physical information-oriented) response. In this vein, Deutsch and Gerard (1955) have shown that social influence on perception is decreased when either public or private commitment has been obtained. After all, one would now admit to the experimenter that one is lying, were one to go along with the errant group.

Another issue that has emerged in the area of perception in the presence of others concerns the effects of "ambiguity" of the experimental situation and of subjective response "uncertainty." Apparently, the ambiguity of the experimental situation has effects on the degree of conformity, a result one might expect. In addition, research by Wiener, Carpenter, and Carpenter (1957) and by Wiener (1958) has shown that a *complex* relationship between ambiguity and certainty must exist (cf. also Flament, 1959). Ambiguity appears to function only in association with changes in response uncertainty. Nonetheless, the two are far from identical. It seems that at least for some subjects a form of dimensional integration takes place, where the two dimensions of stimulus ambiguity and response uncertainty are affecting one another. Yet variance still remains unexplained, suggesting that the ambiguity/uncertainty interaction represents an integration of relatively high order. Following the arguments of Wiener (1958) and Flament (1959), Tajfel (1969) suggests that this variance should be due to (a) group attributes suggesting credibility of the group, (b) group response attributes, leading to divergent confidence levels, and (c) individual experience by the perceiver, suggesting a level of confidence in himself. Again we have dimensional attributes that might require integration. Of course, the effects can also be explained via joint effects of multidimensionality and individual differences on the GIAL (cf. Chaps. 5, 8).

How are these different "confidence" levels combined into a "confidence of judgment" for the two opposing points of view? They might be merely added, viewed as part of a single dimension running from true to false, and resulting in a judgment favoring (possibly only slightly) one side or the other. For some unidimensional subjects, that might be the case. But if that were generally true, then the data on differences in anonymity vs. non-anonymity could not be accounted for. Alternatively, one might propose that there are three entries on a single dimension, all of them potentially irreconcilable. As Streufert and Driver (1967) have suggested with regard to the impression formation task, additional dimensions and differentiation or integration of these dimensions must be generated, if any solution other than nearly random or predetermined selection of a response is to occur. Assuming that some integration does take place, then both the variety of responding and the additional effects of other variables (as the effect of anonymity) provide no further problems for explanation.

Based on the discussion so far, some hypotheses might be proposed:

7.1 Given information in a multifaceted physical and social environment, opposing physical and social information can lead to differentiative and/or integrative perceptions, particularly for more multidimensional persons.

7.2 Increasing normative group influence, or group salience, or the reduction of stimulus quantity and diversity should produce lower level dimensional responding (where previously present) and may result in conformity or nonconformity to group pressure in a reliable but experimental-design-specific fashion.

7.3 A person's differentiative or integrative perceptions will be based on (his individual) dimensions underlying his views of the characteristics of the group, his view of the self, and on the ambiguity of the perceived stimulus.

7.4 Presented with inconsistent physical and social information, resolution stress should be greatest for more unidimensional persons, intermediate to low for integrators, and low or absent for differentiators.

PERSON PERCEPTION

It is well known that the perceptions people develop of each other are a function of the information they receive and the views they hold before the information reaches them. In the complex settings of the real world, the views people already hold are themselves produced by large quantities of previous information, and are quite possibly multidimensional (cf. the research and methodologies of Bieri, 1955, 1961; Gollin & Rosenberg, 1956; Jackson, 1962; Jackson & Messick, 1963; Mayo & Crockett, 1964; Sarbin, 1954; Schroder, Driver, & Streufert, 1967; Shrauger & Altrocchi, 1964; Todd & Rappoport, 1964; Tucker, 1963). The additional stimuli relevant to current perception are often quite varied as well (cf. Tagiuri, 1969) and may be placed on one or more relevant, previously established dimensions. In some cases, they may even be ordered on one or more new judgmental dimensions that are potentially developed in response to stimuli that cannot be placed (or distorted to fit) onto already existing dimensions. It is likely that the perceptual outcome of receiving (moderately novel or moderately inconsistent) information from a complex social source is then as, or in some cases even more, multidimensional than previously stored relevant information.

An example might be useful. Let us take the frequently used psychological concept of "empathy." Certainly, empathy would be possible if the source of information and the receiver of information utilized the same dimension and placed the information at the same point of that dimension. What, however, would happen if the two used different dimensions to place the information, or placed the information on divergent (incongruent) points of the same dimension? To achieve empathy, at least minimal multidimensionality appears necessary here: The receiver must switch the perceptual dimensions he is utilizing to *match* those of the information source *and* must place (if only temporarily) the perceptual information on the same point of each of the dimensions to "put himself in the other person's shoes." Without at least differentiation this feat is impossible.

The necessity for a multidimensional view of person perception appears obvious. Nonetheless, much psychological theory, and particularly much psychological research, has not taken multidimensionality into account. Often the experimenter avoids multidimensionality by exposing his subject to a highly novel (unfamiliar) situation, i.e., one with which the subject has very limited experience, where his previously obtained dimensions cannot be brought to bear. Through manipulated salience, the experimental interpersonal information is brought into single focus. Certainly, again, this procedure has considerable advantages. Dimensions which could introduce "noise" into the data are eliminated. Reliability of the response may be increased. Subjects are more likely to perceive (and respond on) the experimentally provided dimension, even if it might be a dimension that is not understood or used by subjects in their normal life. However, subjects' answers are more apt to be relevant to the theory tested in the research.

One might ask: How realistic is this experimental procedure? In some cases it can be. If (1) a particular subject typically responds unidimensionally in the real world (e.g., because of lack of experience), or (2) if the subject matter lends itself best to unidimensional perceptions, if (3) the experimenter manages to match the experimental dimension to the subjects' dimension, or if (4) individual differences in the content of the selected single dimension are greatly limited, then this approach is not only experimentally reasonable, but probably also externally valid. It seems unlikely that this would often be the case.

Nonetheless, real-world situations do occasionally exist which may be paralleled by the above-mentioned experimental methodology. When persons are exposed to real-world situations with which they have not previously dealt, i.e., where there are no relevant reference dimensions in their experience, it may be more likely that a single *externally provided* dimension (supplied by the experimenter or some external real-world source) would be utilized, at least initially. The success of political demagogues with politically disinterested and uninformed people might provide a good example.

But even where the experiment of "reduced complexity levels" in contrast to what Tagiuri called "higher order variables" has little immediately applicable value (as was suggested in Chap. 1), it does provide information about the *components* of perceptions in the real world. It does not provide the essence of real world perceptions, however. Additional information about other theoretical components of the higher order integrative interaction of dimensional variables is necessary to predict perceptions in settings that are likely to result in perceptual multidimensionality.

An Example of Dimensional Person Perception: Impression Formation

Another Asch design (1946) may serve to illustrate dimensionality in person perception. Asch developed a task to measure primacy and recency. Subjects responded to two sets of adjectives; e.g., first they described a person with attributes "intelligent, industrious, impulsive," then another person with the attributes "critical, stubborn, envious." Typically, the first person turned out to be a good guy, the second one a bad guy. Their third task was to combine the adjectives; they were to describe someone who is "intelligent, industrious, impulsive, critical, stubborn, and envious." The task was difficult: On a typical good to bad scale, the two "persons" of the earlier tasks had been perceived on opposite ends of the dimension. Where only one judgmental dimension (e.g., good–bad) was available to a subject, the third stimulus person needed to be described as either "good" or "bad"; in other words, one of the two sets of adjectives had to be ignored, leading to either primacy or recency effects. Unfortunately, not all subjects responded with either "primacy" (good guy) or "recency" (bad guy) answers. Why not?

As Streufert and Driver (1967) have shown, differences in the dimensional responses of subjects on such a task can be clearly observed. Subjects who respond more unidimensionally indeed must choose either a primacy or a recency response and ignore or deny the remaining adjectives. Multidimensional differentiators view the described person as both "good" and "bad." For example, he might be viewed as "intelligent and industrious" at work, and "impulsive, critical, stubborn, and envious" when he deals with wife and children.[2] Multidimensional integrators have no problem with the task; all attributes seem to fit into a "whole" personality. For example, the person may be described as an industrial executive who worked hard, used his intelligence to get ahead, made decisions (intelligent ones based on hard-work experience) more rapidly than others, jealously worked his way up, critical of errors in subordinates and superiors, stubbornly pursuing his goal of getting to the top.

Clearly, these differences in response characteristics demonstrate how dimensionality is dependent both on the stimulus (integrated responses are not

---

[2] If this impression formation test were scored for differentiation, so that integrative responses would attain the same score as more unidimensional responses, it should correlate positively with such measures of differentiation as Kelly's REP test.

typically made to the first two tasks!) and on the characteristics of the responding perceiver.

The Development of Dimensionality in Person Perception

Certainly, people are not born with multidimensional perceptions. As Piaget (e.g., 1954; Inhelder & Piaget, 1958) has shown, perceptions are initially quite simple and unorganized. However, the opportunity for perceptual social multidimensionality is probably given relatively early in life. Parents tend to provide their children with "categories" for organization of novel stimuli. These categories can easily develop into dimensions if the conditions for "differentiation" (cf. Chaps. 2, 3) are given. On the other hand, categories may merely turn into ordering points on a single (e.g., an evaluative) dimension if the child is forced to organize stimuli primarily or only according to one specific cognitive operation, e.g., what is "good" vs. "bad." Often, some debating experience, or even teaching a child to "see things from the other point of view," can aid in developing perceptual social dimensionality (cf. Chap. 3). Multidimensional research by Sandra Koslin (personal communication) has shown that children in early grades are quite able to perceive other persons along a number of dimensions. Unfortunately, that ability is often destroyed by the unidimensional emphasis (right vs. wrong in all its connotations) of school experience.

Whether a child develops the capacity (maybe it would be better to say the "style") to view the world multidimensionally, apparently depends on the experiences to which he is exposed. Overprotected children who are not exposed to information that potentially conflicts with their cognitive organization have little opportunity to develop multidimensional perception. If all received information can be easily placed (or distorted to fit) on a single perceptual social dimension, there is no need to develop additional dimensions. Similarly, children who are over-exposed to stimuli, particularly if the stimuli are incongruent, may be forced to "escape" into perceptions that simplify or distort stimulus configurations, so that they can comfortably be placed on a familiar single dimension. On the other hand, moderate exposure to incongruity may—if other conditions are favorable (cf. the statement on development of complexity in Chap. 3)—produce the capacity to perceive multidimensionally. In other words, various kinds of experiences may lead to quite different methods of "assembling" or "integrating" social information, including weighted algebraic summation (Triandis & Fishbein, 1963), averaging (Anderson & Jacobson, 1965), or integration (Streufert, Driver, and associates). It appears that some intermediate amount of stimulation with information that does not comfortably fit previous perceptual dimension(s), an information quantity that allows the child time to examine the perceived information for potential fit or allows him to develop new cognitive organizations for his perceptions *before* additional information is added, would more likely lead to greater perceptual multidimensionality.

We might, then, state that:

7.5 All other things being equal, the more often moderately incongruent information has been presented to a person at moderate load levels, the higher his multidimensionality of perception is likely to be.

Information from others is apt to be varied. One's responses may, at times, be positively and, at times, negatively reinforced. As long as this reinforcement is not relevant to one dimension only and does not vary randomly (Pavlovian neurosis induction), it should generate perceptual conflict that might require reorganization. Consequently, we might propose that:

7.6 All other things being equal, a moderate varying reinforcement history for existing perceptual dimension(s) should serve to increase multidimensionality of perception.

On the contrary, one might propose that:

7.7 A constant (positive or negative) reinforcement history for existing perceptual dimension(s) should serve to stabilize or decrease multidimensionality of perception.

The above propositions explain why individual differences in dimensionality of perception should exist (cf. also Chap. 3). But, these differences should not only exist across persons (cf. the research of Streufert & Driver, 1965), but should also exist across domains within persons (cf. Chap. 3). In some domains, whether through lack of conflicting information or through information overload, dimensionality may not develop, even though multidimensionality of perception is present in other cognitive domains. However, the experiences with developing multidimensional perceptions in one domain should aid—if other phenomena (e.g., affect) do not interfere—in the later development of multidimensionality in other domains.

We might, then, propose that:

7.8 All other things being equal, the development of multidimensional perceptions in one cognitive domain is more difficult to achieve and/or takes more time if multidimensionality of perception is not present in any other cognitive domain of the same person than when it is present in another domain.

The greater the number of cognitive domains within which multidimensional perception is present, the greater should be the ease with which it is developed in new cognitive domains. Of course, the easier "transfer" of dimensionality should be aided by the similarity, and hindered by the dissimilarity, of cognitive domains. Distant domains often show divergent dimensionality from each other. For example, many persons who demonstrate perceptual multidimensionality in domains of the nonsocial cognitive area may be quite unidimensional in their social perceptions.

The ease of developing perceptual multidimensionality in any cognitive domain should, in part, depend on the function of affect associated with the perceived stimuli. Multidimensionality may be developed most easily in a "playful" manner, i.e., when the situation within which a perception occurs is not stressing (i.e., represents some degree of positive affect). Just as information overload or excessive levels of incongruity tend to produce stress, any threat associated with perceived events may result in stress that tends to distort perceptions and reduce dimensionality. We may state that:

7.9 All other things being equal, the greater the stress associated with perceived events, the less likely the multidimensionality of perception for these events.

In other words, if any perception has relevance to other cognitions within the person which are associated with negative affect (e.g., fear, anxiety, or the like), or which are considered of grave importance by the person, then he is less likely to reorganize his cognitions in the face of novel stimuli to develop greater dimensionality, even if this would be advantageous to him. But there need not even be stress involved. Well-established connections among various cognitions and among their perceptual components tend to make the process of dimensional cognitive reorganization more difficult, because several cognitions in several domains are likely to be in need of change. We might say that:

7.10 All other things being equal, the greater the number of previously existing cognitions within and across domains that are associated with a perception, the less likely will be (e.g., in the face of incongruent stimuli) the development of new or additional multidimensionality as a result of that perception.

The organization of cognitive dimensions (as presented in Chap. 3) and their associated perceptions differ from person to person. The concepts of differentiation and integration and the individual differences in complexity need not be discussed here, since we have spent some time on these concepts in Chapters 2 and 3. Just like measured behavior, perceptions can be more unidimensional or multidimensionally differentiated or integrated. However, in this context, we should spend some additional time on the differentiators. In some cases, differentiators demonstrate a perceptual process that seems much more rarely evident in their behavior. We know from standard research that some persons develop very fine discriminations among stimuli on some single dimension. Similarly, some persons seem to develop extensive dimensional differentiation. Typically, these persons find it difficult to integrate, perhaps because the amount of information available in the form of dimensions constitutes an overload. They seem to operate with an inordinate number of orthogonal dimensions on which few or single events may be placed. In contrast, it appears that persons who develop *moderate* perceptual dimensionality (moderate differentiators) are much more likely to learn to integrate these dimensions.

We might say that:

7.11 While the attainment of moderate perceptual differentiation appears to be an aid to potential perceptual integration, high levels of differentiation appear to be a hindrance to perceptual integration.

Empathy and Attraction

The organization of information cannot occur in a vacuum. If it does, the organization is likely to be faulty, because it has not been subjected to reality testing. However, much perception is a process leading to behavior, which in turn produces changes in the world surrounding an individual. This behavior and its effects are then perceived, allowing for something of a reality check. Assuming that our subject is operating in a world which permits potential perceptual complexity (multidimensionality), and assuming that others around him respond at least in part on the basis of multidimensional cognitions, then the match of an individual's dimensional perceptions with those of his social partners is likely to be increased, and the usefulness and number of his dimensions may also be increased. We might then state that:

7.12 All other things being equal, the more feedback a person receives as a result of his own actions at moderate information load levels, the higher is his likely multidimensionality of perceptions,

and

7.13 The longer (over extended time periods) the interaction between persons (in the absence of conflict), the greater is the likely match of content and dimensionality of their perceptions.

Matching levels of dimensionality between two persons (cf. the previous chapter) would produce optimal potential for communication, and with it optimally accurate perception of the other (empathy). Empathy, however, is difficult to achieve with another person whom one rejects. Consequently, empathic perception should work for more unidimensional persons only, if they view the other as similar to themselves (if he places judgments of information generally in the same fashion on a single relevant dimension). In other words, for more unidimensional persons, *content* becomes a salient factor in perceptual accuracy. For the more multidimensional persons, particularly for integrators, this may not be necessary, since (a) a number of dimensions for comparison are available, and (b) alternate ordering of stimuli on various dimensions may be achieved by a reintegration process, even a temporary "empathic" one. For example, the multidimensional perceiver might say: If I were placed in his situation, I would be able to see the world as he does.

We may then propose, *all things being equal*:

7.14 *Matching perceptions with another (empathy) is possible between more unidimensional persons only when they are similar in their placement of relevant stimuli on a relevant single dimension.*

7.15 *Potential accuracy of perception of persons placing relevant stimuli differently on various dimensions is more likely with increasing (primarily integrative) multidimensionality of the perceiver.*

7.16 *Greater empathy in social perception is a function of the accuracy of perceptions on a number of dimensions (if present) and their integration into superordinate judgments.*

We may add, the frequently found attraction on the basis of similarity (e.g., Byrne, 1971) and the inverse (Secord, Backman, & Eachus, 1964) should also extend to dimensionality:

7.17 *All other things being equal, the greater the dimensional similarity of persons, the greater their attraction to each other.*

This latter proposition should hold particularly for persons with multidimensional perceptions. As fewer and fewer perceptual dimensions are available, the content of the dimensions should take on greater and greater importance. For more unidimensional persons, attraction should be based on identical placement of content (e.g., attitudes) on one or few dimensions.

Information Load, Complexity, and Perception

Predictions for the separate and joint effects of interpersonal differences in dimensionality and for the effects of information load on perceptual complexity should parallel the predictions that were made in Chapter 3 with regard to complexity in general, and with regard to behavioral complexity in specific. In this case, we are, however, not only concerned with the interaction of interpersonal differences with load, but also with novelty vs. familiarity of the information that is received by a target person. In other words, we must also consider whether the information he is receiving is addressable to his present cognitive dimensionality.

We might predict that:

7.18 Saliently (e.g., in an experiment) provided information with relevance to a single dimension that is clearly communicated to the target by the source, or information provided to the target on a single dimension with which he is sufficiently familiar, will be perceived by the target as intended by the source of the communication.

7.19 In the absence of novel or conflicting (incongruent) information, often at low levels of information load, the dimensionality employed by the target perceiver will not change, and the number of dimensions employed in perception are likely to be minimal.

7.20 Novel highly incongruent information that is not addressable to the current dimensional system will likely be perceived unidimensionally (via distortion onto an existing dimension or via placement onto a dimension which is formed to accommodate the information—potentially temporarily—in the absence of other usable dimensions).

7.21 Moderate load levels of information addressable to the present dimensional system will likely be placed by the target perceiver on more than one dimension, as long as several dimensions relevant to the information exist in the cognitive structure of the target.

7.22 Perceptual integrative dimensionality should be highest at moderate levels of moderately incongruent novel information load. Increases in novel incongruent information or increases in load beyond that level should result in decreased perceptual integrative dimensionality.

7.23 Persons with generally higher levels of perceptual dimensional capacity should exceed persons of generally lower levels of perceptual capacity in perceptual complexity on measures of perceptual integration, particularly when information load is moderate. They should exceed persons of generally lower levels of perceptual capacity in perceptual complexity on measures of perceptual differentiation when information load is moderate and when it is high.

ATTRIBUTION

Some segments of the work on person perception have recently been known under another name: "attribution." When we attribute certain characteristics to ourselves or to the environment, we perceive persons along one or more dimensions. To attribute a characteristic, we might either express a judgment on some dimension, or we might integrate single judgments on a number of dimensions into one or more combinatory judgments.

Attribution, then, is one of the processes of person perception. But, from the point of view of complexity theory, it is not just a new name; there is also (at least in many cases) evidence of a more multidimensional approach than is utilized in the study of other person perception processes. The experimenter often provides the subject with information about a number of characteristics of the stimulus person (or of himself), and assumes that the perceiving subject will utilize these diverse informational characteristics to produce some (often single) measured judgment. For instance, the perceiver may be told that the stimulus person has committed a severe or a minor crime, that this is his first or tenth crime, and that he is attractively or unattractively dressed. The perceiving subject has to decide upon the level of responsibility to be attributed to the stimulus person.

In many cases, the diverse characteristics of, or behavioral categories ascribed to, the stimulus person may be conceived—or are even intended—as information on a number of independent dimensions. While the "categories" may not necessarily be dimensions in themselves, they may represent end-points of or the spaces between dimensions. Weiner's and associates' utiliza-tion of the stable-unstable and the internal-external dimensions to generate a matrix of perceptual categories are discussed below. Can and do subjects perceive the information on these dimensions?

We have stated repeatedly that dimensionality is *not* inherent in semantic stimulus information, unless we are specifically dealing with a message of specific dimensionality sent by a source to a target. Dimensionality exists in the mind of the perceiver. However, many theorists and researchers, par-ticularly in the area of attribution, appear to assume that experimentally provided information is specifically multidimensional (or at least multifactorial or multicharacteristic) in nature. The experimenter may select the dimensions that appear obvious to *him*, and assume that the subject will utilize the same dimensions in his perceptions and attributions as well. We would propose that it is unlikely an experimenter would be able to determine in advance the dimensions on which a particular subject will perceive information provided to him, unless that informational dimension is made highly salient to the subject. Shaw and Sulzer (1964), for example, designed an experiment in which they gave subjects information about environmental characteristics surrounding the action of a stimulus person and, in addition, provided information about the internal state of the stimulus person. When the information about the internal state was left ambiguous, subjects responded with their attributions to the en-vironmental characteristics. On the other hand, when internal states were pre-sented saliently, the attributions varied with the internal state of the stimulus person, not with environmental characteristics. In other words, subjects responded to either one *or* the other of the informational dimensions. Apparently they were able to use both dimensions, but tended to choose the more clearly defined or, if possible, the more salient one.

However, subjects do not always respond on the basis of a single dimension alone. Unfortunately, whether they do or do not is often difficult to determine. Most experiments have not been designed to allow for a check on dimensionality. We have already stated that it is typically the experimenter who selects his "dimensions" on which the stimulus material is presented (cf. also Bem, 1972). The subject may or may not respond multidimensionally to this information. In some cases, it may be possible to determine whether he did or did not by a look at the dependent variable. But it may also not be possible. Often the dependent variable is a single one, e.g., a measure of attribution of responsibility, or attribution of intent, etc. To determine whether multidimensionality did play a part in the responses of the subjects, we might study the diverse effects of the information variables on attribution responses.[3] If all variables have the same, or highly similar effects, then the responses of the subjects may well have been unidimensional. Take a subject who is asked to assign a responsibility attribution value to a stimulus person who is either described as having committed a serious, in contrast to a minor, crime, as being pleasant vs. unpleasant in appearance, and as having a previous criminal record vs. not having such a record. If the subject perceives unidimensionally, for example, on a good-bad dimension, then he may view committing a serious crime as more "bad" than committing a minor crime, being pleasant in appearance might be good as opposed to being unpleasant in appearance (bad), and having a criminal record may be another indication of badness. The subject may merely "add" or "average" the information he has received on a single dimensional scale and produce the appropriate judgment. A graphic representation of such additivity would show parallel lines.

Multidimensionality may (but need not) be demonstrated by interactions among the informational variables on the response measure, or by curvilinear relationships among them. An interaction can, however, be produced by other effects as well, for example, by the inversion of an additive unidimensional scale. Usually a careful look at the data will tell.

Frieze and Weiner (1971) report an experiment in which subjects repeatedly judged the causes of success or failure which stimulus persons experienced in a task. Ability, effort, task difficulty, and luck were employed as the effects of Weiner's 2×2 stable-unstable and internal-external

---

[3] Of course, we are typically dealing with "between" designs. Consequently, we can often only infer from others in the sample what dimension(s) a subject *might* have used if he had been placed in a different cell.

dimensional matrix.[4] The experiments of Weiner and associates typically make the experimental dimensions quite salient to the subjects. Apparently the subjects of Frieze and Weiner did perceive the informational "dimensionality" and used the information dimensionally. In the first experiment reported by Frieze and Weiner (1971), effort and ability (the personal variables) may have added (unidimensionally) into the attribution response. However, luck and task difficulty appeared not to be additive. In a second experiment, the authors obtained results suggesting potentially additive effects of luck and task difficulty, but nonadditivity between these two and the remaining dimensions. Apparently, the subjects did perceive the stimulus information on more than one dimension (quite possibly even those intended by the experimenter).

Again, salience produced specific perceptual characteristics. In the experiment of Shaw and Sulzer (1964), it resulted in unidimensional, in the latter experiment in multidimensional perception. But not all experiments manipulate their variables with as much salience, and not all real-world situations (if one is interested in external validity of experiments) have highly salient characteristics. Of course, other variables may have similar consequences. In an experiment by Carroll and Payne (1976), experience in the relevant task had similar effects. While those unfamiliar with the experimental task combined information additively, experts appeared to make multidimensional (multiplicative) integrative decisions on an attribution problem. What would occur if salience and differences in experience are not given, but the information provided to a perceiver is sufficiently high in quantity and diversity to produce potential multidimensionality of perception?

If an experimenter designs a study to measure the effects of a number of informational characteristics (selecting the dimensions that appear reasonable or even inherent in the environment *to him*), the subject may perceive them unidimensionally, multidimensionally differentiative, or multidimensionally integrative. Only in the last case will the response be based on several dimensions at the same time (i.e., will not be an additive or averaged response on a single dimension). What dimensions are integrated in the judgment of the information, how great a part they play in an integrated response, and consequently what the integrated response will be, would possibly depend on *any* specific characteristic of the stimulus situation. Changing a small part of the stimulus situation would not greatly change the response of a person who uses the information additively on a single dimension, but could greatly change, even invert, the responses of someone who perceives that information integratively. With any change in the integration process, any degree of change in the response is feasible. The consequence may be an *apparent* instability of

---

[4] Research by Weiner, Heckhausen, Meyer, and Cook (1972) had shown that data collection based on a locus of control dimension alone results in confounds. Rather, two separate dimensions (those used by Weiner and associates) are needed to produce meaningful attributions.

experimental results. Changing the subject population, e.g., Weiner and Kukla (1970) and Menapace and Doby (1976), or making minor changes in instructions or in the background situation of the experiment, may produce major changes on the dependent variable. The experimenter who is unaware of the part played by the dimensions of the integrating perceiver is likely to credit the discrepant experimental results to error or worse. If he had taken dimensionality of the perceiving subject into account, he would have been able to explain the discrepancy and to utilize it in designing his next experiment. We will provide an example of this kind of problem later, i.e., experiments by two authors who have obtained opposing results in research on attribution of responsibility with some relatively minor changes in the experimental design.

Dimensionality and Attribution Theory

Attribution theorists typically credit the perceiver with the ability to consider a number of phenomena in determining whether and why a person acted in any particular fashion. These phenomena reflect potentially different dimensional judgments (but need not be). Kelley (1971), for instance, describes a cube employing three dimensions of judgments: distinctiveness (a task dimension), consistency (a time dimension), and consensus (a dimension of person comparison). Kelley, moreover, credits the perceiver with the ability to use these dimensions jointly (we would say either add or integrate them). Based on the location of the stimulus on the three dimensions, the perceiver should be able to conclude whether the stimulus person's action was intentional or accidental, whether it is person specific, etc. Data from research testing Kelley's model has generally been supportive. However, some studies have shown that relatively *small* differences in manipulation of variables (e.g., Hansen & Lowe, 1976) or order of information (e.g., Ruble & Feldman, 1976) can produce considerable differences in attributions. Feldman, Higgins, Karlovac, and Ruble (1976) have provided evidence that Kelley's (experimenter induced) dimensions function well only as long as the subjects have limited experience with the area in which attributions are made. Familiarity appears to eliminate at least one of the experimenter induced dimensions.

If the dimensions proposed by Kelley were indeed those that are used by the various subjects in attribution experiments and by the man on the street when he is attributing characteristics to some actor in the real world, then we should find these dimensions as well in the theories of others.

However, that does not appear to be the case. For example, Davis and associates (e.g., Ossorio & Davis, 1968; cf. also Maselli & Altrocchi, 1969) view the perceiver as attempting to determine whether the stimulus person is trying to accomplish something (e.g., has a reason for doing what he does), has the know-how to do it, is engaging in an act that would accomplish the goal, and whether a result is produced that is not due to accident or coincidence but rather due to skill and competence. Jones and Nisbett (1971) believe that the perceiver may utilize the following data in his attributions: (1) effect data including the nature of the act, the outcome of the act, and its effect on the actor; (2) cause data including the environment and intention, effort, etc.; and (3) historical data (similar to Kelley's theory) including consensus, distinctiveness, and consistency of the act. We have already mentioned the work of Weiner who (working in a somewhat different area) uses a two-dimensional system (stable–unstable and internal–external) to define four attribution categories (ability, effort, task difficulty, and luck). Yet other theorists and researchers in the attribution area use other dimensions of attribution.

It seems unlikely that *all* subjects would use *all* these dimensions or categories provided by the various theorists and researchers with dimensional relevance. It is probably more likely that subjects can be brought to use the categories or dimensions either unidimensionally or multidimensionally (if they have the capacity) under conditions of experimentally produced salience for the relevant perceptions. As Streufert and Streufert (1969) have shown, there should at least be some differences among subjects in the dimensionality of attributional responses. But even if subjects use several salient "provided" dimensions, they may find it difficult to do so, something that would not be the case when they are using their own familiar dimensions. As a result, their responses on the attribution measure should be experimentally "better," the fewer externally provided dimensions are contained in the information. The finding of Orvis, Cunningham, and Kelley (1975) that their subjects responded more meaningfully to two than to three provided informational dimensions may be due to this phenomenon. (Alternatively, it may be due to the strain of integration produced by a larger number of experimentally provided dimensions on the more unidimensional subjects in the sample.)

A resolution of the theoretical problem of which specific dimensions should be considered valid and reliable perceptual characteristics of persons in an attribution task would be quite helpful. Only when we can accurately tap the potential dimensionality (and the actual dimensionality) of our subjects, can we develop theories that will not only hold in the laboratory, where salience can be easily induced, but will also hold in the "real world."

Dimensionality and Attributions of Responsibility

One of the attribution theories is directly relevant to attributions of responsibility. Shaw (1972) has proposed a number of variables (dimensions?) which should apply to responsibility attributions: (1) the stimulus person's internal state, including his intent, motivation, ability, and abnormality (if any); (2) the stimulus person's characteristics, including his similarity to the perceiver and his normative characteristics; (3) the outcome of his action, including the likelihood of the outcome (cf. Kelley) and the positiveness, negativeness, severity, etc., of the outcome; and (4) the situation in which the stimulus person operates, including whether or not he had a choice when he engaged in the action. Further, Shaw considers the characteristics of the perceiver as well. The perceiver is viewed in a Piagetian sense; e.g., the adult is expected to include more (e.g., situations) stimulus variables (dimensions) than the child in producing an attribution judgment. Alternatively, he would have more (single) perceptual dimensions available to him from which he may select one (or more) for an attributional judgment. We might say that the adult is considered more multidimensional than the child (cf. the research of Shaw & Sulzer, 1964). It appears, then, that attribution of responsibility might occur on different, or simultaneously on several, dimensions.

Shaw (1972) predicts a curvilinear relationship between outcome likelihood and attributions of responsibility, a relationship which also suggests the operation of more than one dimension. More recently, Pepitone (1976) has suggested that a complex set of dimensions underlying judgments leading to attributions of seriousness of an act for which a person is responsible and to recommendations for punishment. Pepitone lists seven such dimensions. Nonetheless, much of the research on attributions of responsibility has not considered the potential multidimensionality inherent in responsibility perceptions. This research typically describes some event and then asks the perceiver to indicate whether the stimulus person described in the story is responsible, guilty, should pay a fine, etc. The results obtained by the various research have been less than uniform. Particularly, the research data of Walster (1966) and Shaver (1970) stand in direct conflict with each other. Nogami (1973) and Streufert and Nogami (1973) have proposed that various groups of subjects—because of subtle differences in the instructions which likely defined the meaning of relevant dependent variables—may have understood the meaning of the term "responsibility" differently.[5] In other words, what the experimenters may have viewed as a single concept (responsibility), may have been utilized by their subjects on the basis of two divergent (orthogonal and potentially interactive) dimensions. In one case, the experimental instructions may have made a dimension of "moral responsibility" the salient response dimension; in the other case, the instructions may have made a "causality" dimension the salient one.

[5] Previous research (Kerr, Atkin, Stasser, Meek, Hold and Davis, 1976) has shown that subjects can be cued to attribute guilt divergently depending on the experimenter's definitions of relevant terms.

Let us consider that possibility in greater detail. As in many psychological experiments, the subjects of Walster (1966) and Shaver (1970) were placed in a somewhat novel situation, a situation where no clear previous dimensionality may have existed. The story, of course, produced references to previously established dimensions—in Shaver's work, e.g., that of "justice in a court of law." The court issue did not occur in Walster's experiment. In one case, subjects were cued to indicate whether the culprit had initiated (i.e., caused) the event; in the other, they were cued to indicate whether he had intended the event and/or had been negligent. In both situations, however, subjects were responding in terms of "responsibility." It might have been better to ask for two different judgments, for "causality" and "responsibility." Later experiments of our research group appear to show that "causality" and "responsibility," when measured under conditions of increasing seriousness of an event, tend to interact: attributed responsibility decreases with increasing seriousness, while attributed causality (logically) increases. This finding might resolve the differences between Walster and Shaver, but it does more than that. It points out that subjects in a novel situation are likely to be seduced into using the experimenter's (or in the real world, some communicator's) dimension of judgment.

7.24 All other things being equal, in unfamiliar situations (including many laboratory settings), persons will tend to accept the externally communicated dimension(s) for perceptual judgments.

Nonetheless, these communicated dimensions may be short-lived, or may be modified as additional information becomes available. Conclusions drawn on the basis of externally communicated dimensions, even in unfamiliar situations, may also be short-lived. In some situations, however, they may be very realistic. Take, for example, the argument of Streufert and Nogami (1973) that persons assigned to a jury without previous experience may well be subject to perceptual influence through the manipulation of "responsibility" and "causality" concepts. If the dimension "guilty–not guilty" is associated by a lawyer with causality in his statements to the jury, then increasing severity of an accident should result in greater probability that a guilty verdict will be attained. On the other hand, should the lawyer associate guilt with responsibility, then the likelihood of a guilty verdict should decrease with increasing severity. This argument reflects the underlying proposition that

7.25 In unfamiliar situations (including many laboratory settings), persons may accept the equivalence of two or more externally provided dimensions, if equivalence is stated or implied by the communicator.

There are still other ways in which an information source is able to potentially distort perception by reducing perceptual dimensionality in the target, even in situations of "familiar" stimulation. Often the introduction of a preliminary statement (on which critical attention is not focussed) succeeds in dimensionality reduction. The communicating source merely might say: "Since it is obvious that event A cannot be viewed as . . . . , we must deal with it as . . . . Therefore, ..." If the perceiving target does not pay very close attention, the initial statement has eliminated one or more dimensions of judgment, leaving only the dimension on which the communicator chooses to focus the attention of the target.

REFERENCES

Anderson, N. H., & Jacobson, A. Effect of stimulus inconsistency and discounting instructions in personality impression formation. *Journal of Personality and Social Psychology,* 1965, **4**, 531-539.

Asch, S. E. Forming impressions of personality. *Journal of Abnormal and Social Psychology,* 1946, **41**, 258-290.

Asch, S. E. *Social psychology.* New York: Prentice-Hall, 1952.

Asch, S. E. Issues in the study of social influence on judgment. In J. A. Berg & B. M. Bass (Eds.), *Conformity and deviation.* New York: Harper, 1961.

Bem, D. J. Self perception theory. In L. Berkowitz (Ed.), *Advances in experimental social psychology* (Vol. 6). New York: Academic Press, 1972.

Bieri, J. Cognitive complexity–simplicity and predictive behavior. *Journal of Abnormal and Social Psychology,* 1955, **51**, 263-268.

Bieri, J. Complexity–simplicity as a personality variable in cognitive and preferential behavior. In D. W. Fiske & S. R. Maddi (Eds.), *Functions of varied experience.* Homewood, Ill.: Dorsey, 1961.

Bovard, E. W. Group structure and perception. *Journal of Abnormal and Social Psychology,* 1951, **46**, 398-405.

Brown, R. *Social psychology.* New York: Free Press, 1965.

Byrne, D. *The attraction paradigm.* New York: Academic Press, 1971.

Carroll, J. S., & Payne, J. W. *Causal attributions as mediating factors between seriousness of crime and severity of prison term.* Paper presented at the convention of the American Psychological Association, Washington, D.C., 1976.

Deutsch, M., & Gerard, H. B. A study of normative and informational social influences upon individual judgment. *Journal of Abnormal and Social Psychology,* 1955, **51**, 629-636.

Feldman, N. S., Higgins, E. T., Karlovac, M., & Ruble, D. N. Use of consensus information in causal attributions as a function of temporal presentation and availability of direct information. *Journal of Personality and Social Psychology,* 1976, **34,** 694-698.

Flament, C. Ambiguité du stimulus, incertitude de la résponse et processus d'influence sociale. *Anneé Psychologie,* 1959, **59,** 73-92.

Frieze, I., & Weiner, B. Cue utilization and attributional judgments for success and failure. *Journal of Personality,* 1971, **39,** 591-605.

Gollin, E. S., & Rosenberg, S. Concept formation and impressions of personality. *Journal of Abnormal and Social Psychology,* 1956, **52,** 39-42.

Hansen, R. D., & Lowe, C. A. Distinctiveness and consensus: The influence of behavioral information on actors' and observers' attributions. *Journal of Personality and Social Psychology,* 1976, **34,** 425-433.

Hudson, W. Pictorial depth perception in sub-cultural groups in Africa. *Journal of Social Psychology,* 1960, **52,** 183-208.

Inhelder, B., & Piaget, J. *The growth of logical thinking from childhood to adolescence.* New York: Basic Books, 1958.

Jackson, D. N. The measurement of perceived personality trait relationships. In N. F. Washburn (Ed.), *Decisions, values and groups* (Vol. 2). New York: Pergamon, 1962.

Jackson, D. N., & Messick, S. Individual differences in social perception. *British Journal of Social and Clinical Psychology,* 1963, **2,** 1-10.

Jackson, J. M., & Saltzstein, H. D. The effect of person–group relationships on conformity processes. *Journal of Abnormal and Social Psychology,* 1958, **56,** 279-281.

Jones, E. E., & Nisbett, R. *The actor and the observer: Divergent perceptions of the causes of behavior.* New York: General Learning Press Module, 1971.

Kelley, H. H. Causal schemata and the attribution process. In E. E. Jones, D. E. Kanouse, H. H. Kelley, R. E. Nisbett, S. Valins, & B. Weiner (Eds.), *Attributions: Perceiving the causes of behavior.* New York: General Learning Press, 1971.

Kelman, H. C. Processes of opinion change. *Public Opinion Quarterly,* 1961, **25,** 57-78.

Kerr, N. L., Atkin, R. S., Stasser, G., Meek, D., Holt, R. W., & Davis, J. H. Guilt beyond reasonable doubt: Effects of concept definition and assigned decision rule on the judgment of mock jurors. *Journal of Personality and Social Psychology,* 1976, **34,** 282-294.

Maselli, M. D., & Altrocchi, J. Attribution of intent. *Psychological Bulletin,* 1969, **71,** 445-454.

Mayo, C., & Crockett, W. H. Cognitive complexity and primacy-recency effects in impression formation. *Journal of Abnormal and Social Psychology,* 1964, **68,** 335-338.

Menapace, R. H., & Doby, C. Causal attributions for success and failure for psychiatric rehabilitees and college students. *Journal of Personality and Social Psychology*, 1976, **34**, 447-454.

Nogami, G. Y. Attributions of social causality and responsibility. Purdue University: ONR Tech. Rep. No. 15, 1973.

Orvis, B. R., Cunningham, J. D., & Kelley, H. H. A close examination of causal inference: The roles of consensus, distinctiveness, and consistency information. *Journal of Personality and Social Psychology*, 1975, **32**, 605-616.

Ossorio, P. G., & Davis, K. K. The self intentionality and reactions to evaluations. In C. Gordon & K. Gergen (Eds.), *Self in society*. New York: Wiley, 1968.

Pepitone, A. *Judgments of criminal aggression*. Paper presented at the convention of the American Psychological Association, Washington, D.C., 1976.

Piaget, J. *The construction of reality in the child*. New York: Basic Books, 1954.

Ruble, D. N., & Feldman, N. S. Order of consensus, distinctiveness and consistency information on causal attributions. *Journal of Personality and Social Psychology*, 1976, **34**, 930-937.

Sarbin, T. R. Role theory. In G. Lindzey (Ed.), *Handbook of social psychology* (Vol. 1). Cambridge, Mass.: Addison-Wesley, 1954.

Schroder, H. M., Driver, M. J., & Streufert, S. *Human information processing*. New York: Holt, Rinehart & Winston, 1967.

Secord, P. F., Backman, C. W., & Eachus, H. T. Effects of imbalance in the self concept on the perception of persons. *Journal of Abnormal and Social Psychology*, 1964, **68**, 442-446.

Shaver, K. G. Defensive attribution effects of severity and relevance on the responsibility assigned for an accident. *Journal of Personality and Social Psychology*, 1970, **14**, 101-113.

Shaw, J. I. Reactions of victims and defendants of varying degrees of attractiveness. *Psychonomic Science*, 1972, **27**, 329-330.

Shaw, M. E., & Sulzer, J. L. An empirical test of Heider's levels of attribution of responsibility. *Journal of Abnormal and Social Psychology*, 1964, **69**, 39-46.

Shrauger, S., & Altrocchi, J. The personality of the perceiver as a factor in person perception. *Psychological Bulletin*, 1964, **62**, 289-308.

Sieber, J. E., & Lanzetta, J. T. Conflict and conceptual structure as determinants of decision-making behavior. *Journal of Personality*, 1964, **32**, 622-641.

Streufert, S., & Driver, M. J. Conceptual structure, information load and perceptual complexity. *Psychonomic Science*, 1965, **3**, 249-250.

Streufert, S., & Driver, M. J. Impression formation as a measure of the complexity of conceptual structure. *Educational and Psychological Measurement,* 1967, **27**, 1025-1039.

Streufert, S., & Nogami, G. Y. Time effects on the attribution process: Does attribution of causality differ from attribution of responsibility? Purdue University: ONR Tech. Rep. No. 16, 1973.

Streufert, S., & Streufert, S. C. Effects of conceptual structure, failure and success on attribution of causality and interpersonal attitudes. *Journal of Personality and Social Psychology,* 1969, **11**, 138-147.

Tagiuri, R. Person perception. In G. Lindzey & E. Aronson (Eds.), *The handbook of social psychology* (Vol. 3). Reading, Mass.: Addison-Wesley, 1969.

Tajfel, H. Social and cultural factors in perception. In G. Lindzey & E. Aronson (Eds.), *The handbook of social psychology* (Vol. 3). Reading, Mass.: Addison-Wesley, 1969.

Todd, F. J., & Rappoport, L. A cognitive structure approach to person perception: A comparison of two models. *Journal of Abnormal and Social Psychology,* 1964, **68**, 469-478.

Triandis, H. C., & Fishbein, M. Cognitive interaction in person perception. *Journal of Abnormal and Social Psychology,* 1963, **67**, 446-453.

Tucker, L. R. Implication of factor analysis of three-way matrices for measurement of change. In C. W. Harris (Ed.), *Problems in measuring change.* Madison: University of Wisconsin Press, 1963.

Walster, E. Assignment of responsibility for an accident. *Journal of Personality and Social Psychology,* 1966, **3**, 73-79.

Weiner, B., Heckhausen, H., Meyer, W. U., & Cook, R. C. Causal ascriptions and achievement behavior: The conceptual analysis of effort and reanalysis of locus of control. *Journal of Personality and Social Psychology*, 1972, **21**, 239-248.

Weiner, B., & Kukla, A. An attributional analysis of achievement motivation. *Journal of Personality and Social Psychology,* 1970, **15**, 1-20.

Wiener, M. Certainty of judgment as a variable in conformity behavior. *Journal of Psychology,* 1958, **48**, 257-263.

Wiener, M. Carpenter, J. T., & Carpenter, B. Some determinants of conformity behavior. *Journal of Social Psychology,* 1957, **45**, 289-297.

CHAPTER 8

CONCLUDING
COMMENTS

THE GIAL AND COMPLEXITY

This volume has dealt with two separate theories: Complexity theory and GIAL theory. In Chapters 6 and 7, we pointed out how complexity theory and, to some smaller degree, GIAL theory, relate to various areas of human, particularly social, psychology. But we have not related the two theories to each other to any great degree. This section should do that, as far as it is possible at the current state of knowledge.

We remind the reader that the two theories have one thing in common but, on the whole, have many more differences than commonalities. Both theories view perception and behavior in a multidimensional fashion. While complexity theory deals with the dimensionality of human perception and behavior directly, GIAL theory views one segment of human perception (and to some degree behavior) in a multidimensional way. So far the commonalities. There are many more differences; only some of them will be mentioned. Complexity theory tends to be general and interacts with many other theoretical propositions. GIAL theory is specific and deals only with human handling of information, specifically with the incongruity and the inconsistency (see Chap.

5) of information. As such, it relates to fewer other positions. While complexity may only be in part a learned style and in part hereditary, a person's GIAL appears to be primarily due to past experience. Complexity describes the degree to which a person has the competence to process information in a particular way; GIAL is concerned with an adaptation level related to the processing of information. The GIAL holds no implication of competence.

Nonetheless, both theories deal with information processing. If both influence the quantity and/or the kind of information that is processed, and if they in part determine how it is processed, then we should find some interactive effects of complexity with GIAL. These effects are more closely examined below.

Interactive Effects in Development

Dealing with incongruity tends to be difficult for the young organism whose GIAL is still at a very low level. In the infant, incongruity typically results in crying, bringing the responsible adult to the scene, who will—if he or she can determine the cause of the problem—recreate the comfortable congruent environment with which the young human is "familiar." Nonetheless, the infant is for a time exposed to some level of incongruity, potentially resulting in the first rise in an incongruity adaptation level. As we can see from observation of infants, some amount of incongruity is—or quickly becomes—expected, sought, and maybe pleasant, even during the first year of life. Even before the infant can focus sharply, the blurry shapes and colors of a mobile hold some apparent interest. Slowly a SIAL, at least for visual stimuli, is likely to develop toward a somewhat higher level, before semantic communication is widely understood. At this early age, semantic incongruity cannot yet occur.

After the development of semantic understanding, the first dimension for the placement of semantic stimuli becomes a possibility. Only when incongruity arises on this dimension does multidimensionality of semantic space become useful and possible. As long as it is easy to place all incoming stimuli without conflict on a single existing dimension, there is no need for the development of additional dimensions. We might consequently state that:

8.1 Perceived (semantic) incongruity is the basic necessity for the development of (semantic) flexible differentiative or integrative dimensionality.

We do not mean that a child cannot be *taught* to read particular stimuli on one dimension and other stimuli on a second (or third, etc.) dimension. In that case, however, he is merely categorizing the world, not differentiating it (cf. the discussion in Chap. 2 on categorization and categorizing measures of cognitive structure). Differentiation is present only when the same stimulus can be placed on several different dimensions. An interesting observation which relates to categorization in childhood is the "spurious dimensionality" that is at times displayed by children. The child may be exposed to a stimulus word that is (unknown to him) identical in meaning to another word he already knows. Initially, he believes that the word means something different, that it relates to a different overall concept, etc. He develops a dimension on which this stimulus word (and likely others) are placed. When the child finds out that the word is identical in meaning to another word in his vocabulary, the dimensionality often collapses (without incongruity if the dimensions are perfect correlates of each other, with incongruity if they are not).

This "categorizing" phenomenon, however, does not only occur in children. The experiments of Rokeach (e.g., Rokeach & Cochrane, 1972), in which it is demonstrated to subjects that they are dogmatic in an area in which they claim to be undogmatic and liberal, produce attitude change in the direction of lesser dogmatism. The success of these experiments is probably due to increased awareness in subjects that they are "categorizing." For example, subjects may have previously placed a specific stimulus (e.g., the name of some minority group) on only one dimension (e.g., the unfavorable end of the good-bad dimension) and did not relate the stimulus word or their own perceptual process with regard to the word to the liberal-conservative dimension. Indicating to the subject that the stimulus (the semantic label of the minority group) is also relevant to the other dimension (e.g., "If you are liberal, then why do you call this group 'bad'?") results in cognitive restructuring on the evaluative dimension, producing the attitude change.

Incongruities of which a person is made aware, then, must be resolved in one fashion or another. They may be resolved unidimensionally by distortion of the stimulus information. Alternatively, they may be resolved (initially via differentiative, later via differentiative and integrative effort) by the placement of the stimulus or the stimulus configuration on one or more dimensions, without necessarily producing distortions of the information.

In any case, incongruity in the developmental sequence must precede the development of multidimensionality. We can—as far as development is concerned—then only talk about the effects of incongruity and of GIAL on complexity, not the inverse. On the other hand (see below), if we view any current state of dimensionality or GIAL as *existing* (at a more or less constant level) at any point in time, i.e., at any given level of development, then we can talk about both the effect of complexity on the GIAL and the effects of the GIAL on complexity. The next section of this chapter will deal with these influences.

Effects of an Established GIAL on Complexity

The figure 5.11 suggests that a person has established a GIAL at some level, and that inconsistencies in one direction or another will produce different kinds of activity. Extreme inconsistency should result in boredom on one side and in panic or fear reactions on the other side. Neither one of these is likely to result in the kind of information processing that would aid in the development or in the operationalization of multidimensional activities. *Cloze actions,* as seen from the many studies published by dissonance researchers, also are not likely to lead to multidimensionality. Of course, multidimensional activity may occur as soon as incongruity is partially reduced (e.g., to consistency) and as long as enough incongruity remains to allow for differentiation and integration. On the other hand, *complex information search* (not called "complex" without reason) implies that a person who is *not* currently overloaded with incongruity can "explore" the situation, and can—as he reduces existing incongruity, potentially via integrations—develop new incongruities to bring him toward his GIAL. This process allows the utilization or the development of multidimensional stimulus placement *if the preconditions for multidimensionality are otherwise given.* We can thus expect that multidimensionality would most likely occur or increase when the incongruity level to which persons are exposed tends to be at, or somewhat below, their GIAL.[1] We can expect less multidimensionality in the incongruity range from the GIAL toward moderately high levels of incongruity, and we can expect little or no multidimensionality for incongruity levels considerably beyond the GIAL in one direction or another.

Of course, the particular level of incongruity where a person's GIAL may be placed has its own effects on dimensionality. A very low GIAL would not allow much incongruity to occur before cloze actions predominate. The development of multidimensionality may not even be necessary (or useful) for such a person, and may not occur. Similarly, a person with a very high GIAL may be so continuously overloaded that his ability to develop or utilize multidimensional thought processes could be seriously reduced.[2] On a first view, it might seem that a person with a high GIAL might be able to generate multidimensional activities even when incongruity is high, since his "complex

---

[1] The degree to which an organism develops or uses multidimensional structure of cognitions would directly relate to the degree to which his experienced incongruity levels permit the utilization of complex search activities (moderately low to moderate incongruity below or at his GIAL).

[2] For that matter, effective integrative activity for the high GIAL person may be counterproductive. As incongruity is reduced (if possible) through integration of information, the organism would be forced to immediately turn to the search of incongruous information in the service of his GIAL.

search" activities should reach far into the high levels of incongruous information. However, information load is necessarily raised with incongruity, and we have seen (cf. Chap. 3) that load tends to decrease multidimensionality of information processing. In other words, a very high GIAL does not necessarily suggest that a person is dealing with information (whether unidimensionally or multidimensionally) more effectively.[3]

A moderate GIAL (where load may not be as serious a problem)—with its better balance between load and complex search-producing incongruity levels—may aid in the development and utilization of multidimensionality. In this case, complex information search may even produce incongruity on several dimensions (if several dimensions are present). For persons who already are relatively multidimensional, incongruity on a number of dimensions may aid the organism in maintaining his incongruity level at or near the GIAL. Stated inversely, to maintain that GIAL, he may find it useful to search for multidimensional incongruent information. (Conversely, persons with low GIALs may learn to avoid multidimensional incongruity, leading to lesser complexity.) This activity of the moderate GIAL person may, in the long run, result in the development of higher complexity (and subsequently, incongruity) preference levels and (in some cases) in further development of multidimensionality.

We may then state that:

8.2 The degree to which an organism develops or utilizes multidimensional cognitions (in perception or behavior) relates directly to the degree to which his experienced incongruity levels, in relation to his GIAL, permit the utilization of complex search activities (moderate to moderately low incongruity of information).

In other words, it is assumed that complex search activities would lead to more potential multidimensionality than cloze search activities, which in turn would, under some conditions, lead to more multidimensionality than activities generated when the experienced incongruity far exceeds or remains far below a specific person's GIAL. More specific predictions could be made based on that assumption:

---

[3] The divergent effects of congruous information load vs. incongruous load on perception and behavior should be considered in future research. We would suggest that (similar to the effects of success and failure—cf. Chap. 3) incongruity of load may act as a multiplier of load. To the degree to which incongruity of information requires relating the information to several concepts (with which it is incongruous) or requires several actions to resolve incongruity, it contains proportionately more load then congruous information.

8.3 Prevailing incongruity conditions which are highly discrepant from a person's GIAL (i.e., high levels of inconsistency) in one direction or another would likely result in little, if any, development or utilization of multidimensionality in perception or behavior.

8.4 Incongruity conditions which are somewhat above a person's GIAL should result in low to moderate development or utilization of multidimensionality, unless cloze search is integrative and/or differentiative or permits the reduction of incongruity to such a degree that the remaining incongruity can be utilized in differentiative or integrative perceptions and behavior.

8.5 Incongruity conditions which are somewhat below a person's GIAL should result in moderate to high development and (for already multidimensional persons) in moderate to high utilization of multidimensionality.

8.6 Persons with a very high GIAL are likely to develop low to moderate levels of multidimensionality and (unless their multidimensionality level is already very high) are likely to utilize low to moderate levels of multidimensionality. It is expected that the effects of complex search activities which they would generate even at high incongruity levels are offset by the effects of high load levels.

8.7 Persons with a moderately high or moderate GIAL are likely to develop moderate to high levels of multidimensionality and are likely to utilize (if their multidimensionality levels are already high) moderate to high levels of multidimensionality, particularly if their typical experienced (external) incongruity levels remain somewhat below their current GIAL.

8.8 Persons with a low GIAL are likely to develop and utilize low levels of multidimensionality, since their exposure to information requiring multidimensional placement is probably minimized.

It has already become evident (e.g., propositions 8.6 and 8.7) that the effects of GIAL and complexity on each other follow a "circular" pattern. The degree to which a person experiences stimulus information in more or less multidimensional fashion affects how he responds to incongruity (on the basis of his GIAL) and, in turn, affects (1) further development of the GIAL, and (2) development and utilization of multidimensionality. We will deal primarily with the effects of complexity on the GIAL in the next section. For better understanding of our propositions in this section, however, we may have to make some related statements here. Obviously, the detrimental effects of incongruity on the development and utilization of multidimensionality increase with increasing general unidimensionality of the person involved. While even a small amount of incongruity is often difficult to process multidimensionally for a subject to whom multidimensionality is not or is only minimally available,[4]

[4] It may well be these persons who account for the "incredulity" effect in Osgood and Tannenbaum's (1955) theory.

multidimensional persons may be able to deal (integratively) with much of the incongruity provided by a high GIAL. However, there is some point where they also must collapse under the overlaod of information *per se* and specifically the overload of incongruent information. While we then might propose a low but positive correlation between GIAL and complexity, we would expect that the correlation would break down for persons of very high GIAL levels. On the other hand, at already moderate or high complexity levels (low or high level multidimensional integration), a moderate GIAL or even a moderately high GIAL may aid in the development and utilization of further multidimensionality (if the organism can cope with the environment in this fashion and if he is positively reinforced for his coping behavior).

Effects of Established Complexity on the GIAL

We have seen that a moderately high GIAL (but not a very high GIAL) can be an aid to the development and utilization of multidimensionality. A similar effect can be posited in the opposite direction as well. If the incongruous information to which a person may be exposed can be integrated, then incongruity can likely be reduced via the integrative cognitions of a more multidimensional person. This would mean that apparently high levels of incongruity are not, or do not, remain incongruous to that degree for the integrator. But he may not only be able to handle more incongruity than the more unidimensional person (raising his GIAL over time), he may also be exposed to more incongruity: The reduction of incongruous information material vial integration toward lower incongruity levels would sooner call forth complex search, which in turn would again (at a more rapid rate) expose the person to incongruity levels above his GIAL. As a result, the development of the GIAL may proceed faster and to higher levels.

We have stated that levels of incongruity above the GIAL may be reduced via integration. Can integration then represent a "cloze action"? We propose that it can. For the more unidimensional person, cloze actions would more likely take the form of distortions of information, dissonance reduction, etc. For the more multidimensional person, they may also take the forms of differentiation and integration.

Another effect of complexity may have to be considered. Higher levels of multidimensionality might themselves act as a source for additional incongruity. While more unidimensional persons would likely perceive incongruity on only one dimension, more multidimensional persons who are exposed to an identical stimulus configuration may (1) perceive incongruity related to *several cognitive dimensions* and (2) if one or more dimensions are changed and/or newly related to each other on the basis of the stimulus information, perceive incongruity in the *relationship among dimensions*. This incongruity would also likely be reduced via differentiative or integrative activity. This argument suggests that more multidimensional persons would likely experience higher incongruity levels than more unidimensional persons.

We have proposed that the more multidimensional person would experience a higher incongruity with greater likelihood, and would potentially develop a higher GIAL. One might wonder how (before integration occurs) he can cope with the incongruity level without engaging in the escape or distort actions that are proposed on the right side of Figure 5.11. We are not intending to propose that escape or distort actions do not occur for these persons. Multidimensional capacity is not a "good thing" as opposed to a "bad thing." Nonetheless, in many cases, distortion or escape may not be necessary and may not occur. Rather, the high incongruity may be handled via a balancing mechanism among the various SIALs.

We have (cf. Chap. 5) spoken of the divergent incongruity experiences on specific incongruity adaptation levels (with reference to some cognitive area). Incongruity adaptation may not only differ from cognitive area to cognitive area. It may also allow for a balancing of experienced incongruity levels to an average GIAL. In other words, if incongruity in area 1 happens to be excessively above the SIAL, it can be handled without escape or distortion if incongruity in area 2 remains equivalently below the SIAL. For example, a person who experiences high levels of incongruity at his job may be able to handle it if he has the comfort of a very congruous home-life experience. So far, we have proposed specific SIALs for specific cognitive "areas." However, for more multidimensional persons, SIALs may also relate to the various dimensions which are employed in their cognitive responses to information. If that is so, then several SIALs may relate to any received information simultaneously. The reduction (or low level) of incongruity on one dimensional SIAL may permit the increase (or high level) of incongruity on another dimensional SIAL, with associated complex search activity, and with differentiation and integration activity.[5]

We may then state that:

8.9 If reduction of incongruity via integration is possible, then complex (multidimensional) search by more multidimensional persons would more

---

[5] One should, however, be aware that a number of dimensional SIALs relevant to a specific stimulus configuration might not always be additive (to the GIAL), but might in some cases be interactive. If that were so, a decrease in incongruity relevant to a specific dimension may or may not allow for an increase of incongruity on another dimension with relevance to SIAL and GIAL interaction. Rather, increases and/or decreases of incongruity on SIAL relevant dimensions may produce parallel or opposite effects on other SIAL dimensions, depending on the integrative relationships among these dimensions.

frequently produce increased incongruity, leading (in the long run) to increases in GIAL.

8.10 Since multidimensionality tends to lead to incongruity on several dimensions and among dimensions, it is likely to increase the GIAL (in the long run).

8.11 More multidimensional persons may (through balance among several relevant SIALs) be able to maintain (often temporarily) higher incongruity levels on some specific (relevant) SIAL.

8.12 Moderately multidimensional persons who are integrators should be able to develop a moderately high GIAL (but not as high as high level integrators). Moderately multidimensional persons who are differentiators should be able to develop a very high GIAL, since differentiation allows for the immediate reduction of incongruity.

8.13 More unidimensional persons can handle incongruent information with relevance to only a single dimension. If the incongruous information cannot be distorted, and if no aid in the placement of incongruent information on the relevant existing dimension is given, the likelihood is that the GIAL will be low.

We should add that complexity here provides the *potential* for the development of various GIAL levels. It does not, however, produce the GIAL levels. Rather, whether or not an increased GIAL will be produced depends on the amount of information that is provided (or available) to the organism, the degree to which this information is inconsistent above the present GIAL (either on one, or several, or among dimensions), and the duration or persistence of exposure to such information.

Effects of the Environment on Complexity and the GIAL

In discussing complexity theory (Chap. 3) and GIAL theory (Chap. 5), we spoke of the effects of environmental conditions on the development and the utilization of multidimensionality and the general incongruity adaptation level. To show how the two processes are similarly and differentially affected, the effects are summarized in Table 8.1.

A THIRD LOOK AT COMPLEXITY THEORY

We dealt with complexity theory in Chapter 2 (Review) and in Chapter 3 (Theory). By necessity, the theoretical propositions we made had to include some simplifications. We now take another look at some parts of the theory that had to be simplified, and at some other parts of the theory that appear

Table 8.1   Environmental Effects on Complexity and the GIAL

Typical environmental incongruity level	Typical information load	GIAL level	Complexity level
high	high	high	more unidimensional
high	moderate	high	moderately multidimensional
high	low	high	moderately to highly multi-dimensional
moderate	high	moderate	more unidimensional
moderate	moderate	moderate	moderately to highly multi-dimensional
moderate	low	moderate	moderately multi-dimensional
low	high	low	more unidimensional
low	moderate	low	moderately unidimensional
low	low	low	more unidimensional

insufficiently developed. It is hoped that this duscussion will generate further theory development, or will suggest to the interested reader where alternative interpretations or conflicting viewpoints might be developed.

Differentiation and Integration

In our discussion so far, we have dealt with differentiation and integration as potentially complementary, but quite different processes. There may be some doubt as to whether they are indeed *highly* different. Certainly, in their pure forms, differentiation represents a dimensional *analytic* process and integration represents a dimensional *synthetic* process. As synthesis follows analysis, integration of dimensions depends on the differentiation of the stimulus material onto a number of dimensions to make the synthetic integration process possible.

As stated in Chapter 3, there are people who differentiate and do not integrate. Excessive differentiators may even develop and utilize an inordinate number of unintegrated dimensions. But in most cases some integrative activity follows differentiation, and differentiation may be guided by an expected integrative process. In other words, a person involved in differentiation might be aware of the integrative characteristics or limitations of his dimensional structure with regard to most potential stimulus configurations, i.e., he might know there and to what extent integrative activity is feasible. His differentiation may more often utilize those dimensions that are easily usable in the anticipated integrative process.

The implication of this argument is that the processes of differentiation and integration do not only occur in the processing of externally received information, but may also occur in the person's analysis of his own dimensional system and its relationship to incoming stimulus configurations. In other words, the person might be able to differentiate and/or integrate, using the components of his own dimensionality as stimuli.

The differences between differentiation and integration also become less distinct when one views the process of "discrimination" (cf. Chap. 2). Discrimination refers to the (fineness of) divisions for the potential placement of stimuli on a single dimension. Both the more unidimensional persons and the more multidimensional differentiators and integrators do discriminate.[6] Are the same processes involved at the various levels of dimensionality? What kind of process is discrimination? In a way, one may see discrimination as akin to differentiation: Distinctions (shades of grey) are made between positions into which stimulus information can be sorted. On the other hand, discrimination may be seen as a process akin to integration: Comparisons

---

[6] It has been observed that the discriminations by more unidimensional persons may be finer than those of more multidimensional persons. The reason may lie in the "work" that is possible for an organism. If a person can only hold a certain number of distinctions in mind at any time (e.g., 7 plus or minus 2), one could argue that a certain amount of this cognitive activity is required by dealing with dimensions (if present). In other words, it may be that the more unidimensional person has a greater capacity for the discriminations because of the lack of work in the dimensional realm, or might even be able to cope with more stimuli at one time. The more multidimensional person uses part of this capacity by holding dimensional information, and may have less capacity for discriminative cognitions left over.

between similar stimuli must be made in matters of degree to allow for their discrepant placement (note that differentiation does not need "comparison processes" since the placement of stimuli in differentiated categories likely functions according to the inclusion–exclusion principle). When the non-integrating differentiator makes a discrimination on a single differentiated dimension, he does, in other words, use at least the rudiments of an integrative process. When the integrator discriminates, he in turn utilizes something of a differentiative process—not surprising in this case, since, typically, integration relies on previous differentiation.

Differentiation and Unidimensionality: The Problem of Salience

Distinctions between the more unidimensional person and the multidimensional differentiator may become unclear when "behavior" rather than some perceptual characteristic is the focus of our interest. We may ask two questions: (1) When we observe that the more unidimensional person utilizes only one dimension, does it mean that he has only one cognitive dimension available to him, or is he merely selecting a particular single dimension for action? (2) When we observe the multidimensional differentiator, do we obtain behavior on several dimensions simultaneously or subsequently, or do we merely again observe behavior on a "selected" dimension? If the latter were true, one might question whether a distinction between the more unidimensional person and the multidimensional differentiator is a meaningful one, especially for practical purposes. Particularly if salience would determine the utilization of a specific dimension which is common to both the more unidimensional person and the differentiator, we could not expect any "observed" differences between them.

Certainly these questions are intriguing. Indeed, under conditions of high salience for some specific behavioral dimension common to all persons, no great differences between the two groups of persons might be expected. But not all situations provide highly salient single response prescriptions. What would happen if the more unidimensional person and the more multidimensional differentiator were exposed to a common stimulus configuration without salience or with conflicting salience characteristics? For the more unidimensional person, only one relevant dimension would be available. He would likely place the stimuli on that dimension, leaving out stimuli that are incongruent, or distorting them to fit. The differentiator, on the other hand, would avoid problems of incongruence by placement of the stimuli on several dimensions. Of course, he may select (even randomly?) any of the dimensions which are available to him for action. In that case (as—because of distortion—

with the more unidimensional person), only some of the stimulus information would be likely to have behavioral consequences. Alternatively, our differentiator may respond sequentially to the stimulus configuration with a number of responses (looking like trial and error) based on different dimensions, or he may not respond at all, since he might find it too difficult to pick a dimension for action (similarly to the "open" high level integrator who may be unable to close on an integration before his cognitive system "reintegrates" the information with diverse consequences over and over again). In this case, the relative absence of emotional stress we have posited for the differentiator (as for the nonclosing integrator) would, of course, not hold. Inability to make a decision—particularly in a situation in which a decision appears rapidly necessary—can be quite stressful.

We might then conclude that it may be difficult to distinguish between the behavior of a more unidimensional person and a more multidimensional differentiator *if a single unit of behavior is observed.* But, if behavior is considered over time (particularly in the absence of high salience, or in the presence of multiple salience), the differentiator should generate more divergent responses than the more unidimensional person. Of course, the unidimensional person may provide responses that, in part, look like, but are quite discrepant from, differentiation responses, i.e., categorization.

Differentiation and Categorization

Among researchers concerned with cognitive structure, some (e.g., Zajonc, 1960) have been interested in categorization. Tests of this phenomenon (cf. Chap. 2) tend to measure the number of categories into which subjects can sort provided stimulus information. In some cases, these tests may have measured both differentiation and categorization. In some cases (depending on the test procedure), they may have measured only the categories which subjects used. In general, one might state that the degree to which single stimuli fit only into a single category implies a categorization process. For instance, if a certain minority group is described by a subject only on the industrious-lazy dimension, but not (differently) on the strong-weak dimension (unless, of course, the two dimensions are perfectly correlated for this stimulus object), then the person is categorizing. He is differentiating if he is placing the same stimulus object (differently) on several (not highly correlated) dimensions. Categorization (and selecting a category for response due to salience) occurs quite frequently for more unidimensional persons. It would occur less often for more multidimensional differentiators. Differentiation, on the other hand, occurs (logically) less often for more unidimensional persons and frequently for multidimensional differentiators (cf. Chap. 3).

Weighting of Dimensions

We have stated that the differentiator is likely to be affected by salience of the dimensions which he employs. What about the integrator? We are assuming that (if load or other factors are not detrimental) the integrator will base his perceptions and his behavior on the placement of stimuli on a number of dimensions simultaneously and on the relationship among these dimensions. This process eliminates the likely selection of a single (salient) dimension for perception or action (except as suggested below). Nonetheless, salience may have an effect. One might propose that the *weighting* of dimensions in an integration may be highly influenced by salience. Salient dimensions may have more influence on the outcome of the integrative process. For that matter, if the weighting of one dimension is excessively high in relation to the other dimensions, integration may not occur, and the response of the differentiator and the integrator may be identical: i.e., the response may be determined by the placement of the stimulus on the highly salient dimension alone. With decreasing salience, more and more dimensions (depending on their own salience levels) should come into play in the integrative process. As a result, the same stimulus configurations (with differential salience attached) could at various times result in (qualitatively and quantitatively) different integrations and consequently in different responses.

A Graphic Representation of Dimensionality

For some, it may be easier to imagine the meaning of a "dimension" when it is represented graphically, and we will try to do that. Of course, the more unidimensional person should have only one dimension available in regard to some particular stimulus configuration (see Fig. 8.1).

The unidimensional person who is categorizing produces a similar picture (see Fig. 8.2).

For the differentiator, several unrelated dimensions are given for common placement of the same stimulus configureation (see Fig. 8.3).

Of course, we could also have represented the dimensions as orthogonal in multidimensional space, e.g., D_1 and D_2 (see Fig. 8.4).

Certainly, dimensions need not be orthogonal. Assume, for a moment, that some *constant* oblique relationship between two dimensions would exist, so that a stimulus placement on one would affect the stimulus placement on the other (see Fig. 8.5).

Obviously, some integrative process is taking place. But it should be noted that this integration is fixed. The response (except as affected by unidimensional changes and their effects on other dimensions) would be constant

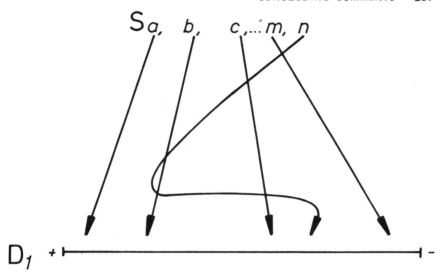

Fig. 8.1. Placement of stimuli "a" through "n" on a single judgmental dimension by a more unidimensional person.

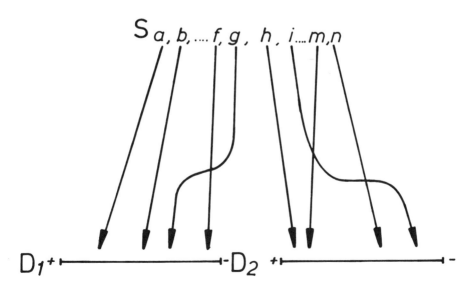

Fig. 8.2. Placement of stimuli "a" through "n" on two judgmental dimensions by a more unidimensional person (categorization, bifurcation).

288

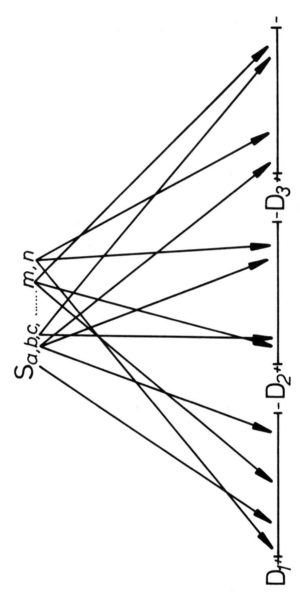

Fig. 8.3. Placement of stimuli "a" through "n" on several judgmental dimensions simultaneously or subsequently (differentiation).

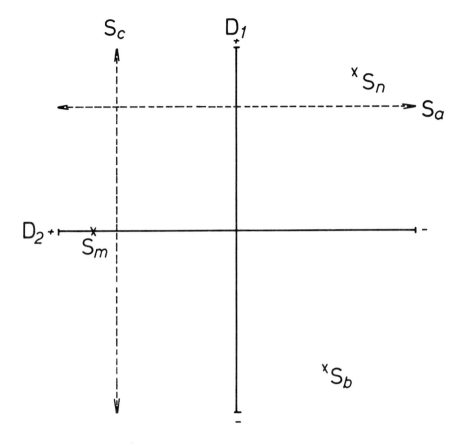

Fig. 8.4. An alternate representation of two dimensions and of the placement of some stimuli based on these dimensions from Fig. 8.3.

across time and events, as long as the stimulus is constant. This graph then represents a hierarchical integrative process (cf. Chap. 3), a process that does not represent the flexible integrative multidimensionality we have primarily focused on in this volume.

How would flexible integration have to be represented? Here we are reaching the limits of immobile two-dimensional paper. We would have to assume the existence of several dimensions on which a stimulus can be placed, dimensions which relate to each other in potentially changing (as a function of the stimulus or as a function of cognitive activity) oblique (i.e., obliquely rotating) fashion. In any case, the dimensions should rotate to some specific

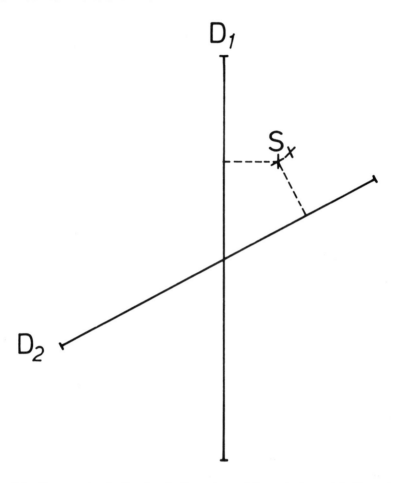

Fig. 8.5. Placement of stimulus "x" on two oblique judgmental dimensions (hierarchical integration).

oblique multidimensional relationship that produces an action. For the purpose of determining this action, the rotation should (at least momentarily) stop, potentially to continue after an action decision has been made (and a potential action may have been carried out). Following the process of action decision (or perception), the rotating motion may reemerge. We have previously talked about the flexible integrator who finds it difficult, if not impossible, to come to an integrative decision because he cannot close. This person is here described by a rotation process that does not stop for action.

DIMENSIONALITY AND THE GIAL
IN ACTION

Throughout the preceding chapters, it has been more or less strongly implied that the concept of a personality "type," either in relation to GIAL or in relation to dimensionality, is misplaced. It has been emphasized that a change of the GIAL and of cognitive structural dimensionality is possible (although difficult to achieve after a certain point in development has been reached). In addition, specific situational influences can, for example, affect the dimensionality of cognitive functioning for short periods of time; environmental alterations of information characteristics can, if they persist and represent a more or less permanent change, produce an altered dimensional structure or a newly-located GIAL. We cannot, then, speak of a "type" in the sense of the older personality theories, which referred to a durable combination of traits having a consistent influence in most situations. It is possible, however, to talk about a person's "typical" dimensionality and about his current GIAL level. And, when one does that, it becomes possible to describe a number of potential "momentary types": the various potential combinations of a person's GIAL, SIALs, and dimensional structure *at one particular point in time.*

The concepts of both dimensionality and GIAL have been viewed in this book in terms of continua, rather than in terms of distinct or distinguishable levels of the variables. This point must be emphasized, for it represents an important distinction between these theories and others in the same area. For the sake of convenience of description, however, we can refer to the overgeneralized and relative categories of high, medium, or low GIAL, and unidimensional, multidimensional differentiative, or multidimensional integrative structure. By a combination of each "level" of GIAL with each "level" of dimensionality, we arrive at nine potential and hypothetical "types": persons with

(a) a high GIAL and multidimensional integrative structure,
(b) a high GIAL and multidimensional differentiative structure,
(c) a high GIAL and unidimensional structure,
(d) a moderate GIAL and multidimensional integrative structure,
(e) a moderate GIAL and multidimensional differentiative structure,
(f) a moderate GIAL and unidimensional structure,
(g) a low GIAL and multidimensional integrative structure,
(h) a low GIAL and multidimensional differentiative structure, and
(i) a low GIAL and unidimensional structure.

We have seen, however, that because of the specific nature of each of these variables and because of the influence they may have on each other (e.g., in development), certain of these combinations are highly unlikely to occur. For example, a person with a low GIAL, developing a multidimensional structure characterized by a high degree of integration, is difficult to imagine. Although this combination is the only one we would, with some degree of certainty, exclude entirely, some of the others can also be viewed as more or less improbable. Therefore, even these pure and hypothetical combinations must be limited.

It has been repeatedly stated that the various "levels" of GIAL and of dimensionality will have differential effects on the processing of information and, therefore, potentially also on resulting behavior.[7] It might be worthwhile to look somewhat more specifically at what may actually occur if one of our hypothetical GIAL/dimensionality mixtures were a real person, in a real situation. It would be possible to write an entire novel from the point of view of the information processing of the main character, resulting from his dimensionality and his GIAL. However, in the interest of space, our descriptions will have to be based on a consciously limited amount of information. Most of the details about the history of our character, the complexities of his current life situation, the nuances of the social environment which he experiences, and the like, will have to be omitted. We will limit our discussion to those factors which have a more or less direct influence on his present situation, both cognitive and environmental. Two cases will be presented and, to provide the optimum amount of information through comparison, the cases will represent two extremes.

Case 1: High GIAL, Multidimensional Integrator

Bruce L. Paulson is 38 years old, married, and has two children, ages 8 and 6. He graduated at 21 from a large northeastern state university in the United States with a Bachelor degree in management science. He earned a Master degree at the graduate school of industrial administration at the same university, completing his studies when he was 23 years of age. Paulson then spent the next several years "trying things out," as he described it.

During this period, he worked in various jobs, some of which were more or less related, others totally unrelated to his training and qualifications. He left these positions voluntarily, remaining in each one between 3 weeks, in an extreme case, to over 3 years. For one period of about 8 months, he lived in

---

[7]We refer here to *potential* differential effects on behavior, because identical or identical-appearing behaviors may result from quite different motivational bases or information processing.

the Haight-Asbury section of San Francisco, supporting himself by working part time in a used clothing store. When asked by older friends during this period for an explanation of his, to them, unexpected and surprising post-graduation behavior, his reply was:

I was really tired of being in the same place all those years, and I got really uptight that I'd get a job when I finished and a house and a family and there I'd be for the next 40 years inside these four walls that kept looking blanker all the time. My God, I can't even imagine doing the same thing everyday for a week—but 40 years! So I just decided I had to do something else. . .even play at being a 'flower child'. Hell, I know that's not what I am. I even know that I'm going to stop doing this and 'settle down,' as my mother always says. I guess I even want to, you know, have all that security and stuff. But right now I need this. And listen, don't think I'm just having fun. . .that that's the reason. Sometimes this whole running scene really hurts.

[Although a high level integrator, at this point, in both his behavior and his explanation of it, Paulson is almost "only" differentiating.[8] He is able to view his behavior as appropriate for the present, although probably not in the long run: a differentiation. He is probably also further differentiating between the utility of his actions and their "correctness." Further, he may find it useful to experience new dimensional placement of stimuli, attitudes, etc. Many of his actions during this period seem to be in the service of his GIAL. He appears to be making up for a cumulative level of incongruity *below* his GIAL during the years of his education. In addition, his predictions of his own reactions to a potential future containing too low environmental incongruity, seem to have created a need to "store" incongruity experience to make up for the coming deficits.]

At the time he was in San Francisco, Bruce met a girl named Anna. She was just finishing her Ph.D. dissertation in sociology. She enjoyed talking to Bruce about the four things she wanted most in life: to be a world famous theoretician and researcher in urban sociology, to have a bunch of wonderful children and dogs, to spend her life exploring places that no travel agent knows how to write a ticket to, and to have a "respectable" husband and a house with a white picket fence. Although he warned her that he did not think he could produce that combination for her, but would try, Bruce and Anna were married when he was 29 and she was 27.

At that point, Paulson decided that the most reasonable thing for him to do was to begin his "career," to begin to set up a basis for security. He did

---

[8] In any case, it will become apparent that, at this rough level of description, it is much easier to recognize *behaviors* that are related to the production or reduction of incongruity than it is to recognize behaviors that are the result of an identifiable level of information processing with regard to dimensionality. Dimensionality can only become apparent at a more subtle level of analysis.

this, in part, out of feelings of responsibility (although he realized that Anna did not need to depend on him for financial support) and, in part, because he felt he had had enough of his life as a free spirit. He found a job in a small but growing manufacturing firm, and experienced some degree of satisfaction in the challenges of the new environment and the applications of his training. He did well in the firm, and was advancing both financially and in terms of the hierarchy; but after 3 years, and the birth of their second child, he and Anna decided to move to the East. They had two reasons: they agreed that for Bruce's advancement, a larger company would provide more opportunities, and they sought a change of scenery . . . literally.

[The explanation for the apparent sudden change of heart in Paulson's decision to marry and "settle down" may lie in two facts. First, he had raised the incongruity in his environment to a point far enough above his GIAL (and on specific IALs, such as interpersonal security and career) that he was beginning to experience discomfort. Some amount of cloze activity was becoming necessary. Second, Anna as an individual, because of her wide-ranging interests, her own relatively high GIAL, and the consequent need to avoid boredom, provided him with the opportunity to combine the satisfaction of a comparatively low SIAL in the domain of interpersonal security, with interesting and potentially incongruity-producing interpersonal inter-action. In addition, the divergent viewpoint of the professional sociologist—as opposed to his business orientation—may have allowed him to view familiar stimuli, as well as new events they experienced together, on additional dimensions, a process that may have aided him in integrative decision making on his job—something that may be particularly useful in a small consumer-oriented manufacturing company.]

At the current time, Paulson is at the middle-management level in one of the divisions of a relatively large, product-oriented corporation. He has been with the company for 6 years (since his move east) and has held his present position for the last 2 years. His job generally provides him with the opportunity to behave multidimensionally, especially when decisions are required, and provides, on the average, a level of environmental incongruity somewhat below his GIAL. His private life is characterized by a relatively low level of incongruity, particularly that type of incongruity created by conflict. This lack of problems between Bruce and Anna, to some degree produced by a discussion of any potential disagreement before conflict actually occurs, is in line with his low SIAL in the area of interpersonal security. Other types of incongruity, needed by both Bruce and Anna, are generally self-generated, through discussion, and particularly through seeking of and participation in novel situations and activities. In addition, their circle of friends is widely varied, including, e.g., a professor of astronomy and a radical feminist author.

At the present time, as we first encounter Paulson, he is in his office alone, working on the preparation of a report which he is due to present at a meeting in 2 days. The work is absorbing, and he is enjoying it; it involves making various potential decisions on the basis of variably probable contingencies. In other words, it is a good task for his multidimensionality and for his GIAL and somewhat high work-SIAL, because it requires making complex integrative decisions on the basis of a number of uncertainties. At the moment, he is operating at a level of environmental incongruity which is somewhat below his GIAL and work-SIAL. The task, however, allows him to operate at nearly his full multidimensional integrative capacity.

In the early afternoon, Paulson's boss, with whom he has positive contact, calls, and asks if the two of them could have a talk sometime during the day. Assuming that it has something to do with the report he is working on, Paulson agrees to meet in the late afternoon. The purpose of this meeting turns out to be quite different from his expectations. Instead of bringing up the report, Paulson's boss enters into a discussion with him about the future development of the company and about the various more or less "official" rumors regarding possible merger or purchase, which have been circulating recently. The central points—of particular relevance to Paulson—which emerged from the discussion, are these: With a probability of about .85, the company in which Paulson is employed will be absorbed by a larger, diversified corporation within the coming year. Further, since the equivalent of his position already exists in the larger corporation, and since the responsibilities and functions covered by that equivalent position are more general, i.e., would subsume the functions of his own position, there exists a probability of about .90 that, should the merger occur, Paulson will lose his job.

[The receipt of this highly incongruous information places Bruce at an environmental incongruity level considerably above his work-SIAL and above his GIAL.]

How does Paulson react to this situation? How does he deal with it? His initial affective response is likely to be a dual one, and a contradictory one. His response to the *content* of the information is, as expected, negative. The prospect of losing one's job (unless it fulfills other motives, e.g., provides a needed excuse to get out of an unpleasant situation) is not likely to be greeted with joy by most people. However, on the level of pure incongruity, entirely apart from the negative content, the information can produce quite a positive response. It provides Bruce with a degree of incongruity to deal with, which has been absent from his environment, and which, because of his high GIAL, he needs. This kind of dual reaction to the content vs. the incongruity of problem situations on the part of high GIAL persons may be the phenomenon which evokes the typical response of "I really get the feeling you actually *enjoy* having problems" from the friends of such people.

One of the first things that Bruce actively does is engage in a number of behaviors which serve to reduce any potential incongruity in other domains, relating to other SIALs. For example, when he returns home that evening, Anna informs him that they have been accepted for participation in an encounter group for three weekend sessions, something they have both been looking forward to. Bruce, after telling Anna about the situation concerning his job, asks her to withdraw their names from the sessions, at least temporarily. The next day, he calls his physician and cancels an appointment, which he has for the following month, for elective minor surgery. He also asks Anna to take his place at a conference at the children's school dealing with a problem the older child is having. Bruce says to his wife, when she seems to imply that he is shirking his responsibilities, "Please try to understand—I'm loaded up to here with things to think about. I just can't take another issue right now. You decide what has to be done. I feel like I'll explode if I have all these things going on at once!" These and similar actions may give the impression of a motivation to avoid wasting time on less central issues, or even of withdrawal under stress. However, in terms of GIAL, the motivation is to lower the incongruity level as much as possible, in all other SIAL areas, allowing all the individual's capacity for dealing with incongruity to be invested in the salient domain, in this case, the work situation. Further, by reducing incongruity regarding these various SIALs, and therefore also re-garding the GIAL, it may be possible for Paulson to raise his work-SIAL relatively rapidly. In other words, if the level of environmental incongruity is low enough in all other areas to compensate for the high level in this one area, the SIAL for the job situation may be established at a higher level. This shift in the SIAL would then permit Paulson to avoid panic or fear responses, and allow him to attempt to deal with the incongruity produced by the threat to his position by both complex search and cloze actions in that specific area.

After reducing other incongruity as far as possible below his usual SIALs in the various areas, Bruce is likely to set out on a number of courses of action simultaneously. These actions are not all observable; some involve long processes of thinking . . . "figuring things out." For someone like Paulson, that means differentiating, integrating, perhaps repeatedly, with information he may already have, and with some he may seek. As already stated, with the avoidance of reactions created by panic or fear (escape, for example), Paulson is able to engage in a combination of complex search and cloze behavior, within the work situation. Since he is multidimensional, he is likely to initiate his search behavior differentiatively, in other words, in a number of different areas simultaneously or successively. One kind of double complex search strategy that he might pursue would involve an attempt to find ways to retain his present position in the case of a takeover by the other corporation. At the same time, he would explore alternative solutions for the eventuality that the retention of his job becomes impossible or unlikely. This he could accomplish, for instance, by gathering information about the personal and professional characteristics of his potential competitor (the individual who holds the equivalent position in the larger company), and about the particular requirements of the job. With this information, it may be possible for him to demonstrate that he is the more suited, the more useful individual for the position. Because of his capacity to perceive and to behave multidimensionally, and therefore to empathize, he probably is capable of considerable insight into the requirements for the job *as perceived* by those who will make the decision as to who gets it. This capacity may offer Paulson the opportunity to manipulate or strategically direct his behavior to produce in the decision makers the desired impression of his qualifications for the job.

At the same time, and still part of his complex search, Paulson may engage in an active attempt to gain various kinds of information about the characteristics of possible new positions with different firms. If he continues to keep the environmental incongruity low enough in all other areas so that fear responses to his job threat are avoided, then it is unlikely that he will pursue this job search with any sense of desperation. Instead, he will attempt to find a job situation (ideally one which he can hold in abeyance as a possibility, without immediately committing himself to it) which best matches his talents, interests, and capacities.

Simultaneously with all this complex search behavior, it is likely that Paulson will engage in cloze behavior in the work situation. He needs to keep incongruity within manageable limits, and, at this point, he has to deal with the original incongruity created by the threat to his job *plus* any incongruity which may arise as a by-product of his complex search. One kind of cloze behavior may involve exploring the characteristics of his present job in comparison with the characteristics of potential other jobs at other firms. This exploration and comparison would be a multidimensional, integrative process, in which various personal and interpersonal factors, ability and utility factors, interests, costs, etc., would be weighed, integrated, and perhaps even redifferentiated and reintegrated. The result of this process may very well be the conclusion that the most useful thing to do—*in any case*—would be to change jobs.

Finally, through a process of further integration of the results of the complex search and the cloze behaviors, Paulson may arrive at an action-oriented decision. He may conclude that, because of the current situational characteristics, this is the time to decide what kind of job is *best* for him at this particular moment in his life. He would then try to match all the potentially available jobs, including the one he has now, with his needs, interests, and capabilities. At the point that he decides which one is optimal, he will direct his energies to getting (or keeping) that one. The work situation incongruity will remain at a relatively high level (although possibly somewhat reduced by a decision to take specific, directed action) until some degree of permanent stability in this area is achieved.

Case 2: Low GIAL, Unidimensional

David S. Alexander is 38 years old, married, and the father of two children, ages 8 and 6. He graduated at 21 from a large state university in the northeastern United States with a Bachelor degree in management science. He earned a Master degree at the graduate school of industrial administration at the same university, completing his studies when he was 23 years old. Alexander then spent the next several years "preparing for the right spot in life," as he described it.

During this period, he worked in a job which was somewhat routine and for which he was probably overqualified. He started in this position immediately after finishing his studies and moving to the west coast, and appeared to be rather content to remain in it. He made no attempts to find a better job and seemed to show no indications of wanting to advance quickly. When asked by older friends at this time for an explanation of his (to them) unexpected and surprising post-graduation behavior, his reply was:

> I really feel I need to prepare myself for a better job, a permanent one. Hell, I know that I'm not going to keep this forever, and that, at least on paper, I could do better. But I've got to know that I can handle things in a more complicated position, and this is a great learning experience. Besides, when I was still in school, everything they were teaching me seemed so clear and straightforward. But when I was getting set to really get out there. . . .God, I began to realize how little I really know about how things operate in a business. I would have fallen flat on my face. And another thing: When I'm ready to settle down, I want everything to be right. You know, have security, money and stuff, not have to be afraid that I'm not going to be able to hack it in a job and fall down on my responsibilities.

[At this point, Alexander is functioning in a typical unidimensional fashion. In terms of his future, he is determined to do things "right," to fulfill his responsibilities, do his job well, etc. His low GIAL presented him with the necessity of dealing with the incongruity, real or potential, inherent in the transition from school to real life. His actions at this time are in the service of *avoiding* incongruity, and that in two ways. First of all, by taking a job that offers less of a challenge than his training has prepared him for, he avoids the incongruity of potential problems in a more difficult or "complicated" job. He is afraid of having to face a situation which is unexpected, for which his training may not have prepared him. Second, he is operating to avoid incongruity in the future. By learning as much as possible now, i.e., by making as many facets of a potential future job as familiar and expected as possible, he will be able to fit into a new and better position without experiencing too much novelty or overload.]

At the time he had been in his job for about 5 years, Alexander met a girl named Shelley. She was working toward her Ph.D. in mathematics education. She told David that she viewed a career as something she would pursue only if she were not married. If she did marry, she would prefer to have children and to be able to have enough time and energy to concentrate on being a good homemaker, wife, and mother. She indicated that a career would only become interesting for her after her responsibilities to home and children were taken care of. She and David decided that the best thing would be for her to drop out of graduate school, and they were married when David was 29 and Shelley was 27.

At that point, Alexander decided, because of the new responsibility he was taking on, it would be wise to obtain a position which held the possibility for advancement and which would offer financial security. He began working at the western division of a relatively large, product-oriented corporation. His new position enabled him to utilize the knowledge and skills he had obtained during his education and during the previous years.

[Alexander's nearly simultaneous decision to marry and to seek out new career possibilities has several interrelated explanations. Because of the fact of living alone, without the security of a permanent relationship, he was experiencing a degree of incongruity above his rather low interpersonal security-SIAL. Through his marriage to Shelley, a bright girl with interests and a personality structure similar to his own, David was able to reduce the incongruity relevant to that SIAL to the point where he was able to better deal with any potential incongruity arising from a new job. A better job became necessary at this point because of the unidimensional need to do things "right," to fulfill his responsibilities. Finally, the decision for Shelley to drop out of graduate school was motivated, for both of them, by the need to avoid incongruity. From David's point of view, having a wife with a doctorate did not match his expectations or conceptualizations of the role of a businessman, and the type of life he should lead.]

After being with the company for 3 years, Alexander was transferred to one of its eastern divisions. This move was made with some apprehension, but turned out to be a successful one. He is now at the middle-management level, and has held his present position for the last 2 years. His job is generally interesting to him, and he has developed a routine which he finds comfortable. He is not usually required to deal with unexpected or novel events alone; innovative decisions are dealt with in a group. The area in which he is involved typically requires making one of a relatively limited range of possible decisions, based on a sufficient amount of reliable information. This activity often produces a feeling of real satisfaction in Alexander. His private life is calm, particularly with regard to interpersonal conflict. The problems that arise between Shelley and David are usually matters of opinion, and these they have difficulty resolving. Their typical procedure in this case is to avoid the topic, rather than getting into real arguments, especially if the issue is unimportant. They lead a fairly active social life, with frequent parties or dinner-plus-theater evenings with their friends, most of whom are contacts made by David Alexander at the company.

At the present time, as we first encounter Alexander, he is in his office alone, working on the preparation of a report which he is due to present at a meeting in 2 days. The work is absorbing and he is enjoying it; it involves a recapitulation of the activities of his area over the past year, the decisions made, and the results of these decisions. It is a good task for both his dimensionality and his GIAL, because it requires dealing with familiar, well-known information and organizing it in a neat, logical, and easily-communicated fashion. It also involves a process of evaluating the decisions that were made, and he feels comfortable in the belief that the right decisions have been made. At the moment, he is operating at a level of environmental incongruity which is barely below his GIAL and work-SIAL.

In the early afternoon, Alexander's boss, with whom he has positive contact, calls and asks if the two of them could have a talk sometime during the day. Assuming that it has something to do with the report he is working on, Alexander agrees to meet in the late afternoon. However, the anxiety created in him by this somewhat unusual request makes it almost impossible for him to continue working effectively. He alternates between worrying about what he has done wrong and about what new demands his boss may want to make of him. The purpose of the meeting turns out to be quite different from his expectations. Instead of bringing up the report, Alexander's boss enters into a discussion with him about the future development of the company and about the various more or less "official" rumors regarding possible merger or purchase which have been circulating recently. The central points—of particular relevance to Alexander—which emerged from the discussion are these: With a probability of about .85, the company in which Alexander is employed will be absorbed by a larger, diversified corporation within the coming year. Further, since the equivalent of his position already exists in the larger corporation, and since the responsibilities and functions covered by that equivalent position are more general, i.e., would subsume the functions of his own position, there exists a probability of about .90 that, should the merger occur, Alexander will lose his job.

[The receipt of this highly incongruent information places David at an environmental incongruity level extremely far above his work-SIAL and GIAL.]

How does Alexander react to this situation? How does he deal with it? Because of the sudden, rapid, and extreme increase in environmental incongruity, his initial reaction is likely to be one of fear and panic. He may engage in some very obvious escape responses, such as immediately leaving the office environment after his discussion with his boss. These escape behaviors may then become more subtle, such as, for example, difficulty in concentrating on his work, or more aimed, such as looking for a new job.

David is likely to attempt to reduce incongruity in relation to all his SIALs by avoidance behavior. When he arrives home on the first afternoon after hearing the news, and attempts to discuss the situation with Shelley, his feeling of panic may make it difficult, almost impossible, for him to talk with her about it. In addition, he is faced with the problem of her potentially strong reactions to this sudden increase in her own environmental incongruity. She, too, may be placed in a panic situation at the very time when he needs to be able to depend on her and to avoid additional incongruity. The interaction of their respective needs and responses may lead to an inability for them to rationally approach the problem together. David is likely to react to any information, regardless of how innocuous it is, with irritability, annoyance, or even anger. It is not unusual for someone with a very low GIAL in such a stressful situation to literally cover up his ears and say "leave me alone." This kind of response represents a hypersensitivity to, and absolute incapability of, dealing with any further incongruity. David may spend a good deal of time withdrawn and brooding, behavior which may give the impression that he is attempting to think through and solve his problems. It is likely, however, that this is another form of escape, and may be quite unproductive. He is also likely to want to avoid any social contacts at this time, for two reasons. First, he needs to avoid additional incongruity, especially that which would be evoked by questions about the situation from his friends. And second, because of his unidimensionality, this threat to his job may be evaluated by David as a negative reflection on himself, and it may be embarrassing for him to face others in this situation.

The positive action David may take will be dictated by his need to escape the current circumstances and by his unidimensionality. Because of this unidimensionality, his job situation, which up to this point has been positively evaluated by him, will have to be placed on the other end of the dimension he is using (a need to place blame, or reduce dissonance: "If I can't have the job, I don't really want it."). If we assume a good–bad dimension, for example (it might also be a utility dimension), David is likely to decide that the takeover by the larger corporation is going to destroy the value of his company and of his position there. Therefore, he would not want to keep the job, even if it were possible. However, he is not likely to reevaluate his own company (before the merger) in the negative direction, because that would have too many consequences for his own self-evaluation. He would then have to say that he has been associated with a "bad" organization all these years, making him also "bad." If, on the other hand, the other company is the "bad" one, then it is possible for him to comfortably feel that both he and his company are merely innocent victims.

Once he has reached the conclusion that his company and his position there are likely to be "ruined," made bad or useless, by this new corporation, he has no choice but to find a new job. Because of the desperation he feels and the pressing need to get out of this intolerably incongruous environment, Alexander is likely to jump at the first alternative he can find. It is unlikely that he will give much consideration to factors such as suitability, interests, even salary. His primacy motivation is escape, and that at almost any cost. He is, therefore, apt to make a decision which will place him in a situation of continued, albeit different, incongruity.

A Closing Note on Both Cases

The persons described in the two cases were exposed to a highly incongruous experience: the probability of losing their jobs. The reader might have come to the conclusion that the more multidimensional integrator with a high GIAL behaved more adaptively than the more unidimensional low GIAL person. Is it then "good" to be like the former, and "bad" to be like the latter? This problem has already been dealt with in another chapter. Which characteristics are likely to be more adaptive would, to a great extent, depend on the environment and the demands to which a person is exposed. Had we described a situation in which the person would have had to cope with a relatively uniform (congruent) environment, in which the rewards were obtained by always making the "correct" decision according to some criterion which was well understood, our high GIAL, more multidimensional person would have been quite maladapted. On the other hand, his low GIAL, more unidimensional counterpart would probably have done very well. In other words, an "evaluative" approach to GIAL and complexity—apart from a look at the environmental and task characteristics—is not very useful.

One more thing might be added. The descriptions probably have made it clear that no personality or ability differences between our two persons were assumed or implied. Both of them are intelligent, etc.; merely their style of dealing with information is different.

A FINAL COMMENT

A rather extensive set of propositions has been presented in this book, based primarily on two sets of theories. To some degree, the theories have required that the reader consider psychology multidimensionally, i.e., we have asked the reader to employ his own complexity. We have presented considerable incongruity, asking the reader to make use of his ability to potentially overload his psychology-SIAL. We have done the same in writing the book. But, there is one more incongruity we want to present. We would like to suggest that we have "closed" somewhere in the development of this theory, so that we could put it down on paper and communicate it to others. That does not mean that we consider the theories to be in their final form.

Temporary closing appears to be necessary. We know of one well-known psychologist (repeatedly referenced in this book) who had to be threatened with a lawsuit by his publisher, so that something would appear in print. The fact that he had to—even if temporarily—close was (among other things) very helpful to us. Yet his theory is not yet finished, and may never be, as long as he continues to think about psychology. We view that phenomenon of continuing theory development and revision as a "good thing" (if we may be permitted to utilize a single evaluative dimension for the moment).

Even though we have "closed" to write this book, the theories we have presented are not yet final products. Even while writing, a number of additional ideas occurred to us: they are not yet included. More of them will probably develop with further thought and with research data. As we have suggested before: We would like to invite the reader to join with us in this development of theoretical veiws on behavior in the complex environment, a level of complexity with which we, as human beings, must deal in this century.

REFERENCES

Osgood, C. E., & Tannenbaum, P. H. The principle of congruity in the prediction of attitude change. *Psychological Review,* 1955, **62**, 42-55.

Rokeach, M., & Cochrane, R. Self-confrontation and confrontation with another on determinants of long-term value change. *Journal of Applied Social Psychology*, 1972, **2**, 283-292.

Zajonc, R. B. The process of cognitive tuning in communication. *Journal of Abnormal and Social Psychology*, 1960, **61**, 159-167.

AUTHOR INDEX

Abelson, R. P., 132, 133, 156, 165, 204
Adams, D. K., 63, 69
Adams, J. S., 229, 236
Adams-Webber, J. R., 35, 54, 69, 70
Ajzen, I., 209, 237
Albert, S. M., 231, 237
Alker, H. A., 51, 70
Allport, G., 134, 156
Allyn, J., 229, 237
Alter, R. D., 13, 74
Altrocchi, J., 50, 81, 253, 265, 270, 271
Anderson, L., R., 209, 227
Anderson, N. H., 70, 227, 237, 256, 269
Andrews, S. L., 146, 159
Appley, M. H., 152, 157
Argabrite, A. H., 65, 78
Argyris, C., 147, 156
Aronson, E., 132, 141, 143, 156, 159, 165, 204, 229, 241
Asch, S. E., 14, 26, 70, 85, 227, 237, 248, 255, 269
Atkin, R. S., 267, 270
Atkins, A. L., 13, 20, 50, 70
Atkinson, J. W., 172, 204
Attneave, F., 36, 70
Austin, G. A., 13, 14, 71

Backman, C. W., 208, 242, 260, 271
Bailey, S. T., 49, 70
Baldwin, B. A., 44, 70
Ballachey, E. L., 208, 240
Balloun, J. L., 231, 237
Barrios, A. A., 26, 70, 227, 237
Barron, F., 166, 204
Bass, A. R., 67, 70
Becker, L. A., 231, 237
Bem, D. J., 51, 70, 123, 129, 140, 156, 263, 269
Berelson, B., 231, 240
Berkowitz, L., 133, 134, 156, 223, 237

Berlyne, D. E., 144, 145, 146, 152, 153, 154, 156, 157, 170, 180, 181, 182, 184, 204
Berry, J. W., 14, 85
Bickman, L., 209, 237
Bieri, J., 13, 14, 15, 20, 26, 33, 34, 35, 43, 47, 49, 50, 53, 54, 55, 56, 57, 58, 67, 70, 76, 78, 84, 166, 253, 269
Black, H. K., 63, 71
Blacker, E., 35, 43, 54, 70
Bottenberg, E. H., 49, 71
Bovard, E. W., 251, 269
Bradburn, W. M., 35, 70
Brehm, J. W., 141, 157, 171, 204, 228, 229, 237, 238
Briar, S., 13, 20, 50, 70
Brock, T. C., 106, 227, 229, 231, 237, 239
Brodbeck, M., 229, 237
Brown, L. B., 65, 71
Brown, R., 208, 237, 249, 269
Bruner, J. S., 13, 14, 48, 71, 209, 242
Bryson, J. B., 60, 68, 71
Bushinsky, R. G., 43, 63, 82
Butler, R. A., 181, 204
Byrne, D., 62, 63, 71, 139, 157, 234, 235, 237, 260, 269

Campbell, D. T., 42, 71, 208, 209, 210, 227, 238, 241
Campbell, E. H., 227, 238, 239
Campbell, V. N., 54, 71
Canon, L., 143, 157
Carlson, E. R., 209, 238
Carpenter, B., 252, 272
Carpenter, J. T., 252, 272
Carr, J. E., 13, 45, 49, 56, 57, 71, 79, 83
Carr, R. A., 64, 73
Carroll, J. S., 264, 269
Cartwright, D., 138, 157, 209, 238
Castore, C. H., 32, 43, 59, 62, 63, 66, 67, 82, 168, 192, 194, 195, 200, 206
Centers, R., 63, 76

Chandler, A. R., 149, 157, 183, 192, 194, 204
Chapanis, A., 140, 157
Chapanis, N. P., 140, 157
Chapman, R. M., 149, 157
Clapp, W., 189, 205
Claunch, N. C., 45, 71
Cochrane, R., 275, 303
Cofer, C. N., 152, 157
Coffman, T., 59, 76
Cohen, A. R., 141, 157, 171, 204, 219, 225, 228, 229, 237, 238
Cohen, H. S., 25, 71
Cook, R. C., 263, 272
Cooper, E., 224, 225, 238
Corfield, V. K., 62, 72
Cox, G. B., 49, 72
Crano, W. D., 53, 72, 232, 238
Crawford, J. D., 13, 77
Crockett, W. H., 26, 27, 28, 41, 42, 46, 49, 51, 52, 54, 55, 56, 57, 58, 72, 78, 79, 80 253, 270
Cropley, A. J., 68, 72
Cross, H. J., 13, 72
Crouse, B., 63, 72
Crutchfield, R. S., 208, 240
Cunningham, J. D., 266, 271
Cummings, L. L., 110, 129
Curtis, T., 223, 244

Davis, J. H., 267, 270
Davis, K., 229, 238, 265, 271
De Haan, J., 225, 243
Delia, J. G., 57, 72, 79
Dember, W. H., 145, 157
Dermer, J., 67, 73
Deutsch, M., 189, 204, 251, 252, 269
Dillehay, R. C., 225, 238
Dinerman, H., 224, 225, 238
Di Vesta, F. J., 209, 238
Doane, B., 180, 205
Doby, C., 265, 271
Dopyera, J., 13, 75
Drabeck, T. E., 6
Driver, M. J., 12, 13, 25, 31, 32, 39, 46, 47, 50, 58, 59, 60, 62, 63, 67, 68, 71, 72, 80, 82, 83, 100, 104, 105, 127, 129, 130, 132, 153, 154, 157, 160, 161, 166, 168, 170, 177, 192, 204, 205, 206, 227, 229, 231, 232, 233, 238, 242, 243, 248, 252, 253, 255, 256, 257, 271, 272

DuCette, J., 56, 57, 81
Duffy, E., 145, 157
Dyk, R. B., 14, 85

Eachus, H. T., 260, 271
Earl, R. W., 145, 149, 157, 158
Ehrlich, D., 229, 238
Emmerich, W., 13, 72
Epstein, Y. M., 62, 83
Epting, F. R., 35, 49, 72, 73
Evans, M. G., 67, 73

Farr, S. P., 68, 79
Faterson, H. F., 14, 85
Feather, N. T., 64, 73, 125, 129, 144, 145, 157, 171, 205, 229, 231, 238
Feldman, J. M., 25, 62, 71, 73
Feldman, N. S., 265, 269, 271
Feldman, S., 133, 157
Felknor, C., 13, 73
Fertig, E. S., 57, 73
Festinger, L., 140, 141, 142, 143, 144, 148, 149, 157, 158, 164, 165, 192, 209, 228, 229, 230, 231, 237, 238, 239
Fiedler, F. E., 67, 70, 73
Fine, B. J., 224, 239
Fiske, D. W., 42, 71, 145, 146, 158, 208, 210, 238
Fishbein, M., 209, 237, 239, 256, 272
Flament, C., 252, 270
Flynn, J. C., 35, 73
Foa, U. G., 13, 73
Franklin, B. J., 64, 73
Freedman, J. L., 142, 158, 229, 230, 231, 239, 242
Freedman, N., 14, 79
French, J. R. P., 223, 225, 239, 240
Freud, S., 12, 13, 73
Friedman, F., 14, 79
Frieze, I., 263, 264, 270
Fromkin, H. L., 6, 9, 32, 33, 82, 142, 158, 178, 205, 207, 212, 228, 231, 237, 243

Galanter, D., 164, 167, 172, 206
Galinsky, M. D., 35, 70
Gardiner, G. S., 13, 44, 73
Gardner, R. W., 12, 14, 47, 48, 73, 74
Gaudet, H., 231, 240
Gelman, R. S., 144, 157
Gerard, H. B., 251, 252, 269
Gergen, K. J., 2, 9

Giambra, L. M., 59, 80
Gilbert, E., 209, 242
Goldman, K. S., 13, 72
Goldstein, K., 43, 74
Gollin, E. S., 253, 270
Gonyea, A. H., 57, 72
Goodenough, D. R., 14, 79, 85
Goodnow, J. J., 13, 14, 71
Gourd, E. W., 57, 74
Granit, R., 111, 129
Greaves, G., 62, 74
Guetzkow, H., 32, 74
Guttman, I., 229, 238

Haber, R. N., 150, 154, 158, 182, 205
Hadley, H. D., 225, 239
Hagen, R. L., 58, 83
Halverson, C. F., 45, 75
Hansen, R. D., 265, 270
Harary, F., 138, 157
Harburg, E., 142, 160
Hardt, R. H., 13, 75
Harlow, H. R., 145, 158
Harré, R., 2, 9
Harrington, G. M., 144, 158
Harvey, O. J., 13, 28, 29, 30, 31, 42, 44, 45,
    47, 49, 51, 52, 53, 57, 61, 62, 63, 64, 69,
    73, 74, 80, 84, 97, 127, 129, 166, 189,
    205, 228, 239
Haun, K. H., 153, 161, 168, 192, 206
Haywood, H. C., 154, 158, 168, 205
Hebb, D. O., 145, 146, 149, 150, 151, 152,
    153, 154, 158, 168, 180, 181, 182, 183,
    205
Heckhausen, H., 263, 272
Heider, F., 23, 24, 75, 133, 135, 136, 137,
    138, 139, 158, 165
Helson, H., 150, 158, 172, 205
Heron, W., 180, 205
Herzman, M., 14, 43, 85
Heslin, R., 61, 63, 69, 75
Heynes, R. W., 209, 243
Higgins, E. T., 265, 269
Hill, K., 60, 75
Hilterman, R. J., 62, 73
Hoffmeister, J. K., 13, 74
Holt, R. W., 267, 270
Holzman, P. S., 13, 47, 73, 75
Holzkamp, K., 2, 4, 8, 9
Homans, G. C., 139, 158
Hovland, C. I., 55, 75, 218, 219, 220, 224,
    225, 227, 228, 239, 240

Huber, G. P., 110, 129
Hubert, S., 227, 237
Hudson, W., 248, 270
Hughes, H. M., 231, 242
Hunt, D. E., 13, 28, 29, 30, 31, 42, 44, 45,
    47, 51, 74, 75, 76, 78, 79, 80, 83, 97,
    127, 129
Hunt, J. McV., 147, 148, 149, 150, 152, 153,
    154, 158, 163, 164, 165, 166, 167, 168,
    170, 171, 172, 180, 181, 182, 184, 189, 205
Hunter, R., 209, 239
Hutte, H., 67, 76

Inhelder, B., 256, 270
Insko, C. A., 225, 238
Irle, M., 140, 143, 158
Irwin, M., 56, 76

Jackson, D. N., 47, 54, 73, 81, 253, 270
Jackson, J. M., 251, 270
Jackson, P. W., 126, 127, 128, 129
Jacobson, A., 256, 269
Janicki, W. P., 53, 76
Janis, I. L., 220, 239
Jaspars, J. M., 34, 62, 76
Jecker, J. D., 229, 239
Jones, E. E., 229, 238, 266, 270
Jensen, A. R., 13, 76
Johnston, S., 63, 76
Joyce, B. R., 13, 76

Kahn, L. A., 208, 210, 240
Kamenetzky, J., 225, 243
Karlins, M., 13, 59, 63, 72, 76, 80, 232, 233,
    235, 240
Karlovac, M., 265, 269
Karp, S. A., 14, 85
Katz, D., 2, 9
Kelly, G. A., 14, 15, 17, 18, 19, 20, 27, 33,
    34, 51, 76
Kelley, H. H., 139, 161, 220, 223, 239, 241,
    255, 265, 266, 267, 270, 271
Kelman, H. C., 218, 219, 240, 250, 270
Kennedy, J. L., 66, 76
Kerr, N. L., 267, 270
Kiesler, C. A., 132, 140, 141, 142, 158, 170,
    180, 205, 208, 240
King, B., vii
Kingsley, R. C., 45, 76
Kivy, P. N., 149, 158
Klapper, J. T., 228, 240
Klein, G. S., 13, 14, 47, 73, 76

Kliejumas, P., 209, 241
Kliger, S. C. (*see also* Streufert, S. C.), 62, 82
Komorita, S. S., 209, 241
Koslin, S., 99, 256
Kothandapani, V., 210, 240
Kretch, D., 208, 240
Krohne, H. W., 57, 58, 76, 77
Krueger, S., 66, 70
Kuiken, D., 60, 75
Kukla, A., 265, 272
Kuusinen, J., 34, 77

Lamm, H., 59, 76, 232, 233, 235, 240
Lanzetta, J. T., 53, 65, 66, 81, 192, 194, 195, 205, 230, 242, 248, 271
La Piere, R. T., 209, 240
Larsen, K. S., 64, 77
Larson, L. L., 67, 77
Latané, B., 229, 238
Lawlis, G. F., 13, 77
Lawrence, D. H., 141, 158
Lazarsfeld, P. F., 231, 240
Leach, C., 35, 81
Leaman, R. L., 13, 20, 50, 70
Leuba, C., 150, 159, 168
Leventhal, H. S., 49, 54, 77
Levy, N., 149, 157
Lewis, H. B., 14, 43, 85
Lewin, K., 12, 13, 23, 27, 77, 127, 129
Lilli, W., 60, 77
Linder, W. K., 144, 158
Linton, H. B., 47, 73
Little, B. R., 49, 77
Lowin, A., 143, 159
Lowe, C. A., 265, 270
Luchins, A. S., 26, 77, 106, 227, 240
Lumsdaine, A. A. 225, 239

Maccoby, E. E., 229, 240
Maccoby, N., 229, 240
Machover, K., 14, 43, 85
MacNeil, L. W., 43, 50, 77
Maddi, S. R., 127, 129, 144, 145, 146, 147, 155, 158, 159, 166, 168, 170, 195, 205
Mahood, S., 57, 72
Mahut, H., 149, 158, 181, 205
Maier, N. R. F., 225, 240
Maier, R. A., 225, 240
Mandell, W., 224, 225, 227, 239

Mann, R. D., 209, 241
Marrow, A. J., 225, 241
Maselli, M. D., 265, 270
Massari, D. J., 45, 76
Mayo, C. 54, 55, 57, 73, 77, 78, 253, 270
McClelland, D. C., 150, 159
McGuire, W. J., 4, 9, 132, 133, 144, 145, 147 148, 155, 156, 159, 165, 166, 170, 171, 178, 195, 204, 205, 208, 209, 210, 220, 225, 241
McKeachie, W. J., 225, 241
McLachlan, J. F. C., 13, 78
Mead, G. H., 13, 78
Mednick, S. A., 63, 78, 126, 129
Meek, D., 267, 270
Meissner, P. B., 14, 43, 85
Meltzer, B., 41, 55, 78
Menapace, R. H., 265, 271
Mervin, J. C., 209, 238
Messerley, S., 35, 55, 70
Messick, S. J., 47, 73, 126, 127, 128, 129, 253, 270
Metcalfe, R. J., 34, 35, 78
Meyer, W.-U., 263, 272
Miller, A. G., 49, 54, 78
Miller, G. A., 110, 130, 164, 167, 172, 206
Miller, H., 13, 20, 50, 56, 70, 78
Miller, N., 227, 241
Mills, J., 143, 159, 229, 238, 241
Mitchell, T. R., 67, 78
Mock, T. J., 46, 72
Moerdyk, A. P., 13, 78
Montgomery, K. C., 145, 149, 159, 160, 181, 206
Moscovici, S., 2, 10
Munson, P. A., 208, 240
Murphy, G., 127, 130

Nagay, J., vii
Nataupsky, M., 229, 238
Newcomb, T. M., 132, 138, 139, 142, 147, 156, 160, 165, 204
Nidorf, L. J., 28, 54, 56, 65, 78
Nisbett, R., 266, 270
Nogami, G. Y., 62, 82, 245, 267, 268, 271, 272
Nydegger, R. V., 67, 78
Nystedt, L., 34, 77

O'Connell, M. J., 110, 129
Odem, R. D., 144, 160
Ogilvie, L. P., 68, 79

Oltman, P. K., 14, 79
Oppenheimer, R., 42, 79
Orvis, B. R., 266, 271
Osgood, C. E., 6, 10, 53, 79, 139, 140, 148, 160, 164, 165, 166, 167, 169, 171, 206, 210, 223, 241, 278, 303
Osofsky, J. D., 13, 79
Ossorio, P. G., 265, 271

Payne, J. W., 264, 269
Peak, H., 209, 241
Pepitone, A., 133, 134, 144, 160, 267, 271
Perin, C. T., 55, 79
Peterson, C., 25, 26, 79
Petronko, M. R., 55, 79
Pettigrew, T. F., 13, 79
Phares, J. O., 13, 80
Philips, C. G., 111, 129
Piaget, J., 12, 79, 91, 130, 256, 270, 271
Platt, J. R., 146, 160
Posthuma, A. B., 13, 79
Prather, M. S., 13, 74
Press, A. N., 54, 57, 72, 79
Pribram, K. H., 12, 79, 148, 164, 167, 172, 206
Price, K. O., 142, 160

Quastler, H., 111, 130
Quay, H. C., 150, 158

Rank, A. D., 13, 83, 99, 130
Rappoport, L., 41, 83, 253, 272
Raven, B., 209, 223, 239
Razran, G., 148, 160
Reed, S. C., 49, 79
Reich, J. W., 31, 44, 57, 68, 74, 79
Reynolds, R. J., 13, 79
Rhine, R. J., 230, 241
Richardson, L., 49, 80
Riecken, H. W., 2, 10
Ring, K., 2, 10, 223, 241
Robinson, H., 143, 159, 229, 241
Rohwer, W. D., Jr., 13, 76
Rokeach, M., 64, 80, 98, 125, 128, 130, 209, 241, 275, 303
Romney, A. K., 229
Rosen, B., 209, 241
Rosen, S., 209, 229, 241
Rosenberg, M. J., 132, 140, 160, 165, 204, 209, 242
Rosenberg, S., 253, 270

Rosenkrantz, P. S., 41, 52, 54, 55, 78, 79, 80
Ross, A., 143, 156, 229, 230, 241
Rowland, K. M., 67, 77
Ruble, D. N., 265, 269, 271
Rule, B. G., 43, 77

Saenger, G., 209, 242
Salapatek, P. H., 144, 157
Saltz, E., 14, 84
Saltzstein, H. D., 251, 270
Sarbin, T. R., 253, 271
Sample, J., 209, 242
Sawatsky, D. D., 43, 64, 80
Schachtel, E. G., 13, 80, 128, 130
Scheerer, M., 43, 74
Schneider, G. A., 80
Schoen, R. A., 12, 14, 47, 48, 74
Schönbach, P., 229, 238
Schroder, H. M., 13, 25, 28, 29, 30, 31, 32, 42, 43, 44, 46, 47, 49, 50, 51, 53, 58, 59, 63, 66, 67, 72, 73, 74, 76, 77, 80, 82, 97, 105, 124, 127, 129, 130, 153, 154, 160, 161, 166, 168, 231, 232, 233, 238, 242, 243, 253, 271
Scott, T. H., 180, 205
Scott, W. A., 12, 23, 25, 26, 36, 37, 38, 40, 51, 52, 54, 62, 64, 67, 79, 80, 81, 166, 206
Scriven, M., 2, 10
Sears, D. O., 209, 230, 231, 239, 242
Sechrest, L., 54, 81
Secord, P. F., 2, 9, 208, 242, 260, 271
Segall, M., 149, 160
Sève, L., 2, 4, 8, 10
Shrauger, S., 49, 50, 81, 253, 271
Shaver, K. G., 267, 268, 271
Shaw, J. I., 266, 267, 271
Shaw, M. E., 262, 264, 267, 271
Sheffield, F. D., 225, 239
Sherif, M., 228, 239
Shore, R. E., 13, 45, 72, 76
Shulman, A. D., 2, 10
Sieber, J. E., 53, 65, 66, 81, 230, 242, 248, 271
Signell, K. A., 13, 40, 81
Sikand, J. S., 68, 72
Silverman, I., 2, 6, 9, 10
Singer, D. L., 49, 54, 77
Singer, J. E., 133, 136, 137, 138, 141, 160, 174, 199, 206
Smith, M. B., 209, 225, 238, 242
Smith, S., 35, 81

Solomon, L., 189, 204
Solomon, R. L., 223, 242
Soucar, E., 49, 56, 57, 80, 81
Spence, D. P., 47, 73
Stager, P., 66, 81
Star, S. A., 231, 242
Stasser, G., 267, 270
Steiner, I. D., 229, 242
Steiner, G. A., 231, 242
Stevenson, M. W., 144, 160
Stewart, R. H., 227, 242
Stogdill, R. M., 67, 81
Streufert, S., 6, 9, 12, 13, 25, 31, 32, 33, 39, 43, 44, 46, 47, 49, 50, 51, 58, 59, 60, 61, 62, 63, 66, 67, 68, 72, 74, 80, 81, 82, 83, 102, 104, 105, 106, 110, 124, 127, 129, 130, 132, 153, 154, 157, 160, 161, 166, 168, 170, 177, 192, 194, 195, 200, 204, 205, 206, 207, 211, 212, 215, 222, 227, 228, 229, 231, 232, 233, 238, 242, 243, 248, 252, 253, 255, 256, 257, 266, 267, 268, 271, 272
Streufert S. C. (*see also* Kliger, S. C.), 7, 10, 13, 61, 66, 67, 82, 105, 106, 110, 130, 211, 243, 266, 272
Suedfeld, P., 13, 31, 44, 49, 58, 59, 60, 62, 83, 99, 105, 111, 130, 192, 206, 223, 225, 233, 243
Suci, G. J., 6, 10, 139, 160, 241
Sullivan, E. V., 13, 76
Sulzer, J. L., 262, 264, 267, 271
Sweet, J. S., 45, 76

Tajfel, H., 14, 48, 62, 71, 76, 246, 247, 251, 252, 272
Taguiri, R., 245, 247, 253, 272
Tannenbaum, P. H., 6, 10, 53, 79, 132, 139, 140, 148, 156, 160, 161, 223, 241, 278, 303
Thibaut, J. W., 139, 161
Thistlewaite, D. L., 225, 243
Thomas, M. M., 68, 83
Todd, F. J., 41, 83, 253, 272
Tomkins, S. S., 44, 49, 83, 149, 150, 161, 179, 180, 184, 186, 187, 206
Tomlinson, R. D., 13, 83
Townes, B. D., 13, 83
Triandis, H. C., 256, 272
Tripodi, T., 13, 20, 34, 50, 53, 56, 58, 70, 76, 84

Tsukiyama, K., 149, 161
Tucker, L. R., 253, 272
Tucker, W. H., 44, 49, 83
Tuckman, B. W., 43, 44, 51, 59, 62, 84
Turner, J. L., 13, 73
Turney, J. R., 67, 84

Uhlman, F. W., 14, 84

Van de Geer, J. P., 62, 76
Vannoy, J. S., 12, 48, 69, 84
Van Ostrand, D., 189, 206
Vernon, J., 60, 83, 223, 243
Vinogradova, O. S., 149, 161

Walker, E. L., 149, 158, 168, 209, 243
Walster, E., 267, 268, 272
Wapner, S., 14, 43
Ware, R., 44, 52, 53, 74, 84
Warland, R., 209, 242
Watson, S. R., 58, 84
Weiner, B., 262, 263, 264, 265, 266, 270, 272
Weinstein, A. G., 209, 243
Weiss, W., 218, 219, 239
Welker, W. I., 145, 146, 149, 161, 182, 192, 194, 198, 206
Werner, H., 13, 27, 83, 127, 130
White, B. J., 13, 44, 64, 74, 84
White, R. W., 145, 161, 209, 242
Wicker, A. W., 209, 243
Wiener, M., 252, 272
Wiggins, J. S., 68, 84
Wilkins, G., 49, 73
Witkin, H. A., 13, 14, 43, 79, 84, 85, 166
Wolfe, R., 13, 85
Wulff, V. J., 111, 130
Wyer, R. S., 30, 38, 39, 40, 44, 57, 74, 85

Yoshii, N. K., 149, 161

Zajonc, R. B., 21, 23, 35, 41, 42, 49, 54, 68, 85, 209, 243, 285, 303
Zander, A., 223, 244
Zener, S. L., 144, 157
Zimbardo, P. G., 6, 133, 149, 160, 161
Zimring, R. M., 50, 85
Zingle, H. W., 43, 64, 80
Zipf, S. G., 223, 244

SUBJECT INDEX

ABX Model, 138–138
Achievement, 119
Acquiescent response set, 125
Activation, 146, 154, 155, 172–174, 177, 188–189, 195
Adaptation level (*see also* GIAL, SIAL), 150–151, 164–204, 274
Adaptation to the environment, 98–99, 170
Adrenalin, 154
Affect (*see also* Cognition vs. affect), 42, 50, 68, 94, 101, 105, 117–121, 147–156, 178–190, 196–204, 208–210, 213, 234–235, 249–250, 258
Affect, positive vs. negative, 119–120
Affective balance, 24
Aggression, 32, 65
Ambivalence, 23, 26, 33
Ambivalent image, 25
Applications of psychology, 2
Area of complexity, defined, 88

Arousal, 68, 146, 149, 151–153, 168, 170, 180, 182, 188, 190, 208
Articulation, 20–21, 23–24, 25, 27, 36–41
Artifacts, 69, 208, 210
Attitudes and attitude change, 3–4, 23, 26, 32, 33, 57, 60–61, 61–62, 122, 133, 135, 137, 139–140, 207–212, 218–219, 222–223, 225–228, 232, 234, 236, 275
Attitudes and behavior, 209
Attitudes, cognitive vs. affective vs. conative components, 208–210
Attitudes, dimensionality of, 207–212
Attraction, 62–63, 150, 234–236, 259–260
Attractiveness (of a source), 222–223
Attribute, 21, 24, 25, 36
Attribution, 123, 132, 142, 211, 261–269
Authoritarianism, 29, 48, 65, 125

Balance–Imbalance, 23, 26, 131, 137–139, 171

Beliefs (*see* Attitudes)
Bias (*see also* Artifacts), 8
Boomerang effect, 228
Boredom, 197–202, 203

Categorizing, 21–23, 35–36, 275, 285–286
Category width, 14–15, 48
Causality, attributions of, 267–269
Central Nervous System (CNS), 146, 148–149, 152, 154, 155, 168, 172, 185
Centrality (Centralization), 23–24
Centrality–Peripherality, 30
Choice behavior, dimensional, 120
Clarity–Ambiguity, 30
Clinical psychology, 13, 58, 68, 120
Cognition vs. Affect, 117, 119, 147, 149–156, 180, 188
Cognitive complexity–simplicity (*see* Complexity)
Cognitive control, 13–15
Cognitive domain (*see also* Area of complexity), 24, 25, 33, 35, 40, 46, 50, 67, 102–103, 120–122, 147, 174, 210–211, 214, 233, 257–258
Cognitive domain, defined, 88
Cognitive space, 12
Cognitive structure (*see* Structure, cognitive)
Cognitive style, 13–15, 120, 125, 136–137, 246, 250, 274
Cognitive universe, 21–22
Collative variables (Berlyne), 152–153
Communication, 120, 178, 212–234, 260, 274
Communication, effectiveness of, 214–218, 260
Compartmentalization–Interrelatedness, 30, 175
Complex environment (complex real world), defined, 89
Complex persons (*see also* More multidimensional persons) 26, 27, 31–33, 41, 46–47, 52–69
Complex vs. simple persons (*see* More multidimensional persons, More unidimensional persons, Complex persons, Simple persons)
Complex search activity, 192–201
Complexity (Multidimensionality) (*see also* Environmental complexity) 17, 19–20, 20–21, 22–69, 88, 119, 166–168, 172, 188, 191

Complexity, areas of, 93–95, 121–122
Complexity, area of, defined, 88
Complexity, defined, 88
Complexity, development of, 91–98, 256–259, 274–275, 278–279
Complexity, domain of (*see* cognitive domain, area of complexity)
Complexity, dimensionality of, 122
Complexity, environmental, 31–33, 181, 194
Complexity, generality of, 12, 28, 35
Complexity, hierarchical, defined, 88
Complexity, interactive, 31–33, 46–47, 58, 65–67, 87–129
Complexity, measurement of (*see* Measurement of complexity)
Complexity, perceptual vs. executive, 46, 92, 93–95, 121, 124, 214
Complexity, research on (*see* Research on complexity)
Complexity, review of, 11–85
Complexity Self-Description Test (CSDT), 47
Complexity, social vs. non-social, 46, 93–95, 121, 122, 124
Complexity, stability of, 35
Complexity, style vs. preference vs. ability, 66, 90–91
Complexity tests, comparability of, 122
Complexity theory, defined, 87
Complexity, unitary characteristics of, 48, 50, 68–69, 122
Compliance, 218, 223
Concealed Figures Test (CFT), 14
Conceptual Systems Test (CST), 45, 49,
Concreteness–Abstractness, 29–31, 42–46, 47, 48
Conditioning, 66, 134
Confound, 5
Cloze activity, 192–202, 203, 204, 220, 228, 230, 276–279
Conflict, 148–149
Conformity, 30, 175, 248–251, 252–253
Congruence seeking, 140–156, 164–169, 203–204
Congruity–Incongruity, 53, 92, 102, 120, 131, 136, 139–140, 163–166, 168–204, 220, 230, 234, 256–258, 261, 274–282, 284
Congruity–Incongruity, defined, 169, 171–172

Congruity–Incongruity, desirability of, 163–166
Conservativism, 125
Consistency, 23, 52–53, 54, 131–156, 169–172
Consistency, affective–evaluative, 24–25
Consistency, redefined, 131, 170–172
Consistency–Inconsistency effects (as redefined) 172–204, 273–274, 276, 278
Consistency–Inconsistency (standard psychological definition) (see Congruity–Incongruity)
Consistency Theory, 131–156, 169–172, 179, 202, 203
Consonance–Dissonance, 131, 140–144, 155, 171, 220, 228–230, 232, 276, 279
Constructs (see also Personal constructs), 27, 48, 56
Content (vs. structure), 16, 19, 23, 28, 89–90, 119, 121–125, 129, 207–212, 214–218, 234–236, 259
Creativity, 30, 63–64, 100, 125–129
Credibility, 218–222, 225
Critical psychology, 8
Criticism of psychological theory, 2, 4
Cultural differences, 122–123, 177–178, 202

Decision making, vi–vii, 6, 32, 58, 59, 61, 65–67, 92, 102, 120, 148, 285
Decisive simplicity vs. flexible simplicity, 47
Development, 13, 29–30, 40–41, 175–176, 202, 274–275, 276, 278, 291–292
Development, critical periods in, 97
Development, stages of, 93, 97
Differentiation, 14–69, 88, 91, 93, 96, 98, 102–103, 107–108, 109, 110–112, 114–117, 119–122, 123–125, 127, 128, 211–212, 222, 235–236, 250, 251–253, 254–255, 258–259, 260–261, 264, 275, 278–280, 282–286, 291
Discrimination (on a dimension), 15–16, 19, 21, 25, 26, 31, 36–41, 48, 88, 283–284
Differentiative multidimensionality, defined, 88
Dimensional habituation, 100–101
Dimensional versatility, 20
Dimensionality, v–vii, 4, 5, 6, 7, 15, 18, 21, 24, 25, 36–41, 46, 52, 58–59, 61, 64–65, 89–129, 132, 166–168, 174, 208–236, 245–269, 273–292
Dimensionality, acquisition and utilization, 95–97

Dimensionality as intelligence, 125
Dimensionality, defined, 88
Dimensionality, measurement of, 121–124
Dimensionality, reduction of, 92, 94, 97, 99–101, 269
Dimensionality, spurious, 275
Dimensionality, training of, 101–103, 256–259
Dimensions, correspondence across persons, 123
Dimensions, discovery of, 96–97
Dimensions, independence of, 123
Dimensions, relevance of, 123
Distortion, 96, 175, 195, 197, 201, 202, 203, 204, 214, 261, 269, 279–280
Dogmatism (see also Openness–Closedness) 64, 65, 67, 102, 125, 128, 275
Drives, 133, 136, 141, 147, 149, 151–152, 154, 180–181, 183–185, 189, 199

Education and Training, 13, 29–30, 91–93, 178, 256–259, 274–275
Electroencephalogram (EEG), 90, 149
Emotion, 179–180
Empathy, 91–93, 253–254, 259–260
Environmental complexity (see Complexity, environmental)
Environmental effects, 104–113, 146, 175–176, 178, 181–201, 202, 203, 210, 281, 291
Escape, 195–197, 200–201, 202, 203, 256, 280
Eucity (see also Success), 32, 105, 119, 154
Evaluation and Complexity, 100–101
Exchange theory, 139, 147
Exploration, 30, 144–146, 147, 170, 174, 176, 203–204
External validity, 5
Extinction, 136
Extinction of structural styles, 120
Extreme judgments, 64–65

F Scale (see Authoritarianism)
Factor analysis, 6, 41, 48, 49, 63, 69, 123–124, 210
Failure (see also Noxity), 32, 59, 61, 66, 105, 119, 194–195, 200, 263, 277
Familiarity, 132
Fear, 149, 183–186, 198, 201, 203, 258
Field dependence–independence, 14, 43

Flexibility, 23, 26, 30, 63–64, 66, 98, 102, 103, 125, 128, 137
Flexible complexity, defined, 88
Flexible–Constrictive, 14
Freedom of behavior, 119
Frequency of interaction hypothesis, 27–28, 56, 57, 58
Frustration, 148, 175
Functional autonomy, 134

Galvanic Skin Response (GSR), 60
Genius, 126–127
Gestalt psychology, 133–135, 136, 138
GIAL (General Incongruity Adaptation Level), 132, 147, 163–204, 228–231, 233, 234, 252, 273–282, 291–303
GIAL, defined, 173
GIAL and Development, 274–275, 281
GIAL, case example, 292–302
GIAL, individual differences in, 171, 176–178, 188, 202, 229, 276–277, 282, 291
GIAL theory: style vs. preference vs. expectancy vs. utility, 177–178, 179, 188, 200
Goal attainment, 147–148, 154
Group structure, 32

H Statistic, 37–41, 51–52, 62, 64, 65, 67, 68
Hierarchical complexity, defined, 88
Homeostasis, 135
Hypnosis, 64

Ideational fluency, 48
Identification, 218, 249
Ideographic, 6, 122–123
Image comparability, 24
Images, 24
Impression formation, Impression Formation Test (IFT) (*see also* Primacy-Recency), 26–28, 39–40, 46, 51, 53–58, 121, 125, 252, 255–256
Incongruence seeking (*see* Variety motivation)
Incredulity, 139–140, 278
Individual differences in complexity-dimensionality (*see* More unidimensional persons, More multidimensional persons, Simple persons, Complex persons)

Individual differences in congruity vs. incongruity seeking (*see* GIAL, individual differences in)
Infinite regress, 3, 5
Information, 26, 53–58, 104–107, 119–120, 124, 135, 137, 148, 165, 167–168, 169–171, 175, 179, 203, 204, 211–212, 215, 220, 222, 225, 229, 247, 253–254, 256, 259, 261, 264, 273–274, 278, 280–281, 285, 291
Information load (*see also* Sensory deprivation and Overload), 32, 58, 59, 66, 92, 105–112, 114–118, 153, 194, 200, 233, 257, 260–261, 277–278, 282, 286
Information load, defined, 88
Information orientation, 58–60
Information processing, 5, 31–33, 137, 147, 168, 215, 232, 274, 276, 283, 292
Information relevance, 105–107, 111–113, 114–117, 261
Information search (*see also* Variety motivation) 32–33, 58, 59, 63, 65–66, 105–107, 108, 117–118, 142, 143–145, 147–148, 164, 167–168, 177, 190–204, 215–216, 228–230, 233, 250, 276–280
Information theory (*see also* H Statistic), 36, 104
Information transmission, 58, 60
Information utilization, 58, 59, 60
Instincts, 134
Integration (*see also* Integration, hierarchical, Integration, flexible), 16–69, 88, 93, 98, 102–103, 107–108, 109, 110–112, 114–117, 120–122, 124–125, 200, 211–212, 222, 227–228, 233, 235–236, 247–248, 250, 251–253, 255–256, 258–259, 260–261, 262, 264–265, 275, 278–280, 282–284, 285–286, 291–292
Integration, Case example, 292–298, 302
Integration, flexible, 16, 25, 47, 96, 103–104, 127–128, 129, 235, 289–290
Integration, hierarchical, 16, 23, 25, 27, 35, 40, 41–42, 47, 48, 96, 102, 103–104, 127, 286–289
Integration Style Test (IST), 46–47
Integrative multidimensionality, defined, 88
Intelligence, 49, 90, 124–125, 126, 129
Intelligence and Dimensionality (*see* Dimensionality as intelligence)
Interactive complexity theory, defined, 87
Internalization, 218, 223, 249

Interpersonal Discrimination Test (IDT), 45, 49
Interpersonal Judgment Scale (IJS), 63
Interpersonal perception and Judgment (*see also* Perception) 27, 28, 35, 253–261
Interpersonal Topical Inventory (ITI), 43, 49, 51, 62, 64–65
Introversion–Extroversion, 60
Irrelevant responding, 108, 109, 111

Laboratory research, 6
Latitude of acceptance–rejection, 228
Leadership, 67–68
Learning (*see also* Education and Training, Reinforcement), 125, 136, 139, 168, 177–178, 190, 274
Learning theory, 134, 140, 147, 227
Least-Preferred-Coworker Scale (LPC), 67–68

Manipulation, 144, 147
Marxist psychology, 8
Mastery, 119
Measurement of complexity, 33–51
Message, 212–218, 224–228
More multidimensional persons, 31–33, 92, 98, 104, 107, 116–118, 122–124, 210–236, 245–269, 277–286, 288, 291
More multidimensional persons, Case example, 292–298, 302
More multidimensional, defined, 88
More multidimensional persons, evaluation of, 98–99
More unidimensional, defined, 88
More unidimensional persons, 31–33, 92 104, 114, 117–119, 123–124, 210–236, 245–269, 277–287, 291
More unidimensional persons, Case example, 292–302
Motivation, 27, 50, 65–66, 104, 131–156, 231
Motivation, molar vs. molecular, 135–156, 169, 177
Multidimensional scaling, 121
Multidimensionality (*see* Complexity, Dimensionality, Minimum multidimensionality)
Multidimensionality, defined, 88
Multidimensionality, minimum, 5
Multidimensional unfolding, 41

Neurosis, 120
Nomothetic, 6, 122–123

Novelty, 33, 59, 60, 100, 102, 145, 149, 152, 167–168, 169–170, 175–176, 188, 192–194, 203, 212, 230–231, 258, 261, 268
Novelty, dimensional, 167
Noxity (*see also* Failure) 32, 105, 119, 154

Omnibus Personality Inventory (OPI), 49
One-to-one (retaliatory) responding, 107–108, 109–112, 114–116
Openness–Closedness (*see also* Dogmatism), 30, 48, 63, 98, 203, 222, 230–231, 285, 290
Optimality, 31–33, 66–67, 107, 110–112, 119–120, 146, 150–151, 153–154, 155, 163–204, 214
Organization, 23, 35–36
Orienting reflex, 148
Overload (*see also* information load), 117, 119, 175, 233, 258–259, 276, 278–279
Overprotection, 29–30

Paragraph Completion Test (PCT) (*see also* Sentence Completion Test), 44, 46–47, 51, 65
Perception (*see also* Social perception, Interpersonal perception and judgment), 5, 14, 58, 91–93, 94, 134, 172, 180, 277
Perception, dimensionality of, 214–218
Perception, veridicality of, 26
Person perception (*see* Interpersonal perception and judgment)
Personal constructs, 17–20
Personality structure (*see* Structure, cognitive)
Physiological characteristics (*see also* CNS), 125, 136, 138, 141, 148, 214
Physiological limitations, 110–111
Polar Contrast Index (PCI), 45
Political process, 13
Power (of an expert), 223–224
Power (of a source), 223–224
Primacy–Recency (*see also* Impression formation), 26, 33, 46, 53–58, 227–228, 255–256
Problem solving, 32, 102
Propaganda, 60, 254
Punishment, 139

Rebellion, 29
Reinforcement (*see also* Reward, Punishment), 66, 67, 100, 102, 119–121, 134, 142, 229, 235, 257, 279

Remote Associates Test (RAT), 63, 126
Rep Test (*see* Role Construct Repertory
    Test)
Repression–Sensitization, 68
Research on complexity (Dimensionality)
    51–69
Research procedures, 3
Respondent decision making (*see* One-to-one
    (retaliatory) responding)
Responsibility, attributions of, 262–263,
    265, 266–269
Retaliatory behavior (*see* One-to-one
    responding)
Reward, 139, 223
Rigidity, 23, 65, 102
Role Category Questionnaire (RCQ), 41–42,
    49, 52, 54, 55–56, 64–65
Role Construct Repertory Test (Rep), 14,
    17, 33–35, 41, 42, 47, 48, 49, 51, 54,
    56, 60, 63, 64, 67, 121
Rorschach test, 35

Salience, 32–33, 61, 100, 101, 102, 117–
    118, 125, 144, 190, 212, 221, 224–227,
    230, 236, 247, 250, 251, 253, 254, 261,
    262, 264, 266, 284–286
Selective exposure, 228–234
Self-concept, 190
Semantic differential, 139
Semantic space, 123, 262, 274
Sensory deprivation (*see also* Information
    load), 31, 60–61, 111, 117, 119, 233
Sentence Completion Test (SCT) (*see also*
    Paragraph Completion Test), 43–44,
    46–47, 48, 49, 51, 56, 58, 59, 63, 65,
    66, 94, 121, 124, 125
Sex differences, 55, 56
SIAL (Specific Incongruity Adaptation
    Level), 172–204, 235, 274, 280–281
Simple persons (*see also* More unidimen-
    sional persons), 26, 27, 31–33, 41, 46–
    47, 52–69
Simplicity, decisive vs. flexible (*see* Decisive
    simplicity vs. Flexible simplicity)
Simplicity of cognitive structure (*see*
    Complexity, Dimensionality)
Simulation, 6, 32
Situational Interpretation Test (SIT), 43,
    51, 53
Sleeper effects, 219–221

Social class, 92
Social desirability, 117, 200
Social influence (*see also* Attitudes), 33,
    61–62, 212–234, 251
Social perception, 246–253
Social structure, 26
Sociometry, 62–63, 67
Stroop Color Word Test (SCW), 14
Source, 33, 212, 214–218, 218–224, 234,
    269
Socialization, 13
Stimulus complexity (*see also*
    Environmental complexity), 60
Strategy, strategic responding, 108, 122,
    236
Stress, 30, 31, 58, 91, 102–103, 119, 213,
    250, 253, 285
Structure, cognitive, 12–13, 16–17, 19, 22,
    23–26, 27, 28, 36–41, 41–42, 89–90,
    119, 121–125, 129, 168, 207–212, 214–
    218, 234–236, 259, 275, 285, 291
Structure vs. process, 40
Success (*see also* Eucity), 32, 61, 105, 119,
    263, 277
Symmetry, 60
Systems theory, 28–31, 42–46, 58, 62, 64,
    65

Target, 33, 212–218, 218–231, 234, 261,
    269
Task performance, 65–67, 67–68
Task satisfaction, 110
Theory in psychology, 1–5
This I Believe Test (TIB), 30, 44, 51, 52–53,
    57, 62, 63–64
Tolerance for ambiguity, 67, 175
Training (*see* Education and Training)
Trait consistency, 57

Uncertainty (*see also* H Statistic), 252
Unidimensionality (*see* Dimensionality)
Unidimensionality, defined, 88
Unity, 22–23, 25, 35–36
Utility, 127–128, 142–143, 212, 230–231

Validity, 5
Value of Life Questionnaire (VLQ), 62
Values, 23
Variety (incongruity) motivation, 145–156,
    165–170, 174, 195, 203
Verbal ability, 48, 133
Vigilance hypothesis, 26, 56, 57, 58